P9-BYM-761

A FATAL PASSION

A
FATAL
PASSION

The Story of
Victoria Melita,
the Uncrowned
Last Empress of Russia

MICHAEL JOHN
SULLIVAN

RANDOM HOUSE   NEW YORK

Library of Congress Cataloging-in-Publication Data

Sullivan, Michael John.
A fatal passion: the story of Victoria Melita, the uncrowned last
Empress of Russia/by Michael John Sullivan.
p.   cm.
Includes bibliographical references and index.
ISBN 0-679-42400-8
1. Victoria Melita, Grand Duchess Cyril of Russia, 1876–1936.
2. Princesses—Russia—Biography.   3. Russia—Kings and rulers—
Biography.   4. Princesses—Great Britain—Biography.   5. Russia—
History—Nicholas II, 1894–1917.   6. Soviet Union—
History—1917–1936.   I. Title.
DK254.V45S85   1996
947.08'092—dc20   95-15823

Random House website address: http://www.randomhouse.com/
Printed in the United States of America on acid-free paper

2 4 6 8 9 7 5 3

FIRST EDITION

Book design by Carole Lowenstein

For my mother,
Mary Ann Sullivan

Acknowledgments

During the several years of research for this book, many individuals contributed invaluable help. First and foremost, I would like to thank my agent, Laurens R. Schwartz, for his great skill and patience in guiding this project and his constant faith and encouragement, and my editor at Random House, Robert D. Loomis, whose considerable talent, taste, and creativity enriched my book and whose unfailing thoughtfulness and kindness made the endeavor an absolute pleasure. The book would not exist without either of these two very remarkable men.

Also essential to this project was the late Grand Duke Vladimir of Russia, the head of the House of Romanov and the claimant to the imperial throne for more than fifty years. Vladimir was noble in every sense of the word. He graciously confronted adversity and disappointment, never losing his great faith and hope in the future. An affable host, the grand duke welcomed me into his home and shared his thoughts and memories with me, educating me on the history of his homeland and his illustrious family, particularly his parents, Victoria Melita and Kirill. It was Vladimir who nurtured my fascination with the remarkable fate of his family, showing me priceless relics of the imperial past and giving me not only books and articles but much time and attention. I visited his home, Ker Argonid, in Brittany, and so became familiar with the setting of much of this book. Very sadly, while I was still working on the book, Vladimir died suddenly of a heart attack—ironically, on my birthday—and did not live to see it finished.

Additionally, I would like to express my gratitude to Vladimir's widow, Grand Duchess Leonida, who was as gracious as her husband in offering me hospitality, seeing to my every comfort and even cooking a special Russian dinner for me. After her husband's death, Leonida took over his correspondence and invited me to visit her home in Paris to discuss my book.

It was during this visit that I met Leonida's beautiful and charming daughter, Grand Duchess Maria, who has inherited her father's claim to the Russian throne and, as his only child, is now head of the imperial House of Romanov. Spending an afternoon with Maria while the rest of Paris celebrated Bastille Day and the fall of royalty, I enjoyed her confidence in and support of my project. I would like to thank this very capable and accomplished woman for her insights and remembrances, and most especially for the gift of numerous family photographs with her request that they be used in this book.

Next, I wish I could express my gratitude personally to Mr. Ivan Bilibin, the chancellor of the Russian imperial court in exile since 1934. Alas, Mr. Bilibin died just before the completion of this book. A kind and generous man, he devoted a great deal of time and effort to helping me obtain vital research materials and interviews. Ivan Bilibin devoted his entire life to the imperial cause and unfailingly lent it great strength through his quiet dignity and sincerity.

A colleague of Mr. Bilibin who was of almost equal help to me was Peter Koltypin-Wallovskoy, a commander of the Order of the Imperial Union of Russia. He took considerable time and trouble to secure for me rare documents and memoirs, kindly offering helpful insights and observations.

I would like to express my thanks to Her Majesty Queen Elizabeth II for her gracious permission to publish many letters from the Royal Archives at Windsor Castle. Miss Pamela Clark, the deputy registrar of the archives, was exceedingly helpful and kind in providing the full resources available and assisting me during my stay at Windsor Castle.

Also, I wish to thank King Michael and Queen Anne of Romania for their generous interest and support. Welcoming me into their home on Lake Geneva, sharing memories of their relatives, and then sending me special books and research materials, Michael and Anne of Romania showed remarkable kindness, and I am indebted to them for allowing me an opportunity for genuine personal engagement with my subject.

In addition, I would like to acknowledge the contributions made by King Michael's late mother, Queen Mother Helen of Romania. The eldest daughter of King Constantine I of Greece, this saintly woman overcame a tragic early life to spend her remaining years in the peace and beauty of an exquisite villa in the hills of Fiesole above Florence, Italy. With her great charm and quiet graciousness, Queen Helen made me feel a most welcome guest in her home. She shared her memories of the past and gave me precious glimpses into the personal lives of many of the fascinating royal characters in this book. Introducing me to other members of her family, serving me lunch and afternoon tea, lending me her limousine and chauffeur, and never forgetting to send notes and Christmas cards, Queen Helen was a true friend with a beautiful nature, who will be missed by all who knew her.

Another member of the Romanian royal family who was extremely helpful in the research of this book was King Michael's late aunt, Princess Ileana, who, after her divorce from Archduke Anton of Austria, became a nun of the Orthodox Church, founded a monastery in rural Pennsylvania, and became known simply as Mother Alexandra. Whether asking questions over the telephone and by mail or meeting with her in her daughter's Salzburg home, I always found Mother Alexandra to be entirely helpful, candid, thorough, and direct in her responses. An unusually wise and objective woman, she fully understood the importance of documenting the personal side of history and generously cooperated in sharing all she knew.

Two of my most generous contributors were Prince and Princess Patrice Golitzin of Paris. Taking it upon themselves to thoroughly educate me not only in the history of Russia but in its culture, music, cuisine, and sensibility, this exceedingly charming and generous couple took me into their home and introduced me to the inner circle of the famed society of Russian émigrés. The prince, a former history professor, shared a wealth of knowledge with me and offered firm and valuable guidance, while the princess, a beautiful and delightful lady, patiently explained the vagaries of the Russian spirit and charmingly served as translator.

Among my other hosts and hostesses who provided valuable assistance in helping me understand the lost world of royal Europe, I would like to thank Prince George of Hanover who, as the grandson of Kaiser Wilhelm II, brother-in-law of Prince Philip of England, and brother of Queen Frederika of Greece, was in an ideal position to explain to me the workings of the complex web of family relationships among European royalty. A gentle and kindly man, Prince George conscientiously assumed my royal education as almost his own personal obligation, and I will always be grateful to him for so pleasantly and humbly giving me so much guidance and sharing with me his time, his books, and his interest. Archduke Otto of Austria, the claimant to the Austro-Hungarian throne, was also generous in inviting me to his home on Lake Starnberg near Munich and thoroughly educating me in the intricacies of royal politics in modern Europe. Otto's mother, Dowager Empress Zita, was equally kind in receiving me at her retirement home in Zizers in the Swiss Alps and granting me an interview, as was King Constantine II of Greece in London, and Archduke Dominic of Austria in Vienna.

I would like to acknowledge the assistance and contributions made by the staffs and services of the Library of the British Museum in London, the Yale University Library, the Library of the University of California at

Berkeley, the Graduate Research Library of the University of California at Los Angeles, the State Library of Hawaii at Honolulu, and the Loyola Marymount University library.

Thanks are also due Tom Zimmerman for his photographs and his advice on the selection and preparation of the historical photographs in this book, and to the biographer Jon Van der Kiste for meeting with me at his home in southern Devonshire and very generously sharing his research and his knowledgeable insight into Victoria Melita and the English royal family. I also wish to thank Hannah Pakula for her insights and advice and her excellent biography of Queen Marie of Romania, and Robert K. Massie for his incomparable works on imperial Russia.

I was fortunate in having the professional services of a very patient and reliable typist, Christine Srubek. Christine thought nothing of working around the clock to meet deadlines; she always smiled and never complained.

Many other people went out of their way to contribute to this book. Miss Elizabeth Hannay, a native of Mississippi who moved to Dinard, in Brittany, with her parents after World War I and has lived there ever since, was able to share her memories of growing up in the social circle of which Ducky was a part. Miss Hannay closely observed Ducky and her family as they and the Hannays exchanged visits. In dealing with the section of this book that is set in Finland, I would like to express my appreciation to Elissa Ketososki Della Rocca for her lectures, guidance, and translations. Many thanks are due Dr. Jasper Blystone, who did the German translations.

Finally, as always, I want to thank the best family anyone was ever blessed with: my mother and father and my two beautiful sisters, Karen Sullivan Gaffney and Kathleen Sullivan Ciraulo.

For all the time and effort it took, writing this book was an experience I enjoyed from start to finish.

MICHAEL JOHN SULLIVAN
Los Angeles, 1996

Contents

Monday, June 4, 1917

Gunfire had echoed through the streets of St. Petersburg during the afternoon. The elegant walls of the Vladimir Palace had been badly chipped and pitted by bullets. Now, as the sun finally began disappearing from the sky and shadows covered the city, a terrifying silence froze the air.

In an upstairs bedroom of the palace two pretty little girls, aged eight and ten, were sleeping peacefully. Their mother, Grand Duchess Victoria Feodorovna, paced nervously outside the door. For hours she had been waiting for her husband to return home. But he never did.

He had left after breakfast to pick up their exit visas at the headquarters of the Provisional Government only two miles away. It took great courage for a Romanov to make such a request, and Victoria's husband, Grand Duke Kirill, had been warned by everyone not to go. But he and his wife were desperate to get their children out of the country. Imprisoned in their home, they knew each day was bringing them closer to a horrible fate.

Kirill should have returned by noon. Everything had been packed for days and ready to go. They had planned to leave on the evening train. But no one had heard from him, and as night fell Victoria Feodorovna grew more fearful. To her, "it was not a natural calm" but like an "ominously threatening sky before a typhoon."

During the last five months Victoria's privileged world had been totally destroyed. Her rank and position, which had been among the most exalted on earth, were now in ruins. Her great wealth was gone. The man she loved—the one for whom she had sacrificed everything—was probably never coming back.

And it seemed likely that Victoria Feodorovna herself would soon be meeting the same violent end.

As the oppressive quiet continued, she must have thought of the irony of her life. She had given up all she had to arrive at where she was now. Following her heart, she had been disgraced and had suffered one of the most shocking scandals of the century. Now fate seemed to be playing a vicious trick on her. Just three months ago Emperor Nicholas II had been forced to abdicate the Russian throne and he and his wife, Alexandra, and their five children had been held captive in their country palace ever since. All the other members of the imperial family of Romanov were now being hunted down and captured like common criminals.

For more than a hundred days the revolutionary forces had been victorious throughout Russia. The monarchy had been abolished, and violence and chaos reigned in its place. At first, Victoria and her husband had hoped that they would be allowed to go quietly into exile. But during the last few weeks conditions had become desperate. The moderate Socialist government had rapidly lost power, and the radical Soviet and Bolshevik parties were struggling to seize control. And regardless of their ideological differences, the Soviets and Bolsheviks agreed on one thing: Every member of the imperial family must be exterminated as quickly as possible.

It didn't seem to matter that Victoria and her husband had been the ones who, in their attempt to save the Romanov throne from certain disaster, boldly challenged the suicidal course of their cousins Nicholas and Alexandra. They had rallied the rest of the family against the misguided emperor and his unbalanced wife, and had fought for the removal of the corrupt Rasputin. During the first months of the revolution, Victoria and Kirill had continued to fight for a more liberal form of imperial rule, one based on the liberties and freedoms of the British system.

The imperial crowns were now empty and waiting. Victoria and Kirill, the most popular and respected members of the Romanov family, were the rightful successors to the dispossessed Nicholas and Alexandra. But the senseless savagery of the revolution had quickly turned this honor into a death warrant.

Staring into the darkness of the night, Victoria might have heard the firm voice of her grandmother Queen Victoria of England, warning her about this "horrid, corrupt country" with its "miserable climate, pernicious society, and wicked, villainous and atrocious government." Wise old Grandmama Queen had always feared for any member of her family marrying into the "arrogant and false" Romanov clan, who she insisted were capable of nothing but violence and hatred.

But Queen Victoria was a kindred spirit of her granddaughter and namesake, in that both shared a passionate temperament that dominated and colored every aspect of their lives.

It was this passion that had led the beautiful Victoria Feodorovna to defy the world and sacrifice everything for the only man she had ever loved. It had also brought her to this disastrous June night in St. Petersburg.

And it was a passion that would eventually prove fatal.

Ducky's
Place in the English Royal Family

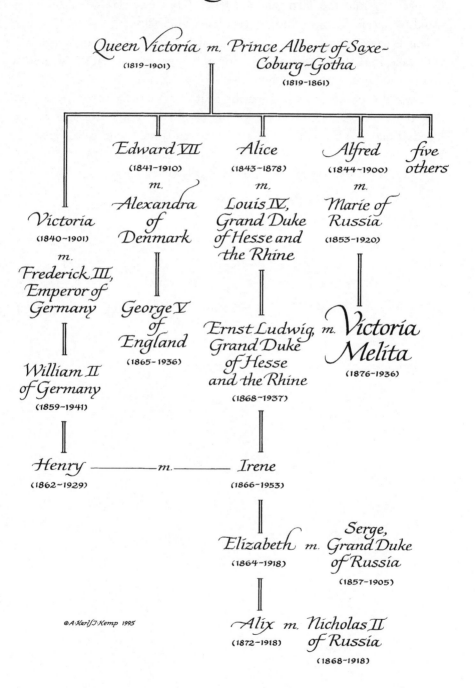

Queen Victoria m. Prince Albert of Saxe-Coburg-Gotha
(1819–1901)
(1819–1861)

Edward VII
(1841–1910)
m.
Alexandra
of
Denmark

Alice
(1843–1878)
m.
Louis IV,
Grand Duke
of Hesse and
the Rhine

Alfred
(1844–1900)
m.
Marie of
Russia
(1853–1920)

five
others

Victoria
(1840–1901)
m.
Frederick III,
Emperor of
Germany

George V
of
England
(1865–1936)

Ernst Ludwig,
Grand Duke
of Hesse
and the Rhine
(1868–1937)

m. Victoria
Melita
(1876–1936)

William II
of Germany
(1859–1941)

Henry ———— m. ———— Irene
(1862–1929)   (1866–1953)

Elizabeth m. Serge,
(1864–1918)   Grand Duke
of Russia
(1857–1905)

Alix m. Nicholas II
(1872–1918)   of Russia
(1868–1918)

© A. Karl / J. Kemp 1995

DUCKY's
Place in the Russian Imperial Family

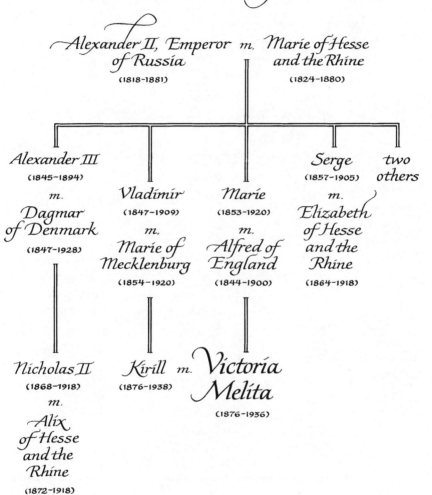

Alexander II, Emperor of Russia (1818–1881) m. Marie of Hesse and the Rhine (1824–1880)

Alexander III (1845–1894) m. Dagmar of Denmark (1847–1928)

Vladimir (1847–1909) m. Marie of Mecklenburg (1854–1920)

Marie (1853–1920) m. Alfred of England (1844–1900)

Serge (1857–1905) m. Elizabeth of Hesse and the Rhine (1864–1918)

two others

Nicholas II (1868–1918) m. Alix of Hesse and the Rhine (1872–1918)

Kirill (1876–1938) m. Victoria Melita (1876–1936)

Ducky's Family

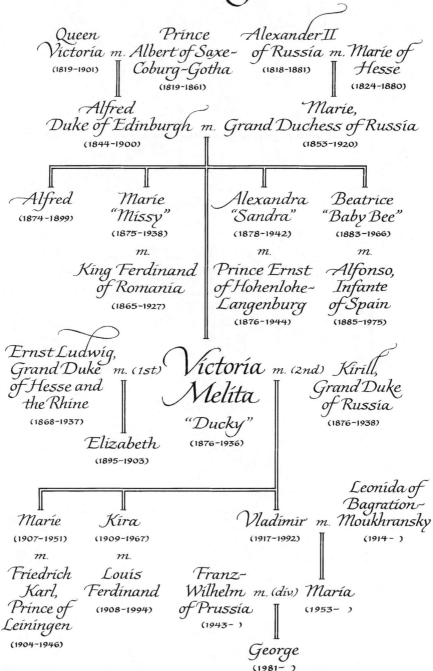

Queen
Victoria m. Prince
(1819–1901)   Albert of Saxe-
            Coburg-Gotha
            (1819–1861)

Alexander II
of Russia m. Marie of
(1818–1881)   Hesse
            (1824–1880)

Alfred
Duke of Edinburgh m. Marie,
(1844–1900)   Grand Duchess of Russia
              (1853–1920)

Alfred
(1874–1899)

Marie
"Missy"
(1875–1938)

m.

King Ferdinand
of Romania
(1865–1927)

Alexandra
"Sandra"
(1878–1942)

m.

Prince Ernst
of Hohenlohe-
Langenburg
(1876–1944)

Beatrice
"Baby Bee"
(1883–1966)

m.

Alfonso,
Infante
of Spain
(1885–1975)

Ernst Ludwig,
Grand Duke m. (1st)
of Hesse and
the Rhine
(1868–1937)

Victoria
Melita
"Ducky"
(1876–1936)

m. (2nd) Kirill,
Grand Duke
of Russia
(1876–1938)

Elizabeth
(1895–1903)

Marie
(1907–1951)

m.

Friedrich
Karl,
Prince of
Leiningen
(1904–1946)

Kira
(1909–1967)

m.

Louis
Ferdinand
(1908–1994)

Vladimir
(1917–1992)

m. Leonida of
Bagration-
Moukhransky
(1914–)

Franz-
Wilhelm m. (div.) Maria
of Prussia   (1953–)
(1943–)

George
(1981–)

PART ONE

Princess Ducky

CHAPTER ONE

The
Golden Crust

T HERE WERE NO SHADOWS on the lives of royalty in the late
nineteenth century—only a brilliant shaft of light that shone
straight down from heaven, illuminating these privileged beings and un-
mistakably identifying them as God's chosen. Royalty ruled the world
"from duty, heritage and habit—and, as they saw it, from right." They
did not trouble themselves with concerns for the future. The present was
so sumptuous, so safe and secure, that no one with a crown on his head
deigned to notice the ominous cracks and strains that threatened to destroy the entire system of the monarchy.

In the year 1876, when Victoria had herself proclaimed empress of
India and the power of her sovereignty was reaching its peak, an important world event was happening far away on the North American continent. The United States was celebrating its first hundred years of
independence, and the American centennial celebration, an international
exposition, opened in Philadelphia on May 10 to showcase the buoyant
survival and prodigious economic growth of the infant institution of democracy. When the multitude of visitors from every corner of the globe
strolled through the giant exhibition halls in Philadelphia, they were awed
and overwhelmed by the displays of the latest scientific and technological
wonders. They were made aware of a new and rapidly transforming world
where each day brought greater additions and alterations to every facet of
existence. People dramatically came face-to-face with a future that could
no longer depend on the proven and accepted traditions of the past.

Interestingly, few members of royalty ventured to Philadelphia to visit the International Exhibition of Arts, Manufacturers and Products of the Soil and Mine, as the centennial exhibition was formally known. Had they made the trip and witnessed the exhibits and displays, they would have had to confront not only the anachronistic nature of their exalted rank but also the specter of monarchy's demise.

In 1876 European royalty enjoyed being entertained by the eccentricities and talents of the adolescent American nation. When a huge, bushy-bearded man named Alexander Graham Bell arrived at Windsor Castle in England that year, Queen Victoria and her family favored him with their regal attention while he demonstrated his latest invention, an instrument that made it possible to talk at a distance through a tiny wire. The queen, who believed in practicality and convenience, arranged for the new "telephone" device to be installed in the castle.

Most of what the crowned heads of Europe knew about the United States they read in the newspapers, which presented them with a picture that was not only amusing but strange.

Essentially the monarchs of Europe were baffled by the new democracy but were inclined not to take it too seriously. The rigid class system, surmounted by the crown, was still as strictly adhered to in the Europe of 1876 as it had been during the Middle Ages.

As that year approached its conclusion, the royal families of Europe focused their attention on the island of Malta, in the eastern Mediterranean Sea, where a grandchild of Queen Victoria would soon be born.

The arrival of the child was eagerly anticipated by every royal house in Europe. The continent's rulers had been intermarrying for so long that royalty was now one large, multirelated family. The baby would have aunts and uncles and brothers and sisters and cousins who occupied all the thrones of Europe, not to mention grandparents who ruled more than half the land on earth. The birth would, indeed, be a most tangible symbol of the joining of two great empires—the British and the Russian—immense and powerful, and as different from each other as night and day.

Queen Victoria, whose nine children and numerous grandchildren were routinely exchanging wedding vows for prestigious crowns, had assumed leadership of this confusingly intertwined family scattered across all of Europe. She always referred to it affectionately as the Royal Mob, and was the uncontested matriarch, the one who made the rules and whose word was command.

The British empire covered almost a third of the earth's surface, and it was literally true that the sun never set on the diminutive queen's domain.* Thanks to the supremacy of the English navy and an early entry in the Industrial Revolution, Great Britain had become the world's largest landlord and its economic, social, and military leader. When the future emperor Nicholas II of Russia made a world tour as a young man, he irritably complained to his mother back home, "How stifling it is to be surrounded again by the English and to see red uniforms everywhere."

But the Russians weren't doing too badly themselves. Next to the British marvel, Russia was a very respectable second. An awesome country covering vast swaths of the world's largest landmass, Russia was geographically contiguous, and not a recent collection of distant territories and colonies. Much more primitively organized than England and the rest of Europe, the Russian empire had retained a great deal of its medieval character. The country's almost unimaginable wealth was distributed so unfairly among the emperor's 130 million subjects that the small and exclusive Russian aristocracy lived a life of unrivaled luxury and splendor, while the landless peasants dwelled in abject misery. The members of the imperial family of Romanov were the wealthiest individuals in the world, making new-minted American millionaires such as the Rockefellers and the Vanderbilts look merely well-off by comparison.

Emperor Alexander II had ruled Russia since 1855 as a liberal reformer who tried to improve the lives of his people. His sensitive spirit had once impressed Queen Victoria when they had danced together as teenagers at Buckingham Palace; afterward, she confided to her diary: "I never enjoyed myself more . . . I really am quite in love with the Grand-duke; he is a dear, delightful young man." Enamored of his tall, slim physique and his astonishingly handsome face, especially the poetic look in his blue eyes, Victoria cherished this memory of Alexander for decades, even as British relations with Russia gradually deteriorated.

Victoria's romantic recollections of the young Alexander conflicted strongly with her deeply rooted hostility toward the Russians. "They will always hate us and we can never trust them," the English queen stated time and time again. Toward the Romanovs themselves she main-

---

* The land surface of the earth is estimated to be 52 million square miles. The British empire at this time occupied almost 17 million square miles, while the Russian empire covered approximately 9 million square miles.

tained the harshest judgments and the most prejudiced opinions. Because Victoria's quiet, refined, and almost saintly husband, the late Prince Albert, had been her ideal of what a man should be, she was shocked and repelled by the boisterous Romanov grand dukes and critical of their extravagant, sensual lifestyles, which she censoriously characterized as "half-Oriental."

Queen Victoria abhorred the idea of any of her children or grandchildren marrying into the Romanov family. Fortunately, there was a religious barrier: The Romanovs belonged to the Russian Orthodox Church, while the British royal house was Church of England. And, religious differences aside, since Alexander II's five sons had gone no farther west than Germany to find brides, Victoria felt confident she would not face the horror of having the Romanovs as in-laws. There had never before been a dynastic alliance between England and Russia, and the English queen never dreamed that it would be possible to share grandchildren with her first teenage idol, now the Russian emperor.

Victoria had not paid much attention to Alexander's sixth child and only daughter, Marie. Ordinarily a girl like Grand Duchess Marie, with her plain face, stocky figure, and blunt personality, would not fare well in the marriage market. She would seem especially unlikely to capture a young man as dazzlingly handsome and lively as Victoria's second son, Prince Alfred. But the queen didn't fully appreciate her practical son's deep mercenary strain. Alfred simply liked money more than anything else. And Marie was the richest princess in the world.

Against tide and tempest, the clever and calculating Prince Alfred began campaigning for the hand of Marie. It was a classic example of exchanging cash for beauty. At first, Marie's parents were as opposed to becoming related to the English royal family as Queen Victoria was to being connected to the Russian.

But finally the determination of youth prevailed, and Prince Alfred of England and Grand Duchess Marie of Russia were married. Queen Victoria summed up her feelings about the matter with one brief comment: "The murder is out!"

The marriage of Alfred and Marie was the first and last time in history that the children of an English and a Russian monarch became husband and wife. In the delicately balanced Europe of 1874 it was an occurrence of enormous significance. Although they were not closely in line to inherit their country's thrones, their union was the symbol of the joining together of the world's two great empires.

With Queen Victoria's eldest daughter now the crown princess of the new German empire and her eldest son and heir married to the daughter of the king of Denmark, future family dinners at Windsor promised to be lively and politically charged affairs. The personal relationships among brothers and sisters and nieces and nephews and aunts and uncles and parents and children would be factors in international politics. A feud between two incompatible family members could possibly lead to a Continental war.

As for Alfred and his Russian wife, now known as the duke and duchess of Edinburgh, their new life together outwardly appeared happy enough. After less than three years of marriage they were about to have their third child. The duke, an officer in the British navy, had been temporarily stationed on the island of Malta, an outpost of the empire located in the Mediterranean, directly south of Sicily and near the coast of Africa. There he lived with his wife and two infant children in an ornate stone villa, the San Antonio Palace, which overlooked the picturesque harbor of the island's only major city, Valletta.

It was here, in the duchess's large corner bedroom, that a daughter was born on the last Saturday of November, the twenty-fifth, in the year 1876.

The gregale, a northeast winter wind of the Mediterranean, had been blowing with almost hurricane force for more than two days when Marie went into labor shortly after midnight. Just as the strong-willed Marie might have planned it, the labor was a swift and no-nonsense one. The baby was given the name of her grandmother Queen Victoria, and, with a poetic flourish, the ancient name of her birthplace, Malta: Victoria Melita.

For the rest of her life she would be known to her family as simply Ducky.

Holding her new infant daughter, the duchess could not have realized the irony of the situation—that she had to leave Russia and marry her English prince in order to have a child who would grow up and become what she herself had wanted to be above all else, yet, because of her very low rank in the line of succession, could never be: the empress of Russia.

CHAPTER TWO

A
Daughter
of Two Empires

*T*HE SUNNY, SUBTROPICAL CLIMATE of Malta was a dramatic contrast to the almost constant ice and snow of the duchess of Edinburgh's Russian home, which she had left behind. Still, as the mother sat with her baby in the warm Mediterranean sun and gazed north across the sea, she longed to be back with her parents amid the splendors of St. Petersburg. Though she had become frustrated and increasingly unhappy in her marriage, Victoria Melita's mother remained a remarkably strong, accomplished and complex woman in an age when feminine passivity was the expected norm. Nothing intimidated the supremely confident duchess of Edinburgh—not even Queen Victoria herself.

In the multinationally extended English royal family, the queen's merest disapproving frown could cow sovereigns and warrior princes; the Russian-born duchess of Edinburgh became known as the only member of the family who could not be dominated by the fearsome little figure in black. In fact, it was this spoiled daughter of "the world's haughtiest Imperial Highnesses" who made the great Victoria visibly uneasy—the only person known to have this amazing effect.

Therefore, it was not surprising that the iron-willed duchess would be the primary force in her children's lives. And it was upon her new baby, Victoria Melita, that her influence would be most complete. She would give to this favorite child her deep love of Russia and her indomitable spirit, and she would reinforce the passionate temperament and honest character that Victoria Melita had inherited from Grandmama Queen.

Although Russia and the Romanovs would play an important part in Victoria Melita's life, the Romanov blood that flowed in her veins really wasn't Russian at all. Having taken almost exclusively German brides for centuries, the Romanov emperors had diluted their original Russian blood to such an extent that Victoria Melita's generation of the imperial family was less than 1 percent Russian. They were now practically pure German.

However, the Romanovs still considered themselves more Russian than the Russians, even though "by education, language and taste, they were part of the cosmopolitan aristocracy of Europe." Reveling in luxury and sensual delights, they lived lives far removed from the harsh realities of their native land. They spoke French better than they spoke Russian. Dwelling in French- and Italian-style palaces decorated with French- and German-style furniture, they dined on French and German cuisine and "traveled in private railway coaches from hotels at Biarritz to villas on the Riviera," being seen more often "as guests in English country houses or palaces in Rome than on their family estates beside the Volga or the Dnieper or the Don."

By the end of the nineteenth century the Romanovs were the most self-indulgent royal family in Europe, much less interested in their traditional duties and obligations than in fully exploiting their unrestricted privileges.

This most powerful dynasty in the world had gradually evolved from a grim and primitive beginning. In 1547 a rough seventeen-year-old Muscovite prince named Ivan brazenly proclaimed himself czar (the Russian for "emperor") of Russia and took a bride from a popular noble family, the Romanovs, of Moscow. The premature death of his wife a few years later helped drive Ivan into a mad rage. After successfully putting down a rebellion in the Ukraine, he calmly watched sixty thousand of his subjects be slowly tortured to death. He soon became known as Ivan the Terrible. Carrying a sharp iron rod with him at all times, he casually used it to impale anyone who offended him. Haunted by the images of his victims, he ended his days in madness.

After Ivan's death, the crown of Russia uneasily bounced back and forth among various claimants until 1613, when a national assembly of nobles elected Ivan's grandnephew, Michael Romanov, czar. From this time until the end of the monarchy more than three hundred years later, the Romanovs occupied the Russian throne.

It was Michael Romanov's grandson Peter the Great who single-handedly dragged Russia into the modern age. With brutal ferocity, this greatest of all Romanov emperors totally changed every aspect of his vast empire. Even the most seemingly insignificant social niceties were enforced, as when the Herculean seven-foot-tall Peter proclaimed, "Ladies and gentlemen of the court caught sleeping with their boots on will be instantly decapitated." To make Russia once and for all a member of the European community, Peter ordered the instant construction of a new capital city on the Baltic Sea and had it named after himself—St. Petersburg. He also changed the title of the Romanov ruler from the Slavic "czar" to the Western term "emperor."

But no matter how relentlessly the energetic Peter tried to bring the blessings of modern science, culture, and literature to his land, he remained unenlightened as an absolute and sometimes cruel monarch. When he came to suspect his own son and heir of working against him, Peter, the great reformer, had the boy savagely tortured and beaten to death.

After Peter's feeble-minded grandson married the insignificant German princess who was to become known as Catherine the Great, the rulers of Russia were reluctant autocrats, doom-laden figures who seemed unable to wield their absolute power wisely. The weight of their crowns produced conflicted lives that sometimes assumed the proportions of Greek tragedy. Whether they admitted it or not, the Romanov emperors of the nineteenth and twentieth centuries knew that their system was woefully out of touch with the progressive march of history, and therefore doomed to oblivion.

"Melancholy, disguised by irony, is in this land the most ordinary humor of mind," was the acute observation of a French writer visiting Russia in the early nineteenth century. The national characteristic of melancholy became the basis of all great Russian literature, but it was nowhere better expressed than in the private lives of the Romanovs.

Even Catherine the Great had struggled to reconcile her patronage of Voltaire's liberalism with her own harsh rule. Because of Catherine's extreme dislike of her rather pathetic husband and his own aversion to her, it is most likely that her son and heir was fathered by one of her numerous lovers and that her husband was the end of the true Romanov bloodline.

Catherine's handsome and charismatic grandson, Emperor Alexander I, resisted Napoleon and eventually brought him to his knees, but he was a strange man who turned his back on all that was worldly and constantly tried to escape from the anxieties imposed by his crown. An idealist in his youth, the dreamy Alexander, always suspected of complicity in his father's murder, became a severely disillusioned and haunted man toward the end of his life. Feeding Russia's hunger for liberty with his pretentious philosophies and grand political schemes, he eventually established a carefully concealed tyranny supported by a system of secret police and government spies. In his mysticism and his narcissistic search for a heaven on earth, Alexander tragically left his country a legacy of hypocrisy, suspicion, and fear.

Alexander I was succeeded in 1825 by his brother Nicholas I, a man so obsessed with discipline that he became known as the Iron Czar. The military was Nicholas's chief passion, and he always remained first and foremost a soldier. With a zeal that almost equaled that of Peter the Great, he sought to control every facet of his immense empire, but his efforts were hampered by a pathological mistrust of every other human being and a steadfast refusal to delegate any of his vast authority.

Nicholas I was as determined to create a solid family as he was intent on remaking the structure of his country. He and his fragile wife, the beautiful daughter of the king of Prussia, produced four sons and three daughters, and established the distinctive good looks of the following three generations of the Romanov family. These seven children and twenty grandchildren of Nicholas became the grand dukes and grand duchesses of the last decades of the imperial dynasty.

Although Nicholas I was a loving and devoted husband and father, many noticed that "he has a habitual expression of severity, which sometimes gives the idea of harshness and inflexibility." Even the young Queen Victoria was intimidated by the Iron Czar when he condescended to make a state visit to England. She was charmed by his "attentions and politeness," but found "the expression of the eyes . . . formidable, and unlike anything I ever saw before."

Nicholas made this same impression on everyone. Tall and magnificently proportioned, he was universally described as the handsomest man of his time. His face and figure were inherited by his eldest son, Alexander II, but not his personality. Unlike his commanding and military father, Alexander possessed a pointed distaste for armies and warfare, preferring literature and the refinement of art and music.

Alexander II, the grandfather of Victoria Melita, was a tenderhearted and liberally inclined man who felt trapped in an impossible role. One of his first acts as emperor was to grant freedom to the millions of Russian serfs who slaved their lives away on the huge country estates of the aristocracy. But like so many reformers before and after him, Alexander's well-intentioned gestures could not change the system, and eventually his idealism resulted in his brutal death.

At least he had the good fortune to pursue true love. Alexander married a relatively minor German princess, Marie of Hesse and the Rhine, and raised a happy family of six sons and a daughter. The boys were all tall and imposing like their father and would become renowned as the handsomest princes of their day, but it was the only daughter, Marie, who was the favorite of both parents, and certainly the apple of her father's eye. It was this spoiled grand duchess who married the son of Queen Victoria, becoming the redoubtable duchess of Edinburgh and the mother of Victoria Melita.

As the grand duchess, Marie grew up in a home like no other. Amid the pomp and splendor of the most magnificent palaces in the world, she enjoyed the unique benefit of not only an extraordinarily exalted public position but also the nurturing love of a devoted family. The combination of a superb education and the affection showered on her by her parents and brothers produced a woman of rare competence and unfaltering self-confidence. Much of her direct and no-nonsense approach to life and her spirit of personal independence may have been the result of being the only girl in a family of six boys. Surrounded by four older brothers and two younger ones, Marie developed a character influenced by manly sensibilities.

Born in 1853, while Alexander was still the Russian crown prince, the grand duchess Marie Alexandrovna was sensitive and intelligent enough to perceive the constant danger that threatened her father's life. Paralleling her own growth to adolescence was the rapid spread of revolutionary activity in Russia. Unfortunately, the chief tactic being used by those who wished to overthrow the monarchy was an unending series of attempts to assassinate the emperor. The entire imperial family lived like trapped animals, imprisoned by their guardians, vigilant every moment of every day. The slightest breach of caution might result in being blown to bits by an anarchist's bomb.

Thus, while Marie "studied long hours by lamplight in marble and malachite salons overheated in defense against the endless Russian winters," she was fearful that at any moment her father and, indeed, her whole family might be murdered.

The stress created by the constant threat of assassination together with the strain of an overly demanding course of study took their toll on Marie's nerves. She coped by seeking refuge in religion—the Russian Orthodox Church. Later remembered by her children as "something of an original," Marie camouflaged her conflicts and terrors by being haughty and good-humoredly domineering in order to create her very own world—a safe and secure world—of unbending rules and strictly correct behavior.

The future duchess of Edinburgh was deeply affected by the invalidism of her mother, a fragile and sickly creature who suffered from one ailment after another, eventually wasting away from cancer. Although "she loved and venerated her mother with all the strength of her soul" and sincerely sympathized with her myriad infirmities, the duchess recoiled from her pale, skeletal form and became determined to seek a life of robust health. Overcompensating, she would always insist on perfect health and daily exercise, no matter what the weather.

Though blessed with the brilliant sapphire eyes of the Romanovs and their perfect clear skin, Marie was not especially attractive. She had a plump round face, a snub nose, fat lips and a square, stocky body. But her personality often made a wonderful impression even on those who were most critical. Upon meeting her future daughter-in-law, Queen Victoria enthusiastically wrote: "Dear Marie has a very friendly manner, a pleasant face, beautiful skin and fine bright eyes. . . . There is something very fresh and attractive about her."

It was at a large family gathering at the Hessian summer palace of Jugenheim near Darmstadt in Germany that Marie first met her future husband. During the hot summer of 1868 the ailing Russian empress brought her children to visit her modest childhood home. Staying with her Hessian relatives was Prince Alfred of England, whose sister Alice was married to the amiable Prince Louis of Hesse and the Rhine. It was appropriate that Alfred and Marie should first meet in Darmstadt and later return to use it as their courting ground: their future daughter, Victoria Melita, would one day marry the only son of Alice and Louis and become the reigning grand duchess of Hesse and the Rhine.

However, during that warm summer of 1868 the encounter between the fourteen-year-old Marie of Russia and the twenty-four-year-old English prince was just the casual meeting of distant cousins. They played games together with the other guests on the terrace of the small, picturesque schloss and went horseback riding through the forests that sloped down to the banks of the Rhine. Having just returned from a tour of duty to Australia, the handsome young sailor prince looked even more striking, his bronzed face making his large blue eyes glow like a clear morning sky. As the plain, straightforward little girl listened to Alfred's tales of faraway adventure, she was consumed by romantic infatuation. Alfred, for his part, certainly enjoyed the ego gratification of such an easy conquest. Hearing reports of Marie's extraordinary wealth, he must have been impressed in other ways too.

Not only is there no evidence that a marriage was seriously considered by any of the principals at this time, but also political and religious considerations would have made such a union inconceivable. When young Alfred returned home to England, his anxious mother, Queen Victoria, was beginning to actively search for a bride for her son. Alfred, however, was still having too much fun sailing the seven seas and conquering feminine hearts to be much interested in settling down to the confines of domesticity.

Beginning to search the royal courts of Europe for a suitable consort for Alfred, the queen might have reflected on the rapid rise to power of her own dynasty. While the Romanovs had ruled Russia for almost three hundred years, the English royal House of Hanover had existed for little more than a hundred and fifty. The English monarchy may have been the oldest on earth—it reached back a thousand years—but many royal families of various backgrounds had come and gone—the native Saxons, the Danes, the French Normans and Plantagenets, the constantly warring Lancasters and Yorks, the Tudors, the Stuarts from Scotland, the Dutch royal dynasty of Orange. There was no reason to believe the German-imported Hanoverians would last forever, any more than their predecessors had.

The English crown truly had been welded of many foreign metals. It would have horrified the Anglophile Queen Victoria to realize that her own exalted family and the despised Romanovs were virtually one and the same. Just as the Russian imperial family was almost purely German, so was the English royal house. For eight generations, all the way back to the early eighteenth century and Queen Anne, each and every English monarch had a German mother. And Queen Victoria herself had married a German, thus providing her son and heir with a German father.

So the Russian and English dynasties had much more in common than either would wish to admit. But the German Hanoverians were not nearly as adaptive in their new kingdom as their German cousins were in Russia. George I, who was imported as the legitimate successor to the English throne, never even bothered to learn the language. He spoke only German until the day he died. Understandably, he never achieved popularity with his new subjects. They considered him stupid and hated his foreign entourage, mocking his two favorite mistresses by nicknaming them the Elephant and the Maypole.

There were to be three successive Georges—the thick German accent and alien manners gradually diminishing but still very apparent in George III. This supremely unlucky monarch was not only spotlighted in history for his chronic insanity and for being the villain in America's struggle for independence, but he is also remembered for producing one of his era's most spectacularly dysfunctional families.

Of the thirteen offspring of George III—thirteen seemed to be his unlucky number, whether in children or colonies—it was his seven sons who brought him the most grief. Emotional instability and bad temperaments appeared to be well-established family traits, but these sons compounded the problem by their undisciplined love lives. Amazingly, because of their knack for choosing totally unacceptable bed partners, such as actresses, Catholics, and commoners, the magnificent seven had thus far failed, one and all, to produce one legal heir to the throne. Racing to reproduce, the family began competing in a baby lottery to see who could provide a legitimate heir to the throne and thus control the future of the monarchy. The contest almost went without a winner until one of the younger sons, Prince Edward of Kent, hastily married an insignificant yet genuinely royal widow and immediately impregnated her. Nine months later a beautiful little girl was born, and Edward, having admirably fulfilled his duty and destiny, died shortly after. The baby girl was given the name Victoria.

The reign of Queen Victoria was one of the most dramatic turnabouts in English history. After sinking over decades to near-incredible ill-repute and public contempt, the royal family was restored to respect and admiration. Brought up by a slavishly devoted mother and isolated from every unsavory influence of the corrupt court, Victoria was a sweet, innocent, idealistic girl of eighteen when she was crowned in 1837. She was also a girl with an iron will, unshakable integrity, and a character so strong that it would, with the further influence of her future husband, change the sensibility and moral consciousness of the entire world.

As Victoria enthusiastically began her rule with a firm but quiet authority and a disarming sincerity, she easily won the affection of her new subjects, who were pleased to notice "the harmony and sweetness of her voice" and happily rejoiced in "what luck it is for this country to have such a jewel to raise the character of royalty."

In one of the most felicitous matings of all time, the remarkable Victoria captured the heart of a man even more remarkable than herself. On February 10, 1840, she married Prince Albert of Saxe-Coburg-Gotha.

Albert, an unimportant young prince from an unimportant little duchy in central Germany, had been blessed with uncommon beauty and brains. He also possessed a gentle charm, a rare purity of spirit, and a true goodness of heart. This paragon of virtue had been groomed since boyhood by his ambitious uncle King Leopold I of Belgium, to be the future consort of the English queen, but was kept in the dark about the plans for the illustrious future marriage until the very last minute.

Evidently, when Victoria first set eyes on him, it was not only love at first sight but was an all-consuming passion that would last a lifetime. This was hardly surprising because, as Albert's hypercritical tutor, Stockmar, said, "he has everything attractive to women, and possesses every quality they find pleasing at all times, and in all countries."

The twenty-one-year marriage of Victoria and Albert was one of history's greatest romances. The astute and patient young husband was wise enough to be the father figure that the queen so desperately needed. Selfless and understanding, he managed to skillfully guide his headstrong and passionate wife in a potentially difficult marriage and succeed in establishing a tranquil and solid family, a new royal family that was worthy of the nation's complete admiration and respect.

The major preoccupation of Victoria and Albert was the raising of their nine children. Although totally devoted and well-meaning, the royal couple were unable, by both temperament and experience, to be the ideal mother and father they so desperately desired to be. Both were the products of pathological childhoods, during which, isolated and unhappy, they suffered the loss of one parent while being smothered by the obsessive love of the other.

Albert dedicated his entire existence to his huge family, patiently giving attention to every aspect of his children's lives, his one aim being the development of perfect little princes and princesses. Predictably, his great

expectations gradually sank into great disappointments. In dealing with
his more unpromising offspring, the less they achieved, the more mercilessly he tried to drive them. Albert—so highly gifted himself in so many
areas—seemed to lack any understanding or sympathy for those who
were not as naturally blessed. Or perhaps it was just the age-old case of a
parent refusing to recognize his or her child as being anything less than
perfect.

But less than perfect most of them were—primarily because of a
heavy dose of Queen Victoria's Hanoverian genes. Not surprisingly,
those children who took most after Prince Albert came closest to his
ideal. His greatest success was his eldest child, Vicky, the Princess Royal,
who was as brilliant and talented as her father. His greatest failure was his
second child, his son and heir, Bertie, who in mind, looks, and temperament resembled his mother to such a remarkable degree that she unhappily considered him "a caricature of myself." Bertie's shortcomings
increased with age, and the Hope of the Nation was soon a spectacular
disappointment to both parents. His youthful romantic indiscretions
drove his father to an early grave, and consequently instilled in his grief-
stricken mother a lifelong aversion to the sight of him.

Despite her many virtues, Queen Victoria was also a spoiled and selfish person who expected to remain the most important part of her offspring's lives even after her children were fully grown and had families
of their own. Possessive, demanding, hypersensitive, and domineering,
Victoria adored all of her children between the ages of three and six but
found them less attractive and more problematic at all later ages. Thus,
the relationship was difficult for both mother and child—an intense and
highly charged bonding based upon affection, need, and intimidation.

The younger children of the royal family generally fared much better,
benefiting greatly from being spared intensive parental attention. With
Victoria and Albert placing such high hopes on the development of darling Vicky and idle Bertie, the rest of the royal brood were allowed to
relax a little bit and make an occasional mistake.

The third child of the family was another girl, Alice. She, though not
a prodigy like her older sister, also took after her father and inherited his
moral sense and many of his abilities. Alice would eventually become the
grand duchess of Hesse and the Rhine and the mother of Victoria
Melita's first husband.

Queen Victoria's fourth child and second son was born on August 6,
1844. He was named Alfred after the great ninth-century English king,

but became known in the family as Affie. With golden hair and large, piercing blue eyes, which Victoria Melita was to inherit, Affie was the queen's handsomest son. During his early youth, he was also her most promising and sweetest-natured child.

At eighteen months of age the angelic-looking little Affie was observed to have "a very good manly temper; much more like that of most children than that of the Princess Royal or Prince of Wales (his obstinate older brother)." Affie was especially fortunate in having Lady Sarah Lyttelton supervising the royal nursery. She was a kind, gentle woman of refinement and great common sense, good humor, and patience. And she was something of an anomaly for her day: Lady Lyttelton did not believe in punishment for children. Her logic was that "one is never sure [punishments] are fully understood by the child as belonging to the naughtiness." Affie fully responded to his kindly nurse, and all his talents and virtues flourished under her faithful care. Approaching five years of age, Affie was enthusiastically described by Lady Lyttelton as having "uncommon abilities; and a mind which will make the task of instructing him most smooth and delightful."

His favorite subject was geography, and he soon developed an obsessive interest in the Royal Navy, which dominated every ocean of the world. This precocious interest in the sea was a happy chance, for the younger sons of the English monarch traditionally pursue careers in the navy.

Affie was amazingly like his father, Prince Albert, in his unusually tranquil and self-possessed disposition and his need to be constantly occupied with some activity of interest. Although Affie had a fine intellect, he also had a passion for anything mechanical. Always curious about how things worked, he often found ways to improve the gadgets he tinkered with, sometimes inventing something new. He was loved by his brothers and sisters for making special toys for them and fixing the broken ones they already had.

When Affie turned eleven, an erudite officer from the Royal Navy was brought to the palace and began tutoring the young prince for his future occupation. There had been serious problems involving Affie's education and a proper decision had been difficult to reach, primarily because he had been chosen by his uncle, Duke Ernest of Saxe-Coburg-Gotha, to be heir to his German duchy.

Duke Ernest was the older brother of Prince Albert. The black sheep of the family, Uncle Ernest lived for pleasure and was now paying the price: a dreadful case of syphilis. Although he had previously produced many bastard children by a steady stream of comely young mistresses, he sadly realized that the disease had put an end to his fathering days. Lacking a legitimate heir, Ernest arranged for his bright and promising nephew to succeed him as the reigning duke.

However, until Bertie married and had children, Affie would remain second in line for the English throne. If anything happened to Bertie before the older prince produced an heir, Affie would one day be king.

With this distinct possibility in mind, it was difficult to give Affie the education appropriate for the future ruler of a German duchy. Ernest, of course, wanted Affie to be sent to Coburg, where he would pursue a very Germanic curriculum and become a good German instead of a proper Englishman. But the lovingly protective Prince Albert would never have allowed his favorite son to go off alone to live under the poisonous influence of the dissolute Duke Ernest.

To avoid having to give in to Ernest's constant demands, Albert played up the possibility that Affie might succeed to the English throne, repeatedly reminding Ernest that "if we make a German of him, it might be very difficult for him and our country." So Affie remained in England and proceeded with his plans for a career in the Royal Navy to precede his succession to the Coburg crown.

Although Affie was still in love with the sea, he also eagerly looked forward to his German inheritance. He adored the cozy isolation of his father's boyhood home, the beautiful and unpretentious Rosenau castle. It was a shared affection that brought father and son very close together.

Affie was in so many ways like his father that, had events not decreed otherwise, he might have grown up to be an equally happy, disciplined, and successful man. Unfortunately, from the early age of fourteen he began gradually losing his father's shrewd guidance and powerful influence. Passing his entrance examinations to the Royal Navy with an outstanding performance, Affie left home, returning only for brief vacations and holidays. After spending his seventeenth birthday with his family at the royal estate in the Highlands of Scotland, Affie set sail for his new station in the West Indies. A few months later he was devastated by the news of his father's sudden death. Prince Albert, exhausted from overwork and worry, was only forty-two when a mild case of typhoid fever killed him in December 1861.

The death of his father completely altered Affie's course in life. Not only did he lose his greatest source of strength, and support, but the loss drove a wedge of misunderstanding and resentment between mother and son that would only push them further apart with time.

Affie sailed home as soon as he could, arriving two months after the tragic death. Though overcome by grief, the young prince tried his best to be cheerful and raise the spirits of those around him, especially his mother.

But the queen was determined to make the very worst of an unhappy situation. She had lost her beloved husband, the center of her existence, and her only interest in life now was to suffer as fully as possible. She indulged in an orgy of masochism that may well have been triggered by feelings of guilt and fear as well as loss.

Her kindly son was in no position to understand his mother's emotional sickness. Affie only knew that in the past he had always cheered her up and brought a smile to her face; now he tried to do the same again. Although she resented and resisted his efforts, she was eventually won over and even laughed out loud, for the first time since Prince Albert's death, when Affie talked his Danish sister-in-law, Princess Alexandra into asking the queen at breakfast one morning if "she had enjoyed her forty winks."

However, such moments of merriment were rare indeed; Queen Victoria only remembered Affie's attempts to amuse her as insolence and later held them against him. Still, he remained her favorite son.

After having spent five tense and gloomy months with his mother at Windsor Castle, Affie returned to active duty in the Royal Navy in the summer of 1862. He was now almost a grown man and leading an independent life, and this separation from his mother was successful in easing the friction in their relationship.

But no sooner had Victoria's feelings toward her absent son softened somewhat than word reached her of his first illicit love affair. Stationed at that time on the island of Malta, the dashing young prince had become romantically involved with a local beauty. The puritanical queen was enraged and shocked by her son's "heartless and dishonourable behavior" and declared it a "heavy blow" to her "weak and shattered frame." She had him sent home immediately to England.

With absolutely no understanding of a young man's need to sow his wild oats, Victoria expected each and every one of her four sons to lead high-minded, celibate lives just as their noble father had done. She refused to tolerate the slightest breach of sexual morality, and considered her boys to be safe from temptation only when they were properly married. Naively, she thought Affie's amorous adventures could be ended by an early wedding.

And "early" meant as early as possible. He was now causing even greater problems by being visibly infatuated with his gorgeous new sister-in-law, Princess Alexandra of Wales, Bertie's Danish-born wife. Affie adoringly shadowed her, spending almost every night with her and her husband at their London home, Marlborough House. Watching the dangerous growth of this potential ménage à trois, Queen Victoria panicked. "He is far too much 'épris' with Alix to be allowed to be much there without possibly ruining the happiness of all three and Affie has not the strength of mind (or more of principle and character) to resist the temptation, and it is like playing with fire," she excitedly wrote her eldest daughter in Berlin. "Beloved Papa always said the feelings of admiration and even love are not sinful—nor can you prevent the impulses of one's nature, but it is your duty to resist the temptation in every way. You may imagine how anxious this makes us."

Very quickly, the queen enlisted her two eldest daughters to find Affie a suitable wife. Although at twenty the young prince was more handsome than ever, finding him a royal mate was not an easy matter. Victoria immediately pushed the candidacy of Princess Marie of Saxe-Altenburg because "it would be such a blessing to have a real German daughter-in-law."

But Affie was unimpressed with his mother's choice, and Victoria's encouraging comment that "possibly the eldest Weimar may turn out less ugly" did not inspire any greater trust. There were several more prospects. The many royal houses of Germany were thoroughly searched for eligible young princesses—the prettier the better. Luckily for Affie, his sister Vicky, the crown princess of Prussia, was just as picky in this department as he was, and since she was in charge of selecting likely candidates, very few made it to the finals. Princess Wilhelmine of Württemberg had been eliminated early because Vicky had found her to be "very plain, not so much by her features as by the unwholesome and unkempt look she has—such untidy hair and a shocking complexion." It seemed that Princess Catherine of Oldenburg, a flashing beauty, might do nicely, but she just wasn't Affie's type and he turned her down.

With health, personal appearance, personality, and politics disqualifying one young princess after another, there remained one increasingly attractive possibility—the notoriously eccentric Elisabeth of Wied, whom Vicky had initially dismissed as being "so odd" and not looking "well-bred or "very ladylike." However, when Affie turned twenty-one and marital prospects began growing slim, Vicky took another and less critical look at Elisabeth, then wrote to the impatient queen that she had "much improved." Vicky admitted that "graceful and elegant her figure and her walk will never be, but she is a very pretty person now." She ended with the tactful query "Have you quite given up all thought of her for Affie?" No, she hadn't. Victoria immediately dispatched her playboy son to Germany to court the young princess.

Elisabeth was truly odd. Gushingly romantic and fanciful, she killed all possibility of a match the moment Affie arrived by insisting that they retreat to the nearby forest, where the embarrassed young suitor was forced to play his violin among her wooded "friends." Affie grudgingly complied, but, the impromptu concert completed, he promptly announced that nothing on earth could ever move him to marry Elisabeth of Wied. Ironically, this same princess would later become Europe's most spectacular royal crackpot as the first queen of Romania—the adversary and predecessor of Affie's future eldest daughter, Marie.

While his personal life was rambling into one cul-de-sac after another, Affie's material opportunities were improving considerably. Suddenly and unexpectedly he was offered the crown of Greece. The Greeks had ousted their unpopular foreign monarch, King Otto, an unadaptable Bavarian prince who had been ruling for the past thirty years as if he had never left Munich. The Greeks liked the idea of having this dashing son of Queen Victoria as their sovereign, and after holding a national plebiscite, they elected Affie the new king of Greece with an astounding 95 percent of the vote.

Unfortunately for Affie's ambition, a previous treaty between the major powers forbade any member of the English royal family to accept the Greek throne, and thus the Danish brother of Affie's adored sister-in-law Alexandra, became King George I of the Hellenes.

In meager compensation for his loss of a crown, Affie progressed to the rank of captain in the Royal Navy, and on his twenty-second birthday in 1866 his mother officially created him duke of Edinburgh and earl of Ulster and Kent. Several months later it was decided that the new duke of Edinburgh would take his ship, H.M.S. *Galatea,* on a lengthy world voyage with an extended stay in Australia. Queen Victoria viewed the trip as a godsend; it offered a convenient solution to Affie's unending platonic romance with his brother's irresistible wife. Victoria disapproved of Affie's wholehearted dedication to amusing parties and the frivolities of society life, and the worried mother hoped "that the responsibility and the separation from his London flatterers will do him good."

"With reluctance and suspicion," Affie sadly left his close circle of family and friends and sailed the *Galatea* to Australia. For his dutiful efforts, he was rewarded with a bullet in the back. A radical Irish nationalist shot him near Sydney, but luckily the cartridge missed his spine and his life was saved by an emergency operation. He returned home to Windsor to recuperate, but soon his popularity was annoying his peevish mother again, the queen bitterly complaining that he got "ovations as if he had done something—instead of God's mercy having spared his life."

It was in an effort to ease tensions at home during this time that Affie fled to Darmstadt to visit his understanding sister Alice—and fatefully met the teenaged grand duchess Marie of Russia.

After their innocent idyll in the lush Hessian countryside, Affie and Marie liked each other, he admiring her character and impressed by her great wealth and she taken with his glowing good looks, but that seems about as far as it went. Soon duty called; Affie concluded his German holiday and returned to the sea. Because a second cruise, which began at the end of 1868, took him completely across the globe to South America, India, and Asia, he did not return home until May of 1871, and thus was kept off the marriage market for two and a half years. Upon his return, Affie was immediately pressed by his mother to find an acceptable wife. "If he can only find a Princess likely to suit and please him," the queen wrote to her daughter Vicky, "I would not mind who she was. . . . I cannot tell you how anxious I do feel about Affie."

Feeling the full weight of the queen's anxiety and impatience, Affie again viewed the available field and firmly settled his choice on his happy memories of Grand Duchess Marie of Russia. Those who knew him best thought it was Marie's immense fortune that made the greatest impression on Affie. His secretary at that time, Sir John Cowell, came to the conclusion that the duke of Edinburgh's mania for money "amounted to a disease." And perhaps Marie was the best cure. Her enormous wealth would certainly free Affie from his reliance on his mother's purse and allow him to finally move out of her shadow and become fully independent.

After the proper diplomatic groundwork was laid, Affie formally met with Marie's father, Emperor Alexander II of Russia, in the summer of 1871 and made his proposal. Disappointingly, the emperor was vague and unenthusiastic toward the handsome young Englishman's suit. Both Alexander and his wife cherished their only daughter and desperately wanted to keep her close to them in Russia. They had no love for England or Queen Victoria and her family, and didn't honestly believe that Marie could ever really be happy in such a life. Most of the Romanov family viewed the queen as simply "a pampered, sentimental, selfish old woman."

Keeping the duke of Edinburgh at arm's length, the alarmed empress quickly introduced her eighteen-year-old daughter to as many eligible suitors as she could find. But apparently because of Marie's limited charms, there weren't that many takers. The empress confided to her Hessian brother that her husband "is still *against* Alfred as a match" even though "Marie inclines much more to him—and especially his position—than to Stuttgart, Strelitz, or Schwerin." The empress betrayed her own feelings by saying to her brother, "If you could find me a *charming Prince* who would be prepared to stay in Russia, I should prefer him to any of them."

For almost two years Marie's parents optimistically waited for that "charming Prince" to suddenly appear, but he never did. They slowly reconciled themselves to their daughter's first choice, especially after Marie began seriously flirting with the better-looking men at her father's court.

In the warm spring of 1873 all animosities and prejudices were put aside and the engagement of Affie and Marie was officially announced.

However, back in England the hatchet was far from being buried. Queen Victoria imagined Marie to be filled with "half-Oriental Russian notions" and believed her as "arrogant and false" as the other Romanovs, and she most decidedly did not want the Russian grand duchess as a daughter-in-law.

Disdaining the Romanovs for possessing the vulgar spirit of the "bourgeoisie" and censuring the Russian empire because "absolute autocracy was wrong and bound to end in tears," Queen Victoria did everything in her power to stop the marriage. First, she begged her prime minister, William Gladstone, to object publicly to the engagement and bring political pressure against it. This he could not and would not do. So Victoria concentrated on the religious question and ranted against the perils of being involved with the Russian Orthodox Church, warning that the marriage "would be the first departure since 200 years nearly from the practice of our family" and saying that "we must be very firm—or else we may pack up—and call back the descendants of the Stuarts."

Victoria tried a variety of other tactics, too, from promoting scandalous gossip about Marie to organizing the family into battle lines, but nothing worked, so she eventually accepted the fact of the impending marriage as "a dispensation of God."

The wedding took place—twice—at St. Petersburg on January 23, 1974. The first ceremony was an ornate Orthodox service at the magnificent Winter Palace. The second was conducted according to the rites of the Church of England. It was the only one of her nine children's weddings that Queen Victoria did not attend.

Her dramatic absence ominously and accurately augured the nature of the marriage to come.

CHAPTER THREE

The Royal War at Windsor

*B*Y THE TIME OF Victoria Melita's birth in November of 1876 the three-year marriage of Affie and Marie had gradually deteriorated to the point where both husband and wife were tacitly admitting its failure and seeking emotional satisfaction elsewhere. For the increasingly cynical and disillusioned duke of Edinburgh, his naval career and a steady supply of whiskey and pretty women occupied most of his time. But for the idealistic and highly principled duchess, her three children had become the sole reason for her existence.

Victoria Melita's mother was one of the most original and independent women of her day, one who was incapable of being dominated, by anyone or anything. Her imperious nature combined with the deep religious and cultural differences between her and the English royal family to produce a monumental conflict. Of all the young women on earth, none could have antagonized the queen of England more than the forthright duchess of Edinburgh.

But those who witnessed the splendor of Marie's wedding at the sumptuous sixteen-hundred-room Winter Palace in St. Petersburg could not help feeling sympathy for the unattractive young girl whose anxiety and insecurity were masked by the appearance of a "permanent scowl" on her face. Perhaps sensing the unhappiness to come in the marriage, the wife of the presiding Anglican minister sadly looked beyond the dazzling regal façade and hoped that since Marie "has always been so tenderly loved . . . it seems quite natural that it should continue so."

An intimation of the permanent storm to come was delivered several months before her marriage ceremony when Queen Victoria insisted that the Russian emperor bring his daughter to England for her approval. Alexander II was so outraged by this demand that he simply responded by calling Victoria a "silly old fool." When Alexander's sickly wife, trying to keep peace, suggested that she bring her daughter to Cologne for Victoria's inspection, the queen exploded. In a flurry of indignant letters to other family members, Queen Victoria ranted furiously that it was beyond comprehension how anyone could expect her, "the Doyenne of Sovereigns," to chase across Europe to meet her son's future wife. Victoria considered the suggestion "one of the *coolest* things I ever heard," and she emphatically made it clear that she was "not like any little Princess ready to run to the slightest call of *the mighty Russians!*"

As it turned out, no one went anyplace, and it wasn't until two months after the St. Petersburg wedding that Queen Victoria finally came face-to-face with her new daughter-in-law. The Edinburghs arrived at Windsor Castle at the end of March in 1874; the bright blue skies that accompanied them might have symbolized the great change in Victoria's feelings toward her son's new wife. After having spent most of her negative emotions in an unending stream of abrasive correspondence with her eldest daughters, the queen had adjusted to the inevitable and had not only accepted the fact of the Russian marriage, but quite intelligently decided to make the best of it. The reports of those who had attended the distant wedding, including her son Bertie and his wife, had persuaded her that Marie, although no beauty, was a woman of admirable character.

Since Victoria was no beauty herself, and likewise always took pride in possessing sterling virtues, which she considered more important than all other qualities, it is likely that she completely reassessed the Russian bride and was pleased to discover what might perhaps be a kindred spirit. Thus, when the duke of Edinburgh arrived with his bride at his boyhood home, his mother was eagerly awaiting them, determined to fully accept the new member of the family.

"I have formed a high opinion of her," she reported to her daughter Vicky. "Her wonderfully even, cheerful satisfied temper—her kind and indulgent disposition, free from bigotry and intolerance, and her serious, intelligent mind—so entirely free from everything fast—and so full of occupation and interest in everything makes her a most agreeable companion. Everyone must like her. But alas! Not one likes him! I fear that will never get better!"

As Queen Victoria charitably tried to find elements of beauty in Marie's plain face, she was primarily concerned that her daughter-in-law's "most pleasingly natural . . . very sensible and frank" character would have a positive effect on her increasingly wayward son. Above all else, the fretting queen was most pleased and impressed by the direct and unyielding manner that Marie displayed toward her ill-tempered spouse, happily noting that Marie was "not a bit afraid of Affie and I hope will have the very best influence upon him."

Had Affie been a different man, his marriage might have overcome the many serious obstacles it faced and become a reasonable success. However, by this point in his life, Queen Victoria's handsomest son could not have made a satisfactory husband for any woman. The sensitive, highly emotional youth who cried so easily and showed such tenderness for his younger brothers and sisters had completely vanished. In his place was a tactless, boorish man who refused to show any tender emotion whatsoever. The tragic loss of his father and an early and complete immersion in the arduous life of a sailor in the Royal Navy had taken a heavy toll on his personality and character. Silent and totally given over to the pursuit of pleasure, he possessed "an abominable temper" and was universally recognized as the most unpopular member of the royal family.

Victoria prayed that somehow in some way marriage would improve her errant son, who she readily admitted was "ungracious, reserved . . . and so little liked." She perceived Marie of Russia as having those qualities of mind and spirit that might best bring about such a rescue. This helps to explain Victoria's initial enthusiasm and affection. The queen had great expectations of her new daughter-in-law—impossible expectations, as it turned out.

Affie was simply beyond saving.

And when it became gradually apparent to Victoria that the qualities of Marie's character were completely impotent in correcting Affie's severe faults, the queen's disappointment turned to anger against the very person on whom she had placed her highest hopes—the "treasure" from St. Petersburg.

Of course it was not Marie's fault that she could not reform her impossible husband. She was just as disappointed in him as was his mother, but she blamed his undesirable traits on his "thoroughly English education." Marie soon came to detest her adopted homeland. It was indeed her unwillingness or inability to adapt to her radically new environment that created a good deal of the tension and conflict in Victoria Melita's mother's frustrated life. Had she at least made a reasonable attempt to fit in and accept the elements of English living that she could not change, the haughty and arrogant Marie would have saved herself a great deal of anxiety and grief. In the beginning, Queen Victoria fervently hoped that the new duchess of Edinburgh would learn English ways "good and fast." But just the opposite occurred.

Feeling vastly superior to the modest English court, Marie complained to her mother that she thought "London hideous, the air there appalling, the English food abominable, the late hours very tiring, the visits to Windsor and Osborne boring beyond belief." Missing the clean beauty of the white, frozen winters she left behind, Marie could never get used to the dreary wetness of her new home with its mist-shrouded landscapes and oppressive, smoky fogs that eternally painted the world in depressing shades of gray.

But what troubled the imperious Russian grand duchess most was the instantaneous reduction of her rank. "Her Imperial Highness" was now simply "Her Royal Highness." She complained to her father, and the emperor promptly informed Queen Victoria that his daughter must still be addressed as "Imperial Highness" rather than in the manner customary for the other English princesses. The queen did not take kindly to this assertion of imperial authority and felt outraged over the none too subtle implication of the inferiority of England's regal rank. When her temper calmed somewhat, Victoria responded that she could care less if "Imperial" was used in the duchess of Edinburgh's new title, provided that the English "Royal" came first.

Thus, Marie officially became Her Royal and Imperial Highness, the Duchess of Edinburgh, the Grand Duchess of Russia. But no sooner was this crisis of etiquette solved than another contest of egos erupted. Having successfully retained her "Imperial" title, Marie then proceeded to use it to gain a superior footing in the royal family. Arguing that it was traditionally recognized protocol for persons of imperial rank to be placed higher than those who were merely royal, she insisted that, as the daughter of an emperor, she be given precedence over all the other princesses of the English royal family, including the Princess of Wales, who was merely the daughter of the king of Denmark.

This, Queen Victoria would not tolerate. There was to be no discussion! The wife of the heir to the throne who would one day be queen of England must come first, and Victoria's eldest daughter, Vicky, who would one day be empress of Germany, must come second. The third ranking position at court for royal ladies was the best that the queen could offer.

Marie took it grudgingly and with resentment that lasted a lifetime. Even the diplomatic cautioning of her good-natured father did not assuage the duchess's injured pride, and it was this minor demotion in regal rank that inspired the permanent and corrosive aversion that Marie would always feel for England and all things English.

Even in the face of Victoria's ruling, the duchess of Edinburgh insisted on observing the full pomp and prerogatives of her imperial Russian title. In progressive and relatively democratic England, the rigid arrogance of Marie became legendary and contributed greatly to her unpopularity.

In defiance of her restricted role at court, Marie retaliated by showing off her collection of jewels—tiaras, necklaces, bracelets, and rings of the world's finest diamonds, emeralds, sapphires, rubies, and pearls—gems so fantastic, so large and perfect, that the jewelry of her sisters-in-law looked tawdry in comparison. When Victoria saw the Romanov jewels at Marie's first drawing-room party, she glowered at them "like an angry parrot," disdainfully narrowing her eyes and "shrugging her shoulders like a bird whose plumage has been ruffled, her mouth drawn down at the corners in an expression which those who knew her had learned to dread."

It seemed that whatever the duchess of Edinburgh did increased her unpopularity. She created a sensation by smoking in public and going about her life as if she cared nothing about what people thought about her. In fact, she didn't. She felt she was above popular opinion, and the only thing that mattered to her was her children.

When she had first arrived in England, Marie was pointedly asked by her new relations when she would be expecting her first baby. Slightly embarrassed, she replied with a laugh that she was "in no hurry," but that her husband was "very impatient." Affie must indeed have been "impatient," for their first child arrived the following October, just a little more than nine months after their wedding. The baby was born at Buckingham Palace and named after his father. Little Alfred had just turned one when the duchess of Edinburgh gave birth to her second child, a daughter this time, whom they named after herself and her mother. This little Marie would eventually become the legendary

Queen Marie of Romania. Another year passed and Victoria Melita made her appearance in Malta.

Ironically, this conflicted and unhappy marriage had the highest birth rate in the entire family.

Avoiding Queen Victoria as scrupulously as she could, the frustrated duchess of Edinburgh also shunned London's fashionable society, which only valued women who excelled in the superficial qualities of beauty, charm, and grace in dancing. The duchess's "rare intelligence and exceptional education" were not appreciated by members of her class in England, but the few friends that she had, such as Lady Randolph Churchill, the mother of Winston Churchill, were devoted to her for life.

Certainly the duchess of Edinburgh's arrogant self-sufficiency was not appreciated by a mother-in-law who was used to controlling every member of her family by an almost automatic intimidation. Queen Victoria had mastered a unique repertoire of subtle yet ominous expressions that enabled her iron will to quietly dominate as effectively as the terrorizing tactics of tyrants. Marie was not the least bit impressed by the queen's power or authority. From lighting fires in the frozen chimneys at Windsor Castle to going riding whenever she pleased, the duchess defied each and every petty edict almost as if to purposely carry on a war with the throne she so despised. Marie even used the magnificent Romanov jewels as a weapon, wearing as many of them as she could, as often as she could, to emphasize her "imperial" superiority.

Poor Queen Victoria suffered a painful jealousy for more than two years until she finally couldn't stand it any longer. Having a daughter-in-law who had a more illustrious title than herself was becoming intolerable. So just a few months before Victoria Melita's birth in 1876, her grandmother arranged to have herself be officially declared empress of India. Now, as queen-empress, she could also use the royal-imperial style of address—and even do her arrogant daughter-in-law one better by being a Majesty instead of a mere Highness.

Sir Henry Ponsonby, Victoria's private secretary, summed up this passionate contest for royal rank and status by humorously quoting Dr. Johnson to his wife: "Who comes first, a louse or a flea?"

If tensions weren't running high enough between Windsor Castle and Clarence House, the London home of the Edinburghs after their return from their sojourn in Malta, in 1877 Russia went to war with Turkey in an attempt to gain control of the Balkans—and Queen Victoria exploded. She considered it nothing less than a slap in the face from

Marie's father, the kindly, sad-eyed Alexander II, who had visited England a few months after Marie had taken up residence there and emotionally placed his precious daughter in the queen's kind care, promising Her Majesty that there wasn't "any reason why our two countries should not be on the best of terms." Now it seemed that the Romanovs were truly as dishonorable as the queen had always believed, and an encore of the Crimean War, with England once again battling Russia, was a distinct possibility for several anxious months in 1877.

Queen Victoria's rage increased with each new bulletin from the eastern Mediterranean. She wrote angry letters to Affie in which she attacked and insulted Russia and the emperor. Unfortunately, she failed to remember that her son was even more tactless than herself, and, with mischievous pleasure, the duke of Edinburgh shared the regrettable letters with his wife. Naturally, the Anglophobic Marie lost no time in passing the contents of the letters to her family in St. Petersburg.

It seemed everyone suffered from the falling-out. Victoria blamed her son and his wife for their almost traitorous lack of discretion; Marie never forgave Victoria for her scathing remarks; and Marie's mother, the empress, blamed the entire English royal family—"The insulting things that the Queen says," she observed, "are worthy of a fishwife. It is a pity that her son has not got more character."

It was a shame that this family crisis occurred when it did, for Queen Victoria's latest grandchild and namesake, Princess Victoria Melita, was about to celebrate her first birthday. Ducky, as she had been affectionately nicknamed, was already taking her first steps and saying "Mama" in an almost uncannily controlled and elegant voice. With auburn hair and large blue eyes that seemed to look earnestly right through things, Ducky greatly resembled her father and her grandfather, the queen's dearly lamented Prince Albert.

This was a grandchild in whom Queen Victoria could really delight, a beautiful baby girl who, unlike her slightly older brother and sister, definitely took after the passionate queen and her serious and high-minded late husband. By the time she was two she was almost as tall as her three-year-old sister, Marie, who was known in the family as Missy. Besides showing signs of exceptional beauty, Ducky was also displaying a precocious intellect. A strong and lively child, she was a natural leader and was already the dominant force in the nursery.

However, because Ducky and her siblings were tightly wrapped in the firm arms of their reclusive Russian mother and because international

events and family conflicts burned intensely during the first few years of
Ducky's life, Grandmama Queen was rarely seen by the children. Fortunately, Victoria and Marie slowly developed a kind of armed truce.
Unlike all of Victoria's other children, the duchess of Edinburgh was
completely independent of her financially. One of the world's wealthiest
women, she didn't want or need anything from her difficult mother-in-
law, and once Queen Victoria realized this and reconciled herself to it,
their relationship went much more smoothly.

And eventually the aging English monarch had to admire Marie of
Russia. While all of her children "avoided discussing her will, and her
veto made them tremble," the queen could always count on Marie to
stand up to her. The duchess seems to have mastered the art of dealing
with her husband's mother right from the beginning. "You only have to
give her a good fright to make her draw in her horns," Marie proudly
boasted to her own mother. Throughout Europe, the duchess of Edinburgh's chief claim to fame was her reputation for being "the sole member of the British royal family over whom Her Majesty does not attempt
to domineer."

Undoubtedly the comparison between the duchess and her dissolute
husband only made her look all the better. One of the most unpopular
men in England, the duke of Edinburgh richly deserved his black name.
Although he knew his duty as a naval officer better than anyone else and
was totally devoted to it, "no-one likes him." Having taken to drink,
Affie was now a full-blown alcoholic interested only in sport and pleasure when away from his ship. And he was away from his ship a good
deal of the time.

"Rude, touchy, willful, unscrupulous, improvident and unfaithful,"
the duke of Edinburgh was a moody and withdrawn man who, between
violent outbursts of temper, seemed to live in his own enclosed world.
No one could trust him, for he took an almost perverse pleasure in making trouble for anyone he could. Even his mother sadly came to the conclusion that Affie was something of a bounder. "I am grieved to say,"
Queen Victoria wrote to her daughter during the Balkan crisis of 1877,
"that Affie has become most impudent in his language and I only hope
he does not make mischief."

At home, Affie barely tolerated his growing family. He hated his wife's
devotion to culture and her intellectual pursuits and was "driven into
temper tantrums over her passions for reading, serious conversation, and
the theater." The duchess did her best to keep the marriage going, but

she bitterly resented her husband's boorish attitude and later confessed to her daughter that she had never felt like anything more than her husband's "legitimate mistress," a role she found "simply degrading" for the daughter of the Russian emperor.

It was to the duchess of Edinburgh's greatest credit that she kept her severe marital problems completely hidden from her children when they were young. Ducky and her brother and sisters never had the slightest suspicion of the secret unhappiness that filled their home. The duchess, retreating from her spouse, centered her emotional needs and prodigious energy on her offspring, especially her daughters (she always "said she liked girls better than boys"). And Ducky was her favorite.

"She made us wonderfully happy," the duchess's eldest daughter, Missy, remembered toward the end of her life, "so of course we children imagined that she was perfectly happy herself. But later on I found out that she had never been really happy, or at peace with herself; many things tormented her, she did not take life easily."

The same thing could have been said of Ducky when she grew to womanhood; another trait she shared with her mother being a relentless quest for perfection that perpetually made her "dissatisfied and critical with herself." Perceived by Ducky and Missy as the victim of a much too severe upbringing and education, the duchess was also seen by her understanding daughter as suffering from the "oppressive influence" of the Russian Orthodox Church to which, "with all her soul," she fanatically clung. "Outwardly she may have appeared haughty, a stickler for form and proud of her rank, but inwardly she was humble, always tormenting herself, tortured with the idea that she had never lived up to the ideal set for her by her parents and those who educated her."

But there was also much that Ducky and Missy admired. "My mother had been very severely brought up, and she herself had strict ideas upon education and behavior, but there was at the same time a wideness of mind about her which made of her an exceptional woman, and above all her generosity was extraordinary. Of course she was wealthy, but she gave even beyond what it was reasonable to give, gave and gave, to big and small, to rich and poor; her very reason of existence was to be able to give."

The chief beneficiaries of the duchess of Edinburgh's inexhaustible giving were her children. They adored her, and contrary to the maternal norm of almost all other royal families of the day, they received her entire time, attention, and devoted love.

The duke of Edinburgh was primarily an absent father, even when he was at home. To his children, who seldom saw him, his taciturn withdrawals were interpreted as an enigmatic exclusivity, which stirred their imaginations. All his faults were concealed by his considerate wife, so his children were free to see his vague presence in the most romantic of lights. Even later in their lives, the duke's daughters did not know enough of his inner workings to understand him fully. They simply remembered him as a "rare" person—by which they meant that "he did not occupy himself actively with his children." They were in awe of the "exceedingly good-looking, sunburnt, blue-eyed" man who would suddenly appear in their home as a "wonderful stranger." But no matter how often they saw their handsome father, they never felt that they were "entirely in touch with him."

On those few precious "red-lettered days" when their moody father would "discover us . . . he would invent some game or amusement that he seemed to enjoy as much as we did. He invented a thrilling game for the winter evenings; the lamps were all put out and Papa would hide in a dark corner pretending to be an ogre. We never knew in which room he was. With fearful trembling we would crawl through the ink-black chambers and suddenly, when all danger seemed over, he would spring out from somewhere and catch us whilst we screamed as though he were really going to eat us up."

Although the innocence of childhood and the kindly protection of Ducky's mother could mask the duke's unsavory character, the extreme friction between the duchess and her domineering mother-in-law was impossible to disguise. Even as a very young girl, Ducky realized that for her mother it was not "easy being Queen Victoria's daughter-in-law."

Leaving the warm, tranquil island of Malta behind while still in her infancy, Ducky sailed into a world of magnificent homes and sumptuous privilege and fame. She also entered a vastly extended family of intricate complexity and impossible conflicts, in which one grandparent was the queen of England and empress of India and the other was the emperor of Russia—not to mention an aunt and uncle who were soon to be the emperor and empress of Germany.

Amid this illustrious and difficult family, Ducky would blossom into one of the most vibrant and original princesses of her day.

CHAPTER FOUR

The Passionate Princess

WHILE HER OLDER brother and sister, Alfred and Missy, took after their Russian mother in looks and personality, Ducky was the only child in the family to closely resemble the duke. With uncommon luck, she seems to have inherited her father's best features—his clear olive skin, his luminous blue eyes, his finely chiseled features, and his beautiful dark hair that brilliantly reflected the softest light. Tall and statuesque, she fortunately did not inherit her mother's bulky figure that her siblings did.

Ducky also shared part of her father's basic temperament—a shyness and extreme sensitivity, which would create many difficulties throughout her life. Unlike her father, however, she never allowed these traits to sour her personality and undermine her character. On the contrary, she steadily developed a remarkably strong spirit and eventually her iron will would make her one of the most formidable women in Europe, and more than a match for her imperious mother and domineering grandmother.

However, the quality that distinguished young Princess Ducky from her earliest years was passion. She inherited from Queen Victoria an almost ungovernable emotional temperament and from Prince Albert, an ardent romanticism. Where her father had demonstrated this same passionate legacy in his early years by bursting into tears at every occasion and later, as an adult, suppressing any emotion whatsoever and withdrawing from relationships, Ducky accepted her own tempestuous nature, always trusting it and exploring its complexity and limits.

From the very beginning, the dark and beautiful little princess was a "difficult child." Serious and purposeful, she took everything very much to heart and was incapable of the slightest degree of insincerity or dishonesty. Ducky also loved unreservedly and resented being disciplined. This "passionate child was often misunderstood," but her sister, Missy, knew and appreciated her better than anyone.

Missy, just a year older, was the physical and mental opposite of Ducky. Fair, with golden hair, she was filled with laughter and had an easygoing, unfailingly good nature. Breezily confident and outgoing, she never felt the need to look beyond the surface of beauty and pleasure. Missy viewed everything around her as a complement to her celebrated beauty and always fancied herself as a central player on the world's stage. Fortunately, a truly loving and magnanimous heart compensated for her self-absorption and shallowness of character. Perhaps one of Missy's finest qualities was her lifelong love for and devotion to her best friend and soul mate, Ducky.

"I took things more easily than Ducky," she later remembered, "and made friends more quickly, but Nana [the children's nanny] liked Ducky best."

Seeing herself as a "true daughter of Eve," Missy reveled in her femininity and cultivated it. Next to this coquettish sister, the bold and straightforward Ducky appeared almost masculine. The contrast apparently suited them both, for Missy seems to have deliberately assumed the softer and more submissive role in the sisterly partnership and Ducky was obviously more inclined toward forceful leadership. These attitudes were expressed in both their day-to-day relationship and the games they played together. Missy would drape gaudy fabrics over herself and pretend to be the great and alluring women of history, while "Ducky usually played the part of my husband, my son or my horse, or all three in turn, according to the necessities of the game. Ducky always played the heroic, brave, self-sacrificing parts, and was almost always a male."

Early in life Missy realized what a special little girl shared her stage: "There was something heroic about Ducky, even at that early age; something a little sombre. She was the one who espoused causes, she was the 'fore-fighter,' the one who discussed and resented, who allowed no nonsense, and had no patience with frauds. She immediately spotted any insincerity and let nothing pass. Tall for her age, she was strong and rebellious, but like the strong she was also a defender of the weak and oppressed, and sometimes she even espoused lost causes with a bravery that we less heroic ones admired without imitating."

Ducky adored her older sister as much as Missy loved and respected her. Assuming the role of protector, Ducky always took the attitude that "whatever hurts Missy hurts me." Inseparable in youth, the two contrasting sisters seemed to form a perfect complement to each other. Their spiritual kinship only grew with age, and indeed, lasted until their deaths.

"Ducky and I were scrupulously fair towards each other," Missy recalled at the end of her life. "We always played the game and never wanted to have separate successes; we could not conceive of a life where we should not be side by side." Although the Edinburgh family included two more daughters—Alexandra, known as Sandra, born two years after Ducky in 1878, and Beatrice, nicknamed Baby Bee, born in 1884—the bond between Missy and Ducky was unique.

Completely sheltered from the many unpleasant realities of Victorian life, the children were not only happy, healthy, and fantastically privileged but also blessed with intelligence, good looks, and, most important, a wise and loving mother who was devoted to them body and soul.

"Mamma loved us passionately. Her whole life was given up to her children, we were the supreme and central interest of her existence. . . . It was Mamma who settled things, Mamma to whom we turned, Mamma who came to kiss us good night, who took us out for walks or drives. It was Mamma who scolded or praised, who told us what we were or were not to do."

As benevolent and loving as the energetic duchess of Edinburgh was with her five children, she never allowed a lapse in her unquestioned authority. The duchess carried out her own definite ideas about their upbringing while being neither "comrade nor companion" to her offspring. So complete was the influence of their mother on their daily lives, and so overwhelming was her presence, that the children never doubted her household sovereignty and always felt confident in the simple belief that "power over good and evil was hers."

Marie's regime was somewhat spartan. Rigid rules and meticulous habits were enforced—precise bedtimes, cold baths early every morning, sensible clothing, perfect manners, proper exercise, eating whatever was put before you, strict punctuality, complete discipline of mind and body. The duchess wanted her son and daughters to be healthy and strong in both body and mind, and she instinctively knew how best to achieve this. Her anti-English prejudices enabled her to avoid the more dubious local customs: She refused to let her children eat rich, fatty foods and retreat from the abominable climate into overheated, airless rooms. Nor were they allowed the indolence that weakened so much of the English aristocracy.

Inactivity was a fault that the duchess could not tolerate. To see one of her brood sitting idle was torture to her. The children were eternally being prompted to get busy, to go outdoors, to play a game or practice a skill or take a ride or go for a walk. Social skills were also high on Marie's agenda. One of her era's most brilliant conversationalists, speaking a half dozen languages fluently, the duchess had been disappointed by the dull society of the English court. Contemptuous of her husband's vacuous relatives and friends, she was determined that her children become masters of the art of conversation. "There is nothing more hopeless than a princess who never opens her mouth," she firmly believed. Thus, the retiring little Ducky was forced to spend a part of each afternoon circling a room of empty chairs and chatting with the invisible company under her mother's supervision. As this rather awkward training progressed, Ducky, at first characteristically resistant, was soon on her way to being as articulate and poised as her mother.

Marie's punctuality, which she also wished to instill in her children, "amounted to a mania, for she was always about ten minutes before time." An early riser, the self-disciplined duchess was always the first one at the breakfast table. "Try as you might you could never be there before Mamma and were continually being scolded for being late."

While Missy would anxiously strive her entire life to obey this maternal mandate of punctuality, Ducky spiritedly rebelled against it at every opportunity.

The duchess insisted that the children eat everything and anything that was put before them, both out of politeness to their hostess, if dining as a guest, and to promote a healthy diet and self-discipline. In refusing to allow her daughter to develop picky eating habits, the duchess enabled Ducky to adapt to a future life of change and to survive the harshest adversity. But as a child, Ducky was unable to see why she had to eat dishes that tasted awful.

"But if they are not good, Mamma?" she would continually implore.

"Then you must just behave as though they were good," her unyielding mother would respond.

"But if they make you feel sick!"

"Then be sick, my dear, but wait till you get home. It would be most offensive to be sick then and there."

Ducky's mother was determined that her children should have invincible "Russian digestions" instead of weak and touchy "English" ones. To this end, she warned them: "Children, don't let English people persuade you that certain foods are indigestible; everything is digestible for a good stomach, but English people spoil their digestion from earliest childhood by imagining that they cannot eat this or that. I always ate everything; in Russia no one ever spoke about their digestions, it's a most unpleasant subject and not drawing-room conversation."

With her mania for good health and a belief that it was the cornerstone of happiness, the duchess refused to allow her children to become sick: "A headache must never be confessed or given way to, a cold did not keep you at home, a fever did not send you to bed." When Ducky finally did succumb to the unavoidable sicknesses of childhood and was forced to stay in bed, her mother extravagantly administered an impressive array of pills and potions ordered from St. Petersburg in staggering quantities. Thinking English medicines and doctors fit only for horses, the duchess contemptuously avoided both and determined that her daughter's convalescence would be as speedy and no-nonsense as possible. Stuffed with remedies and confronted by her mother's disapproving and impatient glare, Ducky learned early in life that to lie in a sickbed was a mark of failure.

To help keep all illness at bay, exercise in all forms was a very important part of the children's lives. The duchess expected performance rain or shine. Whether the planned activity was a walking excursion through the woods or a horseback ride across the gentle countryside, it was never to be changed because of bad weather. "People who use rain or cold or other climate conditions as a reason for not going out and exercising are the people who never go out and exercise at all," the duchess always admonished Ducky and her sisters when they tried to retreat from riding in a storm. "One has to exercise regardless of the weather or else it does one no good whatsoever." As a result, Ducky and her sisters became the healthiest and strongest royal children in Europe.

Strict and unbending in many areas of their young lives, the duchess granted her children a surprising degree of liberty in encouraging a certain wildness and abandon in their games. Watching Ducky and Missy romping with other youngsters, their mother took special pride in the exuberance that her dirt-stained little daughters always displayed. "We were wild children," Missy gratefully remembered later in life, "allowed to get dirty, wet, cold even . . . our lungs were allowed to expand, our faces to sunburn, our legs and arms to get bruised and scratched."

In an era when the upper classes straitjacketed their youngsters in propriety even during playtime, it was amazing that these royal children were encouraged by their mother to romp as freely as urchins from the slums. And, though somewhat taken aback, their grandmother Queen Victoria approvingly noticed the salutary effects of the sisters' boisterous freedom: "All of Affie's girls were so strong!"

Ducky and Missy were the two most extraordinary children of the family, both being "born leaders, but each in quite a different way." Whereas the placid and easygoing Missy always used "gentleness and a deep understanding of the other man's side of the case," the passionately emotional and forthright Ducky used "strength and withering contempt when disappointed."

"We were a strong race," Missy later proudly recalled of them; "the mixture of Russian and English was a strange blend, setting us somewhat apart from the others, as, having strong and dominating characters, we could not follow, only lead."

Having a highly unconventional mother only increased Ducky's independence and nonconformity. The overweight duchess scorned the caprices of popular fashion and quite sensibly refused to stuff her girth into stylish dresses and gowns that would have made her look ridiculous. Instead, she efficiently upholstered herself in a modest camouflage of jackets and skirts and a pair of "funny shaped" boots with small leather bows that were specially made for her in Russia. (One of her many eccentricities was her insistence that the boots be constructed exactly the same for both feet. She confidently proclaimed that it was "nonsense to imagine that you needed a left and right shoe, it was much more rational to have them both alike.")

The second most important person in Ducky's young life was her Scottish nurse, Nana Pitcathly, who had a hatchet face and keen, kind eyes. Loving Ducky and her sisters as if they were her own, "she ruled with a rod of iron and kept us in almost military subjection." Indeed, this disciple of discipline invented a cautionary torture device known in the nursery as the strap, a strip of leather with one end sliced into several fingers. Actually there were two of these straps, a brown and a black one.

They were ominously hung on either Ducky's or Missy's bed as "a warning to the unruly." For some reason, the children perceived the black strap as being the worse of the two, the feared punishment for a major transgression. Although these intimidating weapons were "supposed" to be used for whipping offenders, Ducky could not remember either ever having been used by the bluff, tenderhearted Nana.

Taking a particular pride in the beauty of her two oldest charges, Nana Pitcathly "groomed and cleaned and polished" Ducky and Missy "like pampered horses." But it was easy for everyone to see that "Nana loved Ducky best." The patient old nurse would lovingly spend more time on Ducky's appearance, meticulously fixing her "brown corkscrew curls which Nana rolled over her finger with the aid of a comb." Seeing how the "passionate child was often misunderstood," Nana felt a special sympathy for her honest and sensitive nature and tried to protect her.

Ducky looked at the wonders of life and experienced a "curious sensation of ecstasy" that Missy, who shared it, later referred to as "raptures." Ducky retained a lifelong childlike delight in beauty wherever it could be found. This enabled her to relish the simplest of experiences— a sunset, an unexpected landscape, the shape and shadow of a tree, a stranger's sweet smile, the color and form of a flower. Flowers were a particular passion. All her life Ducky collected, arranged, and painted the most gorgeous floral specimens she could find. Missy described Ducky's ecstasy over flowers as "a sort of prayer-like gratitude for something which delights soul as well as body, eyes as well as heart."

Years later, when talking about her inseparable girlhood companion, Missy was still impressed that Ducky had "felt the same raptures I had for exactly the same things. It was a sort of tightening of the heartstrings, something that brought tears to your eyes and at the same time made you want to shout with joy or fall on your knees and worship or sing hymns of praise and thanksgiving. The causes responsible for these ecstasies were manifold and varied. Some had to do entirely with the eyes, some with scent, some with sound, some entirely with feeling."

Missy particularly remembered a visit to the beach near the family's summer home on the Isle of Wight, off the south coast of England. Arriving with her sister in the late morning, Missy recalled "the indescribable thrill of reaching the Osborne beach at low tide; the stepping out of the wagonette before the coastguard's little castle, with the ever-renewed possibility before us of finding wonderful shells. The sand lay white, damp and smooth beneath our bare feet and half buried in this sand were these treasures only waiting for discovery. . . . Our hearts beat, our eyes glowed; each step might mean marvelous discovery. The fan shells were what we searched for especially, and one day I found a broad, pink fan shell, pale rose pink with deep markings. . . . Ducky and I considered this find almost a miracle."

The leader of these expeditions was always Ducky. Taller than her older sister, Ducky was always the dominant force in their alliance, and the success of this sisterly union set the tone for all of Ducky's future relationships.

Forever challenging authority and refusing to follow convention simply because it was expected that she do so, Ducky always took delight in living her life on her own terms. And loving more intensely than most others, she was a chronic victim of agonizing jealousies and bitter disappointments when it came to romance. Given the restrictions of her era and the rigid obligations of her exalted position, her rebelliousness would create one crisis after another in her life and eventually help establish a reputation so notorious that it was the scandal of the era. Ducky's extreme passion would ultimately bring about her greatest tragedy.

CHAPTER FIVE

Wonderful Eastwell

F OR THE FIRST DECADE of Ducky's life, home was a huge estate of twenty-five hundred acres called Eastwell Park. Situated near the town of Ashford in the county of Kent about fifty miles southeast of London, Eastwell was nestled in the hills of the North Downs and encompassed emerald lawns, lush forests, and manicured gardens, all surrounded by an eleven-mile stone wall.

It was, however, a temporary paradise, as the Edinburghs did not own it. The duke, being faithful to his love of economy, rented the property from the wealthy earl of Winchelsea. The house itself was a massive, sprawling affair of gray stone in a mock-Jacobean style, four stories high and topped by an elegant octagonal tower. Although the entrance to the mansion was framed by a two-story portico with four gigantic marble columns, the structure itself was surprisingly unassuming for occupants of such illustrious rank, "not grand or austere, but lovely, quiet, noble—an English home."

Eastwell contained all the elements of a child's magical and mysterious wonderland. Ducky loved to roam the endless rooms and chambers of the mansion. But the house had a rambling and eccentric plan, with a dark staircase hidden at the back of the mansion. This Ducky and Missy declared was "no place for little girls." Ducky led her sister on secret visits to the "very terrifying place," a wooden well with steep steps that dropped into the distant shadows, seeming "to descend into the very bowels of the earth." An ominous curtain far below billowed to obscure a dimly lit doorway. Ducky had heard the servants call this ghostly marvel the "Glory Hole," and although she never learned what went on behind the mysterious curtain, her imagination told her that it was the very gates of Hell. By continually engaging in this childish game of confronting the most dreaded of terrors, she was unknowingly creating a fearless attitude toward life that would prove useful in her tumultuous and troubled future.

A huge lake in the distant woodlands from the house was another source of terror: a deep hollow in the thick bushes at the far shore emitted an "extraordinary . . . hollow, ghostly sound, as though desperate hands were thumping . . . eternally thumping against dungeon doors." Whenever Ducky and Missy could talk their governess into taking the detour around the haunted lake, the wide-eyed girls would hear the sounds of the "fearful creature . . . our hearts would beat excruciatingly; we would hold each other's hands and try not to hurry past or look afraid" while all the time experiencing "delicious shivers."

A comforting place was the massive cedar tree on the lawn in front of the house. It offered marvelous opportunities not only for climbing but also for hiding in a jungle of drooping branches and tangled, low-sweeping boughs—"a wonderful, cathedral-like mansion in which we children each possessed a room."

Running around the grounds of Eastwell Park and playing American Indians, Robinson Crusoe, pirates, and Robin Hood, or ice-skating and tobogganing in the eagerly awaited winter snows, Ducky and her sisters experienced the most idyllic years of their childhood. Ducky was always to recall Eastwell as "home."

Christmas was among the few occasions when the girls really saw their somber father come alive. The duke, surprisingly, loved the holiday season, and with childlike delight, he meticulously supervised the weeks of preparation: "the stirring of the plum pudding; the servants' party with gifts for each; the setting up of white-draped present tables for each family member; the selection and trimming of the tree." Finally, when Christmas Eve arrived at last, the guarded doors of the library were suddenly thrown open and Ducky and her sisters stared at the towering tree covered with blazing candles. Approaching it shyly, hand in hand, they were enraptured by the thrill of the lights and the "delicious fragrance."

Christmas was also the only time of the year when Ducky's energetic mother relaxed her authority and took a backseat. But no sooner had the season ended than the duchess was in control again. With her husband out shooting with his friends most days and returning in the evening sleepy and silent, the frustrated duchess was free to rule her household as if she were a monarch ruling a kingdom.

A steady flow of relatives visited the family at Eastwell Park. The duchess found that most of her husband's family were just as backward and boring as he was, if not even more so, except for Prince Leopold, Queen Victoria's youngest son, who was her favorite English kinsman. He was a scholar and a lover of culture who possessed a sunny disposition and a keen sense of humor. Leopold's refined tastes were at least partially due to the tragic malady from which he suffered—hemophilia. The only one of Victoria's four sons to have inherited the dread disease, Leopold had virtually led the life of an invalid, avoiding any physical activity that could result in even the smallest cut that could cause his blood to flow uncontrollably; instead, he had devoted himself to a life of the mind.

The duchess of Edinburgh invited Leopold to Eastwell Park whenever she could. He stimulated her starved mind and amused her with his cleverness. Some of his practical jokes, however, were not so funny. One morning Ducky watched in horror as her delicate uncle came hurrying down to breakfast with a handkerchief pressed to his mouth, excitedly crying that he had lost a front tooth. He removed the red-stained cloth to reveal a black hole between his teeth. Ducky's mother nearly fainted: Such a mishap could well be fatal. Just as the duchess was about to rush for a doctor, Leopold burst out laughing and confessed that it had only been "a naughty farce." He had stained his handkerchief with red paint and the hole in his teeth was merely a black piece of gum. At first relieved, Ducky's mother then exploded in rage, giving the repentant prankster "a bit of her mind about causing a loving family such emotion, and Mamma never gave a bit of her mind by halves."

The fact that hemophilia ran in Queen Victoria's family had been recognized, but the extent of the problem had not as yet been understood. Two of the queen's daughters, Alice and Beatrice, would be carriers of the fatal gene, passing it on to some of their sons and, through their daughters, to their grandsons. Alice had married the grand duke of Hesse and the Rhine and was the mother of Ducky's future husband, Ernst Ludwig, and of the future empress Alexandra of Russia. While Ernst would luckily escape the disease, Alexandra was also a carrier, who passed hemophilia on to her only son. It was this that ultimately unhinged the empress and helped to bring about the downfall of the Romanov dynasty, dethroning Nicholas and Alexandra and allowing the imperial crown to pass to Ducky and her second husband.

Of the other family members who came to visit, it was Princess Alexandra of Wales who made the most vivid impression. Aunt Alix, the duke of Edinburgh's former flame, was considered the most beautiful woman of her time. For the precociously aesthetic Ducky, her tall, gorgeous aunt appeared at Eastwell like an "enchanting vision" that could "suddenly fade away." Paying special visits to the nursery to sit and talk with Ducky and Missy while they took their baths, this "magnificent creature" inspired a "speechless adoration."

Ducky's other English aunts and uncles held much less appeal. Most of them were so stiffly formal and reserved as to appear completely indifferent; they "simply looked through you." The only one besides Aunt Alix to shower them with attention was their father's eldest sister, Aunt Vicky, the crown princess of Prussia. Because she lived in far-off Germany, Aunt Vicky didn't see her nieces very often, but when she did, she seemed to try to make up for her absence by overwhelming the girls with numerous courtesies and treats, Ducky's favorite being a tall, "supremely delicious," thickly frosted cake from Berlin called a *Kotputzer Baumkuchen*. Their aunt Vicky would smile radiantly at them as she ceremoniously cut the eagerly awaited dessert; Ducky and Missy could overlook her patronizing manner, but they disliked her expression. "Somehow Aunt Vicky was too nice to you," her observant niece would later recall. "Her smile had something in it of sunshine when the weather is not really warm . . . sunshine with teeth."

A brilliant, ambitious woman who would one day play a significant role in Ducky's life as both critic and protector, Aunt Vicky would always remain a rather distant and unappealing figure. Perhaps it was the perceived "falseness" of the crown princess's personality that created such an unbridgeable gap with her forthright niece.

Regular visits were made to Windsor Castle to see Grandmama Queen—without doubt, the character who loomed largest in Ducky's childhood. The reclusive monarch intimidated her grandchildren even more than she did her children. Ducky and her sisters would be driven along by their nurses "like a troop of well-behaved little geese" down a series of long, soft-carpeted corridors leading to the royal apartments. As "one door after another opened noiselessly, it was like passing through the forecourts of a temple, before approaching the final mystery to which only the initiated had access." With the maids and servants whispering more anxiously the closer they approached, they would finally arrive at Grandmama's door. Now the hush "was awe-inspiring . . . like approaching the mystery of some sanctuary."

The doors slowly opened and there sat Ducky's grandmama dressed in a stiff black silk gown and a white widow's cap, "smiling a kind little smile, almost as shy as us children, so that conversation was not very fluent on either side." Although the formidable queen supervised Ducky's development "with the anxious severity of one who wished that those of her House should do it every honor, no matter where they were placed," she also displayed affection, spending most of the visit inquiring about the children's morals and behavior and the progress of their studies, periodically giving "her shy little laugh and that little shrug of the shoulders which had become almost a trick."

If a naughty misdeed was reported, Grandmama would react with a "shocked and yet amused little exclamation of horror." The queen's reserve would unexpectedly relax for a moment or two and Ducky would experience a true grandmotherly warmth, but then Victoria's innate shyness would quickly return and the difficulty in conversation made them both "secretly relieved when the audience was over."

Ducky most enjoyed visits on which her mother accompanied her. The duchess had the unfailing ability to engage the queen in lively discussion, thus freeing Ducky and her sisters to explore the myriad fascinations of Grandmama's rooms.

Nothing less than a museum to the cherished memory of Prince Albert, the queen's private apartments were a gallery of portraits and photographs of the handsome grandfather Ducky had never known. As Ducky slowly strolled among the bulky furniture, she gazed at visions of Grandpapa in his general's uniform, "Grandpapa in his robes of the Order of the Garter, Grandpapa in kilt, in plain clothes, Grandpapa on horse-back, at his writing table, Grandpapa with his dogs, with his children, in the garden, on the mountains . . . Grandpapa with his loving wife gazing enraptured up into his face."

Ducky fingered the glass treasures on the tables and gingerly touched the other curious objets d'art, looking back again and again at the portraits of her dead grandfather, admiring his beauty and perhaps feeling an unconscious kinship with his dark, glowing intensity.

A screeching pet bulfinch in a large corner cage contrasted shrilly with the hushed, reverent atmosphere. Inhaling the sweet, dizzying aroma of orange blossoms, Ducky would proceed to examine the family photographs cluttering the side tables, "mysterious photographs of dead people, even of dead little children, which, although they made us feel creepy, we always furtively looked at again and again."

Less formal visits were made to Grandmama Queen during the summer, when the Edinburghs stayed with her at Osborne on the Isle of Wight. Osborne House was one of Victoria's favorite homes, primarily because it had been the pride and joy of her dear late husband who had painstakingly created it. An imposing white marble Italianate villa rising rather incongruously on the damp, chilly shore, Osborne was attractive only during the warm summer months, when the inviting beaches and woodlands were a sublime daily diversion.

Here in the informal setting of Osborne Grandmama ate breakfast under her green-fringed ecru parasol on the terrace overlooking the pale blue sea, surrounded by her dogs, her Indian and Highlander servants, and "an aunt or two in nervous attendance or occasionally a curtsying lady-in-waiting." Although still dressed in her perennial black silks, Grandmama was "all smiles," a benign little old lady enjoying the sunshine and speaking in a soft, mellow voice to all those around her.

The long summer stays at Osborne would remain Ducky's happiest memories—a wonderful time of lazy days, of bathing in the sea when the tide was high, and of excursions "through the sweet-smelling woods, past hedges full of honeysuckle."

During these holidays on the Isle of Wight, Ducky and her family occupied a large house misnamed Osborne Cottage that was lent to them by Grandmama and enjoyed enviable privacy because it was located outside the royal park. Amid groves of lime trees, the "Cottage" was filled with flowers and might have existed for Ducky as the perfect setting for an idyllic holiday had her governess and French tutor not been in tow. It being "considered healthy for us and good for our growing backs to lie flat on the floor for about an hour a day," Ducky and her sisters were a captive audience for their strict governess, who used the opportunity to read to them from the classics. The girls were also forced to spend much of their "free" time knitting—"stocking-knitting was for some reason considered a virtuous occupation for little girls."

The French lessons were not so successful: "We children hated speaking French; we considered it an affected language." So they resisted all efforts at being taught the Gallic tongue. The duchess spoke English perfectly, and it was the only language she used with Ducky and her brother and sisters. But she admired French, proclaiming that "it was by far the most elegant language and that a beautiful letter could only be written in French." This would explain why Ducky's earliest letters and obligatory thank-you notes to Grandmama Queen were written in French, whereas all of Victoria's other grandchildren wrote to her in English. Ducky's carefully penned cards to "Ma chère Grand-Maman" were dutifully continued until her ninth birthday, when, perhaps feeling a sudden spurt of youthful rebellion, she dropped the "affected" foreign language and began writing in English.

Ducky was grateful for the opportunity to sit with Grandmama on the terrace in the sun, walk through the exquisite estate gardens with her, and take afternoon carriage rides with her around the beautiful park. It was here, in the peaceful seclusion of Osborne, that Ducky established a closer and more meaningful relationship with her grandmother. A shrewd woman, Queen Victoria quickly perceived the great strength and emotional depth of her granddaughter's character and formed a lasting admiration for the little princess.

Ducky and her sisters romped in the rustic Swiss Cottage, her father's old playhouse, climbed the magnolia trees to escape M. Morsier, their long-suffering French tutor, and scoured the sandy beaches for seashells.

During these summers, the most eagerly anticipated event of all was the royal regatta week at Cowes across the bay, when they would join fat Uncle Bertie and gorgeous Aunt Alix, the prince and princess of Wales, on their magnificent yacht. While Ducky and Missy continued to worship the enchanting Alix, their patronizing uncle proved quite a strain. Uncle Bertie "would chuck us under the chin, pull our ears in a friendly manner, let off a few jokes at our expense and then laugh in his own special way . . . a sort of crackle, a burst of good-humour which crumpled his face up into a hundred little lines."

Alix and Bertie's three daughters, known in the family as the Wales girls, were an unfortunate contrast to the Edinburgh girls. With gangling bodies, long noses, and huge bulging eyes, Victoria, Louise, and Maud (later queen of Norway) had all inherited the full force of their father's homely looks and none of their mother's beauty, whereas Ducky and her sister Missy had been blessed with their handsome father's good looks and none of their mother's plainness. This startling difference in appearance, plus the whiny personality of the Wales girls did not contribute to creating a closeness between the cousins.

Not every summer was spent at Osborne. One year it was decided that Ducky and her sisters would be taken to Balmoral, their grandmother's beloved estate in the Scottish Highlands. Accompanied only by their governess, the girls stayed in a tiny house called Abergeldie Maines that had been lent to them by the queen. When their mother joined them in the early autumn, they moved to a slightly larger house named Birkhall, where Ducky and her two sisters had to share one huge bed.

It was almost a tradition in the English royal family to detest the obligatory annual visits to the queen's Highland home. Although it evoked for Victoria the happiest memories of her married life, Balmoral held no interest for anyone else in the family. Shrouded in a chilly mist and bleakly perched in the middle of nowhere, Balmoral could have been loved only by a lonely old widow or a poet. Therefore it was not surprising that the poetic Ducky and the extravagantly romantic Missy would adore the place, with its mysterious undulating landscape of hazy moors and brooks, and, most of all, the heather—"that wonderful rolling carpet of purple, with an undergrowth of rust, which added that warmth of colour which so completely satisfied the beauty-loving eye."

Returning home to Eastwell Park, Ducky resumed her studies, an education that was becoming "somewhat haphazard because of these many 'displacements,' as it always meant beginning all over again with other teachers and other methods, even in other languages and never for long at a time." Ducky's brother, Alfred, was being given a much more thorough education, which separated him most of the time from his sisters. He was now being sent off to Germany to the grand Edinburgh Palace, which their father had built in Coburg in anticipation of their eventual succession to the duchy. Since Uncle Bertie had two sons, there was slight chance that Alfred would ever inherit his grandmother's throne. Thus it was decided that it was fitting that as the future reigning duke of Coburg he should be brought there. Ducky loved her brother very much, but Alfred gradually became a complete stranger, a troubled youth, and a sad young man who would bring into her life one of its first real tragedies.

Shortly after the birth of her youngest sister, Beatrice, in 1883, Nana Pitcathly, Ducky's Scottish nurse, suddenly died from cancer. Suffering intensely, Nana tried to hide her fatal illness and do her duty to the very end. When the infant Beatrice cried at night, Ducky would peek up from her bed and see the old woman lovingly carry the baby in her arms and walk "up and down, up and down, humming little songs and groaning in between, cruel deep groans which she imagined we did not hear because she thought we were sleeping." Nana died at Eastwell just before Ducky's eighth birthday. She and her sisters were quietly taken up to the death room, where a small service was held at Nana's bedside. Ducky had never seen a dead person before and wept so hard that she had to be taken from the room. She was "inconsolable for a long time." For Ducky, Nana's death was "truly a terrible loss."

CHAPTER SIX

London "Smuts" and Russian Delights

*E*VERY YEAR AFTER Christmas was long over and the social season in the world's largest and richest city was about to begin, the duke and duchess of Edinburgh packed up their children and their household and moved to London for several months.

Ducky and her sisters loved Eastwell Park, but they hated their London residence. It wasn't that Clarence House was uncomfortable or unattractive. On the contrary, it was an imposing mansion with dozens of huge rooms and a large private garden located next to St. James's Palace off the Mall and facing Green Park and Buckingham Palace. What spoiled everything was what the girls referred to as the "smuts," that unique combination of smoke and fog that used to smother the British capital for most of the year and was known as "pea soupers."

The smuts ruined all the magnificence that London could have presented to Ducky and her sisters. Any contact with the filthy London air produced dirty stains, and if they sat or played on the ground in a park or garden it "meant great black stains on clothes, knees or stockings" that also contained a "special greasiness." Even in their own favorite place to play, an aviary hill in a corner of the private gardens at Buckingham Palace that Ducky imaginatively called "the Alps," the earth "was the dirtiest, blackest part of the whole garden" and was "overgrown with incredibly smutty bushes."

Most alarmingly, the "smuts" weren't confined to the crowded streets of the gigantic industrial city. Indoors was every bit as polluted as the world outside. As stately and charming as Clarence House was, "it was hopelessly smutty and everything you touched made your fingers black." To experience a truly remarkable London pea souper, Ducky didn't even need to leave the house, for often she could simply sit at her desk upstairs and stare into "a fog so thick that one could not even see the fire burning at the farther end of the not very large room."

Ducky and her sisters hated the drab outdoors, but were forced by their governess to take brisk daily walks in the local parks. Before the children were allowed to play, they had to put on white smocks, which they were not permitted to remove until they were almost home, by which time the protective garments had turned the color of coal. The only joy to be had from these stiff promenades through the park was the presence of the balloon man at the entrance and the possibility that on some days their governess would be sympathetic enough to buy them one of these magical balls filled with air.

Returning home to her lessons, Ducky entered a house that was more like a museum than a residence. As soon as she walked into the front hall she was greeted by a stuffed bear standing on its hind legs, "a huge, savage-looking beast holding a small tray between his front paws on which visitors left their cards for the gentlemen-in-waiting." Moving past a collection of hunting trophies and bizarre artifacts—the most intimidating for Ducky being a grotesquely grinning warrior in Japanese armor—she would climb the wide main staircase and lower her head to avoid touching the trunk of a colossal elephant head that hung on the wall.

But most fascinating to her were the two rarely used drawing rooms. One was called the Chinese drawing room and was filled with "curios Papa had brought from China, beautiful old weapons and bronzes, ivories and embroideries, and . . . a few precious jades." The second large salon was devoted to the art treasures that the duchess of Edinburgh had brought from her beloved Russian home. There were "all sorts of objects carved from the many semi-precious stones from the Urals: dishes and vases, bowls and cups, Easter eggs and whole writing- and toilet-table sets . . . in the much prized Orletz, an extremely hard stone, dark pink with streaks of grey." What fascinated Ducky most was her mother's collection of Fabergé work—"those 'objets de vertu' so dear to the Romanovs, carved from jasper, malachite, lapis, and rock crystal or enameled in jeweled tones, mounted in gold, and studded with diamonds."

Permeating these rooms was a strong, singular aroma—a curious mixture of fog, oakwood, cigarette smoke, and a pungent fragrance that Ducky's mother had brought from St. Petersburg.

When Ducky grew a bit older the dismal gloom of London was happily mitigated by daily horseback rides in Hyde Park under the anxious supervision of a "fearfully correct old hen" named Mr. Lumley. Although the elderly riding master was often upset and absentminded, he couldn't dampen the girls' high spirits; the sylvan rides were absolute "bliss." By a surprisingly mature and logical agreement between the two sisters, it was decided that Ducky, being the taller, would always get the bigger horse and Missy the smaller.

Galloping side by side down the bridle paths of the London park, Ducky and Missy acquired their lifelong passion for riding. Only a decade later both would win reputations as the finest horsewomen in Europe.

Regular trips to the theater also made the smuts more tolerable. Sitting with her parents in their flower-filled box, Ducky gazed intently at the throng of ladies and gentlemen below, and then, as the lights slowly dimmed and the curtain went up, she marveled at the artistry of Ellen Terry and Henry Irving in *Macbeth* or the profile of the handsome Wilson Barrett in *Lord Harry*. The popular farce *Charley's Aunt* was a favorite with Ducky and Missy and "made us laugh till our sides ached." However, as much as they enjoyed comedy, they had a definite preference for drama.

Because their younger sister Sandra was a docile and passive child who wished only to follow her older siblings, Ducky and Missy either ignored her or treated her with "a certain imperious off-handedness." The auburn-haired Ducky and blond Missy, so close together in age, were perfect complements to each other in almost every way; they formed a partnership so tight and exclusive that they existed in a world of their own. With so much promise and natural talent, they were particularly favored by their energetic and ambitious mother.

The duchess had always cherished the dream of producing a wunderkind, a prodigy with a genius for one or more of the arts. Although Missy was intelligent and accomplished in many areas, her critical mother soon realized that this dainty and romantic child would never excel in anything to an extraordinary degree. So she turned her attention to the more impressive potential of her second daughter.

Ducky's passions and deeply felt moods indicated an artistic temperament of the first order. Talented at drawing and painting, she was also perhaps the most musical member of the family. She was initially given careful training in playing the piano. This created a closeness between mother and daughter, as the duchess herself was a virtuoso pianist. In fact, it was most likely the influence of her mother's piano playing—her "exquisitely soft and velvety" touch and the skillful "running water" flow of her short plump fingers—that inspired Ducky's desire to also be a master of the keyboard. But, alas, the duchess was doomed to another disappointment: it soon became obvious that the highly disciplined and intense young musician would never be the earthshaking genius that her frustrated mother so desperately desired.

Self-critical and never at peace with herself, the duchess of Edinburgh had hoped to find perfection in her daughters. Naturally, when she finally had to admit their limitations, she lost interest in their educations and artistic achievements, and "although she encouraged us, it was always patronizingly and with a touch of contempt."

The acutely sensitive Ducky probably felt this maternal dissatisfaction more than her sisters. It would be years before the Edinburgh girls would understand their "beloved, big-hearted, generous Mama, built on grand lines, but always a seeker, restless in her own soul: one who, in looking for complete perfection, often almost unjustly overlooked what might have been true sources of joy, had she not always been hankering after an ideal implanted in her by those who brought her up."

For all their mother's attention and devotion, there was an emotional distance that could never be narrowed. Relentlessly insisting on the inferiority of the younger generation, the isolated duchess "need not have been so lonely had she only trusted her children a little more." Her daughters sadly realized that "she adored us, gave up her life to us, but for all that she had little faith in us; that was the strange, strange thing."

It may well have been that the very terms of the duchess of Edinburgh's difficult marriage helped to undermine her future relationship with her children. Herself a devout member of the Russian Orthodox Church, Ducky's mother had to sign a formal agreement that she would raise all of her offspring in the Church of England. This she faithfully did. However, the duchess remained staunchly devoted to her own faith, always employing the services of her own Orthodox priest and two Russian chanters. In each of the Edinburgh homes a private area was turned into a chapel for the duchess, and sometimes the thoroughly English little Ducky was allowed to enter and stand beside her mother

while she silently prayed. The overwhelming combination of "heady incense, antique icons, and soul-stirring Russian chants" filled the wide-
eyed princess with a profound sense of awe, and her heart would pound
with the thrilling sensation that she was "very near the Holy of Holies."

Pursuing separate religions must have created a wide gulf of misunderstanding between the duchess and her children, because a vital part
of her soul was automatically shut off from theirs. While her brother
and sisters were content with their Protestant faith and never had the
desire to exchange it for their mother's exotic church, Ducky always
had a strong attraction not only for her mother's religion, but also for
her mother's Russian homeland, its customs and culture and entire way
of life.

The duchess of Edinburgh tried to return home to St. Petersburg as
often as she could. She usually took her children and went without her
husband, traveling through Germany and visiting Coburg, her future
realm, on the way. Accompanying her were also a lady-in-waiting, an
equerry, four nursemaids, four ladies' maids, four footmen, a courtiers,
and a page.

The first visit that Ducky could remember occurred in May of 1880,
when an urgent telegram had called the duchess home to her mother's
deathbed. This was the last time that Ducky saw her Russian grandparents. She would remember her grandpapa, Emperor Alexander II, as a
commanding giant of a man "with grey hair and closely-cut whiskers, a
rather forbidding face but kindly eyes and mouth, which could not
however conceal a perpetual expression of worry."

Ducky's dying grandmother had been an invalid for many years and
was "a pale emaciated woman with a thin, waxen face and long, white
beautiful hands." As the duchess tenderly comforted her suffering
mother, she was horrified to discover that her father had installed his
teenaged mistress, Catherine Dolgoruky, and their bastard children in
the rooms directly above his wife's death chamber. The duchess confronted her father with rage and they fought for the first time in their
lives. Accompanied by the voluptuous Catherine and their small children, the emperor retreated to his country palace, while his heartbroken
only daughter tenderly cradled the empress in her arms and tearfully
watched her breathe her last.

The conflict with her father was shattering to the duchess of Edinburgh. Having just lost her adored mother and blaming the emperor for
much of her final suffering, the duchess stayed in Russia only long

enough for the funeral and then fled angrily home to England. She could not bring herself to forgive her "imperfect" father. Perhaps shamed by his daughter's contempt, Alexander married his young mistress only a few weeks later. However, his newfound happiness was doomed to be tragically brief.

Only nine months after returning from the funeral of Grandmama Empress, Ducky came downstairs one morning in Clarence House and was shocked to find her mother weeping. It was "an overwhelming, unheard-of cataclysm" to see her stern, unbending mother crying uncontrollably. Something terrible must have happened.

And it had: Alexander II had just been murdered by an anarchist.

The emperor had been driving in his carriage when a bomb was thrown directly under the vehicle. Although the tremendous explosion shattered the carriage and mortally wounded the horses and the Cossack escorts, Alexander was miraculously unhurt. Stepping out of the splintered wreckage, he had begun comforting the injured and gently asking about the well-being of the bomb thrower when a second assassin threw another bomb straight at the emperor's feet. In a sudden, blinding "sheet of flame and metal Alexander's legs were torn away, his stomach ripped open, his face mutilated." The gruesome remains were rushed to the Winter Palace, where, moments after arriving, Alexander was pronounced dead.

The duchess of Edinburgh's greatest childhood fear had finally come true. With an uneasy guilt tingeing her great sorrow, she gathered Ducky and Missy together, and quickly returned to St. Petersburg for her father's funeral.

This and future trips to Russia made a profound impression on Ducky. Of all the duchess's very properly brought up English children, Ducky was the one who felt the greatest attraction for her mother's homeland. To Ducky, imperial Russia was nothing less than a page right out of the *Thousand and One Nights,* a fairyland of Byzantine splendor, "uniquely picturesque" and saturated with a special "color and brilliance unlike anything else." A rare, "mysterious gorgeousness" was vividly present wherever she looked—in the colossal palaces with their maze of unending corridors and "over-life-sized halls and drawing-rooms" and expanses of floors so vast and highly polished that she had "the impression of walking on ice"; in the gigantic parks and wonderful fountains and majestic gardens; in the awesome military displays with regiments of "wild-looking" Cossacks "standing in long red coats, high fur caps and armed to the teeth"; in the fantastic religious ceremonies "in churches all glittering with gold"; and, most of all, in the "astounding family gatherings," at which the women wore "jewels so fantastic that you can hardly imagine that they are real."

In these dreamlike palaces, redolent of turpentine, Russian leather, perfume, and cigarette smoke, Ducky looked up in amazement at her mother's five towering brothers, handsome young giants in uniforms, "wonderful and unbelievable, quite like people out of fairy stories that you did not imagine really existed." These enormous, splendid-looking uncles were the opposite of Ducky's vague and preoccupied English relations—they "never looked through you, in fact, they were if anything too aware of your existence and teased you mercilessly; always, on all occasions, public or otherwise, they teased you." They also "loved you and spoilt you and gave you good things to eat or hung lovely little crosses or lockets set with precious stones round your neck" and had friends who "hugged you and made the sign of the Cross over your forehead" and servants who worshipingly "kissed your hands."

First and foremost among Ducky's fascinating Romanov relatives was Uncle Sasha—now Emperor Alexander III, having recently succeeded his brutally murdered father. Uncle Sasha was a six-foot-four Hercules with a flowing chestnut beard and gentle blue eyes, who could twist iron pokers into knots with his bare hands. Although the world viewed Alexander as a fierce despot and a reactionary autocrat, in private he was a good-natured, affectionate uncle who loved to laugh and play practical jokes. The jovial giant led Ducky and her cousins in their exuberant games like an oversized Pied Piper. Uncle Sasha's own special creation was the children's favorite source of fun: a huge net stretched taut above the ground like a trampoline. Climbing up on the net, the bearlike Uncle Sasha would chase his shrieking little nieces back and forth until he cornered them and bounced his huge body down hard in front of them, sending them flying high into the air with hysterical cries of laughter—truly "a game for the gods."

Uncle Sasha's wife, Aunt Minnie—Empress Marie Feodorovna—was as diminutive as he was immense. This oddly contrasted pair had a remarkably happy marriage, he being a totally devoted husband and father and the first Romanov ruler to be completely faithful to his spouse. Petite Aunt Minnie had been born Princess Dagmar of Denmark and was the sister of Princess Alexandra of Wales, Ducky's Aunt Alix. Although not as beautiful as her sister, Aunt Minnie had an equal amount of charm and was "deliciously amiable and much loved . . . the centre of her world, both at home and as Empress."

Of Sasha and Minnie's five children, the eldest, Nicky, was Ducky's favorite. Even though he was ten years older than his beautiful cousin, Nicky was attentive and considerate, a calm young man with an unusually "gentle charm and that kind, caressing look in his eyes, which was his all through life till the day of his tragic death." Nicky would one day inherit his father's throne and rule as Nicholas II.

But Ducky and her sisters were closest to the family of Uncle Vladimir. Slender and slightly less tall than his brothers, the grand duke Vladimir was the handsomest of the Romanov men. He was also the most highly cultured of the grand dukes, sharing his sister's obsession with literature and the arts. Aunt Miechen, his German-born wife, was a regal figure who radiated a seductive, mesmerizing charm. She was also fiercely ambitious, which constantly brought her into conflict with her sister-in-law the empress. The rivalry between the two strong-minded women would increase with time and eventually divide the family into openly warring factions.

Though she couldn't fail to notice the tension that tinged her aunts' smiles when they were together, Ducky was too young to understand the clash of personalities. Nor could she know that her ultimate destiny was to be centered on the family of Uncle Vladimir and its bitterly escalating feud with the throne. Most particularly, it was one of Vladimir's children who would determine the tragic course of Ducky's life.

There were four children—three sons, Kirill, Boris, and Andrei, and a daughter, Helen. "The most beautiful children imaginable," they would become the intimate, lifelong friends of their Edinburgh cousins. Ducky and Kirill, both the same age, were especially close. Attracted to her handsome little cousin from the earliest age, Ducky would follow Kirill around his parents' home with admiring eyes, capturing his friendship with her straightforward manner.

Ducky's only other cousins, Marie and Dimitri, were the children of Mamma's youngest brother, Uncle Paul. The gentlest and most easygoing of the grand dukes, Paul was the duchess of Edinburgh's favorite. Because his wife, Princess Alexandra of Greece, had died very early in the marriage and his children were many years younger than Ducky, Uncle Paul's family was not as close to the Edinburgh family as was Vladimir's. However, these two younger cousins were to play an important part in Ducky's future life; Dimitri would one day murder Rasputin and help bring down the Romanov monarchy.

Ducky's other two uncles had no children. Uncle Alexis was the bachelor of the family. Although an unrivaled connoisseur of beautiful women, this "superb specimen of humanity" could never limit himself to just one. A magnificent, fair-haired Adonis—as enormous as Uncle Sasha—Alexis was a pleasure-loving playboy who irresponsibly carried out his duties as grand admiral of the Russian Navy when he wasn't traveling the world playing the dashing Russian grand duke. "His was a case of fast women and slow ships."

Last but not least was Uncle Serge. Blond and "as tall and slim as the proverbial fir tree," the handsome grand duke Serge was "by far the most frightening of all the uncles, but for all that was our chosen favorite." Rather a strange choice for a young girl's fancy, this rigid and cruel martinet fanatically marched through life along the narrowest path he could find. So tyrannical and reactionary was he that he forbade his wife to read Tolstoy's *Anna Karenina* because he was afraid the novel would arouse "unhealthy curiosity and violent emotion."

Thought by many to have been a severely frustrated homosexual, the emotionally repressed Serge was married to a virginal goddess—Princess Elisabeth of Hesse and the Rhine, known to Ducky and her sisters as Aunt Ella. Her genetic background was a textbook example of the multifamily relationships that were becoming more and more prevalent in the royal houses of Europe. Aunt Ella was actually Ducky's first cousin—being the daughter of the duke of Edinburgh's sister Alice. However, she had now been promoted to the senior level of "aunt," having recently married Uncle Serge, Mamma's brother. Astonishingly enough, in a few years Ducky would marry her Aunt Ella's brother and this cousin-cum-aunt would instantly become Ducky's sister-in-law.

For a young girl as romantic as Ducky, Aunt Ella could not have been better suited to fill this triple role. With green eyes, perfect features, and a tall, slender figure, Ella possessed a rare ethereal quality that led many of her contemporaries to swear they could see a halo. Indeed, this serene and kindly beauty was eventually declared a saint in the Russian Orthodox Church, perhaps as much for her good works as for her quiet fortitude in suffering through marriage to Serge.

Ducky and Missy worshiped this aunt even more than they did their aunt Alix. Wearing gowns trimmed in gold and silver and adorned with fabulous jewels, Aunt Ella created an impression made even more devastating by her spirituality and gentle charm. Ducky and Missy felt their hearts in their mouths each and every time they looked at their aunt—"her purity was absolute; one could never take one's eyes off her, and when parting from her in the evening one longed for the hour when one would behold her again the next day."

Undoubtedly, it was the presence of Aunt Ella that made their "almost menacing" uncle Serge such a highly rated object of their affections. Ducky was too young to understand the sinister implications of her uncle's severe and uneasy personality, and her vague feelings of danger probably were pleasantly titillating.

Alas, the danger would prove to be all too real. Beloved Aunt Ella and Uncle Serge were destined for violent and tragic fates.

But Ducky, throughout her childhood, enjoyed her visits to the home of this unusual couple the most. Because Serge and Ella never had children of their own, Ducky and Missy were given extra love and attention. While in Russia, the girls almost considered their angelic aunt and intimidating uncle to be their second parents.

Parades, church ceremonies, family gatherings, banquets, and quiet country visits—these were Ducky's wonderful memories of the fascinating fairyland called Russia.

Russia. Mamma's home. This was where Mamma belonged. This was where the duchess of Edinburgh was relaxed, happy, and content. And Ducky came to love Russia as much as her mother did.

CHAPTER SEVEN

Return to Paradise

JUST AFTER Ducky turned nine, her secure life at Eastwell Park and Clarence House came to an end. In January 1886 her father was appointed commander in chief of the Mediterranean naval squadron, based on Malta.

Malta! Ducky's birthplace and namesake, a fascinating island, sun-drenched and covered with flowers. The ancient Greeks had considered it a paradisiacal lotusland, naming it Melita, their word for honey. Homer called it the "navel of the sea."

Although Ducky had not returned to her exotic birthplace since those first few months of her life, she was elated by the prospect of going back there to live. The books she had seen and the stories she had heard had set her imagination afire. As the family began hurriedly packing, only one thing diminished Ducky's joy. Her governess, the ugly Mademoiselle, insisted that she and Missy give away almost all of their toys, rather than bring them along. Retaining only a few prized objects, Ducky reluctantly complied.

Mamma's joy was even greater than her daughters'. She would be escaping from this drab, damp, boring country, which always seemed to be disrespectfully placing her second in the hierarchy. The duchess would also be escaping her mother-in-law, Queen Victoria. In Malta, that delightfully dry and sunny garden, she would never have to answer to anyone or take second place. Having thoroughly enjoyed her brief previous stay, Ducky's mother was ecstatic at the prospect of returning.

Queen Victoria was equally pleased to be rid of her troublesome son and her haughty, problematic daughter-in-law. The Edinburghs would now be isolated at a remote foreign outpost. The aging queen was so happy about their departure that she lent them her own yacht, the *Osborne,* for the trip.

It was October by the time the duchess had finally pulled up the family's last roots in England and could begin the long journey east. Traveling across France with her four daughters, she boarded the *Osborne* at Marseilles for a slow four-day crossing through a rough and stormy sea. The yacht was small and unsteady in the heavily surging waters, and Ducky, "a hopeless sailor," was extremely ill for the entire voyage.

When the *Osborne* slowly sailed into the old, fortified harbor of Valletta, Ducky ran to the ship's railing and blinked. The sun had just set; the sky was burning crimson, "as if on fire," and the towering, rock-hewn battlements and waters of the wide harbor reflected the gorgeous glow. The entire Mediterranean fleet was majestically lined up in double rows, their blue-jacketed crews standing impressively at attention, and each ship's band playing "God Save the Queen."

The tiny *Osborne* proudly moved down the center of this spectacular array and docked amid a frenzy of music, cheering, and waving flags and banners. And standing there waiting for them was Ducky's Papa—"Papa at the height of his career, at the height also of his good looks . . . with his deeply tanned face in which his eyes shone extraordinarily, fascinatingly blue." In the lengthening shadows of the evening, the reunited family drove in a solemn procession past cheering crowds through the winding, narrow streets of the town, crossing a series of drawbridges and gliding under massive stone porticoes.

Their destination was the San Antonio Palace, the summer residence of the island's governor, which had been lent to the family for their long stay. Located in the quiet countryside a few miles from the capital, it looked like a dream castle in a young girl's romantic imagination. An Italian Renaissance–style villa, the San Antonio Palace was a sprawling, fanciful architectural creation "with spacious, stone-flagged rooms without end, and long covered galleries running out into promenades upon the top of the high walls, which separated the gardens from each other." What delighted Ducky and her sisters the most were the gardens.

Accustomed to the geometric, formal plans of English gardens, Ducky was amazed by these walled-in, secret-looking oases of lushly overgrown vegetation where "everything grew higgledy-piggledy, a lovely mass of colour saturating the whole place with exquisite fragrance." Above "this medley of flowers hovered a thousand bees and butterflies, and there was a faint buzz in an air which seemed alive with a million wings."

Jasmine, roses, violets, chrysanthemums, verbena, anemones, narcissi, and a hundred other flowers cascaded in sweet-smelling torrents and nearly obscured the narrow paths meandering through the gardens. Ducky's favorite place was the garden outside the bedroom she shared with Missy. Standing hand in hand at the top of the little stone steps leading down to this Eden, the sisters stared with speechless wonder and "its perfect beauty actually made tears of emotion well up in our eyes."

For weeks Ducky and Missy strolled under the arches of orange blossoms and magenta bougainvillea in their new home. Everything they saw was a delightful revelation. The sights, the sounds, the smells—wherever they went an aura of mystery suffused the warm, sunny Maltese landscape.

But what overwhelmed the children most was the sudden change in their daily life. As if liberated by the climate, the two sisters instantly felt a "glorious and blessed freedom."

"Mamma knew how to be severe and there was no pardon for certain misdeeds," Ducky's favorite sister later remembered, "but she also knew how to give us splendid liberty for harmless amusements."

Their most consuming "amusement" was horseback riding around the flat, wild-looking island. The duchess indulged her daughters' "insane passion" by providing each with her own horse, a small and fiery Barbary Arab. These beautiful horses were a Maltese curiosity, having "legs of steel" and tempestuous spirits. Ducky was first given a gray one called Stuart, but he proved too wild and was replaced with a golden chestnut named Scout. Unfortunately, Scout was not as healthy as he looked, and for a time it seemed that Ducky would never find the perfect horse. But when a handsome bay showed up, it was love at first sight. Ducky named her new horse Fearless.

Together with Missy and Ruby, Missy's cream-colored stallion, Ducky and Fearless raced along the island's twisting wall-lined roads and past its sparse pepper trees and pines. "Our ideas about riding were anything but civilized," they later confessed. "We were entirely fearless and our chief pace was full gallop, quite regardless of the ground."

When they weren't galloping through the primitive villages of the island, dodging the startled locals and flying past poky, red-wheeled mule-drawn carts, Ducky and Missy would compete daily in informal races at the Valletta racetrack with the young sailors from their father's ship. These "truly horrible riding-competitions" were pure joy for the Edinburgh sisters; the primary object was to gallop through the muddiest sections of the course and see "who could splash the other the most." But it was never easy to determine the winner, as the mud flew so abundantly that they were "all unrecognizable after one turn."

With their swift horses as the center of their lives and full of the exuberance of preadolescence, Ducky and Missy rejoiced in every aspect of their new home, discovering one wonder after another. These very proper granddaughters of the queen of England had suddenly become "little savages," taking command of the exotic island where St. Paul the Apostle had once been shipwrecked and whose beauty, so resembling that of the Holy Land, had been praised by Thackeray and Sir Walter Scott.

The three carefree years on Malta were to be the happiest of Ducky's life. Wherever she went she felt Malta's seductive charm and "that strange feeling that something is hidden, not yet explored, worlds of beauty, gardens of enchantment you stumble upon at any moment." And it was in this eastern Mediterranean setting that her character was solidly and unalterably formed. Stepping out of the rigid royal confines of her Victorian world, she experienced a degree of independence and freedom such as very few aristocratic children of her time enjoyed. Indulging her love of beauty and freedom, she became a lifelong rebel against meaningless convention.

Galloping around on her horse was not Ducky's only exercise. She liked to run through the fields of knee-high clover and flowers and beans, jumping over the labyrinthine walls that were so numerous that they gave the island the appearance of "an ocean of rock and stone." But most fun of all was climbing trees, an art Ducky and Missy had perfected on a wonderful cedar at Eastwell. Pretending to be monkeys, they struggled to the top: "No tree was too high, nor too difficult, we scaled them all, taking possession of their most unreachable branches whence we seemed to dominate the whole world."

Every Saturday was picnic day. Ducky's mother organized riding parties to some new corner of the small island. With her daughters mounted on their spirited horses and racing off "like a troop of swooping Red Indians," the plump duchess would majestically follow in a carriage filled with her friends.

Sitting on the terraces of the San Antonio Palace with her best friend, a bluff, jolly Irishwoman named Mary Fitzwilliam, the duchess seemed to be completely content at last. Her satisfaction was reflected in her attitude toward her children. Assuming the role of a benevolent dictator, she did very little to restrict their adventures during these "blessed days when everything was joy and all things possible."

However, Ducky and her sisters once went too far and found themselves in disgrace. It happened during one of the Saturday picnic excursions, this one to a bay the duchess had discovered on the far side of the island. As the party toiled up a very steep path, Ducky's mother decided that her delicate friend Mary should spare herself the ordeal of the climb and ride up on one of the girls' horses. Because their stallions had never been ridden by anyone else, the sisters refused.

Enraged and shamed by her daughters' rudeness, the duchess demanded that they give up a horse, which one of the girls reluctantly did. After the climb to the top the horse was returned to its resentful owner and the two women drove off in their carriage. Burning with indignation, Ducky and her sisters, "in floods of tears, like God-forsaken little savages, giving rein to our horses . . . dashed full gallop after the carriage, roaring with rage and sticking our tongues out as far as they would go, whilst we hurled at Lady Mary's head all of the ugly epithets of which our somewhat limited vocabulary could boast."

When the girls finally returned home, their mother was standing at the threshold; with blazing eyes she shouted "hard things that penetrated to the very marrow of our bones." As punishment, the girls' horses were taken away from them for a week and placed in the common public stables in town.

If there was one blight in this perfect Eden, it was the sour presence of the ubiquitous Mademoiselle. Ducky's governess had followed them from England and, seemingly oblivious to the delights of their new home, continued her strict regime of classroom lessons and afternoon back-straightening on the floor. It was Mademoiselle who convinced the duchess that the young girls needed a chaperon on their daily riding trips to the racetrack to compete with the sailors from the fleet.

Perched uncomfortably in her small carriage, the skinny and very correct spinster shadowed her charges as well as she could, following their speeding forms with her tiny, squinting eyes as she shivered in the Mediterranean sun. Mademoiselle's none too silent disapproval of the duchess of Edinburgh's eccentric child rearing eventually created a conflict that sealed her doom.

While Ducky and Missy tramped about and their mother established herself as the social leader of Malta's nobility, their father was busy with his duties of commanding the fleet. Of course when the duke of Edinburgh wasn't off on naval maneuvers he lived ashore with his family. Still a moody, taciturn figure, he found greater and greater solace in his cigars and whiskey and increasingly became a stranger to his children.

Although the southern move had considerably eased the strains of their marriage, the Edinburghs had now drifted apart to such a degree that their union was merely formal. Removed from the critically watchful eye of the queen, they no longer found it necessary to maintain the façade of a happy marriage. And at home it was Ducky's mother who more than ever ran the show.

But even in the distant Mediterranean the queen's presence was felt in every aspect of the family's world. As much as the duchess of Edinburgh continued to resent the power and interference of her mother-in-law, she realized how important it was for her children to stay within the aging monarch's good graces. All of the children were carefully trained to punctiliously maintain a regular correspondence with their grandmother.

Ducky's letters to Grandmama Queen, although conforming to the strict etiquette of the times with their obligatory phrases of respect and affection, reveal the young girl's growing independence. Her letters are written no longer in French but in English. Her childish, uneven scrawl has become a large, boldly written script, and, significantly, she no longer signs her name "Victoria Melita," but instead uses her nickname, "Ducky."

Her first letter from Malta to her grandmother at Windsor was dated the twenty-seventh of November 1886, just one month after the Edinburghs' arrival on the island. It describes her tenth birthday and shows how she and her family were enjoying their new home:

> My dear Grand Mama,
>
> I thank you very much for the lovely little watch you sent me. I got all my presents before breakfast. After, we went to spend the day at St Paul's Bay, it was a very fine day so that Missy and I rode, it took us nearly two hours to get there and we enjoyed ourselves very much, Mama invited two officers from Papa's ship to ride with us, Mademoiselle rode too. We had

luncheon in a house near there, and then we went in a little boat to the lit-
tle island where St Paul's ship was wrecked. We got out of the boats and
walked over the island, but there was nothing to see in it, it was a bare rock
with only the statue of St Paul. We came back from the island and then we
started home, we had hardly started when it began to rain very hard and be-
fore we got home we were all wet through. The weather is very cool but fine.
We were very pleased to hear aunt Beatrice has a little baby, please kiss her
and the baby from us. I hope you are quite well.

> *With much love and many kisses,*
> *Your affectionate grand-daughter,*
> *Ducky*

Ducky, though a year younger than Missy, was maturing very quickly, and by now she definitely seemed the older of the two. With her strong sense of purpose and serious nature, the tall twelve-year-old princess impressed many as being almost like an adult. Having a slim, straight figure, large violet-blue eyes, and thick chestnut hair, which cascaded to her waist, Ducky was blessed with the kind of beauty that was riveting.

When the Edinburghs returned to England for a brief visit in the spring of 1889, Queen Victoria was astonished to discover that her pre-teenaged granddaughter was "nearly as tall as her mother, and such a handsome girl."

The difference between the two older sisters was becoming even more pronounced. Missy was all softness and smiles, an exuberant extrovert who charmed her way through life with feminine gentleness and good humor. With a round, slightly chubby face and pale blue eyes, the princess was an approachable and comfortable presence. Although something of a chatterbox, she projected sympathy and understanding, which made her the most popular and sought-after of the sisters.

In contrast, the tall, slender Ducky was so intense that, on the threshold of puberty, she found that she could cope with the mysterious changes taking place within her only by retreating into herself and guarding her sensitive feelings. By striving to control what she did not yet understand, she ended up stepping back from people and adopting a somewhat somber and watchful manner.

Therefore it was not surprising that Ducky was now found by many to be a shy and difficult girl. Her cousin and future sister-in-law Princess Victoria of Battenberg lived on Malta during this time while her husband, Prince Louis, served with the Mediterranean fleet. She spent many of her afternoons with her Edinburgh cousins, often taking them on horseback rides. She felt closest to Ducky, observing that she was "somewhat farouche, as she was shy."

Had social conventions been different, Princess Victoria could have offered much-needed intimate guidance and advice on her cousin's rapidly approaching womanhood. As it was, both Ducky and Missy alternately reveled in romantic infatuations or retreated into their carefree childhood world of horses and silly games.

Even the prospect of having to lengthen their short skirts threatened their happiness. "We did not want to grow up," they later admitted, "life was too exquisite as it was, we feared any change, anything that might curtail our glorious liberty and independence. We had a subconscious knowledge that there could be no going back. Lengthening skirts was a sign of certain restrictions to our wild ways, it had something to do with the clipping of wings and the putting on of chains, and we were prepared to oppose this innovation with all the strength of our wills, which could become steel when rebellion rose within us."

When the duchess could not persuade her tomboy daughters to lengthen their skirts, she turned to Captain Maurice Bourke, the girls' hero, and enlisted his help. It was testimony to this handsome Irish officer's high place in the Edinburgh girls' affections that it took only one magnetic smile from him to send them looking for thread and scissors.

Captain Bourke was the first man to awaken womanly yearnings in Ducky and Missy. He was a charismatic naval officer, deeply tanned with shining blue eyes and "a delicious smile over extraordinarily white teeth." Captain Bourke was so kind and patient with the high-spirited Edinburgh sisters that he appeared to them as nothing less than a gallant knight for whom they "would have gone through fire and water."

Most important, Bourke provided the girls with an almost perfect father figure. During these years on Malta, the duke of Edinburgh was becoming more and more neglectful of his daughters and was generally absent from their daily lives. While the captain had a thoroughly masculine and romantic image, he was at the same time a comforting presence because he related to them mainly as a trustworthy and kindly uncle.

It was fortunate for Ducky that Bourke appeared on the scene at this time because the princess, on the threshold of womanhood, was in need of an intelligent man's sympathy and guidance. Ducky's adult attitude toward men was shaped by this thoughtful naval officer—her first true love.

There was also another romantic figure in the Edinburgh sisters' lives during this time—their cousin George, the future king George V of England. Stationed at Malta as a fifth lieutenant on his uncle's ship, the *Alexandra,* which was named after his mother, the celebrated princess of Wales, George was a quiet and good-natured young man in his early twenties. However, due to the obsessive attention of his child-like mother, George was still more of a boy than a grown man. Therefore he found himself at ease with his young cousins and "not a bit too grand and grown up." He became Ducky and Missy's best friend, taking "the dear three," as he called them and their younger sister Sandra, on horseback rides through the countryside and jaunts in his two-wheeled dogcart.

In fact, Cousin George became a regular fixture at the San Antonio Palace, staying there when his ship was in port. Miraculously, the bearded, boyish George was also able to capture the affection of both his aunt and uncle, and he, in turn, became devoted to both the duke and the duchess, who he remembered as being "kind, honest and straight-forward and so true." After becoming king, he would always say that the generous-hearted duchess of Edinburgh had always been "like a second mother to me."

Complicating his position in the Edinburgh family was George's growing infatuation with his cousin Missy and her shy reciprocation of his feelings. Because Missy was only thirteen, the flirtation was simply an innocent attachment at this time, but it would eventually develop into a serious romance and a proposal of marriage.

For Ducky, it was a painful episode. The case was not simply that of an adult male showing special attention to one of the three sisters; rather, there was now an exclusive relationship between her sister and someone else who threatened to replace Ducky as Missy's natural soul mate. At first, Ducky resentfully followed along as the couple went horseback riding on the verdant island, glaring all the while at her moonstruck rival.

But the bond between Ducky and Missy was so strong that it soon became apparent that this new intrusion of men and romance would never diminish the relationship that the sisters shared.

Much of the joy of these three years on Malta—between Ducky's tenth and thirteenth birthdays—was derived simply from this special time of life when she was "just between childhood and girlhood, when everything is revelation and all dreams reality. A thick curtain lay over good and evil, no unhealthy curiosity disturbed our peace of mind; there was as yet no desire towards the fruit of knowledge, all was enchantment, no sad blight had ever entered our garden of Eden."

And when it finally came time to leave their island home for good, Ducky was too young to appreciate that it had been a "paradise one never can enter again."

CHAPTER EIGHT

A
Kingdom
All Their Own

WITH AN "unbearable sadness," Ducky and her sisters watched their home being taken apart and carefully packed away. Gradually, the resplendent San Antonio Palace became a forlorn shell of hollow rooms, and the girls fled to the countryside to visit each and every one of their favorite places, their special "beloved haunts," and to say good-bye to their many Maltese friends and acquaintances.

When the day of departure finally arrived, Ducky and Missy wept as they climbed up on the deck of the *Surprise,* the yacht that was to take them across the Mediterranean to Naples. Gazing at the reddish stone amphitheater of Valletta harbor, they felt as if their "hearts were being torn into little pieces" and that they were leaving the best of their childhoods behind them, "a time that had been sheer, unclouded joy and happiness, a time without disappointment or disillusion with never a discordant note."

The only bright spot in this sad time was the presence of Captain Bourke, who, as the commander of the *Surprise,* would be taking them to Italy. Bourke turned a potentially miserable voyage into an unforgettable experience. They stopped and toured the island of Sicily, riding donkeys up Monte Pellegrino to glimpse ruins and famous pilgrim shrines, and then sailed on to Naples, where they spent a day at Pompeii. At night the Neapolitans rowed out to where the royal yacht was anchored and serenaded their illustrious audience.

A few days later the sisters were forced to say a final farewell to their hero. Captain Bourke came to their cabin, and Ducky put her arms around his neck and kissed him for the first and last time.

"Good-bye, little girls," he said, "be good, so that 'Captain dear' can always be proud of you. Never forget that you are a sailor's daughters and that you have the best mother in the world."

Because Eastwell Park had been given up by the Edinburghs when they moved to Malta three years before, there was really no home to return to. This probably had been the duchess's original plan, for she was loath to go back to living in England. The location of their future home, therefore, was an obvious choice: Coburg.

The duchess, who had the final say on family matters, was in love with Germany and all things German, a feeling that had been nurtured by her own German mother and her happy childhood sojourns in Darmstadt. Since her marriage the duchess had made many visits to Coburg and had completely fallen under its spell. Everything about the place suited this difficult woman perfectly—the simplicity, the proud and ancient culture, the beauty of the countryside, the quaintness, the unhurried way of life and, most of all, the total independence and freedom it gave her.

Although the duchess of Edinburgh had been raised in the grandest and most ostentatious court in the world, she had relatively simple tastes. Being physically unattractive only reinforced her natural aversion to the frivolous, shallow world of the aristocratic elite. The gemütlichkeit of cozy Coburg fit the dowdy duchess perfectly. Most important, Ducky's mother would be able to live "entirely according to her desires, uncontrolled by Grandmama Queen and uncriticized by those who were inclined to find her ways foreign and out of keeping with English traditions."

It was evidence of the duchess's conflicted personality that even while she sought liberty and rejoiced that Coburg provided an escape from her mother-in-law's strict authority, the very nature of the German duchy's archaic "social climate of feudalism," with a paternalistic ruler and "simple burghers, uncritical and loyal," appealed to her innately despotic temperament.

Since they would eventually inherit the rule of this little duchy, the Edinburghs had been gradually moving in for the past several years. Even though he was his uncle Ernest's sole heir, however, the duke had always kept one foot on English soil as a possible last-minute candidate for his mother's throne. When the Prince of Wales finally had sons and the duke of Edinburgh's prospects for Windsor evaporated, Affie concentrated more on Coburg, building a fine mansion in the town and sending his only son there to study and prepare for his future inheritance.

Because old Uncle Ernest was aging rapidly, the time seemed right for the Edinburghs to take up residence in Coburg. Both the duke and the duchess had regretted isolating their only son from the rest of the family for the past several years and now looked forward to keeping him and his sisters together. Beyond all this, Ducky's mother relished the prospect of her four daughters being uprooted from their solid English environment and being turned into perfect little Germans like their brother.

In this charmingly picturesque old town, which looked like a page out of the Grimms' fairy tales with its medieval houses and its ancient stone fortress standing guard on a high hill, Ducky noticed how her mamma finally seemed content and happy as the "sole arbiter of her own fate." Here "she was her own mistress; it was a small kingdom perhaps, but her will was undiscussed, she took her orders from no one, and could live as she wished."

The duchy of Coburg was very much like all the other dozens of royal courts in Germany during the last decades of the nineteenth century. In 1889 Germany existed as an empire created and dominated by the awesome power of the Prussian army. The king of Prussia served as the German emperor, ruling over the numerous duchies and grand duchies and small kingdoms and principalities. Each of these German states, no matter how tiny and insignificant, was autonomous, with an absolute sovereign who ruled with the "omnipotent" and uncontested authority of a feudal lord.

Allied by marriage to almost every important royal family in Europe, the handsome and clever sons of the Coburg dynasty had shared the thrones of England, Belgium, and Portugal. With more envy than disdain, Bismarck had called the duchy "the Stud Farm of Europe." However, the current ruler had spectacularly failed in this one vital area. Duke Ernest, although the energetic collector of scores of pretty mistresses, had not been able to produce one legitimate child. This had necessitated the importation of the Edinburghs to carry on the line.

In truth Uncle Ernest was, for the duchess, the chief liability of living in Coburg. The older brother of Prince Albert, Queen Victoria's late husband, Duke Ernest was ruthless, tyrannical, and devoted to every form of vulgarity and vice. He was the exact opposite of the saintly Prince Albert.

Ducky's great-uncle's scandalous court was viewed throughout Europe as nothing more than "a collection of money-lenders, pimps, prostitutes and second-rate actresses." Understandably, the duchess of Edinburgh kept herself and her children as far away from this "ogre in a frock-coat" as best she could. In fact, she was so successful in avoiding the infamous court circle that Uncle Ernest was seen only twice a year, when, lemon-colored gloves in hand and rosebud in his buttonhole, he would briefly invade the Edinburgh home.

Ducky and Missy anticipated these visits with a "fearful excitement." To them, their great-uncle's exaggerated ugliness was both comical and fascinating. A fat, ponderous old man with "the jaw of a bulldog, the lower teeth protruding far beyond the upper and with a pair of blood-shot eyes alive with uncanny, almost brutal intelligence," he would snort amiably and chuck the timid little girls under the chin, calling them "dear, sweet children."

Though too innocent to understand Uncle Ernest's sinister nature, Ducky was astute enough to feel sympathy for his long-suffering wife, Duchess Alexandrine. Formerly a princess of Baden, this meek, martyred creature was a marvel of low self-esteem. True to his character—or, rather, lack of it—Uncle Ernest had married her after having contracted syphilis, a highly infectious and incurable disease at that time. Never a beauty, Alexandrine was by now a "drooping, sad-looking old lady in shabby black . . . with a flat and stayless body. A weak, grisly beard covered her chin and two kindly bleared eyes protruded above a depressed-looking nose, hopelessly pear-shaped."

This pathetic old woman endured every slight by her hostile husband with a smiling serenity, always referring to him as "der lieber gute Ernst" (dearly beloved, good Ernst). The source of her great-aunt's affection for her abusive husband was a mystery to Ducky. All she knew was that she resented how "good" Uncle Ernest contemptuously took advantage of his adoring wife and "treated her as no one else would dare to treat a servant."

Ducky's resentment turned to disgust when, four years later, Uncle Ernest finally died and his widow, at last free from torture, seized on a new opportunity to degrade herself. Taking her husband's last mistress tenderly by the hand, Duchess Alexandrine lavished money and honors on the callous young woman and made her husband's former love nest—a secluded villa in the park—an official shrine, tearfully explaining that "it was there that her beloved Ernst had lived such happy hours."

The piteous example of this perverse old woman was a lesson that Ducky would never forget. Although it made her admire and appreciate her dominating but liberated mother, such self-inflicted suffering must have had a powerful effect on Ducky's passionate temperament. For the rest of her life, Ducky would struggle between her attraction to these two diametrically opposed female role models—strong Mamma and passive Great-aunt Alexandrine.

If Uncle Ernest was reviled by most of his royal relatives—their kindest epithet for him was "that clown from Coburg"—he was surprisingly popular with his subjects and performed his duties with conscientious skill. But sitting like a contented toad in the Ehrenburg, the official residence of the reigning duke, he also spent much of his time eating, drinking, and chasing fast women who were easy to catch. This gave him little time, energy, or inclination to interfere in the lives of Ducky's family while they were occupying their large town house, the Edinburgh Palace directly across the grand city square, the Schlossplatz.

The Edinburgh Palace was a large, square, three-story building with flat, uninteresting façades and scant ornamentation. It reflected the tastes of its creator, Ducky's practical and unaesthetic father. In their upstairs classrooms, Ducky and her sisters gazed wistfully out the window at the "simple and easy" flow of life that, with "its own special charm," centered on the Platz. The other children of Coburg used this huge, formal square for their games and amusements; every day their happy voices could be heard echoing through the rooms of the house. Sunday was the most interesting day of all. Bands played and religious parades filled the square as uniformed infantry officers strutted like the privileged local celebrities they were.

However, it was the Edinburghs' castle, the Rosenau, that was "the real love of our hearts." This unpretentious schloss, inconspicuously situated on a hill above the town and surrounded by fields and forests, was a world unto itself. A felicitous combination of many qualities gave the Rosenau its unrivaled beauty and charm, much like "the same startling effect as an unusual jewel in a perfect setting." The house itself was neither large nor small and was made to look cozy rather than majestic by its pseudo-gothic style with ocher plaster walls and a high roof with two pointed, crenellated façades. Its pièce de résistance was a small tower that contained a sweeping spiral staircase, the only stairs in the house. With a garden on one side and, on the other, a stream cascading over a rocky bed and twisting its way into the forest, the Rosenau seems to have cast a spell over all who saw it. It had been the boyhood home of Prince Albert; when Queen Victoria, saw it for the first time five years after their marriage she was so enraptured by it that she exclaimed: "If I were not who I am—this would have been my real home, but I shall always consider it my 2nd one."

Ducky adored her new home as much as her grandparents had, and so did her mother. And the informality and simplicity of the Rosenau suited the unconventional duchess perfectly.

With her typical energy, Ducky's mother quickly threw out the creaky Empire and Georgian antiques and the florid romantic paintings, completely redecorating the dark mansion. She installed bathrooms, a convenience she had come to appreciate while in England, and modernized the rooms without spoiling their old-world atmosphere. But she firmly resisted some of the new ideas of the coming century, and chose to ignore science's latest triumph, the electric light.

Ducky and Missy and their younger sister were given a large room to share at the very top of the Rosenau's round tower. Imagining it to be the same room where Sleeping Beauty once dwelt, each took possession of one of the deep window alcoves and arranged and decorated it as her own private domain. With a piece of fabric, an earthenware jar, a few special curios, and some fresh flowers, Ducky created her own little world at the top of the romantic-looking tower. She spent hours fixing and arranging her precious objects and dreamily gazing out the tiny dormer window at the forest and villages and town below and the mysterious world beyond, a world she was slowly awakening to.

Coburg was in many ways as enjoyable as Malta. Instead of perpetual sunshine and tropical warmth, the sharply defined seasons of the Thuringian highlands offered a dramatic and fascinating display of constant change.

The duchess, believing more strongly than ever in the moral and physical benefits of outdoor exercise, saw to it that her children were constantly and vigorously involved with nature. Ducky and Missy continued their horseback riding and became known as the best riders in the kingdom. They also took long excursions on foot, bathed in a small local lake, played croquet on their uncle Philip's lawn as well as hard-fought games of tennis. In winter there was sledding and ice-skating, and in spring and fall the duchess led them on mushroom hunts. Ducky displayed the most talent for analyzing nature, and therefore always found the most mushrooms. Her mother also taught her the special pleasures

derived from observing the subtle signs of the changing of the seasons—
the smell of the air, the texture of the leaves and trees and flowers, and
the look of the sun and sky.

There were also indoor games with her brother's friends in the Rosenau's immense attic, "high, shadow-filled and thrillingly haunted by
bats." Twice a week visits were made to that "self-righteous little insti-
tute," the Coburg Theater. Here Ducky watched the romantic and
highly dramatic plays that were favored by the ducal court. The theatrical experience gave form and expression to the intense feelings that
surged through her—feelings she struggled to control and understand. It
also prompted her to give vent to her deepest spiritual sentiments in
games of *Christenvervolgung,* with Ducky playing out the sufferings of the
early Christian martyrs by being tied with ropes and hanged from trees
while her mother presided over picnic lunches in the garden.

Still, there were two shadows that darkened her otherwise happy existence. These were cast by her governess, Fräulein von Truchsess, and
her brother's tutor, Dr. Rolfs.

CHAPTER NINE

Rebellion at Coburg

F OR THE REST of their lives Ducky and Missy would remember how their governess and her fiancé, brother Alfred's trusted tutor, had managed to seize control of the Edinburgh household and unscrupulously dominate it like villains in a gothic novel. The couple had achieved their success by taking advantage of Ducky's mother's two great weaknesses—her hatred of England and her obsessive interest in matters of the intellect. Fräulein von Truchsess was the first governess who had not allied herself with the English servants in the Edinburgh home. By supporting the duchess in her anti-British sentiments and encouraging her passion for all things German, the young Fräulein manipulated the fears and prejudices of her mistress. Alfred's tutor, Dr. Rolfs, was a self-styled paragon of erudition and culture who dazzled the duchess and served as a welcome substitute for her mentally lazy husband.

It must have been a great joy for Ducky's frustrated mother to have, at long last, two such staunch and worthy allies. However, from Ducky and Missy's viewpoint, the couple had merely "wormed themselves entirely into Mamma's good graces."

Very soon, Fräulein and the doctor's "word became law, in all things; their advice was taken, their insinuations were listened to, their ironies and criticisms admitted without discussion." What troubled the sisters most was the intense hatred the smug couple had for everything English, and the very obvious fact that their objective "was to uproot in us the love of England and to turn us into Germans." In quick response, "we resisted this with all our might, pitting our wills against theirs with that magnificent courage of children when their gods are attacked." Thus a bitter war began between the three Edinburgh sisters and their wily superiors. And it was Ducky, with her "steel-like rectitude," who led the revolt.

The pompous German academic was a formidable opponent. Dr. Rolfs personified "German 'Kultur' at its worst, arrogant, masterful, overruling everyone else, turning the best into ridicule, laying down the law, intolerant, tyrannical." Unfortunately, brother Alfred had been placed completely in the doctor's charge in 1883, when he was nine years old. It was apparent to Ducky and Missy that Rolfs was ruining their brother's life. Although Alfred was "eager, blundering, a little swaggering, always getting into trouble, always being scolded," he was also a tender, high-strung boy with "a heart of gold." His sisters loved him with that special feeling attracted by solitary brothers. And nothing upset them more than witnessing the daily abuse Alfred suffered at the hands of his tutor. Worst of all, Dr. Rolfs "liked to ridicule him before others, seeming to delight in making him blush and feel a fool." Ducky wished she could help her brother, but at first she was too young and inexperienced to know what to do. She watched helplessly as the arrogant tutor systematically destroyed every shred of Alfred's confidence and self-esteem.

This brutality awoke in Ducky and her older sister "all the feelings of rebellion that tyrants awake in the hearts of those they overrule." Realizing that they "dared not outwardly revolt or stand up against him"—at least, not quite yet—they took great joy in beginning to make careful plans for his downfall.

However, Rolfs was neither Ducky's greatest nor her most immediate problem. Her governess was her chief nemesis. The young Fräulein charmed and seduced with her "honeyed language . . . and gentle ways" for only one ultimate purpose—to destroy reputations and promote conflict and discord. Her particular ambition seems to have been to destroy the happiness in the lives of Ducky and her sisters.

Perhaps the fact that Fräulein had come from an impoverished aristocratic family accounted for this somewhat pathological desire to punish the privileged elite and bring them down, at least emotionally, to her own level. Ducky and Missy always marveled at "how perfectly she could counterfeit the guileless, almost innocent little girl telling a harm-

less little story to amuse the Duchess. . . . She spoke without accentuating her words, she made them smooth, like beautifully woven silk. . . .
Little by little we came to loathe this gentle relating of innocuous stories . . . knowing that someone's reputation was going to be attacked,
some servant was going to lose his place, some friend was going to be
undermined. . . . It was torture to watch her ways."

Evidently, the young governess was successful in establishing complete
control over the running of the household. "She had wormed herself
into every part of the home's organization," the sisters bitterly observed,
"and her advice was always asked for and mostly taken."

But what enraged Ducky and Missy most was the domination that
Fraulein exerted over their own lives. She had managed to convince the
duchess that her daughters had been seriously damaged by their pampered English childhoods and their years of freedom on Malta. Immediately, hard Russian camp cots were imported from St. Petersburg and
placed in the girls' frilly room in the round tower. A rigorous regime of
instruction began in German, literature, history, geography, arithmetic,
botany, religion, music, painting, French, science, and gymnastics. Plans
were made for them to be confirmed in the German Lutheran Church
instead of the Anglican. And, saving the worst for last, their beautiful
dresses were to be replaced with plainer clothes.

It was one thing to be forced to accept a foreign culture and its tastes
and manners. As distressing as their Germanization had been (Ducky
was now even being forced to write her letters to Queen Victoria in
German), it was nothing compared with the agony of being made to
wear deliberately unattractive clothing. But Fräulein believed that
Ducky and Missy had had their characters ruined by wearing fancy and
elegant clothes. The only solution was to replace their youthful vanity
with somber humility.

To Ducky and Missy, it seemed that this "organically treacherous"
woman was out to destroy every vestige of their considerable beauty.
Soon, "silk underwear and nightgowns were tossed away in favor of harsh
calico." Out went the beautiful colors and pretty dresses that the girls
adored, to be replaced by "humiliatingly ugly gowns, hats and cloaks,
badly shaped shoes—in fact anything that could 'uglify' us in any way."

This was nothing less than "acute torture" for the beauty-loving
princesses. Ducky, in particular, was traumatized by this new regime, and
it served as a vital stimulus for her rebellious spirit. And the Fräulein
found other ways to diminish her charges. In front of their mother, she

led them "to ask questions about the 'hidden mysteries' of life, that aspect of creation the Duchess was most adamant about keeping from them, and then showed them up to their mother 'as nasty little girls with unhealthy minds.' " She also "encouraged and stimulated petty jealousies" between Ducky and Missy, and it was only because of their closeness and devotion that the two sisters remained united during these difficult years in Coburg. What seemed most incredible to Ducky was that her mother could be so taken in by Fräulein and Dr. Rolfs.

The duchess of Edinburgh, no longer finding it necessary to adjust to the undesirable customs of her former English home, began reverting to her old imperial Russian self. Rising in the morning as early as ever, she busied herself with one interest after another. "Her eye was on all things. . . . She did not personally take part in many of the amusements and activities, having in a way aged before her time. . . . But she was the animator, the heart of the whole thing . . . rejoicing over other people's pleasure. . . . She was never out of humour; her wit keen and quick, no one better than she could preside at a dinner-table and make conversation flow."

In the close confines of Coburg, Ducky had a better chance to study her mother's remarkably complex personality. She and Missy noticed that although their mother was "deliciously amusing" and "outwardly placid," she was nevertheless of "an anxious disposition; she took things to heart and worried over them. . . . Clinging to the principles, habits and manners of her youth, she was completely out of sympathy with all modern ideas; if it had been in her power she would have ordered the clock to stand still . . . she was ready to defy the whole advancing world."

Marie's rejection of modernism not only isolated her from society but led her to some rather peculiar beliefs. Because she possessed such an iron constitution and never needed hospitals or doctors or nurses, "she treated all medical innovations as 'modern fads' . . . she repudiated the bacillus theory . . . She positively hooted at those who took their temperature, or blood pressure. . . . As to operations, they were simply a sinful interference with Nature."

Loving simplicity and hating all affectation, the duchess of Edinburgh would always be remembered by her daughters as being "autocratic, conservative, hardened against sickness and pain, proud, courageous, uncomplaining, one who held fast to her old ideas and ideals . . . A curious mixture of tyranny and extraordinary kindness, she could undo at a blow years of patience and tolerance by a sudden hard and often unjustified rebuke."

Ducky suffered the most from the duchess's hypercritical nature and sudden explosions of temper. This was the most disconcerting element in their relationship, and because the young princess tended to be particularly sensitive, her mother's harsh and unexpected reprimands wounded Ducky as nothing else could. There were many nights when the teenaged girl lay awake on her cot in her room at the top of the tower and stared at the vaulted stone ceiling with tears in her eyes.

Not until years later, when Ducky had acquired a Russian husband and moved to St. Petersburg, did she realize the source of her mother's relentless compulsion to "cut off her nose to spite her face." There was "something of the mysterious Russian irresponsibility in her nature, an elemental exasperation against all things and even against herself, which other nationalities in vain try to understand."

Although hidden under the veneer of her earlier English upbringing, it was a nature that Ducky also shared.

The duchess encouraged her children to be communicative about everything except their deepest and truest feelings. Unable to show expressions of love, joy, or grief, Ducky's mother "always had herself in hand, utterly, and hated anything that might have been termed 'sentimentality.' " Her daughters would realize much later in their lives that their mother had "trained us to this attitude and all through life this peculiarity has clung to us four sisters; at moments of deep sentiment or emotion we are disconcertingly dumb. . . . We were painfully shy before any display of feeling . . . the more we felt, the less we showed. . . . This has been an asset but also a hindrance in life."

Of all of the sisters, Ducky was the chief victim of their mother's merciless quest for stoical deportment. Precariously pitted against an intense sensibility, that repression would boomerang alarmingly at the most unexpected times.

Adding to the strains of Ducky's struggles with approaching womanhood was the increased absence of both of her parents. The duchess, now being irresistibly close to the Russian border, traveled home several times a year and also went to the French Riviera in the winter. Because of her daughters' intense educational regime in Coburg, she usually left them behind with Dr. Rolfs and Fräulein.

As for their father, the duke was in love with the sentimental idea of life in Coburg, but he could stand it for only a week or two before he became bored. More devoted to whiskey and women than ever, Ducky's father didn't find the hunting in the local mountains enough to compensate for the lack of other diversions.

Ducky came to rely more than ever on her close friendship with her older sister. She and Missy attended classes together and shared almost every facet of their daily lives. It was this bond of sisterly affection and understanding that made the domination of their arrogant tutor and governess tolerable. In addition, there were two servants—Matilda, the head housemaid, and Meister, the castellan—who loved the girls as if they were their own. Matilda was as devoted to the Edinburgh girls as old Nana Pitcathly had been. A matronly widow, she showered attention on Ducky, baking special biscuits for her and indulging her with special treats such as the sugary, sticky white pastry called *Lederzucker.* However, an unfortunate development brought an end to the happy situation. Matilda, it suddenly became evident, was pregnant. The discovery so horrified Ducky's mother that the poor woman was instantly sent packing. The duchess guardedly told the sobbing girls that the maid had become "sick."

But old Meister was still there. Dwarfish and slightly crippled, this ugly and unkempt creature was the perfect fixture for the fairy-tale setting of the Rosenau, "an irrepressible eccentric beloved by all the family." For Ducky and her sisters, he was a high-spirited clown, a crazy court jester who played directly to their youthful imaginations with his stories and games and discoveries. His greatest accomplishment had been helping Ducky and Missy take an abandoned closet in the thickets beyond the garden and turn it into a "roomy, worm-eaten, and rather decrepit" hut. They painted their private palace grass-green with a big red heart on the door. Outside, Meister hung a bell and tied a horseshoe from its rope for good luck. Inside, a thick tree branch sprouted straight through the room, so the resourceful Ducky carefully put a small cauldron on it and filled it with brightly colored flowers.

Here they entertained their special friends, girls from the Coburg aristocracy. Both Ducky and Missy focused their romantic yearning on the safe territory of their own sex, as many young teenagers do. Missy's crush was the daughter of the commander of the Coburg battalion. For her own true love, Ducky chose "a somewhat 'high flown' girl full of poetry" named Frieda von Lichtenberg. Strolling hand-in-hand, reading and writing each other poetry, exchanging rings, and gazing at the stars with their arms around each other, the two "bosom friends" explored new, mysterious feelings that they failed to fully understand.

But Ducky and Frieda's friendship was perceived by their elders to be too intense and it was brought to an abrupt close, "the authorities considering that her society was not particularly beneficial." Deprived of her best friend, Ducky retreated even further into herself.

Besides the tyrannical Fräulein and Dr. Rolfs, there were erudite instructors whose eloquent discourse Ducky and Missy couldn't quite comprehend. In trying to make them "imbibe all of the knowledge necessary for well-educated little princesses," their teachers concentrated so single-mindedly on a full presentation of facts that they failed to excite their pupils' interest and the bright young princesses were unable to retain much.

By far, Ducky was "the better pupil of the two; she was more quick-witted, eager to learn, had a more retentive memory, and was better at spelling." Whereas her older sister was content to go along with anything pleasant, Ducky was "less ready to accept facts at face value, and with her keen and inquiring mind she relished arguing, not for its own sake so much as out of a desire to question things." As Missy later recalled, "Ducky seldom accepted anything wholesale."

To complicate their young lives even more, the girls were about to be confirmed into the German Lutheran Church following a rigorous course of preparation that involved "complicated theological explanations." It was a "bewildering experience," which left both Ducky and Missy feeling "slightly uncomfortable" and "a little resentful." The end result of this sacred experience in the pretty little rococo church in the village of Oslow, near the Rosenau, was that they both felt guilty for not feeling what they had been instructed to feel. "With all our might we tried to hypnotize ourselves into a sort of religious ecstasy . . . but neither of us experienced the real inner thrill," Missy later recalled.

What they were both feeling most intensely at this time was the unholy emotion of wrath toward their oppressors, Fräulein and Dr. Rolfs, who now had complete control of the household and the children during the frequent absences of the duke and duchess.

But the moment of truth was soon to come.

The formidable couple had set their wedding date, and the duchess of Edinburgh had just left for a visit to Russia. The duke was also away, at his new naval post in England. Fräulein and the doctor now reigned supreme at the Rosenau. The pair went about the little castle "mooning" over each other while the shabbily dressed young princesses sullenly watched and waited.

One evening, while Ducky and her sisters silently ate their dinner, Fräulein, sitting in their mother's place at the head of the table, and the doctor, sitting opposite her at the foot, were having trouble getting an unobstructed view of each other. The problem was a large silver cup, filled with flowers, which stood in the center of the long table. Finally Dr. Rolfs, "in that high-handed way of his," ordered a servant to remove the cup from the table so that he could have a proper view of his beloved.

His command let loose a sudden explosion of protest from Ducky and Missy.

"This was placed on the table by Mamma," Ducky loudly announced. "It is her desire that it should be here—it has always been here—and only Mamma has the right to have it removed!"

The stunned tutor tried to make a joke of this protest, airily dismissing it as foolish and absurd. But Ducky stood her ground. She knew that this was her one chance to be victorious over her oppressors. No matter how small, it was an opportunity that might never come again.

The tutor, growing exasperated and angry, tossed down his napkin and shouted at the children: "Well, it is either I or the pot!"

Without the slightest hesitation, Ducky stretched out her arms and tightly embraced the huge silver cup, glaring defiantly at the doctor.

"We prefer the pot!" she declared.

The shocked man stared with disbelief at Ducky. She returned his stare.

Humiliated, Dr. Rolfs slowly rose from the table and retreated to another room. Under her sisters' admiring gaze, Ducky smiled confidently at the outraged Fräulein and finished her meal.

When the couple married and went off on their honeymoon, Fräulein's eldest sister, whom the girls called Louiserowitch, came to look after the children. Louiserowitch had no great love for her sister and she lost no time in extracting from the children every one of their complaints and grievances against Fräulein and the doctor. As it happened, Ducky's father was spending a week at Coburg, "an event which seldom came to pass." Encouraged by Louiserowitch, Ducky and Missy approached their father and emotionally confessed their bitter feelings about the tyrannical pair.

To their amazement, the duke felt exactly the same way. He despised the arrogant, anti-British couple, and when the duchess returned, "a great row ensued." Fräulein and her new husband were almost dismissed, but the stubborn duchess clung to her faith in them and fought long and hard with her estranged spouse until he finally relented. However, Marie did not reproach her daughters for their denunciation, and she tactfully patched things up between them with concessions on both sides.

Although Ducky and her sisters would always mistrust the defeated couple, who uneasily continued their rule, "the acute epoch of war was over."

CHAPTER TEN

Missy's
Farewell

P RINCESSES MUST MARRY," Ducky's mother firmly believed. And the younger the better. "When they are over twenty they begin to think too much and to have too many ideas of their own which complicate matters."

It certainly would have complicated the duchess's plans. Her teenaged daughters were becoming lovelier by the day, and Ducky and Missy were soon to be recognized as the most beautiful women in Europe. The two sisters—especially Missy, a year older than Ducky and already developing a premature voluptuousness—would be the most sought-after royal brides of their era.

Since the unhappiness of her own marriage had prompted the duchess to lavish all her love and devotion on her children, it seems ironic that she would have wanted to marry them off so quickly, and especially to arrange unions for them that were based solely on dynastic purposes. But this was exactly what she was determined to do.

The aim of the conspiring trio—the duchess, Fräulein, and the doctor—had been not only to turn the young English princesses away from their native culture and make good Germans out of them, but also, more important, to remove them from the marital orbit of the British royal family and maneuver them into solid Teutonic matches. The duchess was clever enough to keep this intention hidden from her romantic daughters.

Naturally the duke of Edinburgh's family did not approve. Ducky's aunt Alix, the Princess of Wales, who was never known for her sharp intellect, was perceptive enough to see what was happening. "It is a pity those children should be entirely brought up as Germans," she wrote to her son, the future King George V, who as everyone knew was then in love with Missy. "Last time I saw them they spoke with a very strong German accent—which I think is a great pity as after all they are English . . . and what do you say to Aunt Marie having *hurried* on the *two girls confirmation*—and in Germany too so that now they won't *even know* that they have ever been English—particularly as they have been confirmed in the German church."

Aunt Alix, abhorring all things German, dreaded the idea of her son's marrying Missy. But the match was being championed by her husband, the Prince of Wales, and by no less a person than Queen Victoria herself. This was too much for the duchess! Determined not to allow her daughter's future, "like most things in the English royal family, to be dictated by the Queen," she conspired to keep Missy and George apart. But this was becoming harder and harder to do.

In the summer of 1890 the duke of Edinburgh began his three-year appointment as commander in chief of the British fleet at Devonport in southwest England. This necessitated his estranged wife's spending much more time in her least favorite country, dividing her residence between grimy Clarence House in London and the small port town on the pastoral coast of Devonshire. The duchess, always a slave to propriety and duty, put in enough visits to keep up appearances and fulfill her social obligations, but she kept her daughters away from England as much as possible, allowing them to visit only a few times a year during their vacation holidays.

Ducky, however, enjoyed these periodic returns to the land of her early childhood. The gentle southern shore of Devonshire brought back memories of summers at Osborne on the Isle of Wight. Her father's official residence, Admiralty House, was an uninspiring mansion with a tiny garden in the back that barely accommodated the children's wild games of croquet. But most of Ducky's time was spent at the seaside gardens of Sir Richard Harrison, the general in command. She became best friends with Violet Harrison, the general's vivacious daughter.

This would be Ducky's last taste of being an English princess and living in the country of her youth; it would also be her father's last naval command. The duke had now reached the top of his career ladder, and this post marked the end of his life as a sailor. Back in Coburg, dissipated old Uncle Ernest was rapidly declining and it seemed that he might finally expire at any moment. Although their mother looked forward to the inheritance of the German duchy, Ducky and Missy were keenly aware that "Papa dreaded the change which stood ahead of him, for he was thoroughly British in taste and habit and bitter was the prospect of expatriation."

Returning to Coburg at the end of the summer of 1891, Ducky and her sisters resumed their frustrating round of lessons. But there was also romance. Their brother's young friends, their former rough-and-tumble playmates, were now shyly pressing flowers into their hands and reciting poetry.

There was the humorous Ribbeck, who never failed to make Ducky laugh, and the dashing Froman, who fascinated her with his supercilious good looks, the dark and enigmatic Arend, and the towering, good-natured Lowel, who blushed deeply and had a crack in his voice.

But in the world of that time there was never any question of a real romance with any of these love-struck Romeos. Princesses were not allowed to carry on love affairs, no matter how innocent or circumspect. They were permitted their casual flirtations and crushes, but their one and only destiny was a suitable royal husband, a consort who would give them rank and status.

In the fall of 1891 it was inconceivable that a royal princess could ever marry a commoner or even a lesser member of the aristocracy. The well-ordered monarchies of Europe would never let such a thing occur. For most, to lose royal status was a fate worse than death. An ill-fated princess of Saxe-Weimar had recently committed suicide because she was forbidden to marry her true love, a baron from a respected noble family. Her grief-stricken father dried his eyes and thanked God for this sad solution—a far better one than the forbidden alternative.

The giddy, self-dramatizing Missy might easily have been carried off in the same dangerous direction as the unfortunate Saxe-Weimar princess had it not been for the influence of her younger sister, who was wary of the pitfalls of allowing passion to run uncontrolled. The constant struggle with her own emotions and feelings had given the fifteen-year-old Ducky a remarkably mature character.

"Sister Ducky was more austere, more unbending than I was," Missy later recalled. "She was always the monitor; the one who would tolerate no nonsense, who admonished or cautioned. Her advice or reproof was listened to and there was a steel-like rectitude about her which commanded respect."

Her sister's guidance became crucial when Missy began a flirtation with the nephew of the Rosenau's head gardener. Although Ducky sympathized, she kept watch on the awkward courtship and stepped in and put an end to it when it threatened to get out of hand.

In the fall of 1891, before either Ducky or Missy had matured enough to have serious romantic feelings for anyone, an event happened that would change their lives forever.

Early one morning while Meister was hobbling spiritedly around the Rosenau garden screeching an operatic aria in his off-key tenor, Ducky's mother, convulsed with laughter by his antics, was handed a telegram from Russia. It announced the sudden death of Alexandra, the "sweet young" wife of the duchess's favorite brother, Grand Duke Paul. She had died during the birth of their second child. The awful news struck them "like a thunderbolt."

The duchess, accompanied by her two eldest daughters, departed for the funeral in St. Petersburg.

It had been several years since Ducky had been in Russia, and this sudden visit gave her the opportunity to see the imperial court through mature eyes for the first time. Rarely do a child's memories fail to exaggerate and enlarge, but Ducky's hadn't even begun to do justice to the magnificence and splendor that the princess now beheld. Ducky was overwhelmed by everything she saw. And she fell in love all over again with her mother's homeland.

The funeral of Ducky's young aunt was held in the great church of the Peter and Paul Fortress, where all the Romanovs had been buried since the time of Peter the Great.

Ducky and her sister shivered at the sight of the colossal tombs of their ancestors, "side by side, in impressive rows, under plain oblong blocks of white marble . . . one tomb exactly like the other, austere symbols of how death levels all things . . . each stone guarding its own secret, the secret of those different lives, many of which had ended in unspeakable tragedy."

The most recent marble monument was for Ducky's brutally murdered grandfather Emperor Alexander II.

Ducky gazed with awe at her mother's family, their dull black mourning apparel "slashed by the bright ribbons of their respective orders, blue for the Empress, red for the grand duchesses." The great pomp of the ceremony thrilled her senses—the "thousands of lighted tapers," the clouds of incense, and the "stupendous chants which rose to the vaults, echoing again from the fortress-like walls." She was moved by the sight of her gentle uncle desperately throwing himself down and having "to be torn away from the coffin of his bride."

After the burial the family gathered together in the Winter Palace. The cousins, almost strangers again because of their long separation, "stared at each other shyly, no one wanting to make advances for fear of rebuffs." But Ducky and Missy couldn't help noticing that "the boys and young men were inclined to like you too much."

One young man liked Missy so much that he excitedly proposed marriage. He was the grand duke George, her second cousin, the son of Grandpapa's brother the grand duke Michael. George had good looks, great wealth, position, intelligence, and a kindly personality.

But the duchess of Edinburgh rejected his offer almost out of hand. She wanted no Romanov husbands for her daughters. Whether it was the sexual immorality of the male members of her family or the ominous storm that she might have seen gathering on the Russian horizon, Marie definitely did not want any of her daughters settling in St. Petersburg.

The Duchess had another worry—the growing attraction between Ducky and her handsome cousin Kirill, who was as appreciative of Ducky's dark beauty as she was of his.

To dampen her daughters' enthusiasms, she shrewdly told them: "Don't you know that the cousins who seem so charming were also kissing the maid behind the parlor door?"

Their mother's cynical warning was more than enough. They found that their exotic Romanov cousins possessed a unique "blending of strength and weakness, kindness and a generosity which almost amounted to lavishness, and yet a touch of cruelty somewhere, undefinable, but you sensed that it was there, dormant, hidden beneath their captivating ways."

Still, neither Ducky nor her sister could help being drawn to these virile young specimens. "We too had Russian blood in us, so we were strongly attracted, but the English side seemed on guard, a little hostile, or anyhow watchful, so that we could not blend entirely, nor feel quite at home." However, English caution aside, they both confessed that they "would have needed but little persuasion" to settle down happily in Russia.

There were visits to Moscow, the semi-Oriental City of the Czars, and to nearby Ilinsky, the country estate of Ducky's aunt-cousin, the beguiling grand duchess Ella, and the grand duke Serge. Ella looked more ethereal than ever in her black mourning, and her teenage nieces gazed at her with an almost worshipful admiration.

Their mother seemed to dominate her Romanov relatives as easily as she did her in-laws back at Windsor. Caustically criticizing the unruly younger generation for being brought up without any manners, the duchess confronted her loud, towering brothers and, "no matter how autocratic her family might be . . . she always had her say."

Watching the frozen landscape disappear as she and her mother and sister returned by train to Coburg, Ducky felt the Russian part of her longing to stay behind. Her mother's homeland had "an extraordinary glamour"; it was "an enormous world of a thousand splendours, of a thousand possibilities, with a feeling of dark mystery as background, something unfathomable and rather awful, a secret no one really possessed."

Back home in Germany, the duchess of Edinburgh concluded that sixteen-year-old Missy would have to be safely placed in an appropriate marriage as soon as possible—"appropriate" meaning German, not Russian or English. After having fielded the proposal of one George, the grand duke George Michaelovich, the duchess was now intercepting love letters from her daughter's English cousin, George of Wales. This George had been counting on Missy's hand in marriage since their platonic romance on Malta three years ago. He was now getting much too serious for comfort.

So the duchess began making discreet inquiries concerning possible candidates, and, of all the available German princes, she decided upon Ferdinand of Hohenzollern-Sigmaringen, docile, painfully shy, jug-eared, and obsessed with the study of botany. He was a member of the cadet branch of the German imperial family, a highly cultured clan that exemplified everything the duchess treasured, and, most important of all, one day he would succeed his uncle as king of Romania.

Having cunningly sent the prince a photograph of her eldest daughter, the duchess was promptly informed of his enthusiasm. A meeting on neutral ground was arranged. The duchess orchestrated the encounter to look like an accident. The Kaisermanöver, Germany's great annual military event, was chosen as the appropriate romantic setting.

Although Ducky was only fifteen and Missy sixteen, the imperial family invited them to the Wilhelmshöhe Palace near Kassel to attend this event. Their mother, having engineered the occasion, accompanied them. This was to be the young women's official debut into the adult world of royal society; clad in matching mauve dresses, Ducky and Missy shyly entered the grand ballroom of Wilhelmshöhe Palace, displaying contrasting images of beauty that would assume legendary status in the decades to come.

At dinner, Missy was strategically placed next to Crown Prince Ferdinand. Because she and Ducky had been brought up speaking several languages and "could make ourselves agreeable to any company," she easily engaged the introverted prince in conversation. Ferdinand's gentle kindliness captivated Missy, and both young princesses decided that they liked him.

The person they didn't like was their overloud and bombastic first cousin the Kaiser. This was their first prolonged exposure to his domineering presence; they found that he "put your back up . . . there was something about him that roused antagonism."

The misogynistic kaiser liked his two beautiful cousins about as much as they liked him. Probably resenting the competition—the girls were diverting gazes from his endless array of elaborate uniforms—the kaiser was to maintain a lifelong antagonism toward both sisters, especially Ducky. Wilhelm tolerated only meek and drab women. His wife, the kaiserin, was exactly such a woman. Ducky and Missy felt sorry for her and marveled at the consistency of her "brave and impersonal smile . . . which she seemed to put on daily with the gorgeous, if somewhat tasteless gowns she was fond of, a smile that finally, as years advanced, seemed actually carved into her face . . . [She was] an automaton, wound up by duty which death alone would unwind."

But the girls were too excited over their "coming out" at Wilhelmshöhe to pay much attention to their unpleasant host and martyred hostess. Missy still had no idea that Ferdinand was intended for her, and she paid him only casual attention. Her heart secretly still belonged to Cousin George back in England.

The determined duchess, building on this first mild success at the Kaisermanöver, now took Missy and Ducky off to Berlin to visit their Cousin Charly. Charly was Princess Charlotte of Saxe-Meiningen, the spoiled daughter of their aunt Vicky and the sister of the kaiser. Charly "moved with deliberate grace and spoke in a soft, melodic purr." She had visited the Rosenau often, and while manipulating Ducky and Missy with the skills of a temptress in order to capture their adolescent love and admiration, she too had contrived with the duchess and Dr. Rolfs to crush their British side and turn them into pure little Germans.

The plan now was for Ducky and Missy to stay at their cousin's home in Berlin, where Ferdinand would be a constant visitor. But the situation backfired. Charly presided over the city's most sophisticated and jaded social set, and the two teenaged girls from the country—sheltered even by the standards of that era—were painfully out of place. Ducky and Missy were ignored by the cousin they had always idolized, and they discovered a very unattractive side to her character that left them feeling crushed and betrayed. Their mother swiftly intervened and took her humiliated daughters back to Coburg. That horrible week in Berlin would be "one of the most painful memories" for Ducky and Missy.

The love-struck Ferdinand, however, was far from lost. He continued his shy pursuit by joining the duchess and her daughters for a few weeks of sightseeing, theater parties, and visits to art galleries in Munich in the early spring of 1892. Missy was now fully aware of what the game was and, most particularly, of what was expected of her. "There was love in the air," she recalled, "it was springtime, and Mama had a happy, expectant face."

Missy's only desire was to please the most important person in her life—her mother, so she made courtship as easy as possible for the almost pathologically shy Ferdinand. With her mother and Charly literally leading him by the hand, a formal proposal was haltingly offered. Missy accepted.

She had no way of knowing that, a few weeks before, her adored Cousin George, who had lost his older brother to influenza and thus suddenly become the next heir to the English throne, had had his parents, the Prince and Princess of Wales, offer to the duchess of Edinburgh his proposal of marriage to Missy. Missy's mother never even discussed the proposal with her daughter. She simply told the Waleses that Missy had just been confirmed in the German Lutheran Church and "that she 'would for nothing in the world, influence' her daughter to change her religion back again to the Church of England."

The refusal rocked the families. Queen Victoria, who desperately wanted the match between her grandchildren, was sadly disappointed and wrote to Charly's mother: "Missy herself would not have Georgie. . . . It was the dream of Affie's life." The angry Prince of Wales stopped speaking to his brother, and the enraged duke of Edinburgh stopped speaking to his wife. It seemed that only the two mothers were happy.

When Missy's engagement to Crown Prince Ferdinand of Romania was announced only a few months later, everyone was horrified at the thought of such a beautiful and promising young girl being sent off with such a dull companion to such a wild and primitive country. Grandmama Queen sent off a battery of outraged letters, then simply resigned herself to the fact that Missy was "a great victim . . . to be enormously pitied."

Victoria wanted Missy married at Windsor Castle like the rest of her English grandchildren, but religious problems made this impossible. The duchess desired that the wedding take place in Coburg, but her in-laws refused to have anything to do with the notorious court of Uncle Ernest, so the ancestral home of the groom, the medievel Sigmaringen Castle in southern Swabia, was agreed upon as the wedding site.

Ducky herself had conflicting emotions. She was happy for her sister, but she was also devastated by the prospect of losing her dearest friend and inseparable companion. The two sisters had hardly ever been apart. When the engagement had been first announced at a huge state banquet at the kaiser's New Palace in Potsdam, Ducky and Missy sat tightly squeezing hands "with something like apprehension." For the bride-to-be, the impending separation from her sister was also the most overwhelming problem she faced. "And above all there was Ducky," she later wrote. "Ducky, dearest of companions and comrades, however should we have the courage to part? Subconsciously I realized that she was full of resentment; I felt that she could not understand my easy consent, that simple-minded acceptance of an almost unknown man; in her heart of hearts she disapproved of this 'Yes,' which had been so quickly, too quickly said. It meant separation, it meant the beginning of something new in which she would have no part; we had always shared everything, and now here was something I was not going to, could not, share any longer."

Ducky, jealous by nature, felt exactly as her sister guessed. This was, so far, the cruelest ordeal of her life. For the next several months, she and her timid future brother-in-law ardently competed for Missy's time and attention. And although she was beginning to fall in love with Ferdinand, Missy realized that "half of me was hankering after Ducky, the companion of my whole life, and this new love was pulling me in another direction. I felt something of a traitor towards my sister, and this was tearing me in two."

During that busy summer and fall of 1892 the duchess and her daughters traveled back and forth several times between Germany and England. It was necessary to attend to numerous details and arrangements, to say nothing of the social obligations of Devonport and of introducing Ferdinand to Missy's cool and disapproving English relatives—first and foremost, Grandmama Queen.

Ducky, though still jealous and resentful, was gradually coming to accept the inevitable. Shrewdly watching the withdrawn prince, she appreciated his sensitive qualities but was wary of his personality and values. With a remarkable precocious wisdom, she gently advised Missy one evening: "To be entirely happy in marriage, the same things must be important to both."

Ducky turned sixteen at Admiralty House in Devonport in November of 1892. The weather was bleak as her spirits. She tried to celebrate this special milestone of her young life, but the fact that her sister's wedding was only six weeks away made her feel more miserable than ever. On the evening of her birthday she wrote Queen Victoria:

> *My dear Grand Mama,*
>
> *It was too kind of you to write to me and to send me those dear little silver trays. I thank you so much for them and for your kind letter.*
>
> *I certainly will miss Missy dreadfully and the time when we are to lose her is approaching fast. But we try not to think too much about it so as not to sadden the last few weeks which we will spend together.*
>
> *We were so sad to hear that poor Aunt Miechen [Kirill's mother] had sprained her ankles; we had heard that she was ill at Paris, but we did not know what was the matter with her. We only hope that she will recover quickly.*
>
> *We will all be so pleased to go to Windsor and to see You again dear Grand Mama; Sandra and Baby have not seen you for such a long time.*
>
> *Once more thanking you for so kindly thinking of me, I remain your affectionate granddaughter,*
>
> *Ducky*

Before they knew it, 1893 had arrived and it was time to set off through the heavy snows of that winter to the remote castle of Sigmaringen. Because their stubborn mother hated luxury and refused to travel in the fancy, comfortable saloon carriages, Ducky and Missy spent their last night together sleeping on the cold and dirty floor of a rickety old train that had neither beds nor hot water.

Up to the very end, the duchess of Edinburgh was determined that her girls be kept as innocent as possible. With amazement Missy later recalled: "A risqué book never reached our hands, we blushed when it was

mentioned that someone was to have a baby, the classics were only allowed in small and well-weeded doses; as for the Bible, although we
were well up in both Testaments, all the more revealing episodes had
been carefully circumscribed." Perhaps this was not the best preparation
for married life.

The wedding took place on the cold, snowy morning of January 10
and was witnessed by most of the Edinburghs' royal relatives from the
four corners of Europe. The kaiser, decked out as colorfully as a Christmas tree, obnoxiously made himself the center of attention, as always.
After three ceremonies—civil, Lutheran, and Catholic—the newlyweds
went off to a nearby hunting lodge for their honeymoon. There was just
enough time for a brief visit home to Coburg before Missy and her new
husband set off for Romania. The night before her final departure Missy
shared a good cry with her sister and was shocked to find even her stoic
mother in tears.

The next morning Ducky and her family and friends gathered on the
icy platform of the Coburg station to say good-bye to Missy and Ferdinand. Sobbing, the sisters hugged and struggled to find the "courage not
to cry out in pain." A moment later the train was slowly moving out of
the station, hands were waving, smoke filled the wintry cobalt sky; the
train became a distant blur and then was gone.

Missy—Ducky's "inseparable companion," her "faithful chum" since
infancy—was gone.

With an "almost unbearable grief," Ducky returned alone with her
family to the Rosenau.

CHAPTER ELEVEN

The Poet Prince

*T*HE WEEKS FOLLOWING Missy's departure were the most painful Ducky had ever experienced. She tried to establish a deeper friendship with her younger sister Sandra, but this dull sibling was a poor substitute for the vivacious Missy. Ducky and her older sister shared a closeness of mind and spirit that neither would be able to duplicate for the rest of her life.

Miserable in her new Romanian home, Missy sent heartbroken letters home to her sister in Coburg begging her to come and visit. Through that long, cold winter of 1893, Ducky wanted to rush to her sister's side, but her mother forbade it; not until several months had passed was she able to journey to the strangely exotic kingdom on the Black Sea. Ducky, with her typical straightforward honesty, accepted the somewhat primitive country and its spartan court life, coming to love and appreciate Romania's uniqueness and idiosyncrasies. She was often to return, and eventually became almost as attached to her sister's new homeland as Missy did herself.

Ducky's thoughts were far from marriage, but the same powers that had masterminded Missy's wedding were now conspiring to bring about another. The duchess, still convinced that "princesses should marry young," was already scouting the numerous German royal houses for an eligible mate for her second daughter. The candidate need not necessarily be a king, but he should have some sort of crown on his head, and one to offer Ducky. The haughty duchess had suffered too much as a nonentity in her own unhappy marriage not to have wanted to spare her daughters the same fate. Again, disdaining the poor candidates in her own Russian family and her spouse's boorish English relatives, Ducky's mother, more in love with Germany than ever, would only consider a very high-ranking German prince.

For once, Grandmama Queen and her rebellious daughter-in-law agreed on something. Victoria had also decided on a German husband for her spectacular young granddaughter, and she had already selected just the right one: her favorite grandson, Prince Ernst Ludwig of Hesse and the Rhine.

Queen Victoria saw Ducky and Missy only on rare occasions; after their long Malta stay, in July of 1890, she had been surprised to find them "very handsome and looking quite grown up. . . . They are very pretty, strong and healthy and dear, good children admirably brought up." As young as the girls were at the time, they still inspired their incorrigibly matchmaking grandmother to take special notice that "they will make excellent *partis* [matches] some day."

A year later, during the autumn of 1891, Ducky visited her grandmother at Balmoral. Her cousin Ernst Ludwig of Hesse was also staying there. "Ernie" was full of his own particular lively charm and high spirits, and, although eight years older than his beautiful teenaged cousin, he devoted most of his time and attention to her. They were amazed to discover that they had much in common. Quick-witted, intelligent, loving everything to do with art and beauty, Ducky and Ernie also shared an appreciation of the ridiculous. They even shared a birthday. Ducky and Ernie dominated every occasion and, as the center of attention, "seemed to rush about in a private world of their own."

Queen Victoria watched and laughed. "Victoria and Ernie are very funny together," she wrote to Ernie's eldest sister, Princess Louis of Battenberg. Indeed, she was so delighted by their antics that she made up her mind that these two young people would be just as happy with each other as she was with both of them.

So she impatiently waited a year and a half for Ducky to mature to a proper age for courtship, in the meantime encouraging her "dear Ernie" to carefully consider the prospect of marriage with his delightfully beautiful Edinburgh cousin. Now, in the spring of 1893, as Ducky approached her seventeenth birthday, her family began actively arranging this perfect match.

Though Ducky's mother had at first opposed Ernie because of his close connection with the English royal family, she had relented in 1892, when he succeeded his father to the throne of Hesse and the Rhine, also known as Hesse-Darmstadt. Since Ernie was now the duchy's ruler, Ducky would be able to enjoy the sovereign role her mother considered so necessary for her daughters. The fact that Ernie was a grandson of Queen Victoria, the duchess was willing to overlook. After all, even though an English princess had recently shifted the focus of the family toward Windsor, the royal house of Hesse was one of the most ancient and illustrious dynasties in Europe. The duchess's mother had been a princess of Hesse, and Darmstadt had served as a meeting place for the family for years. It was almost a second home for Marie.

A land as cozy and relaxed as Coburg, Hesse-Darmstadt comprised "rugged mountains, tall forests, and lush valleys—spanning the Rhine and bordered by the Main just west of the Kingdom of Bavaria." For more than three centuries, it had experienced the usual turmoil of the eternally battling German states. In 1806 its ruler, formerly denominated the landgrave, achieved the rank of grand duke. After the Napoleonic wars the modest-sized grand duchy prospered greatly and began marrying off its princesses to the major crowns of the Continent.

The fortunes of the peaceful grand duchy improved significantly when one of its princesses became empress of Russia in 1855. Five years later the empress's nephew went to England for Ascot Week and fell in love with Queen Victoria's second daughter, Alice.

Alice had inherited more of the prince consort's sterling character than any other of his eight children. Unfortunately, unlike her brother Affie, she had not inherited any of his good looks. Alice was plain, almost homely. She had an unusually fine mind, however, and a warm and loving heart. She also had a strong sense of right and wrong and an almost saintly disposition. Indeed, Princess Alice was so selfless and giving that she often verged on martyrdom.

Naturally, a daughter such as this was precious to a woman as self-centered and emotionally dependent as Queen Victoria. She often took advantage of Alice's kindness and devotion, and by the time her daughter had reached a marriageable age, the queen wrote her uncle, King Leopold of Belgium, "I shall not let her marry as long as I can reasonably delay her doing so."

But she had not anticipated the sudden appearance of handsome young Prince Louis of Hesse. This sensible young man appreciated

Alice's considerable inner resources. The young people's strong mutual attraction surprised and pleased Victoria and Albert. They did all they could to promote a romance; when they invited the shy Louis back to Windsor six months later, he haltingly asked Alice to be his wife and she instantly accepted.

Although Queen Victoria was ecstatic at the thought of having Louis as a son-in-law, she still didn't want to lose a treasure like Alice any sooner than she absolutely had to. Much to the dismay of the ardent young couple, she insisted on a year's engagement. In the meantime, the Hessian prince quickly became Victoria's absolute ideal. The more she saw of him, the more she considered Louis to be "good, amiable, honest, modest, warm-hearted, high principled and unassuming." She looked upon him "as if he was one of our own children."

The fact that Louis was a "bright companion" and so "full of fun and high spirits" didn't hurt his popularity with the queen either. Nor did his appealing good looks. "Beauty I don't want," Victoria claimed, "though I should be glad of it when it was there." But for all Victoria's stuffy idealization of the qualities of the mind and spirit, she was in some ways a superficial woman. Even that paragon, Prince Albert, would never have captivated her had he not been so handsome. She was in love with him long before she discovered his inner beauty. All of her life Queen Victoria was a sucker for a good-looking man, and whenever one of her daughters or granddaughters had a chance to marry some royal Adonis, she gushed over the prospect. When the queen considered the well-built, blue-eyed, pink-cheeked young prince from Darmstadt, she couldn't have been more pleased.

Because of Prince Albert's sudden and unexpected death in December 1861, Princess Alice's marriage did not take place until July of the following summer, at Osborne House on the placid Isle of Wight. Given the crushed spirits of the principals, the ceremony was more like a funeral than a wedding. But Alice was delirously in love with her husband, who fully returned her ardor. In fact, Queen Victoria felt that if Louis had a fault, it was that he was "too sentimental" about his tender feelings.

Alice managed to adapt happily to her new German home; she was to have a greater influence on the Hessian royal family than they were to have on her. She also visited Windsor as often as she could. Having such a good-natured, kind, and generous son-in-law gave Victoria the opportunity to dominate the family as much as she wanted. Between Alice's

English ways and the overwhelming influence of the queen, Darmstadt swiftly became an unofficial outpost of the British empire.

Even the very Germanic Prince Louis had been smoothly converted into the perfect English country gentleman. Only a year after the wedding, when he and Alice returned to Windsor for the birth of their first child, a relative wrote of Louis: "He wears a Norfolk jacket, short breeches and multi-coloured garters, is very fond of sherry and horses, reads as little as possible, and never writes at all."

The happy Hesse marriage produced seven children. The eldest, Victoria, married Louis of Battenberg and became the mother of three illustrious children: Lord Mountbatten, Queen Louise of Sweden, and Princess Alice of Greece, the mother of Queen Elizabeth II's husband, Prince Philip. The next daughter, Elizabeth, married Grand Duke Serge of Russia and became Ducky's idolized Aunt Ella. Irene, the third girl, married the kaiser's brother. Ernst Ludwig, the eldest son, was born in 1868. His younger sister, Alix, would marry Nicholas II of Russia and become the ill-fated Empress Alexandra. Two other children, a boy and a girl, died in early childhood.

Life in Darmstadt was uneventful, only occasionally interrupted by international politics. In 1866 the grand duchy had joined Austria in an unsuccessful war against Prussia. There was much suffering as a result, and Alice found herself nursing the dead and wounded at the local hospitals. The experience had a profound effect on her; she became engrossed in theology, philosophy, and science, dedicating her brilliant intellect and sensitive conscience to finding the true meaning of life and the answers to the serious moral questions that so troubled her, much to the chagrin and disapproval of her mother.

A more immediate result of Hesse's challenge to Prussia was the ignominious result of defeat: Forced, with the myriad other German states, into the new German empire, Hesse found itself subordinated to the hated Prussian Hohenzollerns. And the proud grand duchy's natural resentment of this imperial oppression only increased local alienation from the other principalities. So the path toward the English sensibilities of Princess Alice was broadened.

During the first fifteen years of their marriage—before Louis became the reigning grand duke—Alice and her family lived in a large, comfortable house in the center of Darmstadt across from the beautiful park of linden and chestnut trees where the Renaissance-style ducal palace stood. Surrounded by the quaint Teutonic trimmings of a German medieval city—narrow, twisting cobblestoned streets among ancient steep-roofed houses decorated with picturesque carvings—the English princess made her home as much a little piece of England as she could. The walls were filled with paintings of British palaces and English landscapes and numerous portraits of Queen Victoria, Prince Albert, and the other members of the family Alice had left behind. Even an English governess, a Mrs. Orchard, had been imported to bring the strictly ordered, no-nonsense ways of Windsor to Alice's nursery.

Ernie grew up a healthy and happy little boy, sensitive and introspective like his mother, but with his father's looks. His early childhood in Darmstadt was a cozy one, with a loving family in a comfortable home. Led by a liveried footman, Ernie drove his own little pony cart through the grand ducal park when he was only four or five, but Mrs. Orchard, known to Ernie and his sisters as Orchie, ran a strict nursery. There were few luxuries, meals were kept basic, and the emphasis was on sunshine and fresh air. Ernie ate a diet of rice pudding and baked apples and was made to follow a precise and unalterable daily schedule. Whereas his sisters embraced Orchie's rigid philosophy of strict discipline and self-denial for the rest of their lives, Ernie had a dreamy, poetic temperament that was incompatible with such an outlook. He resisted the iron rule of his governess and used his charm to evade it. (Later, when he matured, he rejected all self-discipline and fully indulged his artistic and ardent nature.)

In the summer, when the Rhineland boiled, Ernie and his family moved to Wolfsgarten, a beautiful hunting lodge in the cool, forested hills north of Darmstadt. He and his little sister Alix spent their mornings "in a sun-filled courtyard, running up and down a flight of high stone steps and sitting by the courtyard fountain, dipping their hands in the water, trying to catch a goldfish."

At Christmastime, Ernie saw the decor of the palace ballroom turned into a replica of that for the Yule celebration at Windsor Castle. A huge tree bearing wax candles and golden garlands rose magically in the center of the room, and a plump goose and tasty puddings and mince pies filled the dinner table. After the holidays came visits to Hesse relatives all over Germany and Austria.

The most difficult such visit was the one to Berlin to see Alice's older sister, Vicky—the crown princess of the new German empire. Although

Bismarck was made the scapegoat for most of the Hessian hostilities toward the Hohenzollerns' recent conquest, Alice resented not only Vicky's part in Prussia's ruthless domination of Hesse but also her great power and wealth.

The children eagerly awaited the yearly visits to Grandmama, Queen Victoria. Ernie and his sisters were probably the old queen's favorite grandchildren, and their annual stays at Osborne and Balmoral were the highlights of their youth. There was also another special tie between the English queen and her Hesse grandchildren, a sad and dangerous one.

In 1870, when Ernie was two, a second son had been born to Alice and Louis. He was named Frederick William after his uncle the crown prince of Prussia, but was called Frittie by his family. Shortly after his birth, Alice was proudly writing to her mother how healthy and strong Frittie was, "the prettiest of all my babies." A little more than a year later the happy tone of Alice's letters suddenly changed. Now she nervously remarked that big lumpy bruises kept mysteriously appearing on his tiny body. Desperately wiring her mother and the renowned royal physician, Sir William Jenner, for advice, she bravely tried to keep up her spirits: "I trust he may outgrow this."

When the bruising became more severe, the agonized mother suddenly remembered her own younger brother Leopold, who had slowly developed the same symptoms when he was a baby.

Leopold suffered from a dread disease: hemophilia.

Soon there could no longer be any doubt: Frittie was also a victim of this rare and often fatal condition, which had become known as "the royal disease." The blood of hemophiliacs did not clot properly, and the consequences of this fact were terrible.

Hemophilia would be the curse of the next several generations of Queen Victoria's far-flung family. Because the disease never appears earlier in her family tree, it is generally believed to have originated in a genetic mutation in Victoria herself. (Albert's family history is irrelevant. As a man, he had an X and a Y chromosome. Hemophilia is never carried on the Y chromosome, and a man with the defective gene on his X chromosome would have had hemophilia, which Albert did not. Had he suffered from the disease, he would not have lived long enough to father children, because in his—and Ducky's—time there was no treatment.) Queen Victoria, carrying the defective gene that causes the disease, passed it to one of her sons, Prince Leopold; two of her daughters, Alice and Beatrice, also inherited the gene, becoming carriers and producing hemophiliac sons and carrier daughters. One of these was Ernie's sister Alix, who eventually took it to the Russian imperial family.

Because Ducky and her siblings were the offspring of one of Victoria's nonhemophiliac (hence non-hemophilia-carrying) sons they were not affected by the disease and could not pass it on.

Ernie had been very lucky: He might very well have inherited the disease from his mother, as his little brother had done. But although he was physically unscathed the disease left a deep emotional scar. Sensitive and impressionable, Ernie was often moved to tears by the horrible pain little Frittie endured. The slightest bump or cut could turn the lively toddler into an invalid for days or weeks at a time, as the non-clotting blood filled joints and sockets, twisting and contorting his small body into excruciatingly painful positions. When Frittie was two years old he nicked his ear and almost bled to death. It took three days to stop the flow of blood. Ernie, his little brother's protector and chief playmate, watched with horror.

A year later, on a sparkling May morning, Ernie and Frittie were chasing each other through their mother's bedroom, hiding in the thick drapes in front of the windows. Frittie laughingly disappeared behind one of the drapes—and when Alice went to look for him, he wasn't there. Somehow the small boy had fallen out of the window onto the stone terrace below. Within a few hours blood had flooded his brain and the gentle little Frittie was dead.

The grief-stricken parents never got over the boy's tragic end, but it was four-year-old Ernie who suffered the most. He had nightmares for months, and even two years later he was still consumed by thoughts of Frittie's death. At night he pathetically cried to his stern nurse, Orchie: "I don't like people to die alone; we must all die together!" He also breathlessly recounted to his mother that "I dreamt that I was dead and was gone up to Heaven, and there I asked God to let me have Frittie again; and he came to me and took my hand."

Because of young Ernie's delicate emotional balance, his parents gave him special attention. Now the only boy in the family, he was pampered and spoiled and excused from strict discipline. The fact that he was such an intelligent and handsome little boy, with a warm and lovable nature, further raised his status in the family.

For a while it seemed that the high-strung Ernie was finally adjusting to his brother's death—and then tragedy suddenly struck again. This time there would be no complete recovery.

One afternoon just before Ernie's tenth birthday, in early November of 1878, a year after his father had succeeded his uncle as grand duke of Hesse, his eldest sister was reading aloud *Alice in Wonderland* to him. She struggled with her voice; her throat was sore. By bedtime she had a fever and the doctor was called in. He gravely diagnosed diphtheria. Within a few days, the highly contagious disease "swept through the palace like a plague."

All the children except Ella were ill, and then Grand Duke Louis himself was struck down. For several days Alice nursed her family through the epidemic, watching them hover between life and death. She never slept. Ernie became so desperately ill that when his youngest sister, May, died, his mother didn't dare tell him. Just as the others were beginning to recover, he had a serious relapse and almost died. His mother, overwhelmed with tender pity, kissed him good night and contracted the disease.

The next day, December 7, the still asymptomatic Alice went to the railway station at Darmstadt to meet Ducky's mother, who was passing through on her way home to Coburg. Because of the diphtheria epidemic, Alice could not risk bringing her visitor to the palace, so she and the indestructible duchess socialized in the "draughty chill" of the train station. When Alice returned to the palace that evening she collapsed from exhaustion and felt the first symptoms of the disease. She spent the next day struggling to put her affairs in order and arranging for her family's future. Then she sank into a coma. A few days later she was dead.

Everyone in the family was crushed by the loss, but Alice's little boy was affected more deeply than anyone could have imagined. The death of his mother was an open wound that a lifetime of desperate and frantic diversion and indulgence could never heal. Ernie's emotional strength, never great, was shattered beyond repair; as his English grandmother remarked to his eldest sister, "Poor dear Ernie, he will feel it so dreadfully!"

He remained "dear Ernie" to Queen Victoria for the rest of her life. Always seeing him as a tragically lost and stricken child, Victoria spoiled and protected Ernie as if he were one of her own children. Indeed, all of the Hesse family were adopted by their sentimental grandmother and given privileges and considerations that none of Victoria's other grandchildren enjoyed. There were yearly visits to Windsor; there was an unending flow of letters in which the queen gave detailed instructions to the children's tutors and governesses and doctors. Because the good-natured Louis never remarried, his domineering mother-in-law almost effortlessly assumed command of the Hesse family, dictating its tastes and standards.

In consequence, Ernie and his sisters grew up much more English than German. As the troubled little prince advanced to adolescence he exploited his very lovable but feckless personality, capturing the sympathy and affection of almost everyone who crossed his path. Ernie also resisted discipline and conformity in any form. He did poorly in his studies and constantly caused his grandmother to despair. When he was thirteen the frustrated queen firmly instructed his eldest sister: "I must say Ernie's great absence, inattention and backwardness are becoming serious in his position and at his age. I have not yet written about it to Papa (the Grand Duke Louis) but I think that he ought to go away for 2 or 3 months with Herr Muther [Ernie's tutor] where he could have no distractions and learn steadily without the hope of picnics and expeditions which occupy his mind far too much."

Unfortunately, Ernie's handsome looks were just as effective as his charm in manipulating those around him. With a tall, well-porportioned physique, a broad face with wide-set sparkling sea-blue eyes, high cheekbones, a firm square jaw, and thick auburn hair, the heir to the Hesse throne never failed to attract admiring glances.

But despite Victoria's efforts, well into manhood Ernie still possessed a bubbling, carefree spirit—a commodity he had painstakingly crafted to conceal his inner conflicts. Just before his twenty-first birthday Queen Victoria was still commenting that "Dear Ernie I found as dear and childlike as ever."

Having attended the universities of Leipzig and Giessen, the aesthetic Ernie had been greatly influenced by the Arts and Crafts Movement, whose origins lay in England, with the ideas of John Ruskin and William Morris, among others. But rather than follow his artistic inclinations he was obliged to pursue the course set by his soldier father: He was made a second lieutenant in the Hessian Life Guard Infantry in 1884 and joined the Prussian Foot Guards two years later. Although he did well enough to pass his military examinations in 1888, he gave up the military four years later when his father suddenly died from a stroke.

Now, at the tender age of twenty-three, Ernie was the ruling grand duke of Hesse and the Rhine. But the fun-loving new sovereign liked politics about as much as he liked the military. Reluctant to assume power, at his father's deathbed he had thrown himself despairingly into the arms of his aunt Marie and begged for her help.

Help, indeed, was on the way. Queen Victoria immediately rushed to Darmstadt to straighten out her wayward grandson. She had determined that the first thing Ernie needed was a wife.

CHAPTER TWELVE

The
Queen
Commands

W HEN QUEEN VICTORIA arrived at Darmstadt in April of 1892 it was almost impossible for her to believe that her dearest daughter and favorite son-in-law were now lying side by side in the Rosenhöhe mausoleum. She was solemnly greeted at the station by Ernie and his sisters dressed in black. The Queen looked around the quiet and empty platform and noticed that there was "no Guard of Honour; all [was] silent and sad."

For the next week the seventy-three-year-old monarch gave her frivolous grandson a crash course in the art of governing. Ernie listened well and found his self-confidence growing. The authority of the queen and the popularity of his late parents made the new grand duke's ascension to power in Hesse a simple matter. When it came time for Victoria to depart, she was pleased to see that "dear Ernie" was going to be a fine ruler. The only remaining problem was finding her grandson a wife. Always convinced of the power of a happy marriage, Victoria thought that the imperfections of any man could be put right by a devoted mate.

But in Ernie's life there were special issues, which even the best of matchmaking could not address.

Surprisingly, Grand Duke Ernst Ludwig of Hesse and the Rhine found ruling quite enjoyable. No longer forced to pursue the dreary life of a soldier, he was now free to do whatever he pleased. There was no one to answer to, and his every whim could be carried out as a command. And life in Hesse was also about to change dramatically.

The death of Ernie's mother fourteen years earlier had seemed to plunge the grand duchy into permanent mourning. There had been nothing to replace her brilliant and beautiful influence. But now, Darmstadt began to bloom again.

Ernie personally supervised the redecoration of the grand-ducal palace, enthusiastically directing the craftsmen to create the realization of his dreams. His next project was Wolfsgarten, the family summer home in the northern hills. The young grand duke, who had a particular interest in gardening, restyled the rustic lodge into a country villa.

There were no limits to Ernie's artistic interests. He was an accomplished painter, a skillful sketch artist, a writer of verse and dramatic narrative, and a connoisseur of every fine art. The neglected Court Theater flourished as he not only funded it but also regularly attended rehearsals, designed the stage scenery, and nurtured new talent.

The grand duke was caught up in "an eternal search for new ideas" and new amusements. "Spoilt and pampered by his parents and his four sisters" all his life, he was used to being allowed to explore everything to its limits. Now the whirl of his official schedule left "the old ones at his Court panting to keep pace." His constant quest for new amusements and his indulgence in parties, playful diversions, and practical jokes suggest a need for escape from the reality of life, from his problems and fears . . . and from himself.

Few looking at his clear blue eyes and smiling face could have guessed how dark the demons were that haunted Ernie's secret dreams.

Certainly not his grandmother, who was convinced that marriage to a charming and brilliant woman—Ducky—would solve all her grandson's problems. Indeed, "a wish that his [marriage to Ducky] should come to pass had been expressed by his father shortly before his death."

However, since acceding to the Hessian throne, Ernie had seemed reluctant to marry. As far as anyone knew, the popular young prince had never had a serious romance. Although most of the pretty maidens of Darmstadt had lost their hearts to the handsome grand duke and often went out of their way to catch a glimpse of him, Ernie seemed rather indifferent to feminine charms; it was noted that there was no favorite among his many female friends and admirers.

Seeing her grandson's lack of romantic initiative, Queen Victoria proceeded to try to manage his life as thoroughly as she had his father's. Shortly before his death, the old grand duke had secretly married a commoner. When his ex-mother-in-law visited Darmstadt and discovered this, she immediately had the marriage annulled; Ernie's heartbroken father was forced to return home without a wife. With this example still fresh in his mind, Ernie had neither the confidence nor the natural inclination to oppose Victoria's iron will.

The only reservation in the queen's mind was the matter of health. The shadow of hemophilia over the Hesse family brought back painful memories of her late son Leopold. She took great care that a union between her two grandchildren, Ernie and Ducky, couldn't possibly produce offspring with the dread malady. In May of 1892, after returning from coaching Ernie in his new role as grand duke, the Queen had a lengthy consultation with her personal physician, Dr. William Jenner, and reported the results to Ernie's eldest sister, Princess Louis of Battenberg: "When Dr Jenner was here I spoke to him about the possibility of Ernie's marrying one of the Edinburgh Cousins, and he said there was no danger and no objection as they are so strong and healthy and Aunt Marie also. He said if the relations were strong intermarriage with them only led to greater strength and health. I have written this to Ernie himself."

Matters of health having been resolved, the queen impatiently waited for Ducky to turn sixteen and for Missy to be safely married. Shortly after Missy's wedding, while Ducky was still suffering from the sudden separation, Victoria invited her and her parents to Osborne. She also invited Ernie. And she wrote to Ernie's eldest sister, a reliably maternal influence, that she must "hint" to her brother "to be very kind and posé [sedate] and not tease Ducky or make silly jokes, which might destroy our hopes and wishes."

During their brief stay at Osborne, Ernie and Ducky were thrown together as much as possible. They took long walks along the mist-shrouded paths, went riding together, and shared afternoons on the chilly terrace. They enjoyed each other's company as much as ever, but Ducky's mind was completely elsewhere—in the Royal Palace at Bucharest, with Missy. The thought of a serious courtship didn't even occur to her. And Ernie was not interested in romance with his "beloved chum."

This lack of enthusiasm frustrated their grandmother but did not deflect her.

Returning to Coburg, Ducky still resisted all efforts to cheer her, so her mother took her to St. Petersburg "to help her over the parting which she had minded almost tragically, for her nature was deep and loving and always somewhat stormy."

The trip proved successful. Ducky finally snapped out of her depression. But it was not the splendors and imperial wonders of Russia that achieved the result. It was the handsome face of her cousin Kirill. On the threshold of manhood, sixteen-year-old Kirill was already six feet tall. In contrast to Ernie, this serious and reserved first cousin was a self-confident young man who viewed the world with cool arrogance.

Ducky and Kirill engaged in quiet and soulful talks; they held hands and exchanged secrets; and by the end of the visit, they were in love. Had Queen Victoria found out, she would have been furious.

Marie wasn't any too happy, either. The duchess liked her nephew well enough, but she was still leery of the men in her family, those lusty, free-living grand dukes who always made such poor husbands. Besides, the Russian Orthodox Church forbade marriage between first cousins. Particularly for members of the imperial family, who publicly had to be above reproach, such a union was out of the question. The duchess of Edinburgh hurried her moonstruck daughter back to Coburg.

Resenting the machinations of Queen Victoria, the duchess grew less and less enthusiastic about Ernst of Hesse as a husband for Ducky. Realizing how close were his ties to his grandmother and her family, Ducky's mother began looking elsewhere for a matrimonial candidate.

And, back in Darmstadt, Ernie was having serious doubts about whether he even wanted to get married. "Uneasy about being an adequate husband," he was not attracted to Ducky as he felt he should have been. Although they had similar temperaments, that fact seemed insufficient to base a marriage on. Having spent "one particularly cheerful holiday together did not make it a foregone conclusion that they would be ideally suited as husband and wife." And, what was much more important, Ernie was beginning to realize that he "preferred male company."

There was also the critical matter of avoiding the family malady and providing the grand duchy with strong and healthy heirs. Despite Dr. Jenner's advice, Princess Louis of Battenberg, who erroneously blamed hemophilia for her daughter's deafness, was not reassured. She anxiously wrote Ernie from London:

> I still worry rather at the thought that Ducky and you are so nearly [doubly] related. Could you not in a general way ask Eigenbrodt [Ernie's private physician] why he is so much opposed to relations marrying. If he has other reasons besides the fear of an illness like Uncle Leopold's, against our family especially intermarrying, it would be as well to know them, for I

think it is one of the duties of a man in your position especially, to try and have healthy descendants, and I know besides from experience that to see one's children not quite strong, or with some little ailment, like Alice's hearing, is a cause of worry and pain. . . . I hope you won't think I am fussing you, but I so fear the newspapers will soon be discussing engagements between you and Ducky, and then Grandmama etc and Uncle Affie will try again to hurry you.

As Ernie pondered what to do, the queen did exactly as his sister had warned. Trying to drum up family support, she was surprised to find her eldest daughter, Vicky, now the dowager empress Frederick of Germany, disapproving of marriages between closely related persons. On the defensive, Victoria explained that "the same blood only adds to the strength and if you try to avoid it you will marry some unhealthy little Princess who would just cause what you wish to avoid."

Others in the family objected even more vehemently, and not on the grounds of uncertain genetics. Ernie's younger sister Alix, who was enjoying acting as the stand-in grand duchess during her bachelor brother's reign, was desperately unhappy at the prospect of Princess Victoria Melita, "a tall, dark girl, with violet eyes, four years her junior, with the assuredness of an Empress and the high spirits of a tomboy," taking precedence over her at the Hesse court. Nor did the idea of Ducky's imperious mother "playing the dictator around Darmstadt" thrill her. Alix decided that if the "spritely, mercurial" Ducky came, she would leave.

Undaunted by the growing opposition, Queen Victoria kept pressuring her grandson toward Ducky, and he was both unwilling and unable to stand up to his powerful grandmother. A letter he wrote to her a year after his father's death clearly illustrates the extent of his subservience:

Please forgive me for not writing any sooner, but the anniversary of all those awfull [sic] days made us all so unhappy that it was all I could do to keep sisters safe from breaking down. I still cannot believe that it is allready [sic] a year since all this sorrow came to us. But one thing I must say, darling Grandmama, that if it had not been for the great love you showed us in all this time I do not know how we would have got over it, and my one prayer is that you will keep it for us as you have done all these years since darling Mama died, for you have always been a second mother to me. That is the reason why we will all our lives never be able to thank you enough for all you have done to us.

The fact that Ducky was now in England encouraged the queen to make the match immediately. In 1893 her granddaughter had spent late spring in Devonport, where her father was completing his three years of service as commander in chief of the port. On June 2 the entire town turned out for the departure of the popular Edinburghs. A month later another special occasion gave Victoria the opportunity to bring Ducky and Ernie together in a romantic setting. Prince George, Missy's rejected suitor, was marrying Princess Mary of Teck in the chapel of St. James's Palace in London. It was arranged that Ducky would be one of the bridesmaids and that Ernie would escort the queen in the chapel and partner her at the luncheon that followed. That evening Ducky and Ernie together attended a party given by their uncle the Prince of Wales. It was noticed that their relationship was now more relaxed. Trying to forget her hopeless love for her Russian cousin, Ducky enjoyed the gaiety of the event.

But Ducky still had mixed feelings about Ernie. He certainly was clever and handsome, and few people were more amusing or could make her laugh as hard. She enjoyed his company and felt at ease around him. Almost totally ignorant of the facts of life and of what to expect from marriage, Ducky could only contrast her feelings for Ernie with those she had for Kirill. While her smoldering Russian cousin made her slightly nervous, Ernie was calm and comfortable.

After George and Mary's wedding, Ducky returned home to Coburg with her parents. No sooner had they arrived than Uncle Ernest went out hunting one day, caught a chill, and promptly died. He was seventy-five, and what years of wild dissipation had failed to achieve, a sudden cool breeze had neatly accomplished. When Duke Ernest II died, on August 22, 1893, newspapers across Germany took special note that a prince of England—Ducky's father—would succeed him.

The duke and duchess of Edinburgh and the princess Victoria Melita of Edinburgh were gone. Ducky's father was now Duke Alfred of Saxe-Coburg-Gotha; her mother was Duchess Marie of Saxe-Coburg-Gotha; and Ducky was Princess Victoria Melita of Saxe-Coburg-Gotha.

The day after his uncle's death the new duke began his reign by taking an oath in the presence of his detested nephew, the kaiser. It was not easy for Affie to proclaim his loyalty to the arrogant German emperor and to the empire that his duchy had been forced to join. And the occasion was bitter for other reasons as well. Only two months earlier, Affie, who held the highest possible naval rank, that of admiral of the fleet, had sadly ended his brilliant career on the high seas. Although he had been groomed for the grand duchy since his early childhood, he had little enthusiasm for the dukedom or for being reunited with his estranged wife.

The new Duchess of Coburg, however, was filled with joy. "Aunt Marie will love being No. 1, and reigning Duchess, I am sure," the Empress Frederick confided to her daughter Sophie.

After the funeral in Gotha, a grand event attended by both the kaiser and the Prince of Wales, there was a whirl of activity as the new ruling family settled into the ducal palace at Coburg. Meanwhile, Missy was about to give birth to her first child in far-off Romania. The duchess was determined to journey to Bucharest and take charge of the occasion so that everything was done just right—her way.

Queen Victoria seized this opportunity. As she had swamped Ernie with advice two years earlier when he became grand duke of Hesse, she now focused her concentration on the Coburgs, taking advantage of the hectic conditions at the Rosenau to promote the Hesse marriage. She flooded the family with sternly instructive letters. To Ernie's eldest sister, she wrote in September: "I have had it out with Aunt Marie [Ducky's mother] having written kindly but strongly to her. She is most anxious about Ernie and Ducky and I have written *twice* to Ernie about the *necessity* of his showing some attention and interest. Pray tell it him and say he *must answer* me. —Aunt Marie fears he no longer wishes it, which I am sure is not the case. Georgie lost Missy by waiting and waiting. . . . Aunt Marie is at Sinaia [the Romanian summer palace] and in about a fortnight or 3 weeks we may expect Missy's confinement."

No sooner had the duchess hurried off to Romania to be at her pregnant daughter's side than the duke raced over to England to cement his other daughter's future. Ducky's father went directly to Sandringham and consulted with the Prince of Wales. The two brothers decided that if Ducky was to marry Ernie, they would have to act fast. Still crushingly disappointed that George and Missy had not been allowed to wed because of the cunning maneuvers of the duchess, they knew that only a well-organized opposition could possibly defeat her. Rushing down to Windsor, they conferred with the queen.

Victoria fired off another letter to her reluctant grandson, this time leaving him little chance for evasion. Ernie wrote back at the end of the first week in October: "I have not changed the very least and I beg you to let Aunt M. know that I feel just the same as I have done all the time and only for Ducky's sake I have not gone to Coburg because I did not want the people to begin talking about her. When she is back I will try to go and see them."

Back in Coburg, Ducky was busy with her studies and rejoicing over a major triumph: Dr. Rolfs and the Fräulein, now his wife, had finally been dismissed with a generous pension. (Queen Victoria took happy note that the Rolfses "will no longer be a cause of dispute and dispeace.") Wandering the stone corridors of the Rosenau, Ducky still missed Missy and dreamed of Kirill. During the past several months everything had changed so completely that she felt confused and insecure. Even the birth of Missy's first baby—a son named Carol—was something of a miracle to this young girl who still hadn't been informed of the mechanics of sex.

Ducky celebrated her seventeenth birthday at the end of November and a few days later was surprised by a visit from Cousin Ernie. On his return to Darmstadt, the grand duke immediately reported to Grandmama Queen:

> I have just returned yesterday from Coburg, where I spent very happy days. I have very good news to tell you, my prospects are very good. Ducky has been all these days so dear and so kind to me that I have got the very best hopes. I am certain that if I wanted to ask her now she would say yes. But I did not because I wanted to tell it to you first. The situations between Uncle Alfred and me now are so changed since I talked to you last year in England that I want to ask you again about our marriage. Uncle is now a German Prince and is doing everything so wonderfully well that all his subjects are simply devoted to him. I heard all this now when I was there. He has shown so much love and tact that the people simply addore [sic] him. I am afraid that for this reason now that the idea of having my wedding in England will be impossible, for it would harm him so much, he would hurt his people and dissapoint [sic] them at the same time and it would make me miserable to think that I was the cause of bringing him into trouble. I have also asked different people here . . . and they all said the same that if the wedding was in England it would harm him very much and the people here would say about me that I ought to have been sensible and stopped it.

Although Ernie wrote in such confident tones he continued to have serious doubts about marrying Ducky. But whatever his true feelings, he felt compelled to bow to the wishes of the queen.

A hundred years ago "in all Royal and Imperial families the head was bowed down to and considered omnipotent, no one dared discuss his decrees or cross his will." This was especially true of the "Doyenne of all Sovereigns," the redoubtable Queen Victoria.

Several decades after her death, the queen's great authority was still vividly remembered by one of her granddaughters: "In a way she was the arbiter of our different fates. For all members of her family her 'yes' and her 'no' counted tremendously. She was not averse from interfering in the most private questions. She was the central power directing things . . . who seldom raised her voice, except when accentuating certain words. . . . Her sons and daughters were in great awe of 'dearest Mama'; . . . her veto made them tremble. They spoke to her with bated breath, and even when not present she was never mentioned except in lowered voices."

Adding to Victoria's mystique was her severe isolation; she lived "so shut away from the world, surrounding herself with that atmosphere of mournful abstinence from all joys of life." Her contemporaries fully responded to this almost "religious hush," granting Victoria a special prestige that was "fetish-like."

For a grandson as feckless and vacillating as Ernie, there was never any question that he would submit to the queen's command.

"After the gravest heart-searchings" during the Christmas holidays, he journeyed back to Coburg for the New Year. And on the ninth day of 1894, the duke of Coburg joyfully sent off a telegram to his mother at Windsor Castle: "Your and my great wish has been fulfilled this evening. Ducky has accepted Ernie of Hesse's proposal. We are a very happy family party."

Everyone seemed pleased—except the prospective bride and groom.

PART TWO

The Fighting Grand Duchess

CHAPTER THIRTEEN

The
Wedding
of the Century

T HE WINTER OF 1894 was one of the coldest in history. During January and February record-breaking temperatures were recorded all across Europe as Arctic air drifted to the Mediterranean. Winds of hurricane force blew the roof off the central railway station in Berlin; in France, they toppled a recently constructed monument to Napoleon. Thick blankets of snow buried the German countryside, isolating Darmstadt and Coburg from the rest of the world.

It was the perfect climate for dreaming romantic dreams.

Ducky sat by her window at the palace in Coburg and gazed at this frozen world. Everything had been arranged. Her fate was sealed. And all she had done was say yes—a dutiful response to the wishes of her grandmother.

Accepting her cousin's proposal of marriage had been the proper thing for Ducky to do. The seventeen-year-old princess could only rely upon the promises of those she trusted. And they guaranteed her that love would come with time, that friendship was surely the basis for a happy marriage.

Victoria had recognized the wisdom in her grandson's suggestion that, for diplomacy's sake, the wedding should be held at the bride's home. Since Affie had become the reigning duke, said the queen, "my interest in dear old Coburg is *very great now.*" She was pleased to note that he "seems most anxious to do it well" and "has set about everything wisely." The last thing Victoria wanted was to offend Affie's new subjects by forcing him to hold Ducky's wedding in England.

Now the occasion was just three months away. Having suffered the disappointment of not being able to attend Missy's wedding, held in the dangerous dead of winter, Victoria let it be known that she expected the timing of Ducky's nuptials to suit her. She had no intention of missing the first (and, as it turned out, the only) wedding between a pair of her grandchildren. The date was set for April 19, comfortably into the spring, but well before the heat of summer which the elderly queen's health could not tolerate.

On the eighteenth of January, having suddenly realized that she had not written her grandmother since the official announcement of her engagement, Ducky rushed off a rambling note, which displayed her confused state of mind:

> *My dearest Grandmama,*
>
> *You will forgive my not having written to you yet I am sure as the last few days we had scarcely time for anything. I need not tell you how happy I am, I know how fond you are of dear Ernie and you can easily imagine it. It is also so delightful that Darmstadt is so near, it will not seem like leaving home so entirely. We spent such a happy time now all together. It was so nice that Alix [Ernie's sister] came too. I think she enjoyed being here; we had a ball whilst she was here and she danced very much and was very gay. They also have a great deal going on at Darmstadt and had to leave so soon that all that happened in that short time seems still like a dream to me. It was so nice that Missy was also just here and so we were all together but unhappily they too had to leave so soon as they wished to stay still a short time at Sigmaringen.*
>
> *Hoping once more you will not mind this letter coming so late, I remain your very affectionate granddaughter,*
>
> *Ducky*

The queen did mind; she minded all infractions of the strict rules of etiquette she set forth for her large family. But Victoria had no time to chastise Ducky for her tardiness; she was preoccupied by the upcoming wedding. For Victoria, the journey was to be a sacred pilgrimage, a sentimental return to her beloved husband's boyhood home for the uniting of two grandchildren Prince Albert had never known.

The queen waved away the objections of her family to the marriage. Although there was little she could do to mitigate the hostility of

Ducky's anti-British mother, Victoria was gradually winning over her daughter Vicky, the empress Frederick. Ducky's aunt had always possessed a very high opinion of her, and now, writing to her mother, she conceded that her niece was "a charming girl, bright and clever, with plenty of spirit, which is rather what he [Ernie] wants." Because Empress Frederick had always been fond of her late sister, she felt that "it is so nice to think that it will not be a stranger in dear Alice's place." But she was still troubled by the close blood relationship of the bride and groom. "If only she were not his 1st cousin," she wrote her daughter Sophie, "what could be nicer?"

As for the duchess of Coburg, she fumed at having been so cleverly outmaneuvered by her husband's tight-knit family while her attention was elsewhere. Although she liked her charming and cultured nephew, she resented his closeness to Grandmama Queen and was infuriated by the way Victoria ran his life. Having finally escaped Victoria's domination, the duchess feared that her daughter would now be trapped. In a sense, Ducky was marrying a son of Queen Victoria, just as her mother had done—for this was the role that Ernie had been playing for sixteen years.

After the engagement had been announced, the first thing Ducky's mother did was draw Ernie aside and have a long, serious talk with him about Grandmama Queen and "the English family." She vehemently explained to him "why we could not really like them and how often they had been nasty and spiteful to me." She sternly warned her young nephew that "he must not always be dragging Ducky to England in perpetual adoration of Granny." He must also "understand the reasons why we can never adore her."

Ducky's greatest joy during the hectic months before the wedding came when Missy and her husband visited Coburg after the holidays. The reunion of the two sisters was so emotionally overwhelming that forty years later Missy would "still catch my breath merely at the thought of it. . . . Ducky, my sister, my pal, my companion, my chum. . . . As children we had always scoffed at the idea that there could be tears of joy, but on this day . . . I understood the meaning."

As the new crown princess of Romania, the immature Missy had suffered terribly through her first year. She had found the Balkan kingdom harsh and strange. Her husband's uncle, King Carol, was a tyrant who seemed determined to treat her as a foolish child. Worse yet, Missy's husband had turned out to be a boorish cipher rather than a knight in shining armor. The two were almost completely incompatible, and only Ferdinand's lust was making the marriage a productive one. Already, just before her first wedding anniversary, Missy was expecting her second child.

It seems extraordinary that Missy neither confided in Ducky nor explained the facts of life to her. It is a testimony to the age's sense of propriety that even these very close sisters found it impossible to discuss anything of a sexual nature. They had been brought up to keep their feelings secret from the world. Not until decades later, after turbulent lives filled with tragedy, would Ducky and Missy overcome the rigid strictures of their youths and open their hearts to each other. Meanwhile, it was a pity that Ducky's older sister couldn't advise her. The young woman might not have entered her marriage with so many painful illusions. In fact, she might not have entered it at all. But Missy's judgment, at that time, was even poorer than her little sister's. She looked at Ernie's handsome face and simply saw "a pleasant, clever young man and a desirable 'parti.' " "According to worldly appreciation," Missy would later reflect, "this was a match which promised every hope of happiness."

Dynastically, Ducky's marriage was also considered to be the most illustrious of all the four sisters'. Most of the newspapers in Europe during the first months of 1894 praised the brilliancy of this union between Queen Victoria's two grandchildren. The influential *Neues Wiener Tageblatt* of Vienna went so far as to attribute an exaggerated political importance to Ducky's impending marriage:

> The wedding at Coburg and the presence there of . . . the Emperor William and the Russian Heir-Apparent will still further advance the "rapprochement" between the two States. The House of Coburg has already given the country [Germany] Princes devoted to peace. Whether the sons of that House have obtained positions of high influence in London, Brussels, or Lisbon they have everywhere exerted themselves in the interests of peace, a task which has been greatly facilitated by their connections with most of the ruling families. . . . Without going too far in the way of political speculation, it is evident that the Coburg wedding is a striking symptom of peace.

As the day of the wedding approached, Ducky imagined herself deeply in love with her handsome bridegroom. The normally sleepy little town of Coburg had never seen such activity. Suddenly, the small duchy had become the focal point of the entire continent. The ceremony, although rather simple by royalty's standards, was meticulously planned. Special souvenirs were made and elaborate decorations were created. When the unusually heavy winter snows finally began melting in the beginning of April, the bloom of spring seemed to stir the people of Coburg to great excitement. After decades of Uncle Ernest's childless and lascivious rule, the duchy was now about to celebrate the marriage of its first royal bride in almost a century.

As the century moved closer to its conclusion and an era seemed to be approaching its end, the Coburg wedding became a hopeful symbol. The joining of two of Queen Victoria's grandchildren seemed to symbolize the world's greatest empire regenerating its might and majesty.

Victoria had planned the whole year around the ceremony. To escape the frigid English winter, she left Windsor on March 13 with her youngest daughter, Beatrice, and traveled by special train through France and Switzerland to Florence. There she rested in the sunshine at the beautiful Villa Fabbricotti. On April 16 she resumed her journey, arriving in Coburg the next day with a "heart . . . full of memories of the first time that she had made the journey with Albert." As she stepped out onto the platform at Coburg, there to greet her was her entire family, dominated by her flamboyant grandson the kaiser and a squadron of Prussian dragoons. Driving through the colorfully decorated streets to Schloss Ehrenburg, "she was received with great enthusiasm by the population." When she passed under a spectacular triumphal arch built especially for the occasion, two girls dressed in white dropped hundreds of flowers about her.

Perhaps enjoying her success too much, the queen was moved by her conscience to make an outrageous disclaimer: "I am not a matchmaker [nor do I] delight in marriages."

To symbolize the good feeling of the wedding, the duke had amnestied all the minor offenders in the Coburg jails. The night before the wedding he and Marie hosted a magnificent family dinner. A special musical and theatrical performance at the Riesensaal was followed by breathtaking torchlight processions through the town and countryside. (If Ducky was nervous in the whirl of formal events, she didn't show it.)

On the morning of the wedding, Thursday, April 19, 1894, the sun rose warmly in a deep blue sky as thousands of people poured into the immense Schlossplatz in the center of Coburg. A brief civil marriage ceremony had taken place in the privacy of Queen Victoria's apartments an hour before noon. (Victoria wore a very satisfied smile.) Then the small family party entered the royal chapel downstairs, where the guests were beginning to assemble. Because the chapel was within Schloss Ehrenburg proper, the crowd in the Schlossplatz was disappointed: The illustrious relatives of the bride and groom went directly from their rooms to the ceremony without making a public appearance.

The crowd's disappointment was understandable; one of the greatest gatherings of royalty in history had filled the chapel of the schloss. "I never saw so many," Sir Henry Ponsonby, the queen's private secretary, marveled as he surveyed the dazzling array of crowned heads. In addition to the kaiser, there was almost every member of Queen Victoria's vast family: the Prince of Wales, Empress Frederick, the Connaughts (the duke of Connaught, Victoria's son Arthur, and family) and the Battenbergs, Missy and her husband, Crown Prince Ferdinand of Rumania, and dozens of others. Also present was Marie's family—most notably, the czarevitch Nicholas of Russia and several Romanov grand dukes and grand duchesses, including Kirill's parents.

The small church had been decorated with festoons of garlands made from fir twigs, "hung from pillar to pillar, wound around the marble columns flanking the pulpit, which was covered with white flowers." Just a few minutes before noon, as the colorfully uniformed and magnificently bejeweled guests took their places, a band in the nearby courtyard began playing the German national anthem: The royal procession was approaching. Sitting in a tiny private gallery at the lower end of the chapel was the pathetic figure of Aunt Alexandrine, the dowager duchess of Coburg, covered in black and looking frail and vulnerable.

As the clock towers of the city began striking noon and all the church bells rang, the grand marshal of the court, elderly Prince von Ratibor, solemnly appeared at the entrance of the chapel, leading an impressive group of courtiers and officials. With his majestic wand of office, he dramatically tapped the floor three times to proclaim the entrance of the royal procession.

As might be expected, the first to enter was Kaiser Wilhelm, dressed in the uniform of a Hessian general and beaming with high spirits. He escorted Ducky's somber-looking mother, the duchess of Coburg. Behind them walked the sweetly smiling Empress Frederick, followed by her brother the Prince of Wales, attired in the uniform of the First Dragoon Guards. At his side was his nephew, Czarevich Nicholas. Dressed as a hussar of the Imperial Russian Guard, the czarevich was the most dashing figure of all. Behind them streamed a long line of kings and queens, dukes and duchesses, princes and princesses.

After these distinguished guests had been seated, Prince von Ratibor announced the entrance of the bridegroom and the best man, the young duke's uncle Prince William of Hesse. As Ernie slowly marched to the altar, he looked like the hero of a romantic opera. Dressed, like the kaiser, in a Hessian general's uniform, the handsome groom wore a shining helmet with red and white plumes.

There was a momentous hush throughout the crowded chapel, and then the entrance of Queen Victoria was loudly announced. The old queen, dressed as always in black, entered very slowly, leaning gently on the arm of the duke of Coburg. He carefully led his mother to a gilded thronelike chair in the center of the first row of seats.

There was another long pause, and then Princess Victoria Melita of Saxe-Coburg-Gotha began walking down the aisle, followed by her youngest sister, Beatrice, and her cousin Princess Feodora of Saxe-Meiningen.

As the Empress Frederick later wrote to her daughter, Sophie, "Ducky looked very charming and 'distinguée.' She had a plain white silk gown with hardly any trimming, and Aunt Alice's [Ernie's mother's] wedding veil, a light slender diadem of emeralds with a sprig of orange blossom stuck in behind. It all suited her charmingly."

Ducky stood at the flower-draped altar next to Ernie and shyly looked downward. The singing of an anthem began the service; then Herr Müller, the court chaplain, delivered a speech. The bride and groom calmly placed rings on each other's fingers as the service was eloquently read. Then, "the venerable Court Chaplain, who was deeply moved, invoked a blessing upon the young couple in a voice broken with emotion." The Lord's Prayer and a special benediction completed the ceremony.

"During the service Aunt Marie"—Ducky's mother—"was very calm," Empress Frederick reported to her daughter, "but the tears rolled down Uncle Alfred's cheeks, and Grandmama's and mine too."

After the wedding ceremony, the guests were led to the huge, vaulted throne room of the schloss, where breakfast was served. Surrounded by their family and friends, the newlyweds were continuously toasted and congratulated. Queen Victoria sat in the center of the feast and quietly commented that she thought the wedding ceremony had been impressively performed, "but I like ours so much better."

When breakfast was finally finished, the vast crowds in the palace square who had been waiting since dawn for a view of the royal celebrities finally got their wish. A procession of the couple's relatives escorted Ducky and Ernie to the Schlossplatz, where a luxurious phaeton "decorated liberally with spring flowers" was waiting. The crowds cheered the royals' appearance.

As Ducky kissed her mother good-bye, she was surprised to find tears in the duchess's eyes—the first tears she could ever remember seeing. The young bride was swept by a sudden feeling of despair. At that moment she wanted nothing more than to throw herself into her mother's arms and return to the Rosenau—but before she had time to gather her thoughts, her mother firmly took her arm and helped her into the carriage.

The kaiser, the Prince of Wales, and Wales's brother, the duke of Connaught, began heartily throwing handfuls of rice, and the carriage drove off past a sea of waving hands and a shouting chorus of "Hochs!"

While the whole family was waving at the departing coach, four photographers quickly ran into the square and coaxed this amazing collection of royalty to pose for several pictures. No sooner had that been accomplished than the sun disappeared behind a wall of dark clouds and a violent thunderstorm raged for the rest of the day and night, forcing the cancellation of the evening's fireworks display.

For those perceptive enough to understand the natures of the bride and groom, the symbolism of the storm was startling.

But there was another tempest stirring behind the walls of Schloss Ehrenburg. A decision had just been made that would not only shadow the day's gala event and but also change Ducky's life—and the course of world history.

CHAPTER FOURTEEN

Stolen Thunder,
Vanquished
Dreams

THE MORNING AFTER Ducky's wedding Queen Victoria sat quietly eating her breakfast in her apartments at the Ehrenburg when Ernie's sister Ella, the wife of Grand Duke Serge, rushed into the room and excitedly cried out: "Alicky and Nicky are engaged."

For the past several days the royal wedding at Coburg "had been thoroughly overshadowed by the matter of Nicholas and Alix." The two young lovers, both first cousins of Ducky, had been romantically involved for five years, ever since the seventeen-year-old Alix had visited her sister Ella in St. Petersburg. The gentle Nicholas had danced with the beautiful blond princess from Hesse at court balls; he had taken her skating and tobogganing in the afternoons; and they had fallen in love.

But there had been a serious obstacle to their romance. Nicholas's parents, the emperor and empress, did not want Alix as a daughter-in-law. They forbade the match and pushed him toward a variety of other eligible princesses. However, for once in his life, the docile czarevich stood his ground.

Alix "took everything in life seriously, and religion was the most serious matter of all." She had been confirmed into the German Lutheran Church and was fervently devoted to its doctrines. However, as the wife of the heir to the Russian throne, she would be obliged to convert to Russian Orthodoxy. This she seemed unable to do, believing that to renounce her faith would be "a direct affront to God."

After falling in love with Nicholas in the winter of 1889, Alix decided to play a waiting game. Later in the year she rejected the marriage proposal of her cousin Eddy, Prince Albert Victor, the eldest son of the Prince of Wales and the heir to the English throne. Eddy, a rather slow-witted and odd-looking young man, died unmarried three years later, leaving his younger brother George—whom the duchess of Coburg had rejected as a suitor for Ducky—the heir apparent.

This established an interesting parallel between Ducky and Alix. Both of these granddaughters of Queen Victoria had marriages arranged for them by the queen when they were seventeen. Neither young woman was in love with her intended husband; both men were their bride's first cousins. But here the parallel ends. While Ducky was more mature and self-confident than her cousin and future sister-in-law, it was the psychologically fragile Alix who successfully resisted the queen's command. Spoiled and stubborn, the Hessian princess was as coddled by her grandmother as her brother, Ernie, had been. Ducky, on the contrary, was dealt with more harshly, possibly because her mother had removed her from the Queen's influence.

Victoria had pushed the union of Alix and Eddy as passionately as she had that of Ducky and Ernie, and she was disappointed when Alix balked. But rather than being angry at her granddaughter, she greatly admired her resolve: "She says—that if she is forced she will do it—but that she would be unhappy and he too. This shows great strength of character as all her family and all of us wish it, and she refuses the greatest position there is."

But, indulgent of Alix though she was, the queen, hating Russia more than ever, was determined that she would not marry Nicholas. When she finally realized the strength of her granddaughter's feelings for the czarevich, Victoria panicked. A few days after Christmas, 1890, the queen frantically wrote Alix's eldest sister: "This must *not* be allowed to go on. Papa must put his foot down and there must be no more visits of Alicky to Russia—and he must and you and Ernie must insist on a stop being put to the while affair. The state of Russia is so bad, so rotten that at any moment something dreadful might happen."

Queen Victoria seems to have a keener awareness of the impending Russian apocalypse than any of her contemporaries. The personal destinies of several of her grandchildren would have been far happier had they listened to her desperate warnings.

But Alix didn't listen. She was in love.

The romance continued for the next four years. Nicholas sullenly rejected every attractive young prospect his parents presented to him. When he coolly dismissed the most promising candidate of all, the gorgeous Princess Hélène of France, the emperor and empress wearily relented and gave Nicholas permission to propose to Alix when he journeyed to Coburg to represent them at Ducky's wedding.

Alix had settled in comfortably as the first lady of Hesse, serving as the Darmstadt court's hostess first for her widowed father and then for her bachelor brother. High-handed and aloof, she relished her role and took every opportunity to exercise her privileges. As infatuated as she was with the gentle czarevich, Alix seemed perfectly happy in Darmstadt taking care of Ernie and running the Grand Ducal Palace. It wasn't until the beginning of 1894, when her brother announced his engagement, that Alix nervously began thinking of marriage herself.

Not only would Ernie's marriage deprive Alix of her status, but his particular choice of bride made it intolerable to remain in Hesse. Timid and introverted, Ernie's youngest sister was severely threatened by her determined and self-assured cousin. She had never liked Ducky, and in this clash of temperaments, she correctly guessed who the easy victor would be.

Alix had been so angry when she received her brother's telegram announcing the engagement that she refused to send a reply. "Only with great difficulty could she be persuaded by her ladies-in-waiting to send her congratulations to the couple." Supposedly Alix confronted Ernie and "caused a stormy scene," but he, in turn, had sternly responded that "his marriage was none of her business, and if she no longer wished to live in Darmstadt then she was free to take herself off to one of his shooting-boxes with her own lady-in-waiting."

Alix accepted the inevitable and somberly prepared for the arrival of her new sister-in-law. But to the end of her life she would carefully nurse a special grudge against Ducky. And eventually her resentment turned to hatred.

By the time of Ernie's wedding, Alix was more receptive to a Russian marriage, and when Nicholas arrived from St. Petersburg, she was waiting at the station to meet him. During the days before the ceremony, the Alicky-Nicky romance captured the family's attention. Unable to wait any longer, the impetuous czarevich rushed to Alix the very first morning after his arrival and proposed to her.

But no matter how much she wanted to get out of Darmstadt before Ducky moved in, Alix still refused to change her religion.

"She cried the whole time," Nicholas wrote to his mother, "and only whispered now and then, 'No, I cannot.' Still I went on repeating and insisting. . . . Though this went on for two hours, it came to nothing."

When the kaiser arrived the next day he aggressively played matchmaker. Very keen on the idea of his German cousin being the future empress of Russia, the kaiser pressured Alix to accept Nicky's proposal. But he had little success. Alix's older sister, Ella, who had converted to the Russian church when she married Grand Duke Serge, finally convinced her that changing one's faith was "not really so enormous or unusual an experience."

During the day of Ducky and Ernie's wedding, tension over the Russian engagement was reaching its peak. While the couple exchanged vows, Nicholas stared anxiously at his beloved. "At that moment how much I would have liked to have been able to look into the depths of Alix's soul," he confided to his diary.

Alix spent that stormy night making a decision. The next morning she calmly agreed to renounce her Protestant faith and enter the Orthodox Church.

When the announcement was made, Nicholas observed that "the whole family was simply enraptured." This was most notably true of the kaiser; but others were not so optimistic. The queen quickly reconciled herself to the engagement just as she had to Ducky's parents' marriage twenty years before, and immediately took charge of the romance, instructing Nicholas to call her Granny. But her eldest daughter, the perceptive Empress Frederick, was against the match. Always sympathetic to Ducky, her favorite niece, the dowager empress was unimpressed by her other niece and predicted disaster: "Alix is very imperious and will always insist on having her own way, and she will never yield one iota of the power she will imagine she wields; I use the word 'imagine' advisedly because my niece is given to very exaggerated ideas as to her own cleverness and importance."

Although Alix and Nicholas would enjoy a very happy marriage, their partnership would prove disastrous for the precariously balanced Russian empire. As her aunt shrewdly remarked, Alix did not have the character to make a good empress. She also passed hemophilia to the Romanov heir, and turned this personal tragedy into a national calamity.

It was truly a pity that the two marriage-minded couples at Coburg couldn't have changed partners. Ducky would have made a superlative consort for Nicholas II. Not a carrier of hemophilia, she would, most likely, have provided the Romanov dynasty with solidly healthy heirs. Possessing the courage and strength of character the czarevich so desperately needed, his confident cousin would have guided him well. However, no matter how well-suited Ducky was to be empress of Russia, the Russian Orthodox Church strictly forbade first cousins from marrying. Ducky could no more wed Nicholas than she could her first love, Kirill.

As for Ernie and his sister Alix, they would probably have been happiest remaining where they were. History certainly would have been happier. The spinster sister and her bachelor brother would have made perfect rulers for quiet Hesse. Neither was emotionally suited to have families of their own, and in their tranquil childhood home their injured spirits might eventually have healed. Ernie certainly should not have married a woman as romantic and passionate as Ducky.

Departing from Coburg on the afternoon of her wedding, Ducky could not help but feel pushed to the side of the royal stage, despite the cheering crowds who lined the streets and waved at her. Alix's indecisiveness had kept the entire family on tenterhooks during the prenuptial festivities. No one seemed able to talk of anything else. Everyone was anxiously waiting for the petulant young princess to give in and accept Nicholas's proposal. And the longer she held out, the more anxious they became.

Just as Ducky was about to replace Alix at Darmstadt, Alix had hurried to Coburg and made herself the center of attention. Whether deliberately or not, Alix managed to make her own matrimonial problems the center of interest. Ducky didn't appreciate this in the least. The more she saw of Alix, the less she liked her, and now she resented how Alix had manipulated the family and gotten her own way at Ducky's expense. And the new grand duchess of Hesse must have also resented the fact that, unlike herself, Alix was to marry the man she loved.

Ducky and Ernie made a grand state entrance into Darmstadt. She was dressed in pale mauve and wore a small flowered hat as she sat next to her husband in an open carriage overflowing with irises, roses, and lilacs. Smiling and waving, they slowly drove through the twisting streets "filled with happy, cheering crowds." Bands played and all the church bells rang and the whole city was gaily decorated with flags and banners.

Hesse had been without a grand duchess for more than sixteen years, and the arrival of their sovereign's new wife was an occasion for great rejoicing. Incredibly poised and regal-looking for a teenager, Ducky was a very pleasant surprise for the citizens of Darmstadt. Her charm and beauty delighted everyone she met, and here, at the former home of her aunt and uncle, everything was cozy and familiar. Even her husband.

She and Ernie had been chums from childhood, only recently pushed together and told to fall in love. Probably neither had any idea of what love was.

And this was made apparent as soon as they traveled to Wolfsgarten and began their honeymoon. Nervously retiring to their bedroom that first evening, Ducky and Ernie discovered that they were "sexually incompatible." The groom's previous doubts about being "an adequate husband" now seemed very well founded. That night he finally had to face the fact that he "was not attracted to her."

The sexually inexperienced Ducky had no standard by which to judge her awkward husband's inept and unenthusiastic performance, but her first sexual encounters with Ernie left the young bride feeling "completely shattered and disillusioned."

Worst of all, there was absolutely no one to talk to, no one to advise her. The puritanical Marie would never have discussed such an intimate problem with her daughter. And even Missy, Ducky's sister, soul mate, and closest friend, couldn't discuss "things pertaining to the heart."

"Crushingly disappointed in romantic love," the new grand duchess of Hesse and the Rhine accepted her marriage for what it was. Because the other areas of their relationship were satisfactory, Ducky convinced herself that she was happy and her marriage was a success. She and Ernie laughed and joked together more than ever, doing as they pleased and indulging every whim. Rather than calming the feckless young grand duke and bringing discipline and responsibility to his life, his high-spirited consort only encouraged his fun-loving style.

If the proper and conservative Hessians thought that their young ruler was flamboyantly unconventional when he was single, they were shocked to find that now he was utterly impossible. But no one was more upset by Ernie and Ducky's self-indulgence than their grandmother Queen Victoria. The queen harangued Ernie's older sister, begging her to exercise her influence. Citing the newlyweds' failure to answer letters or even respond to telegrams, she angrily wrote that "already there are great complaints. I do wish you could get Ernie to be less neglectful." But even a year after their wedding, Ducky had still not so much as written to thank most of her royal relatives for their gifts.

Independent for the first time in her life, Ducky was becoming her own person, exploring the limits of her new existence. Unfortunately for her, the only way she saw to stretch and grow was by overindulgence and rebellion.

And however "merry and colorful and exciting" her days with Ernie tended to be, her long nights were filled with frustration and broken dreams.

CHAPTER FIFTEEN

God's Gracious Gift

*T*RAPPED IN SUCH a disappointing life, Ducky put all of her energy into her appearance. Almost immediately the well-scrubbed young schoolgirl had become a stylish woman of the world. Her new subjects were delighted at how she had so quickly achieved "a certain regal magnificence." Riding through the streets of Darmstadt in her open carriage, Ducky was admired by everyone. Few could fail to agree that she looked "every inch the Grand Duchess."

But the glorious new façade hid a disillusioned spirit, which was becoming more melancholy day by day. Living "more like brother and sister than husband and wife," Ernie and Ducky charmed the world with their beauty, wit, and elegance. People still gushed over the young newlyweds and pronounced them the perfect couple. Life was a party wherever they went. However, only in a crowd did they succeed as a couple. Ill at ease and restless when they were alone together, they avoided private moments as often as possible. Occasionally there were awkward attempts at making love, always instigated by Ernie, always slightly embarrassed and perfunctory. Within three months of their wedding Ducky was pregnant.

Ernie was filled with joy. After all, his chief reason for marrying had been to provide Hesse with an heir. And his subjects were equally thrilled. But Ducky was not really quite sure how she felt. She had not anticipated that motherhood would come so soon. Only seventeen years old, Ducky was still adjusting to the demands of being a wife.

The child was expected in March of 1895. Ducky passed her first summer and fall in Hesse resting and leading a relatively quiet life. She found the confinements of pregnancy difficult to endure. There was no running about and galloping madly across the countryside on her adored horses. Since Marie was overseeing the birth of her daughter's first baby, things were done exactly her way.

Fortunately, Ernie's difficult little sister had spent very little time in Darmstadt since the wedding. After becoming engaged Alix had been taken directly to England by her older sister Princess Louis of Battenberg, and had spent the entire spring and summer living with her sister and Queen Victoria, receiving a crash course in Russian culture and religion, and taking a cure for her nerves at Harrogate. Perhaps her intimidating new sister-in-law also helped keep her at bay. Alix certainly had no wish to return home and play second fiddle to this almost frighteningly confident young woman. It was bad enough to have lost her cherished position, but it would have been agony for a woman with as many "personality problems" as Alix to have had to sit back and watch her former duties being performed so adroitly by such an obviously superior princess.

However, with her own wedding date so far away, Alix could not remain in England forever. At the end of the summer, when her fiancé had concluded his visit with Queen Victoria and gone back to St. Petersburg, Alix reluctantly headed back to Hesse. She took up residence at Wolfsgarten, where for almost two months she and Ducky kept as far away from each other as they could. Ducky and Ernie conveniently moved back to the capital at the beginning of fall.

Curiously, these two beautiful young women, cousins and sisters-in-law, equally determined and autocratic, never openly clashed at the Hessian court. Possibly Ducky's advancing pregnancy and the constraints it placed on her precluded a direct confrontation. Also, Alix's illustrious future must have brought her a considerable degree of consolation. But there was still a terrific amount of friction, and on those occasions when the two were unavoidably thrown together, their mutual antipathy was plain to see.

A cruel stroke of fate brought Alix's indefinite stay to an abrupt end. Nicholas's father, the Emperor Alexander III, Ducky's bearlike uncle Sasha, was terminally ill with nephritis. The doctors ordered his immediate removal to the balmy climate of the southern Crimea, and the czarevich found himself caught between "my duty to remain here with my dear parents and follow them to the Crimea and the keen desire to hurry to Wolfsgarten to be near my dear Alix."

Although Nicholas chose duty, leaving for the imperial summer palace on the Black Sea coast with his anxious family, he wrote Alix when his father's condition became critical and asked her to come at once. She was on the very next train to Russia.

The emperor died ten days after Alix's arrival. Nicholas was devastated. He tried to put up a good front for his fiancée, who was irritated to find most people taking advantage of his docile nature. She urged him to "show your own mind and don't let others forget who you are." But the young man was so terrified of the future that even encouragement from his beloved was of little benefit. With tears in his eyes, Nicholas took his stalwart brother-in-law, Grand Duke Alexander, down to his room, and collapsed hysterically in his arms.

"Sandro, what am I going to do?" he cried in a desperate voice. "What is going to happen to me, to you, to Xenia, to Alix, to mother, to all of Russia? I am not prepared to be a Tsar. I never wanted to become one. I know nothing of the business of ruling. I have no idea of even how to talk to the ministers."

(Nicholas never did attain complete confidence. And as much as Alix loved him and wished to rescue him from his insecurities, she merely compounded the tragedy to come.)

Returning with the body to St. Petersburg, the family prepared for the state funeral. The crowned heads of Europe and their relatives gathered at the Winter Palace after the burial and stayed on another week for the impromptu wedding of Nicholas and Alix, now known as Alexandra.

Ernie had been one of the first to arrive at his sister's side. He tried to comfort her and give her strength during the long and sad funeral ceremonies, and then witnessed the pomp and splendor of her marriage. But Ducky midway through her pregnancy and suffering all its discomforts, stayed behind at Darmstadt. It was probably just as well that she couldn't make the trip, for the month-long separation from her husband gave them both a much-needed vacation from the tensions of their difficult marriage.

Unlike her disappointed sister-in-law, Alix quickly experienced bliss in matrimony. The morning after her wedding, Alix euphorically wrote in her diary, "Never did I believe there could be such utter happiness in this world, such a feeling of unity between two mortal beings."

Obviously, the disparity in personal fulfillment between these two brides did not endear Alix to Ducky. Alix had stubbornly defied her family and married the man she loved; now she was empress of Russia. Ducky had been forced into a loveless union and was utterly miserable, plus she was a mere grand duchess, stuck in a boring little country.

During this time, Ducky's greatest consolation was the long letters in which Missy cheerfully detailed her tribulations as the crown princess of Romania. Missy's personality and high spirits had created a considerable amount of friction at King Carol's rigid court. Not surprisingly, the young wife of the heir-apparent had rebelled at her austere new life.

"Down there in the new country," Missy candidly wrote later, "I was in harness, I was merely a little wheel in a watch which was keeping Uncle's [King Carol's] time but a little wheel which had to do its part, relentlessly, and no one tried to surround that part with any glamour or make it seem worth while; it was all work and no play, I was with a vengeance the stranger in a stranger land."

Struggling to keep up her spirits, Missy complained to her understanding sister that "everything I did seemed always to be wrong. . . . At Uncle's court everything was denied you, enjoyment was looked upon as frivolity, every word you said was an imprudence, your life was not your own, nor your house, nor your servants, nor even your children!"

But although she and her husband had incompatible personalities, they at least enjoyed an exceptionally passionate love life. In fact, if Missy had a problem in this regard, it was the opposite of Ducky's. Crown Prince Ferdinand was sexually obsessed with his ravishing wife and exercised his marital privileges so often and so violently that the duchess of Coburg finally wrote directly to King Carol and firmly instructed him to tell his nephew to restrain himself before he jeopardized Missy's health.

For the ultra-romantic Missy, however, a vital sex life counted for very little. She, in her own way, was just as disillusioned in marriage and alienated from her husband as Ducky was. The craven and bumbling Ferdinand had failed to touch either Missy's brain or her soul.

Thus, the two sisters had more in common than ever, but circumstance and distance kept them apart. Ducky was trapped in Darmstadt by her progressing pregnancy, and Missy, nearly constantly pregnant herself during the first few years of her marriage, was forbidden by the tyrannical king to travel unless it was absolutely necessary. Exchanging a steady flow of long letters between Darmstadt and Bucharest, the unhappy sisters found "with a pang that we both realized that our ways were parting more and more."

Ducky, as determined as ever, refused to admit how unhappy she was. To the world, she smiled and continued doing the best she could. When her aunt Empress Frederick visited her toward the end of the year, she marveled at how Ducky was looking so "lovely, but very pale, and her figure showing scarcely anything of impending events. She is such a dear and so sympathetic, unaffected, gentle and ladylike."

The first Christmas of her marriage was a somber affair for Ducky. The severe restrictions of her advancing pregnancy that barred any physical activity were taking their toll. She and Ernie were now living like brother and sister, and through the gloom of winter and enforced inactivity, Ducky wistfully looked out the east windows of the Grand Ducal Palace toward Coburg and to Russia far beyond.

The birth was expected just after the first week of March 1895. Always an enthusiastic midwife to her grandchildren, the duchess had already arrived from Coburg and efficiently organized the doctors and the nursery. While Ernie nervously waited, Ducky and her mother calmly prepared for the event.

A few days later, on the morning of March 11, the sun rose warmly in a clear, bright sky and brilliantly illuminated the rolling, snow-covered Hessian countryside. Ducky had gone into labor during the night, and just before noon the church bells of Darmstadt began ringing furiously and distant cannons started thundering their loud salute. Within minutes the excited citizens of Hesse began hearing the news: Grand Duchess Victoria Melita had given birth to a baby girl. It was the first royal birth in Hesse in almost two decades. Although she was not the much-desired male heir, this little princess was cherished by the entire Hessian population. And none treasured her more than her proud father. Ernie had succeeded in doing what he had always secretly feared he could never do: He had fathered a child and produced a family. And the fact that his little girl was strong and healthy and beautiful only increased his love and sense of vindication.

Indeed, the infant was tangible proof that the Ernie-Ducky marriage, that highly controversial union of first cousins, had been a success.

Ducky couldn't fail to notice her husband's true emotions when he visited her bedside for the first time: He turned his polite smile away from her expectant face and embraced his new daughter. From this moment on, Ernie centered all of his love on the baby.

Ironically, with enormous violet-blue eyes and lush chestnut hair, the infant looked just like her mother.

Against the wishes of Queen Victoria, the baby was named neither Alice, after Ernie's mother, nor Victoria for the queen herself. Instead, Ernie decided to name his daughter Elizabeth, after his Hessian grandmother.

As much as Ducky adored the baby, she found it increasingly painful to watch her husband shower her with all the warmth and affection he denied his wife. At first, Ducky tried to compete with Ernie in caring for the child, but within months that proved hopeless.

Obsessively haunting the nursery, the grand duke succeeded in completely taking over the baby's life. Deprived of her husband's companionship, Ducky found motherhood surprisingly empty and somewhat sad. With father and daughter forming an uncommonly tight bond, mother was left out in the cold. Ernie very quickly enlisted Elizabeth into his private world of fantasy and beauty. He managed to communicate with Elizabeth before she even learned to speak. When she was only about six months old he decided to let her select the wallpaper for her new bedroom. He held up various samples and carefully watched Elizabeth's reactions. Whenever he held up mauve ones, "she made happy little noises." Sensing that she liked one mauve sample in particular, Ernie confidently decorated her room in that shade.

When Elizabeth learned to talk her relationship with her father became even more intense. However, as complete as his devotion was, Ernie was not totally fulfilled by this lovely little gift from God. In some ways he seemed more restless than ever, desperately searching for something that even he himself might not have known or understood.

Ducky certainly didn't. The longer her marriage continued, the less she seemed to know her husband. And Ducky hated mysteries. She had no patience with them.

CHAPTER SIXTEEN

Babylon
on the Rhine

HOPING THAT DISTANCE would make her husband's heart
grow fonder, Ducky spent part of the summer of 1895 far from
Darmstadt and Ernie. Missy had miraculously managed to pry a foreign
vacation out of the tyrannical Romanian king; she had made plans to
visit England, attending the Ascot races and passing an idyllic month on
the Isle of Wight with her two children, Carol and Elisabetha. Ducky
quickly decided to join her and take three-month-old Elizabeth.

In early June, Ducky stood in the palace courtyard next to the nurse
carrying the baby and said good-bye to her tall, handsome husband.
Ernie awkwardly leaned forward and gave her a polite kiss on the
cheek, then turned to his small daughter and took her in his arms, tearfully covering her face with kisses. This display "brutally struck deeply
into [Ducky] and left her with a painful wound from which she never
recovered."

During the long journey to England Ducky became more and more
depressed. The sight of the gently rolling Kent countryside brought back
memories of childhood and of her youthful romantic fantasies, now
turned to ashes. But as soon as she reached London and flung herself
into Missy's waiting arms, her sorrow temporarily dissolved.

Laughing as she hadn't laughed since her marriage, Ducky delighted
in her older sister's high spirits and sense of fun. Dressed in white, the
two attended the Ascot races and appeared at one gala party after another. Although they were both wives and mothers who held important

positions in their respective countries, Ducky and Missy were still teenaged girls, who were just beginning to realize how much they had missed by marrying young.

After Ascot, the sisters and their children went together to the Isle of Wight, the Eden of their youth. Happily, Grandmama Queen lent them a large cottage at Osborne. There, next to a tranquil beach amid "the sun-warmed woods" with high hedges of honeysuckle and wild roses, Grand Duchess Victoria Melita of Hesse and Crown Princess Marie of Romania became children again.

For Ducky and Missy, "it was pure joy being once more in the cherished places of our childhood." During that summer of 1895 they spent their days experiencing the "exquisite delight" of rediscovering everything they had loved as children—the woods and parks and beaches and farms and gardens of their grandmother's retreat. Once again combing the ocean sands for those fan shells in such delicate pink shades, Ducky also joined her sister in watching the coast guard at work and walking "alongside the slippery pier with its multicoloured seaweed."

They took turns driving a small one-pony trap around the island, occasionally rolling it up onto the old ferry and going across the bay to Cowes where they passed whole afternoons browsing in gift shops for presents for the sailors who had become their children's slaves as enthusiastically as they had once been theirs.

But the dominating presence on the island was still tiny Queen Victoria sitting placidly beneath her green-lined tent-parasol on the terrace of Osborne House, surrounded by her Indian and Highlander servants and her retinue of well-trained dogs. Although daily appearances at breakfast were still mandatory and Victoria "was full of searching inquiries about our new homes and general behavior," there was now something very comfortable and less intimidating about Grandmama Queen. Now that Ducky was independent and held sovereign status, she no longer felt so vulnerable to her grandmother's austere authority. They certainly were not equals, but the gulf between them was not nearly as wide as before.

Reunited with her sister and back home in the peace of her favorite childhood refuge, Ducky had a great deal of time to reflect during that quiet and isolated summer. She had returned to her past and then proceeded forward again, but looking at things from a completely different angle. By the end of her stay she had come to a very important conclusion: She regretted her marriage. It had been a dreadful mistake.

But there was nothing to be done. She could only go back and make the best of it.

Ducky and Missy arranged to return to the Continent together. To ease their traveling with small children, the queen generously lent them her yacht, H.M.S. *Osborne,* for crossing the Channel. Extending their holiday for as long as possible, the sisters decided to go back via Holland, a country they had never visited. The *Osborne* docked at the old port of Middelburg, whose inhabitants still wore the costume of centuries past. The royal visitors experienced the enchanting new scene together and found the unspoiled beauty "almost too good to be true."

The two then proceeded to Darmstadt, where Ducky persuaded her sister to stay on for several days at Wolfsgarten. With Missy at her side, the unhappy grand duchess of Hesse galloped her horse along the sandy woodland roads.

When Missy finally returned to Romania, she left her sister an invaluable gift. The summer they had spent together had served as a transfusion for Ducky's dying spirit. Missy's resilient character, which enabled her to triumph over her own very unsatisfactory marriage, inspired Ducky to attempt to do the same. And because Ducky was far more courageous and strong-willed than her older sister, she convinced herself that she could do it.

The solution seemed to be the same one Ernie had chosen: diversion. Ducky's husband filled every moment of the day with a whirl of pleasant people and pleasurable pursuits.

Thus, the grand ducal court of Hesse quickly became Europe's most hedonistic. The unwritten rule was that anyone over thirty was "old and out." The elderly aristocrats of Hesse quietly retired to their serene drawing rooms, "sipping tea and shaking their heads, and dreaming of the days of Grand Duke Louis and his uncle before him."

However, many of these decorous critics would have been surprised to learn how innocent most of the young royals' "wicked pleasures" really were. Although the art of flirtation was perfected, the sexual mores of these pleasure seekers remained quite conservative, compatible with those of Grandmama Queen. Adultery was still taboo between the members of the same social class. Many royal husbands had mistresses, and some royal wives took lovers, but these affairs were kept scrupulously private and always involved partners of a much lesser rank.

Certainly Ducky could never have been involved in a casual affair. To have engaged in a sexual relationship simply for excitement or physical pleasure was an impossibility for someone of her character and background. Given her uncompromising nature and her beliefs in very definite rights and wrongs, Ducky, who always "hated frauds and insincerity more than anything else," placed great value on faithfulness and fidelity. Even though she had failed to find in her marriage the love she craved, she still cherished her moral and romantic ideals.

For a woman as passionate as she, it must have been difficult to resist the temptation to find affection elsewhere. Her beauty and charm attracted considerable masculine attention. But the grand duchess displayed a fidelity to her indifferent husband that was a true proof of her remarkable character.

Only a great, true love could have challenged her resolve.

As for Ernie, no one really knew where he was satisfying his sexual urges, or if he was satisfying them at all. Ducky often wondered. There had recently been whispers throughout the small court about a certain young woman of Darmstadt who received evening visits from the grand duke; there had also been talk of his unconventional friendships with the male members of the flourishing artistic community of Hesse.

But much of Ernie's energy was being spent in patronage and guidance of a movement of local artists and architects who were working in the style known as art nouveau. Setting aside the Mathildenhohe, a forested hill on the northern edge of Darmstadt, Ernie had organized a colony of these artists, subsidizing their creation of an entire village. As the century turned, art nouveau would dominate the sensibility of the entire continent.

The restless grand duke also concentrated his attention on the Darmstadt Court Theater. He delighted in selecting his favorite plays and supervising every detail of their production—designing the sets, casting the lead roles, and directing the director. And his interest in the performing arts brought him into the company of many young actresses. The sage gossips of Darmstadt began whispering of certain young beauties who received the grand duke's special attention during extra rehearsals held privately at night.

Meanwhile, at home in Wolfsgarten, he and his wife struggled to create the only tolerable life together, one filled with a crowd of other people: relatives and friends, each as clever and amusing as possible.

Far from the Babylonian hotbed of vice that their shocked elders vividly imagined, Ducky and Ernie's home life simply anticipated the rapid changes in the world. Not only did people feel the usual anxiety brought about by the ending of a century, but tension was further charged by the rapid advances in technology and the impending death of Queen Victoria, a colossal mother-figure who had set the rules of the day. Horses and carriages were beginning to share the streets with automobiles and bicycles. Electric lights were being installed everywhere. Telephones and phonographs were entering every wealthy home. Airplanes were almost a reality. Motion pictures were the latest novelty. And radio was the dream of the future. Very little of the past seemed relevant to the exciting present. And strict standards of conduct and behavior were viewed as meaningless and obsolete.

(The personal freedom that Ernie and Ducky fostered was also extended to their child. As soon as she could walk, little Elizabeth was given a specially built miniature house all her own. It stood in its own garden, and adults were forbidden to enter—"much to the frustration of royal nurses and tutors, who could be seen pacing up and down impatiently outside as they waited for their high-spirited young charges to stop their games and emerge.")

For many royals who as children had been subjected to the most merciless discipline, the advent of a new era was an invitation to toss away the straitjacket of intricate etiquette and do as they please. No place represented freedom and the glorious promise of the new century more than Ernie's court at Hesse. With its progressive artistic and intellectual community presided over by its young, party-loving rulers, Darmstadt was a paradise for Europe's youthful royals. To visit Wolfsgarten was like being "schoolchildren on a holiday." Ducky's cousin Prince Nicholas of Greece considered his stay there "the jolliest, merriest house party to which I have ever been in my life." These do's were "the most informal . . . titles gave way to nicknames, and everyone behaved as they wished."

Ducky and Ernie threw such a continuous succession of parties that it was difficult to know when one ended and another began. Guests constantly filled the bedrooms of Wolfsgarten. As they arrived, instead of being offered a visitors' book to sign, they were led by the laughing grand duke to a special windowpane in the main salon and instructed to scratch their names in the glass. Led by the grand duchess, visitors rode wildly through the Wolfsgarten forests, "a wonderful place for riding." and engaged in races and equestrian games. Other less daring guests mounted large bicycles and held jousting tournaments. On rainy days everyone sat on the floor and painted imaginative pictures in the style of "cheeky, impertinent modernism, with its usual contempt for established principles." Classicist Victorian sketching was definitely out.

There were excursions to the races at Frankfurt, to the casinos of Wiesbaden, to the spas of Baden-Baden. There were cruises on the Rhine and picnics in the woods. Many frequent guests, such as Nicholas and Alexandra, had their own private trains standing by to take groups on any impromptu expedition they might desire.

Ernie was always the energetic and irrepressible master of ceremonies. Two of his greatest delights were hot-air ballooning and his water slide. The grand duke kept his own giant balloon docked near the Wolfsgarten stables. To either their horror or delight, guests would be escorted to the balloon's spacious gondola and lifted inside for an abrupt rise over the estate. To drift high above the Rhine valley while enjoying an aerial picnic became one of the greatest thrills of a visit to eccentric Wolfsgarten, and Ernie unfailingly took visible pride in his cleverness.

The water slide was a creation entirely Ernie's own. His inspiration had been a small pond in the woods which was filled with mud, covered with duckweed, and surrounded by bulrushes. The pond had a steep bank on one side. Ernie had a large water chute constructed in a way which would allow it to be used as a slide. The object was to ride a small boat down the long chute into the pond. When the boat hit the pond, the occupants would be drenched in a muddy spray.

The water slide was used mostly by the male visitors to Wolfsgarten. However, on one notable occasion a distinguished lady guest was inveigled into riding. Lady Buchanan, the wife of Sir George Buchanan, the British ambassador to Hesse, was a sedate older woman who was used to being treated with great respect and affection by the grand-ducal couple. Feeling more mischievous than ever, Ernie persuaded the ambassador's wife and one of the younger ladies-in-waiting to climb into the boat with him at the top of the slide. Whatever Lady Buchanan was thinking, it was a major mistake to be wearing her "new and very best dress," a flawless pink creation of which she was very proud. Ernie conspired with the boat's other occupant, Prince Nicholas of Greece, to deliberately overturn the vessel when it hit the water; Lady Buchanan, screaming, flew into the mud and then slowly crawled out, "a limp, black creature" struggling up on the bank. Her exquisite dress shrank so much after being washed that it fit only her small daughter.

Seeing that Lady Buchanan had actually enjoyed the prank, Ducky quickly enlisted her as an accomplice in several of her own jokes. A few days later everyone was sitting in the huge courtyard of Wolfsgarten peacefully having lunch. Looking up, they were surprised to see two un-kempt peasant women with colored handkerchiefs on their heads and wearing checked aprons walking casually through the open gates and preparing to join the elegant party. At first completely nonplussed, the servants eventually gathered their wits and approached the poor crea-tures to demand that they leave. Everyone gasped with astonishment when the women suddenly took off their camouflage and revealed themselves as the grand duchess and Lady Buchanan, "both helpless with laughter."

At Wolfsgarten, many evening parties lasted until dawn, and when the revelers weren't dancing new dances or inventing new games, they would darken the room and read aloud from shockers such as *Dracula* and *Frankenstein* as a single candle threw eerily flickering shadows on the wall. One of Ducky and Ernie's favorite evening amusements was a game called Consequences, which they played "with scant respect for the feelings of others." One person would ask a delicate or probing question; the one questioned was required to give a completely honest answer. One of Ducky's closest friends, Princess Daisy of Pless, a famous beauty and fellow Englishwoman, played Consequences during one of her visits and remembered Ducky asking the question "Why does virtue take so many different forms?"

"Because, being a woman, she likes to change dresses," a wit promptly replied.

Later in the evening the grand duchess became pensive and sullen.

When her next turn in the game came, she quietly asked:

"Why does one so often hurt the person one loves best?"

There was no answer to her question.

CHAPTER SEVENTEEN

The Little Spitfire

A S THEIR UNHAPPY MARRIAGE began its third year, Ducky and Ernie drifted still further apart. The grand duchess was not a woman to suffer quietly. While theatrical Missy loved to play the martyr, Ducky was much more like their mother, the duchess—a "strong and rebellious 'fore-fighter.' "

Ducky was always to remain something of a stranger in her new kingdom. Because the former rulers of Hesse had deliberately turned their backs on the modern era and "kept progress in retard," it was difficult for someone as sophisticated as she to adjust to the dreary local sensibility. Also, there had been no grand duchess in Hesse since the tragic death of Ernie's mother in 1878. This nearly twenty-year vacancy created idealized expectations that no one could possibly have met.

But Ducky didn't even try. By now, it was obvious to her that Ernie had married her solely to provide Hesse with an heir and a grand duchess; his only interest in her was her performance as "die Landesmutter," the Mother of the Land. Angry at his indifference, and wishing to hurt him as much as he was hurting her, she extended her resentment to his entire kingdom. In retaliation for his failures in private life, she refused to play her assigned public role. Having little patience anyway with the rigid constraints and boring traditions of the Hessian court, Ducky simply did what she pleased.

The grand duchess's bewildered subjects had no idea of how much she was suffering in her miserable marriage. All they saw was "a highly volatile young woman, plunging from moods of jubilation to those of deep melancholy."

Ducky was constantly irritated by the numerous duties of a grand duchess, most of which seemed both dull and trivial. So she conveniently "forgot to answer letters; she postponed paying visits to boring old relations; at official receptions she often caused great offense by talking to somebody who amused her, and ignoring people whose high standing gave them importance."

These tactics had exactly the desired effect. Ernie was outraged. Although irreverent and fun-loving and fond of wild parties, he was an attentive and conscientious ruler who "had been well schooled by his father and Queen Victoria, and he respected the legacy of his mother whose health had in part been sacrificed to shouldering burdens beyond the call of duty." He saw Ducky's disregard of her duties as an insult to his mother's memory and a direct affront to their subjects. His continual reproaches provoked equally continual displays of Ducky's "ungovernable temper." Shouting, dropping tea trays, smashing china, and taking careful aim at her husband with "any handy object," Ducky created the only passion in their marriage. The servants soon became accustomed to the sound of china being smashed against the walls.

Exasperated at her granddaughter's consistently tardy replies to her letters, and with complaints from other family members reaching her ears, Queen Victoria sadly concluded that instead of having the desired steadying effect on Ernie, Ducky was making things worse than ever.

Like her grandmother, most critics harshly condemned Ducky's behavior. Their expectations had been high, and now their disappointment was proportionate. None of them knew of the emptiness of her home life, and many forgot that their glamorous grand duchess was still just a teenager.

Ducky desperately needed an outlet for her vigorous drives. Predictably, she put all her passion into her favorite hobby: horses. She had always adored them, but now they became her entire life. The stables at Wolfsgarten were the finest in Europe. Magnificent steeds were imported from everywhere on the Continent—wild stallions from Russia, "a wonderful collection of white Lipizzaners" from Vienna, and exquisite ponies from England. Even Missy was impressed by the quality of her sister's stable, with its "first-rate horses of every kind, from the light-footed Arab to the heavy Irish hunter."

Most contemporaries credit Ducky with being the best rider they had ever seen. Missy often proudly proclaimed that Ducky "was a splendid horsewoman"; she fondly recalled the "many gay riding parties even by moonlight when the forest became ghost-like and strange, so that it became difficult to stick to the road."

While her husband considered horses only "a means of transport" and nervously kept his distance from the more high-spirited ones, Ducky delighted in recklessly fast riding, the more dangerous the better. Or she would take out her carriage, guiding four or sometimes even six huge stallions along Wolfsgarten's narrow dirt roads at a speed that "made others fear for her safety."

When she finally returned to the palace after one of these rides there was much to answer for. She usually had forgotten a string of appointments and engagements—and, worse, she seemed utterly unconcerned by this. If Ernie scolded her, she would accuse him of being a lazy coward who hadn't had the strength and courage to accompany her.

Ducky's favorite horse was a black stallion named Bogdan, sent all the way from the steppes of Russia. Bogdan was the terror of the palace. Let loose in the courtyard, he would chase the frightened servants and attack anyone who got in his way. One day he even attacked the grand duke, charging after Ernie and tearing out the seat of his pants "as he bolted up the steps to seek safety in the house." The sound of "Ducky's laughter ringing out across the courtyard at this undignified sight did not further the cause of marital bliss."

The beautiful grand duchess of Hesse and her magnificent horses created a sensation wherever they went. When Missy was taking a cure at Bad Schwalbach, near Darmstadt, Ducky drove over in her carriage with four white Lipizzaners "harnessed Hungarian-wise with attractive trappings." On afternoon excursions with Missy through the local countryside, Ducky and her white horses attracted so much attention that "we were considered 'fast.' " Indeed, the sisters found that "whatever we did used to bring censure down upon our heads, we seemed to have the faculty of shocking our betters." One such adventure was a harmless drive to the Frankfurt races "which has remained notorious."

Herr von Riedesel, the master of the Wolfsgarten stables, delighted in the grand duchess's "passion for horses which gave special importance to his beautifully run stables. He was her most devoted slave and liked to turn out her carriage and riding-horses as perfectly as possible." When

Missy and Ducky decided to go to the Frankfurt races "in grand style," the enthusiastic stablemaster decided to outdo himself. Inspired, Ducky and Missy decided to dress up "with as much 'chic' as we could, but in our own special style which often met with disapproval."

The sisters' "simple but striking" outfits consisted of plain white skirts, long and bell-shaped, and tailored jackets, Ducky's of pale mauve and Missy's a pleasantly contrasting turquoise. The jackets were perfectly cut to show off the sisters' figures and had crystal buttons. With white hats and shoes and gloves to match their skirts, they tied broad white tulle bows under their chins and pinned bouquets of blue and mauve hydrangea to the fronts of their jackets. "It was this unexpected finishing touch that was considered the most reprehensible."

With Ducky driving, Missy at her side, and two grooms seated back to back, off they paraded to the gala races at Frankfurt in their flashy carriage pulled by the wonderful white Lipizzaner horses. To their joy, they "reaped all the success we had expected" and it was easy to see that their chic simplicity "outshone the more heavy finery donned by others for the same occasion."

However, their triumph had its price. Their aunt Empress Frederick, who was also at the races, looked on in shock at the unconventionally flamboyant appearance of her two beautiful nieces. Scandalized by their breach of decorum and fashion, the empress immediately wrote to the duchess of Coburg to denounce their transgressions. The duchess, in turn, fired off harsh letters to Ducky and Missy scolding them for their "sinful love of dress" and their "affection for wanting to look different from other princesses."

Empress Frederick was just one of four empresses who found themselves closely involved in the emotional crisis of Ducky's marriage. A brilliant woman who herself had suffered a tragic life, Empress Frederick was a shrewd judge of the members of her vast family. Of all her royal nieces, it was Ducky who had her greatest respect and affection. To a certain extent, the two women were kindred spirits. Having been unhappy in her own private life, Ducky's aunt must have had a rare insight into the nature of the Hesse marriage and the character of her favorite niece.

She supported Ducky and smilingly appreciated the nickname her son, the kaiser, had bestowed upon her: the Little Spitfire. (Others at the Berlin court referred to Ducky as the Fighting Grand Duchess, some with admiration, others with disapproval.)

Whenever the Empress Frederick spoke of her niece, she had only praise for her. She declared Ducky even more beautiful than her husband's Hessian sisters. During the spring of 1896 when then-famous artist Heinrich von Angeli was at Darmstadt painting Ducky's portrait, the empress candidly commented: "I envy him, she is so handsome that it must be a real pleasure. I admire her still more than her sisters-in-law, Ella and Alicky, lovely though they are."

In particular, the empress admired Ducky's unusual hairstyle, which "suits her wonderfully and shows up her pretty white young brow." Ducky, she wrote, "is wonderfully handsome with the graceful fashion she wears her hair, in large waves back over the head showing the roots turned back in the middle of the forehead, which is so pretty because one sees that it is a person's own hair. The towsel and fringe like a thick sponge over the forehead suits Aunt Alix [the Princess of Wales, later Queen Alexandra] but no one else. It spoils Maudie [the future queen of Norway]'s pretty face, and May [the duchess of York, later Queen Mary] wears a wig front."

The three other empresses involved in the Darmstadt imbroglio were Queen Victoria (empress of India); her touchy granddaughter, Empress Alexandra of Russia; and the wife of Victoria's grandson, Empress Augusta of Germany.

Victoria, the mastermind of this unhappy union, realized that her two favorite grandchildren were seriously mismatched. She vowed to never arrange another marriage ever again.

Her high-handed granddaughter Empress Alexandra was in the delicate position of being both Ernie's sister and Ducky's first cousin. But her loyalties were with her brother. As the marriage continued to come apart, Alix stood behind him, blaming Ducky for every problem.

In direct contrast to the disparaging Alix was the kaiser's self-effacing wife, Empress Augusta Victoria, known in the family as Dona. This dedicated and simple woman admired Ducky almost as much as Empress Frederick did. Ducky and her cousin Dona had much in common. Both loved horses, and both had negligent husbands. (Time would eventually reveal that the kaiser and Ernie shared certain predilections.) So the empress—eighteen years Ducky's senior—"had great sympathy for her in her marriage difficulties." (However, Dona's understanding of her husband's psyche was even more limited than Ducky's knowledge of Ernie's.)

As her marriage worsened, Ducky found temporary refuge at the German imperial court in Berlin. The court's grandeur and pageantry were much more to Ducky's liking than Darmstadt's modesty or Windsor's formality.

At the military parades the kaiser so proudly staged, Dona and Ducky presented an unintentionally comic contrast: While the slender grand duchess gracefully pirouetted in her saddle, the fat, awkwardly bouncing empress looked exactly like "a sack of potatoes."

But Ducky couldn't live her whole life at the Berlin court. And as things at home got worse, her temper became even more celebrated.

Partial relief arrived in April with the wedding of Ducky's younger sister at Coburg. Sandra was marrying Prince Ernest of Hohenlohe-Langenburg, a grandson of Queen Victoria's half sister, Fedora, and would be living nearby at Schloss Langenburg. But Ducky and Missy and much of the family opposed the match, on account of the groom's princely house occupying the lowly status of entry-level royalty. But on the other hand, Marie found Sandra "the most uninteresting specimen" of her four daughters, a meek and jealous creature often ill with headaches. However, the marriage turned out to be uncommonly happy.

While the family was assembled for Sandra's modest nuptials, an invitation arrived at Darmstadt for Ducky and Ernie to attend the coronation of Nicholas and Alexandra in Moscow. As the brother of the woman about to become empress of Russia, Ernie would be one of the most important guests. Naturally he and his wife quickly accepted.

The trip would change Ducky's entire life.

CHAPTER EIGHTEEN

Journey to Moscow

THE CORONATION OF Nicholas and Alexandra in May of 1896 was the most magnificent spectacle in Russian history, capturing the imagination of the entire empire. It was as if "the past and the present had combined in a last great effort of joy before the gloom was to fall upon them . . . the last great flare-up of a candle before it was to be extinguished."

For Ducky, the occasion was not only exciting and glamorous but also a family reunion. The duke and duchess of Coburg and all their children were attending. Ducky and Missy rejoiced at the thought of being reunited again; both sisters realized that the celebration in Moscow represented their first and perhaps only chance to savor all the royal splendor that thus far had been denied them. They were determined to make the most of it.

Ducky and Ernie scooped up baby Elizabeth and climbed onto a special train into the vast expanse of her cousin's empire. Ernie, seemingly in a world of his own, kept his distance from his moody wife for most of the three-day trip.

Being so closely related to the Russian Imperial Family, Ducky and Ernie "belonged to the inner circle," with special status among the numerous royals attending the coronation. They stayed in the sumptuous Moscow house of Ernie's sister Ella, the wife of Ducky's uncle Grand Duke Serge.

However, since Missy and her family were staying in a mansion nearby, Ducky avoided Ernie's sisters as much as she could; she and Missy made it their object "to come together as much as possible." They discovered that "to share things still heightened our pleasure in life." Immediately, they put on their finest dresses and jewels, and without half trying, the "dark and somewhat somber and melancholy" grand duchess of Hesse and the blond and "always amused" crown princess of Romania conquered the festivities and captured most of the male hearts of Moscow. It was difficult for anyone to dispute that "of all the Royal beauties the daughters of the [former] Duke of Edinburgh were among the most radiant."

As Ducky and Missy dazzled "a large following of admirers," their mother looked on with narrowed eyes. The stern duchess still treated the sisters like children; "her eye was all-seeing, her word was law, and her dissatisfaction when expressed was never lightly set aside." During the coronation she kept them "in severe order, often thoroughly disapproving" of their clothes and behavior. "Her withering criticism of the way we wore our veils under diadems, which she considered too picturesque and not orthodox enough," still made the sisters burn with rancor forty years later. Marie contemptuously dismissed their "tendency towards picturesqueness" as mere "affectation," and Ducky and Missy quickly realized that "when we knew she would be present, we had to refrain from too much artistic imagination."

Was the duchess really that austere and narrow-minded? Or was she simply jealous?

Having grown up as the Russian emperor's only daughter, in a family of six brothers, Ducky's mother had been the uncontested center of masculine attention. However, when she married and left home, her monopoly came to a very swift end. Unattractive, overweight, and charmless, the duchess was poorly equipped to compete with other women on almost any level. Intellectuals appreciated her mind and moralists prized her character, but society either ignored her or laughed at her behind her back.

How frustrating it must have been for the dumpy, heavy-featured duchess to have produced two spectacularly beautiful daughters.

Luckily, Ducky and her sister had at least one powerful supporter in Moscow: their great-aunt Sari, Grand Duchess Alexandra, the lively and stylish widow of Grand Duke Constantine. When Marie began scolding her daughters, Sari would quickly leap to their defense: "Let the children look as nice as they can; I like to see the young have ideas of their own and your daughters seem to have good taste."

The official coronation ceremonies began on May 18, 1896. On Thursday, the twenty-first, Nicholas and Alexandra made their state entrance into Moscow at the head of a magnificent procession. For the past several days they had been secluded in a monastery beyond the walls of the city "so as to prepare themselves in all humility for the coming sacrament."

As thousands of church bells rang and a million eager spectators crowded the streets, the procession began with the trotting squadrons of the Imperial Guard cavalry, their golden helmets and cuirasses flashing in the warm afternoon sun. Next came the Cossacks of the Guard, "wearing long coats of red and purple, their curved sabers banging against their soft black boots." They were followed by the numerous members of Moscow's nobility, adorned with "gold braid and crimson sashes with jeweled medals sparkling on their chests." Behind them marched the court orchestra, the imperial hunt, the court footmen in their red knee breeches, and the solemn-looking officials of the court wearing lavish, gold-embroidered uniforms.

There was a long pause in the procession; then Emperor Nicholas dramatically appeared, alone, on a tall white horse. He was "not clad in gorgeous apparel but in the simple dark green uniform all [were] accustomed to see him wear, on his head the round tight-fitting astrakhan cap, characteristic of the Russian army."

"Small, almost frail-looking," Nicholas sat straight and rigid in his saddle, his face "drawn and pale with excitement" as he kept his right hand raised to his visor in a continuous fixed salute. There was "a gentle, almost wistful smile on his lips" and in his bearing was "the quiet dignity of one deeply conscious of all he represents."

Following at a distance were Nicholas's uncles and cousins, the Russian grand dukes, each wearing the colorful uniform of his own regiment. The most dashing was nineteen-year-old Grand Duke Kirill, mounted on a gray charger that had been a gift to his father from the emir of Bukhara. Next rode the royal representatives from all of Europe and Asia; then came the huge gilded carriage of Catherine the Great, drawn by eight cloud-white horses. Nicholas's mother, Dowager Empress Marie, sat inside, smiling and waved graciously to the crowds with that special "charm peculiar to her family," the rulers of Denmark. In a second and slightly less fantastic golden coach sat Empress Alexandra, dressed in a pure white gown covered with glittering diamonds. With a tight mouth and eyes devoid of all happiness, the new empress sat somberly, "as though darkly guessing that life might be a foe, she must set out to meet it sword in hand."

The immense procession wound through the decorated streets of Moscow, which looked "like a city of fairyland," and at last entered the Kremlin by the Nikolsky Gate. Having blended "the best that art can produce with the dignified proportion of exquisite taste," the event had been "a drama acted in complete harmony with the surroundings."

Five days later, on Tuesday, May 26, a cloudless blue sky overlooked the Kremlin's majestic Ouspensky Cathedral, where the coronation of Nicholas and Alexandra took place. The cathedral "was packed with humanity"; although "the religious rites seemed interminable, and . . . one had to stand the whole time in a stifling atmosphere of heat," the ceremony was thrilling, a spectacle seen "once and only once" in a lifetime.

Ducky stood solemnly next to her husband, at the very center of the sacred ceremony. She was swept by mixed feelings as she watched her sister-in-law, the new Russian empress, enter the cavernous cathedral with her cousin Nicky while the anthems of the Orthodox Church triumphantly sounded. This was the world of Ducky's mother, and, now, more than ever, Ducky felt that it was her world too.

Imperial Russia suddenly beckoned with all its grandeur to the granddaughter who had been banished to the backwoods of central Germany. Although Ducky had never wanted to marry Nicky—and in any case, dynastic and religious law would have forbidden the union— she couldn't help feeling that the crown of the Romanov consort had been perfectly crafted for her own head.

After all, Ducky was a true Romanov, with the blood of that ancient dynasty flowing through her veins. Her mother was the daughter of the Emperor Alexander II. Submerged since the beginning of her life in the chilly austerity of Victorian England and the rigid severity of rural Germany, Ducky had had only glimpses of her mother's native land. Although she had always felt a special affinity for Russia and was strongly attracted to its passion and exotic splendor, Ducky had so far seen it through a child's eyes.

Now, for the first time in her life, the indomitable Victoria Melita was discovering the most important part of herself. She had found a land with a spirit to match her own.

Listening to the glorious choir, "composed of the finest known male voices in the whole land," Ducky trembled. The "celestial" singing thundered through the vast church and then suddenly dwindled "to a still whisper." The chorus "implored, it triumphed, and it sorrowed, it conveyed an idea of the infinite, and while it lasted brought heaven down to earth."

As the chants echoed to the domes of the Ouspensky Cathedral's five golden cupolas, "a fragrant haze of incense" filled an atmosphere of pure golden light and made everything seem "more like a dream than reality." Wherever one looked, there was "gold, nothing but gold, with here and there the flash of a precious stone, red, blue or green." It seemed as if "every inch of wall and ceiling was covered with luminous frescoes." Before the altar stood the great iconostasis, a golden screen covered in a mass of jewels; "the light, filtering down from the cupolas and flickering from hundreds of candles, reflected off the surfaces of the jewels and the golden icons to bathe everyone present in iridescence."

The ceremony lasted five hours. The cynosure of every gaze was, quite naturally, the imperial couple, who sat on the altar in huge ancient thrones made of ivory and covered with hundreds of diamonds, rubies, and pearls. Ducky and Missy carefully studied the enigmatic empress. While admiring her beauty and sympathizing with her tragic childhood, they had always found her cold and difficult personality rebarbative. Ducky and Alix, in particular, had long been close to crossing swords, what with Alix's resentment of Ducky's presence in Darmstadt and of the problems in Ernie's marriage. Besides, the sisters-in-law were almost complete opposites.

Empress Alexandra grimly sleepwalked through the ceremonies, an uncomfortable "tightness about her lips" preventing even the "slightest of smiles." Alexandra "never relaxed this severely aloof attitude. . . . Nothing ever seemed to give her pleasure, she seldom smiled, and when she did, it was grudgingly as though making a concession. This of course damped every impulse towards her. In spite of her beauty no warmth emanated from her; in her presence enthusiasm wilted."

Ducky would have agreed with Missy's assessment. They found Alix "serious, earnest-minded, with a high sense of moral duty and a desire to-wards all that is good and right; she was nevertheless not of 'those who win'; she was too distrustful, too much on the defensive, she was no warming flame." To see her convinced them that "life, like all else, needs to be loved; those who cannot love life are vanquished from the very start."

After the coronation there followed several more days of celebra-tions—parades, balls, banquets, and processions. Fireworks illuminated the sky every night, painting the golden domes of the Kremlin with a brilliant rainbow. But amid the whirl came a tragedy that stunned the empire and, indeed, the world. It was a chilling and accurate preview of things to come.

On the morning of May 30 a huge traditional feast for the citizens of Moscow was being prepared on the field of Khodynka, just beyond the city. People had come from all over Russia, eagerly anticipating the free food and clothing and special souvenirs bearing the emperor's portrait. Later in the day Nicholas and Alexandra were to preside over the presentation of these prized souvenirs. But just after dawn a rumor began that there were not enough gifts and that only the first few hundred people would be receiving them. The immense crowd, many of whom were drunk, instantly surged forward and stampeded toward the souvenir booth, "the multitude all rushing at the same moment towards one point." Nearly five thousand men, women, and children were crushed to death. Within an hour the former scene of "rejoicing and good cheer" had been turned into "a bloody disaster as sinister as a battlefield."

The massacre was blamed, in part, on Ducky's uncle Grand Duke Serge, who as governor of Moscow was responsible for the supervision of the proceedings. The imperial family wanted to cancel the rest of the celebrations and go into mourning. The emperor and empress especially wished to call off the ball at the French embassy that evening; but France was Russia's chief ally and politics were politics, so they were compelled to attend.

As public condemnation fell upon Ducky's hapless uncle Serge, his saintly wife's "despair was painful to see." The suffering of Aunt Ella brought her brother and his wife closely to her side. Ernie tried to comfort his sister, but Ducky was confused in her feelings. Having idolized her as Cousin Ella, and then as Aunt Ella, the wife of her mother's handsome brother Serge, Ducky now had to relate to her as an unhappy sister-in-law.

After attending the rather somber French gala embassy on the evening of the gruesome Khodynka tragedy, Ducky and Missy embarked on a whirl of fêtes and balls. During the next week, "one Embassy after the other gave brilliant receptions, the Great Powers vying with each other in pomp and splendour." Giddy almost to the point of euphoria, Missy entered into the festivities with abandon and helped to lift Ducky out of her depression.

But soon Ducky was in posession of "a closely-guarded secret."

Surrounded wherever they went by dashing and handsome admirers, the two sisters, "the most radiant . . . of all the the Royal beauties," engaged in one flirtation after another. All were light-hearted and innocent—except one.

Ducky's superbly handsome cousin Grand Duke Kirill had been cherishing his youthful memories of her as much as she had been thinking of him. Their previous adolescent attraction had been so strong that neither of them had ever forgotten it. Now, seeing each other again at this glorious pageant, during such a dramatically heightened moment in history, with the Romanov family reaffirming itself and proclaiming its power, the cousins discovered the deepest desires of their own hearts.

After three weeks of sitting next to each other at banquets, gazing at one another during ceremonies and parades, talking quietly at family parties, and dancing gracefully together in court balls, Ducky and Kirill realized that they were in love as "their mutual passion grew more demanding."

Ducky did her best to hide her feelings. But it was of little use. While Missy quite openly conducted a playful flirtation with Kirill's wayward younger brother, Boris, and totally escaped censure, Ducky tried to wear a mask of indifference. But for any observant eye, "the birth of the love affair was clear to see."

Ducky and Kirill well knew that there could be no future for them together. Divorce for Ducky was still out of the question, and, even if it could have been arranged, the disgrace would be intolerable. Besides, there remained the bar that had always been present: Russian imperial law and the Orthodox Church forbade the marriage of first cousins.

Ducky forced herself to go off with Ernie for a month's stay at Ella and Serge's country home, Ilinsky, in the forested hills near Moscow, while Kirill dutifully went with his father to the annual fair at Nizhni Novgorod, Russia's great medieval city on the upper reaches of the Volga.

The purpose of going to Ilinsky was "to recover from the fatigues of the Coronation festivities." But the house party soon became much livelier than expected—an unending series of horseback rides, cruises on the river, carriage jaunts, dances, picnics, moonlight suppers, and visits to other country houses. "Amusement followed amusement," and the revelers' every move was accompanied by "wild, wailing, laughing, sobbing gypsy melodies at all hours of the day and night." June was "a period of buoyant, almost mad gaiety, a giddy whirl of enjoyment."

Serge and Ella were thankful to escape the horrible shadow of Khodynka. Nicholas and Alexandra were happy to be out of the public spotlight, relaxing in the informality of the secluded country estate. Ducky and Ernie kept a polite distance from each other. Missy and her husband were staying nearby at Archangelsky, the palace of the wealthy Yousupoff family, and she and Ducky were, as always, inseparable. And of course, Marie had come along too, observing their every pleasure "with a certain disapproval." Continuing to exasperate her daughters with her incessant critical commentary on every aspect of their appearance and behavior, the duchess found a skilled accomplice in her rigid and judgmental brother Serge. Fortunately, most of Marie's time was taken up with fussing over her little granddaughter Elizabeth, who was already showing signs of being a promising candidate for perfection.

Ducky's older brother, Alfred, was also a member of the party at Ilinsky; much to her dismay, he was already showing signs of an unstable personality and rapidly dissipating character. More than ever, she felt helpless to intervene in her twenty-one-year-old brother's downward spiral. He was living an independent life now in the unwholesome military arena of Berlin, progressing from one bad habit to another. But behind his tired blue eyes brother Alfred was as lovable as always.

One afternoon toward the end of the idyllic holiday, Missy was swimming in the river when the strong current caught her and "suddenly began to swirl me away." Just as she thought for sure that she was going to drown, Alfred grabbed her and saved her life. If only his sisters had been able to do the same for him.

July signaled the breakup of this family reunion. Ducky, who had been doing her best to occupy herself with Missy and forget Kirill, broke down and sobbed when it was time to climb aboard their separate trains.

There was very little to cheer the disheartened grand duchess of Hesse as she sat alone in her drawing room on the train while her husband concentrated all of his attention on their baby daughter. The vast Russian landscape unfolded monotonously, baked by an almost constant sun.

Inside the stifling train Ducky was dizzy from the intense heat, but she wished the unpleasant journey home would never end. As the coaches rolled closer and closer to the border, she realized how much she really wanted to stay behind in Russia.

CHAPTER NINETEEN

The
Marble Man

DUCKY AND ERNIE retreated to Wolfsgarten. The unusually warm summer and the exhausting coronation festivities combined to make the young couple lethargic and reflective. For the remainder of that season, a reasonable facsimile of harmony reigned at the Grand Ducal Palace.

Having observed the bliss of Nicky and Alix's marriage, both Ducky and Ernie felt frustrated and depressed by the failure of their own. Separately, they each tried to analyze what had gone so wrong and how it could be put right. Ducky vowed to swallow her disappointments and keep her temper. Ernie awkwardly tried to be more considerate and attentive. But a vital spark was still missing, and neither husband nor wife understood why.

By the time the leaves began changing color, the dispirited couple had to abandon introspection to prepare for a visit from their newly crowned relatives. Right after leaving Ilinsky, Nicky and Alix had begun a tour of Europe, making formal state visits and private courtesy calls on their fellow sovereigns. They went first to Vienna to pay their respects to the aging Emperor Franz Josef of Austria-Hungry, then to Breslau for the ordeal of visiting the overbearing kaiser. After that came ten tranquil days in Copenhagen with Nicky's grandparents the king and queen of Denmark; they then yachted to Scotland to visit Alix's grandmother, Queen Victoria, who was "marvelously kind and amiable to us."

Nicholas and Alexandra's state visit to France was triumphant and exhilarating, with an "outpouring of emotion . . . by the people and soldiers." The imperial couple left reluctantly, and Nicholas instantly disdained the stolid reserve of Germany. He found everything so "black and dark and boring" that he found it "unpleasant to look out of the window" of the imperial train.

Considering the opinion of his wife's homeland with which Nicholas began his stay at Wolfsgarten, it is not surprising that he didn't enjoy himself. Besides, the two brothers-in-law disliked each other. The reason was simple—a polarization of temperaments and interests. While Ernie was flighty and mercurial to the point of giddiness, interested in pranks and in the rarefied atmosphere of the arts, Nicky was serious-minded and sincere, a simple and straightforward fellow plainly devoted to his obligations and duties. Suddenly placed together, the whimsical poet prince and the unimaginative emperor had little to say to each other.

Mirroring their disaffection was the acrimony of their wives. The old resentment Ernie's sister had of his wife was rekindled by the visible signs of the marriage's failure; as for Ducky, she was alternately bored and irritated by the prudish empress's "narrow-minded devotion to 'Kinder, Kirche, Kleider und Kuche' " (children, church, clothes, and kitchen).

It was testimony to the great love between Alix and Ernie that these reunions took place at all. Brother and sister, having been so closely united by the tragic losses of their youth, were to remain deeply devoted to each other for the rest of their lives. And Alix always maintained a strong attachment to her childhood home, where she could escape the tensions and rigid constraints of the Russian court. In an effort to make his illustrious sister at home as much as possible, Ernie erected a golden onion-domed Russian Orthodox church right in the center of his artist's colony, the Mathildenhohe, at the edge of Darmstadt.

After Nicky and Alix departed in the fall of 1896, Ernie and Ducky quickly reverted to discord and strife. Perhaps the example of the imperial visitors only emphasized the impossibility of their own marriage.

During the gloomy autumn and winter of that year, Ducky sank into a depression. What she had hoped she could wipe from her mind slowly crept back into her thoughts and consumed her consciousness:

Kirill.

Where was he now? When would she ever see him again?

Ducky's Russian cousin was as lovesick and frustrated as she was. Hoping to add to his son's education "with an impression of the artistic beauties of Europe," Kirill's father sent him on a tour of Italy in the autumn of 1896; Kirill visited "everything that was worth seeing there from the Lakes in the North to Sicily." When his Mediterranean sojourn was completed, the grand duke tried to forget his cousin during the "uninterrupted succession of balls and parties" that made up a St. Petersburg social season which "was one of the most brilliant that could be imagined." After that, Kirill began his service with the 1st Company of the Imperial Naval Guards.

In a family of astonishing masculine specimens, Grand Duke Kirill Vladimirovich was considered the most handsome and impressive. He had been born at Tsarskoe Selo on October 13, 1876, just a month and a half before Ducky. His father was Grand Duke Vladimir, the third son of Emperor Alexander II and the brother of Ducky's mother. A scholar, "Uncle Vladimir was the most erudite of Mama's brothers." History being his favorite topic, "there was not a name, date, or event he did not know by heart." Genial, humorous, and with a loud, ringing voice, Grand Duke Vladimir was an exceptionally cultured and worldly man who loved to entertain as many interesting guests as possible in his lively home. Like all the Romanov men, he was also a soldier "heart and soul." And, like all of Ducky's Russian uncles, "he could be uncomfortably outspoken and his voice being unusually sonorous and carrying, his remarks could occasionally be disconcerting." His temper and booming voice terrorized his meek nephew Emperor Nicholas II, and he effectively dominated the novice sovereign during the first several years of his reign. But even though he could be intimidating, Ducky's gruff and sophisticated uncle "was the most kindly gentleman in every way."

Kirill adored his father. Admiring his "strict conservative nineteenth-century principles," he saw Vladimir as "an exceedingly kind man, one respected by all for the nobility of his character as well as for his culture and profound erudition." The relationship couldn't have been closer; to the end of his life, Kirill remembered his father as "my dearest friend," to whom he could always turn to for advice and support.

Kirill's mother, the worldly, supremely confident, and accomplished grand duchess Marie Pavlovna, the daughter of the grand duke of Mecklenburg-Schwerin, had been raised in northern Germany. She was known to Ducky as Aunt Miechen. More concerned than her husband was with her social position in St. Petersburg, the grand duchess was often absent from her home, so was not the influence on Kirill and the other children that their doting father was.

Marie Pavlovna, although "an incomparably amiable hostess [who] . . . knew to perfection how to receive all manner of men," was jealous of the emperor and empress and resentful of her husband's secondary rank. Considering themselves far superior to the unsophisticated Alexander III and his family, Marie Pavlovna and Vladimir were highly critical of the throne and contemptuous of the sovereigns. The feeling was mutual, and eventually a feud would develop between the families, thanks primarily to the insatiable ambition of the formerly insignificant princess from Mecklenburg-Schwerin.

What Kirill's mother lacked in political power she made up for in stylish display. Indulged by her husband, "she could spend what she would, every luxury, every comfort, every honour, every advantage were hers and she was one of the best-dressed women of her time: her clothes were superlatively smart and she had the great art of knowing exactly what to wear for each occasion; she never made a mistake." Ducky and Missy appreciated the uniqueness of their aunt Miechen, whom they viewed as "one of life's spoiled children." They were especially awed by her ability to manipulate those around her; Miechen expected "everyone who approached her to continue the spoiling, which they generally did, and yet it was she who appeared to be dispensing favors."

Regardless of her lively wit and charm, however, the self-obsessed Marie Pavlovna must have been a very unsatisfactory mother.

There were four children, three sons and a daughter. Kirill was the eldest, although there had been an older boy named Alexander who had died a year after his birth. Kirill and his younger brothers, Boris and Andrei, were close in age and grew up together inseparable. They, in turn, were devoted to their baby sister, Helen, whom they alternately teased and bullied, once taking turns smothering her with a pillow after having seen *Othello*.

Kirill grew up at the magnificent imperial palace of Tsarskoe Selo. He was a handsome and well-behaved little boy who romped in the woods and rode his black pony, Ugoloek, through the great park. But it was Tsarskoe Selo's large artificial lake that drew him most. Kirill loved to go sailing and rowing on it; these pastimes were, he recalled later, "my first introduction to water upon which I was to pass so much of my life."

Because Grand Duke Vladimir enjoyed the countryside so much, the family stayed at Tsarskoe Selo for as long as they could, not moving back to the city for the winter season until January. Their town house, the Vladimir Palace, stood on the Neva embankment in St. Petersburg. What most impressed the small Kirill about the immense, Florentine-style palace was the novelty of gaslight, which illuminated the endless passageways, and the Carcelle oil lamps, "which were wound up like clocks by special lampmen."

In St. Petersburg Kirill's parents threw famous dinners, parties, and balls, which thrilled even the jaded Russian aristocracy. It was also here that the children received visits from their grandfather Emperor Alexander II. Alexander took a great interest in Kirill and his brothers; they "were Grandpapa's special favourites." He bought them little stuffed soldiers dressed in the various uniforms of the Imperial Guards and "a wooden 'hill'—a kind of slanting platform from which we used to slide down on a carpet one after the other."

The murder of Alexander II was the first tragedy of his young grandson's life. The little prince and his cousin Ducky, both five years old, stood at the windows of the Winter Palace and watched the elaborate funeral procession, fascinated by the street lamps which had been "shrouded in black." The concept of regicide was, of course, beyond the children's comprehension.

The center of Kirill's childhood was his English nurse, Millicent Crofts, whom the adoring children called Milly. Milly loved Kirill as if he were her own, singing nursery rhymes to him in the evening and later reading aloud from *Barnaby Rudge* and *Oliver Twist*. Because of her, the first language the youngsters learned to speak was English.

When Kirill reached his eighth birthday, his father called him and his two younger brothers into his study and momentously announced: "You are to have a supervisor for your studies; obey him as you obey me."

At first intimidated, Kirill was soon reveling in the adventure of seeking knowledge. The "supervisor" was General Alexander Daller, a retired artillery officer who seemed ancient to the boys. Because Kirill's parents spent much of the year traveling to the warmer climates of Western Europe to accommodate the grand duchess's delicate health, the squadron of tutors selected by the conscientious General Daller became influential figures in the boy's young life.

Daller himself had a strong influence on Kirill and quite capably filled in for the absent Vladimir. An excellent amateur carpenter, he passed on his enthusiasm to his eager young charge and taught him how to work with his hands, a skill which Kirill would cherish his entire life. In the evening Daller fascinated Kirill and his brothers with dramatic readings from the imaginative new novels of Jules Verne.

Next to Daller, the most important guiding force in Kirill's boyhood was his religious instructor and spiritual guide, Father Alexander Diernoff. This pious and scholarly priest gently introduced him to the history and principles of the Russian Orthodox Church and established a profound devotion that would later bring great conflict to Kirill's conscience.

With the exception of an ineffectual history tutor, Kirill's instructors were excellent. Mr. Browne, his English teacher, introduced him to the novels of Sir Walter Scott and the plays of Shakespeare. The German tutor, Herr Kerzerau, was also the physical training instructor. The slender, well-built Kirill became an expert gymnast and grew fond of riding, swimming, skating, and especially golf. And from Herr Kindiger, the music professor, Kirill acquired a passion for music and learned to play the piano. He would later boast that "all my life I have been a keen musician."

When Kirill became a teenager his parents took him on their foreign sojourns. His first trip abroad was to the Swiss resort of Vevey on Lake Geneva. In Paris they stayed at the Hôtel Continental on the rue de la Paix; at San Sebastián on the northern coast of Spain, the grand ducal family visited the Spanish royal family and swam in the chilly ocean using the queen's wondrous "bathing machine," a large compartment on rails that was lowered into the water and pulled out by a steam engine to adjust to the changing tides.

When Kirill turned fifteen, in the autumn of 1891, he began training for the naval college. He continued his regular lessons in literature, language, history, religion, music, and the arts, but also undertook to study mathematics, chemistry, mechanics, and the other sciences, which were "virgin soil" for him.

Kirill not only met this academic challenge but used it to his advantage, being inspired to organize his time, "to divide the hours of the day, and set aside time for rest, and physical exercise, without which the mind is more apt to exhaust itself." Even at this early age, Kirill had set himself toward success. The importance of academic achievement in Russia during this time had created a mercilessly competitive atmosphere; fear of failing darkened every young student's life. Indeed, "examinations were always considered a matter of family honor," and any "boy or girl who failed in them was a disgrace."

While Kirill was struggling with the principles of navigation, he was also being introduced to the rules of St. Petersburg high society, trivial but "necessary equipments for setting out upon the course of life." At dancing lessons and parties arranged by his mother, he met girls of his own age for the first time. His favorite was a pretty young aristocrat named Dally Cantakouzene.

But no sooner had his romantic education begun than it, and his youth, came to an abrupt end. It was time for Grand Duke Kirill Vladimirovich to begin his naval career. At the age of fifteen, in the summer of 1892, he went to sea, as a midshipman on His Imperial Majesty's Ship Moriak.

The shock of leaving home and being alone in a crude and violent environment "was a rude awakening" to the young prince who, until then, "had experienced nothing but the very best examples of polished manners, of kindness, justice, and exalted moral and ethical standards in a home that was typical of the very best traditions of a brilliant and cultured period."

Although Kirill had never been pampered, nothing could have prepared him for the brutality of life on a Russian ship. H.I.M.S. Moriak was a top-heavy, poorly constructed, entirely unseaworthy vessel, "a monument to inefficiency, an embodiment of the conception of failure."

As if his physical environment weren't daunting enough, the human factor was even worse. The Moriak's commander was an obscene, bullying sadist, "a pestilent fellow" who lived only "to ill-treat the crew like a devil." From morning till night, his "savage outbursts of violence" and cursing brutalized the crew. Kirill, "who had scarcely ever heard an angry word spoken" in his home, now listened to an unending stream of the most violent language imaginable, which "excelled itself in unadulterated filth."

As traumatic as this new life was, the young prince managed to adapt quickly, making friends with the other boys apprenticed on the training ship. For Kirill, who had so successfully organized his life and mastered his previous studies, the brutal challenge of the Moriak was just another opportunity to perfect his natural skill at making the most of what life offered. And the thrill of training aloft mitigated the tyranny of shipboard life. Because it was necessary to know every detail of the sails and ropes and riggings, Kirill spent much of his time clambering about "like a little monkey."

Finally, the head of the naval college board of examiners arrived to test the midshipmen's knowledge and skills. Kirill passed with high marks, bringing his hideous days on the *Moriak* to a welcome conclusion. In time he came to believe that, although "it was a rude entry into the world," it had been an invaluable experience for his future life.

Kirill's next concern was the important naval college examination he was scheduled to take in three years. The test covered an enormous range of knowledge and required long, intensive study. He returned home to Tsarskoe Selo in the winter of 1892 and spent the following year with special tutors, absorbing facts and figures as fast as he could.

In the summer of 1893 he went to sea again. Unfortunately, this experience was little better than the first. His training ship, the *Prince Pojarsky,* was of the same "antediluvian design" as the *Moriak,* and it also, unhappily, featured a similar "continuous flow of abuse" from a brutish captain "addicted" to beating the crew. Cruising the placid Gulf of Finland, Kirill and his fellow cadets slaved away while continuing to study for the naval college exam. It was a relief for Kirill to leave the ship in the autumn of 1893 and accompany his parents, brothers, and sister to Spain.

With his historian father as a perfect guide, Kirill discovered the treasures of the Iberian peninsula, traveling to Madrid, Barcelona, Valencia, Valladolid, Saragossa, and many other cities and towns. They completed their tour with a short voyage to the Balearic Islands. Kirill marveled at the "luxuriant and ethereal beauty" of Majorca.

On his return, Kirill buried himself with his tutors at the Vladimir Palace in St. Petersburg, working night and day to make up time on his studies. The following summer he joined his third training ship, the frigate *Vovin,* which, he happily discovered, was of the latest design and commanded by an unusually civilized captain.

A few months later Kirill's uncle Sasha, the emperor Alexander III, died suddenly after a short illness. The perceptive eighteen-year-old realized that the emperor's passing was far more significant than a personal loss: "His death was the beginning of the end." It had been Uncle Sasha's policy "to keep the Imperial Family united in a bond of friendship and peace." But now that Kirill's passive cousin Nicky was the ruler of Russia, "never again was there to be that same spirit of understanding among us, that easy fellowship and gay merriment. All that had come to a final conclusion."

Ironically, Kirill and Nicky were the best of friends at the start of the new reign. The young grand duke was the best man at Nicky's wedding. But Kirill had little time to spend with his relatives. In the months after Nicky's accession he studied harder than ever for his naval examinations; he passed with excellent scores and was promoted to the rank of petty officer. In the summer he was assigned to his fourth and last training ship, the *Vernyl,* and spent several gloomy months drifting in the heavy fogs of the Baltic Sea.

That autumn he made his first solo trip abroad, climbing the mountains of Switzerland and paying a short visit to Coburg to see his aunt Marie and uncle Alfred, Ducky's parents. Kirill had a special fondness for his father's only sister, and for her husband, who had had such an illustrious career in the glorious English navy. While his young nephew sat listening with shining eyes, the duke of Coburg recounted one sea adventure after another. Other evenings were spent performing music with the duchess. The affection between Kirill and his aunt and uncle helped greatly to increase his infatuation with Ducky. And he found it very easy to fall hopelessly in love with his cousin during the excitement of Nicky's coronation the following year.

Their parting after the Coburg visit had been much more difficult for Ducky. While she had little more to look forward to than the continuation of a miserable marriage, he gazed ahead to a future of unlimited promise. Naturally inclined to lightheartedness, Kirill responded to his romantic difficulties with buoyant determination. The seeming impossibility of their love was just another challenge to be met head on. With the arrogance of youth, the twenty-year-old grand duke knew what it took to be a winner.

As Ducky suffered through the spring of 1897, sharing lunch and dinner and little else with her husband, Kirill was beginning life in the Naval Guards. In March he went to Cannes with his brother Boris, taking the opportunity to visit Ducky's parents at their winter home, the Château Fabron in nearby Nice. Because Affie "was very proud of his Russian relations, and liked them to meet members of the English Royal Family," he arranged for his favorite Romanov nephew to meet his mother, who was staying at the Hôtel Cimiez. Kirill anticipated this meeting with mixed feelings. Having grown up in a very anti-English home—his father despised the queen for her supposed ill-treatment of his only sister, the duchess of Coburg, and his mother was "an ardent supporter of Bismarck and Emperor William II"—the young man didn't quite know where his loyalties should lie. Although he admired his uncle, he prepared for the worst.

Joining the queen for lunch at her hotel, Kirill was pleasantly surprised by her agreeable manner. He departed with "a very favorable impression" of Victoria and came to the conclusion that "there was something quite distinctive about her, which only a strong personality can convey on the first acquaintance."

Returning to Russia, Kirill quickly established himself in St. Petersburg society. Within the next few years, this handsomest and most charming of all the grand dukes would become something of a legend among his own generation.

The other members of the imperial family regarded Kirill with envy. His cousin Grand Duke Alexander Mikhailovich, described him as being "built like an Apollo, kind-hearted and gay." And he was in awe of the "highly pleasing combination of social virtues which made [Kirill] immensely popular and left nothing to be desired even by the fastidious maître d'hôtel of the Ritz in Paris. He tipped lavishly, he traveled often, he danced well." Even Kirill's uncles, who had established the dashing reputation of the Romanov men, easily conceded his attraction: "We, the elders of the clan, felt slightly jealous of his endowments. Wherever we went we met people who expected us to measure up to the standards of handsomeness and generosity established by our nephew."

Smiling and confident, "the idol of all women and the friend of most of the men," Kirill "ruled over the 'younger set' in St. Petersburg, resplendent in his uniform of the Sailors Regiment of the Imperial Guard, benevolent and towering."

However, not everyone was completely dazzled. There was a dissenter, a very important one: Missy.

She referred to Kirill as the Marble Man—beautiful and majestic, but cold. "I don't think you would like Kirill," she confided to one of her close friends; "he is an extraordinary cold and selfish man, you never can feel really happy and jolly with him, he seems to freeze you up, has such a disdaining way of treating things and people."

Missy's hostility may have been the result of simple incompatibility, but possibly it was due to an unconscious jealousy. If Kirill's privileged place in her sister's heart wasn't threatening enough for Missy, his looks

and confidence were. While Missy had an understanding word for almost every human who crossed her path, and felt empathy even for her
enemies, she was hostile to men she considered "too handsome." Kirill
certainly fit into this category. Perhaps, used to being the center of attention, Missy secretly resented the competition of a male beauty who
escaped her charm.

But even if the handsome, cocksure Kirill did look at the world
through cool gray eyes "with an expression of fastidious contempt," he
seemed exactly what Ducky so desperately needed.

CHAPTER TWENTY

The
Awful Truth

"T RAVELLERS, LIKE POETS, are mostly an angry race," Sir
Richard Burton had written in his journal more than forty years before. This observation certainly applied to the restless young grand ducal
couple of Hesse. The unhappy husband and wife had exhausted the escape offered by their social life; early in 1897, when they suddenly tired
of playing host and hostess to their numerous relatives at the royal playground of Wolfsgarten, they fled, lest they be forced to face each other
and admit the failure of their marriage.

The choice of where to go was an easy one.

Ever since visiting Missy in her new homeland four years earlier,
Ducky had longed to return to Romania. The country appealed enormously to her passionate nature and she was eager to explore it. She was
equally anxious to be with Missy again, to share the laughter of their
carefree youths, and to commiserate with each other over the frustrations of their empty marriages.

Ducky and Ernie journeyed east by rail across Germany, Austria,
Hungary to the towering Transylvanian Alps, and then down to the flat,
broad plains of Wallachia where Bucharest, the gay and elegant "Paris of
the Balkans," awaited them like a marvelous vision from a fairy tale.
Missy and Ducky's "joy at being together and sharing all things again,
knew no bounds."

Missy later confessed that "we were probably looked upon as two
frivolous young ladies, and were no doubt severely criticized by those

wiser and steadier than we were. But for both of us it was a period of magnificent enjoyment which the disapproval of others could not mar."

As always, the most challenging obstacle to Missy's fun was her nemesis, the king, who continued to dominate his family as thoroughly as he did his country. King Carol was determined to make a success of the new Romanian monarchy; if his transplanted German dynasty was to take permanent root in this hostile Balkan soil, his actions and those of every member of his family would have to be beyond reproach. Unfortunately for the high-spirited Missy, the king's dynastic insecurity produced a mercilessly rigid code of conduct. Almost all forms of frivolity were taboo.

Missy and her husband, Ferdinand, known as Nando, couldn't make a move without the king's approval. Although they "would never dare accept an invitation without his special consent," the crown prince and crown princess found Ducky's visit a perfect opportunity for at least momentary freedom. "Having visitors who had to be entertained, we were able to reach out towards a certain emancipation up to the present denied us," Missy later remembered. "With 'the fighting Grand Duchess' to back her up," Missy "broke through most of King Carol's restrictions" and joined her sister in a whirl of laughter and fun. For Missy, "to have Ducky as a companion was unutterable happiness."

At parties, balls, and banquets, Ducky and Missy discovered the hedonistic Romanian nobility. The first thing these two proper young granddaughters of Queen Victoria realized was that only two matters concerned this unique aristocratic circle: love and power. The Romanians never thought to control their desires or "temper their immediate gratification." Supposedly, at that time there was no word in the Romanian language for self-control—"the term and idea being equally untranslatable to the Roumanian mind."

Ducky and Missy marveled at the web of love affairs that surrounded every member of society. The sisters came to the conclusion that in Bucharest "life was not a pilgrimage toward character development, but a game of intrigue played with a nimble mind and a passionate heart."

Facilitating this free-for-all game of love was the Romanian Orthodox Church. The state church officially sanctioned three marriages for every person. Ducky blinked with amazement as she was continually introduced to society ladies and their past, present, and future husbands, often casually co-existing in the same dining room or parlor.

This pragmatic approach to love and marriage must have had an enormous impact on a beautiful and unhappily married young woman like Ducky. Without considering Romanian hedonism as a possible solution to her own problems, Ducky was comforted by the knowledge that some people were bold and practical enough not to allow themselves to be doomed to a life of unhappiness.

But Ducky had little time to think at length about anything during her Romanian sojourn. From morning until late each night her days were crowded with diversions. Passionate about dancing, the two sisters were the first to arrive at court balls and the last to leave, twirling about the dance floor "till our feet ached." They spent most of their time together, leaving their husbands to amuse themselves. Although Ernie and Nando were complete opposites, they got along very well together, the grand duke's high spirits infecting his withdrawn and apathetic brother-in-law.

Missy also appreciated her sister's lively husband. She found Ernie to be "the gayest of companions" who was "full of almost feverish life." But the crown princess saw trouble beneath this pleasing surface: "There was something effervescent about him, rather restless even; he was highly strung and had the artistic temperament developed to the highest degree."

The highlight of that winter season in Bucharest was a costume ball given by the royal family at the Cotroceni Palace. For weeks both Ducky and Missy planned their special costumes in secret, not divulging their choices even to each other. When the night of the ball finally arrived they were startled and amused to find that they had each chosen to appear as the heroine of a recent Edmond Rostand play, *La Princesse Lointaine*. (She had been played by Sarah Bernhardt.) Even their gowns were similar, the only difference being that Ducky's was white with "large pearly lilies worn over the ears, while Missy wore black and gold Indian tissue with red roses instead of lilies." Because these long, clinging gowns made dancing almost impossible, the sisters withdrew before the cotillion began and, this time carefully coordinating their efforts, reappeared in different costumes—Ducky dressed as the moon, and Missy as the sun.

During the day, as the weather improved, Missy arranged picnics and riding parties to the forests beyond the city. She and Ducky "were in the saddle nearly every day." Galloping across the flat Wallachia countryside, the sisters imagined they were children again in Malta, racing toward life, chasing dreams of wonder and romance.

As reckless as they were restless, Ducky and Missy extended their equestrian excursions to the forbidden peasant villages and Gypsy camps hidden in the woods. Missy was quick to realize "now that I had Ducky as a companion I could indulge in that suppressed desire to know Roumania more intimately from that side which made it so different from the Western countries to which we were accustomed. She took the same interest in it as I did, so that everything became worth while."

The Gypsies fascinated the sisters the most. Leaving the safety of their carriage, they would march forward and "penetrate undismayed among the tents, climbing over heaps of indescribable refuse, gazing about us full of interest but not without a shudder."

"Bewildered, dazed, half attracted, half repelled," Ducky and Missy were most fascinated by the old Gypsy women, who looked to them like fairytale witches. "Crouching above mysterious black pots, standing motionless at the dark mouths of their tents, leaning on their staves, gazing with bleared eyes at visions of their own or coming slowly towards us through the dust, wrinkled, toothless, crooked, they were almost too good to be true."

After returning from such adventures, the sisters put on their finest dresses and spent the late afternoon and early evening riding in their carriage up and down the Chaussée Kisselev, a large open park at the end of Bucharest's main boulevard, the Calea Victoriei. Lined with four rows of lime trees and surrounded by villas and fashionable outdoor cafés, the chaussée was a perfectly Parisian setting. It was the custom in Bucharest for society to gather there during the last hours of sunlight and parade back and forth in their carriages, showing off their exquisite attire and magnificent horses. Trotting out across the park, the carriage horses would then return at walking speed, "so as to let the horses regain their breath and allow a mutual review of the ladies' smart dresses."

Always riding together in the same carriage, the sisters "would dress up in consequence, careful that our gowns, hats, cloaks, or parasols would be in pleasant harmony." Ducky and Missy "liked being as smart as possible." They often dressed alike and engaged in "certain eccentricities of attire." Their favorite get-up was a white drill cloth riding habit made "tout d'une pièce," "very tight-fitting as though moulded to our bodies, worn with a belt around the middle." The sisters wore matching white boots, and their hats, huge, boat-shaped Empress Eugénies, were made of black felt with two flowing plumes, one white and the other black.

The future German chancellor Count Bernhard von Bülow encountered the sisters on the chaussée one afternoon and later remarked that "a prettier picture could not be imagined than Grand Duchess Victoria, side by side with her blond sister."

Ernie and Nando also participated in these daily promenades, although not with their wives. They drove in their own carriage, and, each time they passed by, saluted Ducky and Missy, who "answered with becoming grace." The men of the royal family enjoyed the privilege of driving with a magnificent-looking chasseur perched next to the coachman and dressed in a green and silver uniform with long plumes flying from his bicorne hat. The women "had to content themselves with a mere footman."

The "giddy and frivolously inclined" sisters, dedicated to "purposely exaggerating our affectations," decided that they wouldn't be happy until they also had a chasseur. They begged Nando for permission, but the crown prince, a chauvinist and a slave to rules and regulations, dismissed their request.

"But it looks so much smarter," they insisted. "Why should your carriage be smarter than ours?"

Nando stood his ground, and the more his wife and sister-in-law insisted, the more adamant he became.

But the mischievous sisters were determined to have the last laugh.

Stealing the uniform of King Carol's chasseur, Ducky and Missy convinced a young officer to put it on and ride with them in their carriage. Ernie had been let in on the secret so that everyone's ride through the chaussée that afternoon could be timed for the very best effect. As the carriages approached each other, Nando recognized the uniform of his uncle's chasseur and raised his hand in a special salute he reserved only for his sovereign. Only when the carriages were side by side did the crown prince realize that he "was not honouring his august uncle, but instead his wayward young wife and sister-in-law." Turning pale with rage, the mortally embarrassed Nando said not a word.

Although Ernie roared with laughter and tried his best to convince his humorless brother-in-law that it had all been a fine joke, Nando seethed all the way back to the palace. He scolded the women that evening, but Ducky and Missy felt that the trick had been well worth it for the sake of "the horrified look on his face."

Ducky and Ernie had already prolonged their visit for much longer than they had originally planned. The Romanian air had seemed to stimulate their appetite for fun and ease the tensions of their marriage. Ernie seemed more relaxed than ever, and Ducky was so happy to be with her sister that she forgot how hopeless her life had been back in Darmstadt.

When Ernie's conscience told him that it was time to get back to running his own kingdom, he returned to Hesse. But Ducky remained in Bucharest. She was "so happy" being with Missy again that she "could not bear to tear herself away from her beloved sister." Here she was free to do as she pleased, free from the strict "code of behavior expected of a 'Landesmutter' at Darmstadt."

Although the dancing season was over, spring brought daily horseback rides, picnics, and excursions to villages of moss-covered cottages with ramshackle gardens, peculiar churches, and crumbling graveyards. One of Ducky and Missy's favorite pastimes was venturing to the hidden corners of Bucharest where fashionable society never went and searching through the odd little shops for "locally-produced leather, wood, pottery and metalcraft." The sisters would return home with their carriage "piled high with these strange acquisitions at which the servants scornfully turned up their noses."

Week after week Ducky and Missy frolicked like children. "We sisters 'let ourselves go,' " Missy wrote in her memoirs, "in the exhilarating delight of being together and each day we invented something new." At last their mother, back home in Coburg, became aware of their frivolous antics.

The duchess at once picked up her pen and fired off a warning to Ducky and Missy. She accused them of being "only too ready to get rid of your husbands. . . . Flirt, amuse yourselves, but don't lose your heart, men are not worth it and if you could, really could see their lives, you would turn away in disgust, for you would find there nothing but dirt, even in the lives of those who seem to you good and noble."

As summer approached, it was time for the delinquent grand duchess of Hesse to return to Darmstadt. Ducky had already stayed far longer than was considered proper. She had been separated from her husband for almost three months, and her prolonged absence was becoming difficult to explain. When the officers of Missy's honorary regiment, "who had a great admiration for my sister," began decorating Ducky's saddle with garlands of flowers, she finally realized that it was time to go home.

Once again, her sister's plucky handling of her own marriage inspired Ducky to try even harder to get along with Ernie. When she boarded the express and began her long journey to Darmstadt, she had almost reconciled herself to accepting her husband's neglect.

But in Hesse she was struck by a subtle change in her husband's demeanor. Ernie seemed more distant and nervous than ever, and the Wolfsgarten palace felt "awkward and strange, as if it had changed owners during her absence and she was now an unwelcomed visitor." Several of the servants, especially, seemed remote and somewhat secretive, whispering in corners and sometimes laughing together when Ducky passed by. Others appeared embarrassed and avoided looking her in the eye.

Ducky was at a loss—until one fateful morning when, searching for her husband, she entered his bedroom unannounced.

Exactly what happened will never be known, but to judge by what Ducky told her niece years later, she saw Ernie in bed with one of the teenaged boys employed in the palace kitchen. So great was the shock that Ducky was physically ill for several days, unable to face her husband or anyone else in the palace.

As she gradually regained her composure a deep sense of shame replaced her grief. For apparently almost everyone in the palace knew of the grand duke's proclivity. While Ducky had been away in Romania, he had been left alone to freely indulge it, and he had apparently carried on in the most indiscreet manner. "No boy was safe," Ducky bitterly told her niece, "from the stable hands to the kitchen help. He slept quite openly with them all."

The knowledge of Ernie's homosexuality devastated Ducky; the mere thought of it filled her with revulsion. She had had no previous experience of homosexual people and was at a complete loss. In fact, she could scarcely believe that such a thing as homosexuality existed. As far as she knew, her husband was the sole practitioner of this unspeakable vice.

Of course, Ernie was far from being alone in his sexual tastes. In the late nineteenth century "homosexuality lay at the very heart of Imperial Germany's politics, culture and society." Presiding over this male-glorifying civilization was Ducky's abrasive cousin Kaiser Wilhelm II—himself a latent homosexual.

Although the emotionally unstable kaiser "went through his life neither realising nor accepting his own homosexuality," the hidden existence of his true desires "helped to explain several of the peculiar characteristics of the emperor and—some would say—of his empire."

Ironically, male homosexuality in the Second Reich "was the vilest of offenses—and, paradoxically, the most prestigious." Under Paragraph

175 of the German penal code "anyone remotely associated with inversion was an unspeakable criminal" and subject to a long prison term of hard labor.

In 1906 the kaiser's closest companion, Prince Philipp von Eulenburg, would be exposed as a homosexual and brought to trial, causing a scandal that almost brought down the empire. For the rest of his life "Wilhelm never resolved his feelings for Eulenburg, never understood them, and certainly never labelled them." The kaiser was almost strangulated by his relentlessly hypermacho pose.

From the throne down, homosexuality occurred at every level and in every area of the German empire. Even the Fatherland's most cherished hero, Frederick the Great, had been a homosexual, as had been that eccentric castle-building Bavarian monarch Ludwig II, and another of Ducky's cousins, Prince Charles Edward of Albany, the son of her late Uncle Leopold and the future heir to her father's kingdom. Another Coburg cousin, Bulgaria's imported King Ferdinand, was married twice but spent most of his free time seducing the handsomest soldiers he could find, while the brother of the Austrian emperor, Archduke Ludwig Viktor, was romantically involved with the male masseur in a Vienna steambath. The old king of Württemberg "was in love with a mechanic," and all three of the kaiser's aides-de-camp, the kaiserin's private secretary, and the court chamberlain were sexually active homosexuals.

Even if Ducky had known that "the most virile men in the empire wrote gushing letters to one another," it is doubtful that she would have felt any better or been the slightest bit inclined to accept her husband's "disgusting nature."

With royal divorce taboo, Ducky seemed condemned to continue her hopeless marriage. Because sex, and most particularly "deviant sex," was a subject not even discussed between intimates, there was no place for Ducky to go with her grief. Most women would have been crushed by this experience, either collapsing into victimhood or searching for assistance. But Ducky, as proud, self-possessed, and independent as ever, stood her ground and silently planned the best possible course of action.

It was fortunate for her that she decided on discretion. Had she, in anger or confusion, attempted to expose Ernie's illicit conduct, the results could have been disastrous for her. Only five years later a similar situation arose in another illustrious German family, with a chilling and tragic conclusion.

The Krupp family were the wealthiest and most highly respected members of the Second Reich. Friedrich—"Fritz"—Krupp had spent a lifetime creating an industrial colossus, supplying the arms and munitions that made Germany the world's most formidable military power. Fritz was a close friend of the kaiser's. He was also a homosexual who kept a stable of young boys at his vacation playground on the Isle of Capri. Fritz indulged his pederasty to such an extravagant extent that he was eventually hounded out of Italy by the local police.

In 1902 some vengeful soul collected a batch of damning letters and photos and sent them to Krupp's wife, Marga. Understandably shocked and outraged by the revelation of her husband's "perversion," Frau Krupp could think of nothing better to do than to go directly to the kaiser himself and ask for his assistance in bringing Fritz to book.

But rather than offer help, the kaiser was furious at the distraught Marga for trying to make trouble. Wilhelm notified Fritz's friends, who decided to quiet the outraged wife by declaring that she suffered from hallucinations and was "in urgent need of prolonged treatment in an institution for nervous disorders." Fritz uneasily agreed.

The day after going to see the kaiser, a "wild-eyed and hysterical" Frau Krupp was taken from her home, dragged off to the mental hospital at Jena, and secretly locked in a padded cell. The night before he was to sign the papers commiting his wife to the asylum for life, Fritz committed suicide.

Had Ducky tried to make trouble, she might have suffered a similar fate.

Instead, she decided to ignore Ernie's vice and go her own separate way, embittered by his hypocrisy and duplicity, determined to one day exit the marriage at any cost.

Not until more than three decades later, when Missy's youngest daughter, Ileana, discovered that her handsome fiancé, Prince Lexel of Pless, was homosexual, would Ducky express her agony. In the meantime, she searched for an immediate escape from her humiliating situation at Wolfsgarten.

A few days later it came. A telegram arrived from Missy saying that Nando had come down with a virulent form of typhoid fever and was near death.

Without a second thought, Ducky packed her bags and rushed back to Bucharest and her sister's comforting arms.

CHAPTER TWENTY-ONE

A Royal Scandal

B ECAUSE NANDO'S PARENTS were unable to come from Sigmaringen, King Carol had forbidden Missy's family to rush to Romania to be with her, lest it suggest an unfavorable comparison. But as always, Missy's sister was a special exception; Nando's uncle "could not prevent Ducky from coming back" to be with the crown princess during the crisis.

Ducky arrived at the Cotroceni Palace in Bucharest in late May. Summoning every ounce of strength she had left, she comforted Missy as well as she could. Together, they kept vigil around the clock, watching Nando slip closer and closer to death as the days passed. "Several times he was at death's door" as the typhoid was aggravated by serious complications, including double pneumonia that almost killed him. He was kept alive only by "injections of salt water in great quantities, which tortured, but finally saved the patient."

Nando's convalescence was a "long and wearisome" one with numerous relapses of dangerously high fevers. To avoid the intense summer heat of the capital, the crown prince was moved to the cool air of the royal mountain retreat at Sinaia. Confined to his bed, the pale and exhausted young man appeared "almost a stranger" to his wife and sister-in-law. With a "gaunt waxen face, sunken cheeks and skeleton-like hands," Nando was permanently ravaged by the disease. His suffering had left him bald and old before his time. Missy's handsome husband was gone forever; in his place sat "a rather touching, bearded scarecrow."

Ducky wished she could have stayed through the summer, but since she had already spent most of the year in Missy's kingdom and her brother-in-law was now out of danger, it was impossible to stay away any longer from her own duties. And, there was an even more pressing reason for immediate departure. Grandmama Queen was celebrating her Diamond Jubilee in London, and all of her far-flung family was gathering for the festivities.

Of course, Nando and Missy could not attend. Ducky solemnly boarded her train in the middle of June and headed back to Darmstadt to face Ernie.

There was little time to deal with the problem of her marriage, however. Almost contemptuously ignoring her husband, Ducky immediately packed up her finest dresses and headed for London "in a sombre frame of mind," with Ernie quietly in tow.

The Diamond Jubilee, marking the sixtieth anniversary of Queen Victoria's accession, was the most magnificent celebration the British empire had ever seen, "a masterpiece of imperial propaganda." Ducky's grandmother had reigned longer than any other English monarch and, "held in that veneration which longevity inspires, she was beyond reproach." To her three hundred fifty million subjects across the globe, "like the sun and the moon, she was part of the order of nature."

On June 21, 1897, the old queen left Windsor Castle and went to London. As cheering crowds lined the streets, she was borne by carriage to Buckingham Palace, where a banquet was held that evening. The hundreds of royal guests were seated at tables of twelve chairs each; Ducky and Ernie were placed prominently at the queen's table. Ducky found herself sitting opposite her illustrious grandmother and between the exotic-looking crown prince of Siam and her handsome uncle the grand duke Serge of Russia. Although Ducky and Ernie's favored positions at her table might have been partially inspired by her special affection for them, it also seemed "as if Grandma particularly wanted to keep a close eye on these two grandchildren." Having heard rumors of the domestic problems at Darmstadt, the shrewd old woman peered out through her thick spectacles and searched for the truth herself.

The next morning Jubilee Day began with a cloudy sky, but as soon as Queen Victoria climbed into her carriage, the dark clouds drifted off and bright sunshine flooded the city for the remainder of the day. A "gorgeous procession" featuring the royal family and a colorful collection of the leaders of the empire's myriad nations streamed through the

streets of London from Buckingham Palace to St. Paul's Cathedral. Because the seventy–eight–year–old Victoria didn't think she could manage
the steep flight of steps leading up to the cathedral, the religious service
was celebrated on the pavement in front. (When Victoria's crusty old
cousin the grand duchess Augusta of Mecklenburg-Strelitz, witnessed
this unusual arrangement, she indignantly exclaimed, "After sixty years
of reign, and nothing better could be devised than to thank God in the
street!")

Also attending the jubilee celebration was Grand Duke Kirill. On his
first ship as a naval officer, he was on the maiden voyage of the *Rossya,*
Russia's newest and most impressive battleship, which had made its first
stop at Devonport as an official emissary to the jubilee. While the *Rossya*
was receiving a fresh coat of paint, Kirill went up to London and stayed
with his uncle Alfred and aunt Marie at Clarence House. In his memoirs
the tactful Kirill simply mentioned that "they had with them their
daughter Victoria Melita, then Grand Duchess of Hesse." Ernie's sister
the grand duchess Elizabeth of Russia and her husband, Serge, were also
guests at Clarence House, and this provocative grouping must have created a fascinating set of interpersonal dynamics.

It was awkward for Ducky and her estranged husband to be residing
with the man she truly loved. Ducky and Kirill had not yet become
lovers, but the more fate placed them in each other's company, the closer
they were coming to an understanding.

Also staying at Clarence House was Ducky's brother Alfred, looking
pale and unwell and more dissipated than ever. He was put on the same
floor as Kirill and, a lover of music, often invited his Russian cousin into
his rooms to play the "very ancient piano which he had." Seeing her
brother again, Ducky was alarmed by his deteriorating condition.
Plainly, Alfred was continuing his downward drift, but there seemed to
be nothing anyone could do.

The Jubilee Day ceremonies were "a continuous series of parties and
balls." Kirill was somewhat hindered by a "violent attack of hay fever."
He had to guide his horse in the procession with one hand while using
the other to hold his handkerchief to his nose. But he still managed to
have a good time and became one of the court's most popular dance
partners, enjoying himself "excellently" as he appreciated the beauty of
the women.

Ducky was also determined to enjoy herself. She went to every ball
and danced every dance, but seldom with her husband. For once,

"Ducky's flirtations seemed to amuse the Duchess." Indeed, Marie took "some measure of malicious delight" in seeing how much her English in-laws were upset by the obvious failure of the Hesse marriage. Since the duchess of Coburg had always resented Queen Victoria's imperious arrangement of the match, she was now gratified to find her daughter producing so much worry in what she disdainfully called "the English camp." Ducky's father had used the jubilee celebrations to indulge his alcoholism, and in consequence had enjoyed himself immensely, but her mother, true to form, passed the time ranting and raving about every characteristic of the British way of life.

Queen Victoria thought that time and further additions to their family would solve whatever problems were plaguing Ducky and Ernie. Less than a year before, she had written to Ernie's eldest sister, Princess Louis of Battenberg: "Your account of Ducky gave me great pleasure and I am sure she will become of more and more use to Ernie and she should be able to hold her own to be of use to him. I hope there will be another Baby—a Son, let us hope. Is there 'nothing' coming?" There was nothing.

By the time the jubilee festivities came to an end, Ducky and Kirill were even more deeply in love than before. Ducky so much wanted to divorce Ernie that she seriously considered approaching her grand-mother and asking her permission, but Grandmama Queen would never allow a divorce in her family. And feeling herself the perfect victim of Victoria's matchmaking, Ducky laid the responsibility for her misery right on the doorstep of the English royal family. The fact that Ernie still gushed like a schoolboy over "my own darling Grandma" and main-tained "his cheerful, unquestioning submission to her wishes" didn't im-prove matters any.

During this time Kirill had a much more positive attitude than Ducky toward Queen Victoria. His uncle Alfred had personally led him up to the queen and proudly said, "May I present to you my young nephew, who is on a Russian battleship." Seated in a low chair, the diminutive monarch smiled and spoke very kindly to the tall grand duke, who had to stoop down rather awkwardly to hear her. Since he had met her a few months before on the Riviera, Kirill was struck by a strong sense of déjà vu. But he was even more impressed with Victoria than he had been be-fore. Seeing her now in the full pomp and splendor of her court, he ad-mired the great authority she conveyed and marveled at her "very distinctive and striking" personality.

Before the jubilee came to an end, Kirill had to rejoin his ship and depart for the Pacific and the Far East. Unable to show her feelings, Ducky had to watch her love depart from Clarence House as if she were a casually affectionate cousin.

Ducky returned to Darmstadt that summer feeling more miserable and frustrated than ever. There seemed no solution to her problems, no hope of ever obtaining the happiness that she now could feel just beyond her reach. And, as if this were not enough, a scandal was about to make her life even more unbearable.

Ducky had not been as successful as she thought in hiding her passion for her Russian cousin. Although nothing overt had happened between them, the love they shared was visible to any perceptive observer, and whispers began spreading throughout the royal courts of Europe about the shocking scandal in Hesse. Further fueling the gossip were rumors of Ernie's homosexuality.

In such a tight-knit, small country, "it was impossible to keep secrets." From the court, rumors filtered out to military circles, and then to the citizens of the grand duchy. It was said that the dashing ruler of Hesse and the Rhine "showed a marked fondness for male kitchen hands and stable boys."

The whispers soon turned to talk. And the talk grew malicious. Throughout Darmstadt, "old ladies, over their tea, passed around photographs of the Grand Duke Kirill, remarking how good-looking he was." And the bohemian parties at Wolfsgarten inspired "strange and wild" tales. Suddenly, Hesse was crediting its handsome ruling couple with an imaginative list of unspeakable depravities.

When the gossip finally reached Queen Victoria at the beginning of 1898, she reluctantly summoned Sir George Buchanan, her chargé d'affaires in Darmstadt, to Windsor Castle. It was soon obvious from what he said that in the Hesse marriage "all was not well." Sir George was visibly embarrassed at "being unable to conceal from Victoria how tense relations were between her grandchildren." In answering his monarch's questions, "he chose his words with great care," but he couldn't help giving a fairly accurate description of the disintegrating marriage.

The old queen's eyes filled with tears.

"I arranged that marriage," she said very sadly. "I will never try and marry anyone again."

Queen Victoria might have felt guilty for having created such an unsatisfactory alliance, but she insisted that the marriage continue. And when Ducky and Ernie finally implored their grandmother to allow them to part, she "not only would not hear of it but expressed herself very strongly about the proposition."

The queen was not being deliberately cruel, nor, in her opinion, was she being foolishly rigid and closed-minded. In the romantic and idealized world of Victoria, compliments of Prince Albert, honor and duty and family came far above all else in life. Suffering was an important part of this world, as was self-denial. Marriage, being sacred, could not be terminated at convenience or will. And if children were involved, then the welfare of the unhappy parents was not to be considered.

Ducky and Ernie's daughter, three-year-old Princess Elizabeth, was the elderly queen's great joy. When she reached eighty the following year, 1899, it was this child whom Victoria asked to see first and to have wish her a happy birthday. The queen called Elizabeth "my precious," and Elizabeth called her "Granny Gran."

What bothered Victoria most about the failure of the Hesse marriage was its effect on little Elizabeth, whose happiness must not be jeopardized by the selfishness of her parents. With the child's well-being foremost in her mind, the queen determined that, no matter how miserable they might be together, Ducky and Ernie should never separate.

Ducky accepted this defeat, which was only temporary: Her grandmother was of an advanced age and in failing health. Riding furiously across the Hessian countryside, the discontented grand duchess vented her rage in the saddle, escaping from the hostile, gossipy atmosphere as often as she could. She was becoming ever more unpopular in the conservative homes of Darmstadt. Now, any comparisons with Ernie's saintly mother were made only by people with a cruel sense of humor.

To avoid her husband and his narrow-minded court, Ducky often stayed at Coburg, at the imperial court in Berlin, and with her younger sister Sandra in nearby Langenburg.

Meanwhile, Kirill was doing a good deal of traveling himself. The *Rossya* carried him through the Mediterranean and the Suez Canal to India, China, and Japan. Along the way he had climbed the Great Pyramid of Cheops, Egypt, walked through the Acropolis in Athens, and enjoyed the pleasures of a dozen different ports. But the grand duchess of Hesse was constantly in his thoughts, as he was in hers.

By coincidence, the *Rossya* had made an extended call at Malta, Ducky's birthplace and spiritual home. When it was time to leave, an eerie and "very odd" thing suddenly happened. The practical and level-headed Kirill explained it as "a phenomenon of Nature" but confessed that he "had never seen anything like it before."

Just as he and his fellow officers had boarded a steam launch and were proceeding across the harbor of Valletta toward the awaiting *Rossya,* "all of a sudden a strong wind blew upon us, violently and in gusts, as though from nowhere." Before they knew what was happening, the calm and cloudless day had instantly given way to a vicious and invisible storm that descended upon their small boat. The mountainous swells of the sea almost consumed them, and it was with "great danger and difficulty" that they were finally able to reach their battleship.

Although fully understanding the meteorological explanation for this bizarre occurrence, the shaken grand duke couldn't get over the impression that the savage storm "had been let loose upon us specially, by some malignant spirit of the place."

Indeed, for lovers as star-crossed as Ducky and Kirill, the storm was a perfect preview of what fate had in store.

CHAPTER TWENTY-TWO

Death and Reconciliation

A S 1899 BEGAN, Ducky was eager to leave the gloom of Darmstadt and journey to her parents' schloss for the celebration of their silver wedding anniversary. Although the duke and duchess of Coburg had maintained their marriage for twenty-five years, their relationship "had fallen apart in all but name." Only the winter before, when the duke had taken a yachting vacation to the south of France, the duchess had written to her daughter, "If you only knew how easy and comfortable life is without him." Still, all of their relatives had been invited to come pay homage to their achievement. The duchess's brothers and their wives had made the long trip from Russia, and several of the duke's English and German relations had also braved the heavy January snows to attend. The focus of the anniversary was the home of Ducky's parents, Schloss Friedenstein, a huge palace in the shape of a squared horseshoe perched on a hill above Gotha. After the formal celebration came a family dinner and an elaborate theatrical presentation.

But there was an empty chair at the head of the banquet table. Ducky's brother, the hapless Prince Alfred, lay dying in a dark, secluded room on the palace's lower floor.

The official story was that the hard-living young man was "suffering from consumption." But the truth was far more tragic and sinister.

Ducky's only brother had long been a cause of concern to the entire family. Having inherited the duchess's unattractive looks, young Alfred was an unhappy contrast to his beautiful sisters. Docile and good-natured, the boy had desperately needed extra care and understanding, but his tyrannical masters at Coburg, Dr. Rolfs and Fräulein, had mercilessly destroyed his ego and his self-confidence, so that he became the perfect victim for the barracks of Berlin. Appointed to the First Regiment of the Prussian Guards while still a teenager, Alfred quickly progressed from one dissipation to another.

Aunt Vicky, the dowager empress Frederick, thought her nephew should never have entered the German army. She wrote her daughter Crown Princess Sophie of Greece: "It is true that he was giddy and wild, as many young men alas are, and that he contracted an illness, of which I know next to nothing, as I have never asked or heard anything about it, one dislikes thinking about it. . . . This was neglected and the poor boy led a dissipated life besides. Potsdam!—that was not the place for him."

If Ducky's brother had been fortunate enough to marry well and early, he might have seen saved from this "life of debauchery and excess." However, Alfred remained a wild young bachelor until his twenty-fourth year, when he impulsively married an Irish commoner, Mabel Fitzgerald, at Potsdam in 1898. This union was invalid under England's Royal Marriages Act of 1772, and Alfred's outraged mother insisted it be annulled immediately. What happened next is "still shrouded in mystery," but it appears that Mabel was pregnant; and that "the father-to-be pleaded in vain against his mother's decision." Tragedy followed: Alfred quietly retired to his room and shot himself.

The wound was serious, and the young man languished week after week in his parents' isolated palace. His dangerous condition was apparently further complicated by the fact that he "was suffering from venereal disease."

The entire episode was humiliating for the straitlaced duchess of Coburg. Having sought perfection in herself, she refused to accept anything less in her children. And poor misguided Alfred was about as far from perfection as a human could get.

While the others celebrated the silver wedding anniversary in the huge banquet hall and ballroom of the schloss, Ducky and Missy went down to the dark, hidden room and visited their suffering brother. They found him "pale and emaciated," "his young life wasting away." Missy later wrote her sister Sandra: "He hardly recognizes anyone and often does not know what he says, poor boy."

Anxious that the embarrassing truth not be discovered, the Duchess concealed Alfred's suicide attempt even from Ducky and Missy. She continued to maintain the charade that he had tuberculosis, and insisted that he had to be promptly taken to dry, sunny Merano, a popular health resort on the southern slope of the Alps. The doctors objected to the move, telling the duchess that if he was moved from his sickbed Alfred "would die within the week." But, as always, Marie had her own way. Right after the anniversary guests had departed, she arranged for Alfred to be put on the next train south with a tutor and a medical attendant. The duchess planned that after a few weeks convalescing in the high mountain valley Alfred would travel to Egypt with Ducky and Ernie for the rest of the winter.

Neither Marie nor Affie chose to accompany their only son and heir to Merano. This seemingly heartless decision was almost exclusively the work of the duchess. After decades of "heavy drinking and smoking," the duke of Coburg was suffering from the first stages of cancer of the larynx, and was more vulnerable than usual to his wife's iron will.

Young Alfred was shipped off to Merano and his suicide attempt was successfully hidden. However, the doctors were soon proven correct in their warnings. On February 6, 1899, only a week after Alfred's removal, a telegram arrived at the schloss in Gotha announcing his death.

Of course, now it was easier to conceal the truth than ever. The press was told that Alfred had died of consumption, and this was the official medical cause of his death. The same story was presented to the family. Not until several years later did Ducky and Missy discovered what had really taken place. The truth finally came as a shattering blow to them.

Had Ducky and Missy known the real reason for their brother's demise, their grief might have been tempered. Although "it was unbearable to think that he had died all alone," Alfred's sisters were particularly unnerved at how the hand of death had so unexpectedly touched their family for the first time. "We were all so healthy, so strong, illness was an unknown thing in our family," Missy later wrote in her memoirs.

And this was Ducky's first great loss in life. It left her despondent. She had never expected her twenty-four-year-old brother to die—at least, not until well into the next century. She was overwhelmed by the crushing realization of her own mortality. The effect Alfred's death had on her parents also intensified Ducky's despair.

The day her brother's body was brought back to Gotha, Ducky and her sisters were gathered in her mother's room, all of them dressed in mourning, waiting for the funeral procession to enter the huge court-yard of the silent old schloss. "All of a sudden the church bells of Gotha began ringing and we heard the muffled tones of a funeral march, and Mama, generally so sober of movement, so undemonstrative, sank to her knees, crossing herself many times and then burst into tears."

It was "an overwhelming sight" to see the stoic Marie weeping so un-controllably for her firstborn. "We all went down upon our knees beside her, whilst the bells seemed to be ringing in our heads and our hearts."

Sorrow seemed to descend permanently on Gotha after the heir was buried. Marie and Affie were "racked by guilt" about the circumstances of their son's death. The ailing duke held his wife responsible and de-cided to spend whatever remained of his own life "as far away from her as possible, never to spend another night under the same roof if it could be avoided."

The succession to the duchies of Coburg and Gotha settled upon Ducky's late uncle's only son, the hemophiliac Prince Leopold of Al-bany. The fifteen-year-old boy was quickly taken out of Eton and shipped to Coburg to be "Germanized." This was Queen Victoria's wish and probably an intelligent solution to the political dilemma created by Alfred's death, but it was a painful decision for Ducky's father. With his hopes and dreams in ruins, the duke was now a completely broken man.

Ducky had been glad to leave Darmstadt a few weeks before, but now she was looking forward to returning home. After witnessing the honors heaped upon her parents for the survival of their sad mismatch, Ducky might have wondered if she wasn't expecting too much of life. Perhaps longevity, not quality, was the mark of a successful marriage. Surrounded by the marital failures of her parents and her beloved sister, the frustrated and confused grand duchess of Hesse reexamined her own relationship with Ernie. She made up her mind to do everything possible to make their marriage work. Ernie, too, must have been affected by the tragedy at Gotha, for it was apparent that soon afterward he encouraged her to join him in "a determined attempt at reconciliation."

They returned to Wolfsgarten in the early spring; perhaps the season's evidence of rebirth set the stage for their efforts. It was noticed that Ducky didn't try to escape into the forests on horseback as often, and when she did go riding it was at a quiet canter, with her husband at her side. For his part, Ernie tried to control his sexual desire for young men.

It was an awkward and strained attempt, especially the effort to resur-rect the physical aspect of their marriage.

As for Ducky's true heart's desire, Grand Duke Kirill, he was pursu-ing his promising career in the Russian navy. Ducky tried to convince herself that their love had been a mere flirtation or an unattainable dream. Keeping as busy as she could, she struggled to forget her feelings for him.

A few months after Alfred's death, in May of 1899, Ducky and Ernie took their four-year-old daughter with them to Windsor Castle to join their relatives in celebrating Queen Victoria's eightieth birthday. The queen was visibly cheered by the effort her two grandchildren were making to save their marriage, and she paid "special attention" to little Elizabeth, her favorite great-grandchild. Rushing in every day and excitedly trying to jump up into the heavily shawled old woman's bath chair to wish her a good morning, the child fully returned the queen's love. Later in the day, while Elizabeth played with her nanny in the palace nursery, the sound of Victoria's approaching pony cart on the drive below would bring the little girl running out onto the balcony, waving and shouting, "Granny Gran, I'm here." Some of little Elizabeth's more exuberant antics made the queen laugh so hard she had tears in her eyes.

After the birthday festivities at Windsor, Ducky and Ernie followed their grandmother to Balmoral, where Ducky "immersed herself contently in her painting and drawing." Marie Mallet, one of Queen Victoria's ladies-in-waiting, attended Ducky during her stay. As an observer of royalty, Marie could be "extremely critical if not downright scathing," but for Ducky she had only admiration. To begin with, she was amazed at the beautiful grand duchess's artistic talents. "She draws unerringly," the lady-in-waiting marveled, "never rubbing out or correcting a single line, and her taste is excellent. It really is genius thrown away but it makes her very happy and she works as hard as if her livelihood depended upon it." Marie thought Ducky exceptionally gifted as a decorative artist too, and believed that "she could make a very good living by designing wallpapers and chintzes."

In Scotland, Ducky also helped her cousin Thora, Princess Victoria of Schleswig-Holstein, and Marie with their preparations for a charity bazaar to be held at Bagshot in July. Since every article for sale at the bazaar was to be "of Royal manufacture," Ducky worked hard to create useful and attractive items of aesthetic appeal. Although she had suffered under her English grandmother's domination and had to some extent absorbed her mother's prejudices against England, she always retained a special love for the British Isles. Marie Mallet was surprised at Ducky's "loathing of Germans; the grand duchess had spent her entire adult life in Germany and had always given the impression that she was a zealous Teuton. Marie certainly perceived Ducky as being somewhat foreign and different from the other members of the English royal family, but she was struck by how the grand duchess of Hesse "adores England with passion and declares a cottage here is preferable to all the Schlosses in the Fatherland."

Ernie departed for Darmstadt the first week of June. Ducky had planned to follow a few days later, first stopping at London for some shopping. When he arrived in Hesse on Friday, June 9, Ernie telegraphed the queen at Balmoral: "Most heartfelt thanks for your kindness, feel rather low, but hope to be better when Ducky and Baby arrive Monday."

The next day Ducky wired the queen to thank her for the visit and say that already she was feeling "quite homesick for lovely Scotland." Later that same day she received an urgent telegram from Dr. Westerweller, the court physician at Darmstadt: Ernie had fallen seriously ill with a very high fever.

Ducky immediately wired her grandmother what had happened and that she was "leaving straight for Darmstadt tonight."

Traveling all night, Ducky reached home by the next evening and hurried to the palace. She was barred at the door by Dr. Westerweller and given some very bad news.

Ernie had smallpox.

Smallpox, which has been eradicated, was a highly contagious viral disease that could quickly carry off its victims or leave them suffering through a lengthy and painful convalescence. Ducky was immediately given a protective vaccination. She wired Queen Victoria that night that "every precaution taken and am not allowed to see him." The crisis passed just after Ducky arrived home; gradually the grand duke began to recover.

On Monday, June 12, Ducky telegraphed Queen Victoria at Balmoral: "Ernie still doing well. Is terrible not being allowed to see him. Say it may last weeks. Have all been vaccinated. Feel miserable."

With somewhat higher spirits, Ducky wired her grandmother the next day: "Condition very satisfactory. Ernie feeling really better. Doctors think he will recover quicker than at first expected. Sent him your message, still have not seen him. He has two nurses and is being very well looked after. Have ordered bulletins to be sent to you regularly."

On Wednesday Ducky reported: "Ernie getting on admirably—such an infinite relief, weather stormy, cold. Live quite alone with Baby and

Wilhelmine and long to be able to talk to you like in a happy time at Balmoral, no question yet of being allowed to see Ernie."

The following day the anxious grand duchess was happily reporting that her husband was "making rapid progress" and taking a bath for the first time. Two days later, on a bright and warm Saturday morning, she "saw Ernie today for a moment at the window looking really quite well, every trace of illness has disappeared." But the grand duke was still feeling quite weak and frail, and another ten days passed before he was considered safely over the disease. Finally, on June 27, *both* Ernie and Ducky wired their grandmother: "We are so happy to be together again. Perfectly safe."

Having seen them so happy together in Scotland, Victoria now convinced herself that the Hesse marriage had turned out successfully after all. As an expression of her love and sympathy, she sent Ducky a beautiful ring accompanied by a very affectionate letter.

Ernie's serious illness had indeed helped bring the grand ducal couple closer, but the effect lasted only a very short time. The brush with death and the lengthy recuperation made Ernie more restless than ever. By the time summer had ended, he was reverting to his old ways once again, having sex with the more comely young men employed at the palace. However, he had learned to be more discreet, and the gossip was muted enough that it took some time to get back to Ducky.

Just as their marriage was falling back into an uneasy routine, the grand duke and grand duchess of Hesse decided to throw a large family party to celebrate the official consecration of the ornate, gold-domed Russian Orthodox church that Ernie had built for his two sisters and their Romanov husbands. Although most of the imperial family had been invited, Kirill had been tactfully left off Ducky's guest list. But his younger brother Boris had not. On an extended leave from his ship, Kirill had asked Boris to accompany him to Paris.

Boris had a better idea.

He persuaded Kirill to come with him to Ducky's party at Wolfsgarten.

CHAPTER TWENTY-THREE

The End of
Two Eras

THE HUGE HOUSE PARTY at Wolfsgarten in the autumn of 1899 marked the end of an era. It was the last great gathering of royalty in the nineteenth century. And, in a way, it signified the conclusion of an important chapter of Ducky's own life.

The members of Ducky and Ernie's family eagerly flocked to Hesse. Naturally, Nicky and Alix came from St. Petersburg. The petulant Russian empress was surprisingly happy during her visit to her childhood home. Possibly because of the new tranquility of her brother's marriage, she even made an effort—a modest effort—to be friendly to Ducky.

Kirill was determined to mitigate the awkwardness of the situation and enjoy himself as much as he could. He and Ducky were friendly while engaging in group activities, but refrained from being alone together. It was a considerable strain on both of them to suppress their strong feelings, but they tacitly agreed to accept the inevitable. Ducky's decision to rededicate herself to her marriage had doomed her love affair.

Everyone nevertheless managed to have a wonderful time, and Kirill didn't regret his decision to come. Living closely together, like a large happy family, these royal beings acted like carefree children. There were games at all hours of the day and night. In the evenings there were amateur theatricals, with the crowned heads of Europe, dressed in garish costumes, mounting a makeshift stage and zealously performing absurd parts. During the day there were rides and drives in the woods, and picnics on the terrace of the castle. Pranks and practical jokes were the rule rather than the exception, and Ernie was usually the ringleader.

In his memoirs, Kirill called this pleasant stay at Wolfsgarten one of his "happiest recollections." He was one of the last to leave; after a short trip to Paris with his brother Boris, he went back to Germany and spent a few days with his aunt and uncle, Ducky's parents, at Coburg. While he was there, Ducky visited from Darmstadt, ostensibly to see her mother. But it was noticed that she left immediately after Kirill did. Despite their firm intentions, romance was blooming again.

Ducky was still not prepared to give up completely on her marriage. Outwardly, Ernie was trying his best to be a good husband. She wanted to believe that their problems could be solved. About this time, they began sleeping together again—infrequently, but with slightly more satisfying results.

There was also another reason for Ducky's reluctance to leave her marriage now. Missy had just been implicated in a sensational sexual scandal. She had had an affair with a handsome young Romanian officer, Zizi Cantacuzene, and thanks to the spiteful gossip of the old king it had become common knowledge. To complicate matters, she was eight months pregnant with her third child, fathered by Nando.

The duchess of Coburg scolded her daughter for "great sin," reminding her that there was still time "to become a good steady woman." But what outraged the duchess more was the vicious way King Carol had actively spread the story of Missy's transgression to all the courts of Europe. She sent him a scathing letter in which she angrily took her son-in-law apart piece by piece, condemning Nando's infidelity, "his laziness, his indolence, his antipathy for all work, for any serious endeavor, and, worst of all, his sensual passion for Missy," which ended up "repulsing her." She dropped all polite pretense, plainly telling Carol: "Nando will himself avow that he treated his wife like a mistress, caring little for her emotional well-being in order to constantly assuage his physical passions."

As for her daughter, the duchess sternly instructed her to never tell Nando "the whole truth" about her "iniquitous behavior," and to "get herself [home] as quickly as possible." Missy immediately left Bucharest and returned to Gotha. Ducky and her younger sister Sandra also came home. Thus, all the sisters were reunited for the final Christmas and last remaining days of the 1800s in the uncertain atmosphere of their parents' home.

Calm settled over them as they assembled in the schloss's huge central room, where they worked on special handicraft projects, "mostly at wood-carving and wood-burning then so much the fashion." Ducky and Missy also painted and embroidered, finding their tranquil routine both "blissful and harmonious."

While the rest of Europe rushed forward noisily to greet 1900, Missy, Ducky, and Sandra drew together in the safety of their parents' snow-covered home and peacefully retreated into the happiness of the past.

Only a week after the new year began, Missy gave birth to her child, a daughter, blond like herself, whom she named Marie. In early spring, Nando arrived and begged her to return to Romania. The couple reconciled and went home.

The spring also brought unexpected happiness to Ducky: She was pregnant. Because she had already had one miscarriage, in 1900, the energetic grand duchess tried to lead "a very quiet life." But she still had not learned how "to play the passive part of an expectant mother," and continued to ride her horse through the woods, perhaps jeopardizing her pregnancy.

In an effort to get proper rest, Ducky went to Italy with Ernie in April. When they returned to Hesse at the beginning of May, Sir George Buchanan visited them and reported to Queen Victoria's private secretary, Sir Arthur Bigge: "The Grand Duke and Grand Duchess appear to have derived much benefit from their stay at Capri and to have enjoyed it thoroughly. Their Royal Highnesses are both looking remarkably well and are very glad to be back at Wolfsgarten after their long absence. The Grand Duchess is naturally obliged to lead a very quiet life at present, but the Grand Duke has had a good deal to occupy him since his return home."

No sooner had the diplomat written this report than Ducky gave birth to a premature, and stillborn, son.

A week later Queen Victoria, referring to "the disappointment at Darmstadt," and, expressed to Ernie's eldest sister the hope that "as she is so much stronger we shall have another event before too long which will repair this blow." But the queen was being far too optimistic, for the stillbirth was a blow that nothing could repair. It seemed to offer a final symbol for the fate of their marriage. And as if this sorrow were not enough for Ducky, a few days later she learned that her father had inoperable cancer of the larynx.

The family decided to keep the duke of Coburg's fatal illness a secret. Because Queen Victoria's own health was "beginning to give cause for concern" and she was distressed by the suspected cancer of the spine of her eldest daughter, Empress Frederick, it was thought too cruel to burden her with the impending death of her second son.

The duke, in considerable pain, was taken back to his favorite home, the idyllic Rosenau, where the family had spent their happiest days in Germany. Suffering horribly, he refused to see Ducky or anyone else in his immediate family. Missy sent Nando as her emissary to Coburg; the crown prince was shocked to find his father-in-law being "fed from a tube" and the defeated doctors discussing cutting out his tongue.

When it became apparent that death was near, Ducky and her sisters were finally summoned to their father's bedside. Missy persuaded her mother to stay away until the very last moment, as her presence "would only excite him more." With the exception of Missy, who was delayed in Romania, they were all with him when he died on the evening of July 30, 1900. Poor Queen Victoria was probably the duke's most sincere mourner. "Oh, God, my poor darling Affie gone," she cried. "It is hard at eighty-one!"

Although she had never been very close to her errant father, Ducky too was devastated. First her brother; then her baby; now her father— death was becoming familiar.

As for Victoria, from the moment she heard of her son's death, she began a steady decline and slowly lost her will to live. She deteriorated throughout the autumn of 1900; her grandson the future King George V remarked that she was looking "very seedy."

Meanwhile, Ducky felt her marriage finally coming to its natural end. As much as Ernie wanted to change, she knew he never would. And when she allowed herself to think about them, she was still as repulsed as ever by his homosexual liaisons.

There was also Kirill.

Despite their long separations and their efforts to forget each other, their love had grown stronger.

Kirill had been serving with the Russian fleet in the Black Sea. That autumn he returned to St. Petersburg on leave and at once set off for

Wolfsgarten. This time there was no mistaking his purpose. He and Ducky discussed their future and decided once and for all that they would be spending it together. Ducky would divorce Ernie and eventually, somehow, she and her cousin would be married. In his memoirs, Kirill obliquely remarked that "the three weeks which I spent at Wolfsgarten in the autumn of 1900 were decisive for the whole of my life."

He and Ducky now attempted "to meet as often as possible" and immediately went off to Paris together. Even though they were accompanied by Kirill's younger sister, Helen, their holiday created a scandal. But it was worth it. They enjoyed themselves "enormously in the gay and carefree manner of youth."

There was still one major obstacle, which all of their courage could not conquer. But with the beginning of the new year, it seemed that that difficulty would be finally removed:

Queen Victoria was dying.

On January 1, 1901, the queen wrote in her journal: "Another year begun and I am feeling so weak and unwell that I enter upon it sadly." Never before had she greeted the new year without optimism.

Staying at her favorite residence, Osborne House on the Isle of Wight, she passed a "monotonous procession" of sleepless nights and drowsy days, irritated, melancholy, and apathetic. On January 12 a dense fog descended upon the while island, "as if to herald what was coming."

Though Ducky's mother had continually crossed swords with her stubborn mother-in-law in the past, the death of the duke and the queen's feeble health "made all the difference." The two widows had found much mutual sympathy, and when it became apparent that Victoria was rapidly sinking, Marie rushed to Osborne. On the way she stopped at Darmstadt and picked up five-year-old Princess Elizabeth, giving the child a last chance to see her beloved "Granny Gran."

The day after the duchess arrived she took the queen on her last outing. Taking advantage of a short break in the cloudy weather, she had her mother-in-law put into her pony chaise and sat down beside her for a short drive through the forested estate. Always a believer in the curative powers of exercise and fresh air, the duchess must have been disappointed in the excursion's failure to revive the listless queen. Two days later, on the seventeenth, Victoria suffered a mild stroke that left her mentally confused and with difficulty speaking. A heart specialist examined her and announced that the end was near. The next morning telegrams went out to the rest of her family.

Just after sunset on January 22, Queen Victoria died peacefully, surrounded by most of her children and grandchildren. First and foremost was the kaiser, surprisingly humble and tactful, keeping out of the way until he was called to the deathbed. For more than two hours he supported his grandmother's head with his one good arm. Young Elizabeth was brought in and told that Granny Gran was now with the angels. "But I don't see the wings," she whispered.

The Queen's two favorite grandchildren, Ducky and Ernie, were absent. They had gone to St. Petersburg to visit their Russian relatives. Victoria's death, though expected, was a great shock. The Russian *Court Circular* announced that the grand duke and grand duchess of Hesse and the Rhine would be leaving for England on the twenty-sixth to attend their grandmother's funeral and that with them would be Grand Duke Michael Alexandrovich, officially representing his brother the emperor.

But Ernie attended the funeral alone. Ducky had stayed behind in Russia. Perhaps her grief was too intense, or perhaps she was showing sympathy for Missy, who had desperately wanted to go, but had been forbidden by the Romanian king. Whatever the reason, it was an extraordinary omission. Especially since Ducky's beautiful little daughter was there center stage.

During the magnificent funeral at Windsor Castle, Elizabeth sat next to her cousin Prince Edward of York, the future King Edward VIII and duke of Windsor, who was almost the same age. Their aunt Maud, the future queen of Norway, observed them during the funeral and later wrote to Edward's mother: "Sweet little David [Prince Edward] behaved so well during the service, and was supported by the little Hesse girl who took him under her protection and held him most of the time round his neck. They looked such a delightful little couple."

Victoria's passing was a source of great distress. The duchess of York, herself to be the queen of England in only nine years, cried: "The thought of England without the Queen is dreadful even to think of. God help us all!" This plaintive cry to the Almighty seemed to be on everyone's lips. "A sense of desolation was mingled with sudden alarm, for while she lived England's power had seemed to be steadily increasing under the protective shadow of her formidable bonnet." Victoria's death was not just the conclusion of an illustrious reign, it was the passing of an era and the end of a way of life. For better or worse, change would now be the order of the day.

And there would be no greater changes than the ones within the dead queen's family. Without the matriarch to guide their every move, the children and grandchildren of Victoria at last came into their own and could do as they pleased. This was especially true for Grand Duchess Victoria Melita of Hesse and the Rhine.

Ducky was finally free.

CHAPTER TWENTY-FOUR

Divorce
Most Shocking

A FTER VICTORIA'S FUNERAL, the duchess of Coburg went directly to the Château Fabron, her winter home on the French Riviera, for a quiet rest. Located on the heights of Nice, the villa was surrounded by tropical plants and had a view of the sea. Joining the duchess were three of her four daughters: Ducky, Missy, and teenaged Beatrice.

Because of his delicate health, the crown prince of Romania and his wife and children had been allowed by the king to spend the winter in the south of France. For Missy this was an opportunity for unrestricted fun and to be with Ducky again. Ducky was just happy to get away from her husband and the hostile Hessian court.

To no one's surprise, Grand Duke Kirill obtained permission from the Russian emperor to journey to the Mediterranean to visit his aunt Marie. Once again, his younger brother Boris, who was in love with Missy, went with him. Together, the romantic cousins spent most of their time driving along the corniches in an automobile. Kirill had bought a Panhard-Lavasseur, a twelve-horsepower machine with "dangerous brakes" that "spluttered, shook and made fearful noises."

During their more tranquil moments in the garden of the Château Fabron, Ducky and Kirill planned for the future. She would leave Ernie and petition for a divorce. But she didn't know yet exactly how and when. This action would require every ounce of her courage.

When Ducky finally returned to Darmstadt the growing tension in her marriage was noticed by everyone. Dining at the palace, Count von

Bülow was struck by how "stiff and unfriendly" the relationship was between husband and wife. One visit with their Hessian cousins, and the duke and duchess of York, the future King George V and Queen Mary, counted their own blessings. The duchess later wrote to her husband, "After what you told me the other day of the sad lives of poor Missy and Ducky, we should be even more grateful to feel that so much sympathy exists between us two in our married life."

At the end of the exceptionally hot summer of 1901, Kirill journeyed again to Hesse to visit Ducky at Wolfsgarten. He was to leave on a year's voyage to the Far East on his new ship, the *Peresviet,* and he had to see her one last time. It was his presence that, at last, gave her the necessary steel.

One morning in October, a few weeks after tearfully saying good-bye to her lover, Ducky rose early and very carefully and quietly began packing most of her clothes. She had told Ernie that she was going to Coburg to stay for a week or two with her mother at the Rosenau. Her husband took no particular notice of her departure, but the servants wondered why she had hugged her daughter so tightly and cried when she left her behind.

When Ducky arrived at Coburg she immediately informed her mother that she had left Ernie and was determined never to go back. At first, the shocked duchess refused to listen to such nonsense, but after Ducky flooded her with a litany of suffering and sorrow, plus a description of her son-in-law's true sexual nature, she put her arms around Ducky and pledged her support. The duchess might have been a slave to propriety and tradition, but when it came to her daughters, and Ducky especially, she would trade the world for their happiness and well-being. As she had often told them in the past when they had broken her rules, "Your old Mama grieves but will never abandon you."

With her mother squarely on her side, Ducky wrote Ernie that she was going to file for divorce. Surprised, he resisted the idea. Ernie would have liked things to have gone on the way they were. He had hoped his wife would take Kirill as a lover and maintain her own private life so that he would be free to engage in his. It seemed a fair trade—a perfectly even exchange. For the image-conscious Grand Duke Ernest Ludwig of Hesse and the Rhine, no matter what was happening in private, the mask of respectability must be kept firmly in place.

Divorce threatened to rip that mask right off. It was unheard-of for Christian sovereigns to terminate their marriages legally. The scandal might very well shake the Hessian state. It might also give credence to the gossip concerning Ernie's homosexuality. Ernie was staring at personal and political disaster.

And did Ducky care at all about the mess she was about to make?

Yes . . . and no.

Of course she minded as much as he did the great scandal about to crash down on their heads. She grieved over how it would affect their daughter. But she cared little for appearances, meaningless tradition, or public opinion. This was the fundamental difference between Ducky and Ernie: He could live a lie; she could not. Since earliest childhood, she had had "no patience with frauds."

At last, Ernie resentfully agreed to a divorce. In a candid letter to his eldest sister, Princess Louis of Battenberg, he confessed that the last few years had been "a living hell." He also confided, "Now that I am calmer I see the absolute impossibility of going on leading a life which was killing her and driving me nearly mad. For to keep up your spirits and a laughing face while ruin is staring you in the eyes and misery is tearing your heart to pieces is a struggle which is fruitless. I only tried for her sake. If I had not loved her so, I would have given it up long ago."

Of course, Ernie was romanticizing the problems of his marriage and not touching upon the cause of the breakup: his homosexuality. But his sister was much more knowledgeable than he knew. She later wrote of her brother's unhappy relationship with Ducky:

> In October 1901 I had a letter from Ernie, who had been spending a short time at Capri, saying that Ducky had informed him that she had decided to ask for a divorce. I was really less surprised and startled by her decision than he. Though both had done their best to make a success of their marriage, it had been a failure. Their characters and temperaments were quite unsuited to each other and I had noticed how they were gradually drifting apart. As I had known Ducky well from a child, since the time that she lived with her parents at San Antonio [in Malta], she had often spoken freely to me on the subject of her married life. She had confidence, that I hope was not misplaced, in my fairness of judgement and, in spite of my being devoted to my brother, I can only say that I thought then, and still think, that it was best for both that they should part from each other.

Unfortunately, Ernie's straightforward sister was the only sympathetic voice to be heard. Everyone else in the family was horrified. On October 27, when word reached St. Petersburg, Emperor Nicholas immediately wrote his mother, Ducky's aunt Minnie, Dowager Empress Marie:

> I must inform you of a terrible and unexpectedly grave event. Can you imagine—Ernie and Ducky are getting divorced, yes, actually divorced! We heard of it three days before leaving Spala. Victoria [Princess Louis of Battenberg] sent a long letter of Aunt Marie's [Ducky's mother's] to her. In it she explains to all her sisters that, as far as she can see, the relations between Ernie and Ducky had been bad for some time past, that their estrangement was growing from day to day and that, in the end, divorce was the only possible way out. Such is Aunt Marie's opinion and Ducky's too. Ernie, after a long struggle, has come to the same conclusion. It is all quite settled and nothing left to do but for the ministers of Darmstadt and Coburg to arrange the legal side. All of this appeared to us so dreadfully sad and was so very unexpected that at first we thought Victoria must have gone out of her mind. But a few days later Alix and Ella had the news confirmed by letter from Aunt Marie, so that now there is no possible doubt left. All that time, nothing from them direct—not a word. At last, yesterday, a telegram from Ernie, saying that it is all definitely decided. I am intensely grieved and sorry for poor Alix; she tries to hide her sorrow. In a case like this even the loss of a dear person is better than the general disgrace of a divorce. How sad to think of the future of them both, their poor little daughter—and all his countrymen.

Nicholas was speaking for most of his generation when he declared that death was preferable to divorce. Queen Victoria's surviving elderly cousin, the crusty Grand Duchess Augusta of Mecklenburg-Strelitz, was aghast at the subject's mere mention. She wrote her niece the duchess of York on November 4: "What truth is there in the Darmstadt divorce? The Papers openly speak of it; could they not agree? Ernie has been absent some time, in Italy; what can it all mean?"

On December 21, 1901, the grand duke and grand duchess of Hesse and the Rhine were legally divorced by a special verdict of the Supreme Court of the grand duchy. The official grounds were "invincible mutual antipathy."

An important provision of the divorce settlement was the future of Princess Elizabeth, now six. It was decided that she would spend six months a year with each parent, and that upon her eighteenth birthday she would return permanently to Darmstadt.

It was finally over.

Ducky, exhausted, spent a quiet Christmas with her mother at the Rosenau. Marriage, motherhood, death and divorce: She had lived a full lifetime. She had just turned twenty-five.

Most people considered her more beautiful than ever—she was slender, with large, violet-blue eyes, finely carved features, porcelain complexion, and curly chestnut hair.

But her future appeared more uncertain than ever. Though she had shed her husband, marriage with Kirill was still an impossibility. For them to wed would mean defying everyone's laws—their family's, their church's, and their country's.

Perhaps the most bizarre solution to Ducky's problems was put forth by the crazy old queen of Romania, who believed that "God had moulded her for sorrow . . . and . . . she must fulfill her destiny." Instead of trying to run after happiness, Ducky should sacrifice her life to help others. The queen instructed her to "go and learn how to nurse, form a sisterhood of her own, wander about the world in search of all the suffering, all the misery, all those that life has treated hardly. Lead a life of continual sacrifice, that her grand nature was destined for this."

Ridiculous this advice may have been, but as the new year began the "Fighting Grand Duchess" wondered how much longer she could keep up her struggle.

PART THREE

Twilight of Splendor

CHAPTER TWENTY-FIVE

Tide Against Tempest

WITH VERY FEW EXCEPTIONS, everyone from her own international royal family to the working classes bitterly condemned
the former grand duchess of Hesse. Because she had been the one to request divorce, and because only a handful of people knew the real reason, Ducky was blamed for her marriage's failure. She received no
sympathy. Indeed, days after the public announcement, she awoke to find
herself a royal pariah.

She had expected criticism, especially from those who didn't know
her, but she was shocked, hurt, and angered by the reaction of her own
family. Treating her as "a virtual outcast" were her uncle Bertie, now
King Edward VII, and her cousin Willy, the kaiser. For once these two
monarchs "found something about which they agreed." Edward at least
kept a gentlemanly tone in expressing his indignation, but the volatile,
misogynistic kaiser ranted in language that wouldn't have passed the
public censor. But these rulers' censure "was benign compared to the
vindictive fury" of the Russian empress.

Alix had never grown fond of her self-confident sister-in-law. The
gradual estrangement between Ducky and Ernie had fed her hostility.
Now, as far as the neurotic Alix was concerned, her beloved brother had
been stabbed in the back and ignominiously dumped. The divorce was
a deep humiliation and, as Alix saw it, a direct insult to her. As her husband had remarked in his letter to his mother, better off dead than disgraced by divorce. From now on, the Russian empress would openly

display unmitigated hatred for her cousin Ducky. And though the former grand duchess could shrug off the condemnation of her other relatives, the antipathy of her imperial cousin would, in time, almost ruin her life.

During the first months after her divorce, Ducky, wounded and in despair, wrote to her old friend in Darmstadt, Lady Buchanan. She decried the "uncharitable treatment" to which everyone was subjecting her and maintained that she had sacrificed seven years of her youth just to please her selfish grandmother. Now that Queen Victoria was dead it was her turn, finally, to have some degree of happiness.

Amid the hostility, Ducky's two sources of support were, as always, Missy and her mother. Missy was dealing with her own difficult problems in Romania—she was unhappily married, the mother of three children, and at odds with the king and queen—and so was unable to offer as much help as she would have liked; the duchess of Coburg, however, was an untiring and unstoppable force of nature.

The duchess never made any effort to hide the fact that Ducky was by far her favorite child. It could hardly have been otherwise, when they had so much in common, from their passionate Slavic temperaments to their uncompromising honesty. Both women placed integrity, sincerity, and simplicity above all else and despised affectation and duplicity. Both loved all things Russian. (Alone among the duchess of Coburg's five children, Ducky eventually converted to her mother's religion.)

For a woman who mercilessly pushed her children to attain her own ideals of perfection, the duchess found her dreams almost realized in her strong-minded second daughter. (As for her first, Marie voiced her disapproval of the frivolous Missy at every opportunity. She often wrote scathingly critical letters to Bucharest, over which Missy sadly said she "shed tears of humiliation.")

As an avalanche of condemnation descended upon the Rosenau, Ducky's mother felt that a quick retreat might be in order. She packed up the household and took Ducky and sixteen-year-old Beatrice to the Riviera. Beatrice, known in the family as Baby Bee, was becoming a beautiful young woman and a perfect companion for her older sister. Having "always been a child of exceptional intelligence," she was the only one of the four sisters who could effectively manipulate their domineering mother. As clever and unyielding as the duchess was, her youngest daughter "generally outwitted" her and "had most things her own way."

At the secluded Château Fabron, the sun and the sea and the holiday atmosphere slowly helped Ducky out of her depression. Ducky's mother insisted that she get out and do things to keep up her morale. Believing that "they never could have enough exercise," she forced her daughters to go outside in all kinds of weather.

"It is ridiculous to remain at home because it rains," the Duchess would proclaim just as authoritatively as she had when they were children. "People who allow their exercise to depend upon the weather, never take any exercise at all."

So Ducky and Baby Bee were off, rain or shine, riding in the wooded hills, driving along the Grand Corniche, and strolling the Promenade des Anges. The constant activity was meant to keep her mind from certain thoughts—primarily, thoughts of Grand Duke Kirill.

One warm winter morning, as if summoned by a benevolent sorceress, Kirill's ship appeared on the Mediterranean horizon. The *Peresviet,* in transit to Asia, had just called at Toulon, where Kirill's elderly Aunt Augusta, the grand duchess of Mecklenburg-Strelitz, had come on board and expressed herself vociferously upon the subject of Ducky's infamous divorce. This gave Kirill, isolated for the past several months at sea, a painful sample of what his beloved had been enduring. He was gratified when their voyage was unexpectedly interrupted by a five-day stay at the French naval base at Villefranche, a picturesque port only four miles from the Château Fabron.

Ducky came aboard the *Peresviet* as soon as she docked. Kirill very properly and formally gave her a tour of the ship, then entertained her with tea in the dining room with the other officers. After that his good friend Dimitrieff, an excellent singer, performed as Kirill accompanied him on the piano, much to Ducky's delight. Then Kirill discreetly took Ducky back to his cabin. (He remarked in his memoirs that "she was particularly anxious that I should be well lodged on this long voyage.")

Obtaining a brief shore leave, Kirill visited Ducky and her mother at the Château Fabron. The lovers amused themselves as well as they could, trying to stay lighthearted. The duchess remained in the background, leaving the young couple alone as much as possible. On Kirill's last night at the château, the duchess decided that Ducky and her lover should have a special dinner all by themselves, "as this was a farewell occasion."

In his memoirs, Kirill vividly recalled his feelings that night: "She was in exile and I was going to the unknown, to the uncertainty of a blank future. About one thing both of us had no illusion whatever, that a mountain of obstacles to our happiness would arise, that every conceivable wheel of intrigue, coterie and vetoes would be put into motion against us, and that we would be left to fight that sea of troubles alone with thousands of miles between us. By that time I would be at the other end of the world and the woman I cared for would have to defend herself as well as she could and I would be unable to come to her aid."

After dinner, Kirill and Ducky walked in the garden beneath a full moon. They were thinking of the future, but spoke little, knowing that their thoughts were shared. Finally, just before midnight, "feeling that this might be the last farewell," Kirill "plucked up courage" and left to join his ship.

He drove his little Panhard-Lavasseur automobile back to Villefranche, where a steam launch was waiting to take him out to the *Peresviet,* and instructed his French chauffeur to take the car back to the château for Ducky.

Early the next morning, just as "we were casting off, I noticed a carriage driving up to the quay. Ducky and her sister, Beatrice, had come to see me off. The propellers churned up the water, the 'Peresviet' moved slowly out and the quay receded. I stood on deck and watched them until distance hid them from sight."

Ducky sadly returned to the Château Fabron, "left to fight the sea of troubles alone."

CHAPTER TWENTY-SIX

The Curse
of Hesse

I N T H E S P R I N G O F 1902 Ducky reluctantly returned to her mother's home in Coburg. Still in disgrace, she kept to the secluded little Rosenau and awaited the arrival of her seven-year-old daughter.

Princess Elizabeth's first six-month stay was not the joyful visit Ducky anticipated. Since she had left the child behind, Ducky very much appeared to Elizabeth as a deserter. And undoubtedly Elizabeth's hurt and anger at her mother's sudden departure were augmented by Ernie's "immense bitterness towards Ducky after the divorce."

Feeling betrayed and humiliated, Ernie nursed a resentment that time never cured. He removed as much material relating to Ducky from the Hesse grand-ducal archives as he could; even thirty-five years later, when he wrote his memoirs, he dismissed his first wife with a single short sentence.

Elizabeth, a beautiful and precocious child with "sad, anxious eyes," had much in common with her mother. But she and her father were kindred spirits, and because of Ernie's preeminent position in Hesse and the importance and necessity of an heir, their relationship was an unusually close one. Ernie apparently possessed a rare insight into his child's psyche. In his memoirs he speaks glowingly of his daughter, crediting her with a "deep sensitivity and a very large heart." "I never knew a child who had so much influence on adults," he wrote. "Her inner personality was very strong, and she had a natural quality that protected her from being spoiled."

Although Ernie perceived Elizabeth as "always friendly and happy," he realized that she was affected by his unhappy marriage. "Despite her young years, she knew exactly what was happening in our divorce, and she suffered unspeakably, for she knew where she belonged and her whole love was for me. She felt herself to be completely Hessian and nothing made her happier than to hear herself referred to as 'that child from Hesse.' "

Obviously, Ernie's assessment could not be objective, and, besides, he would have influenced young Elizabeth's feelings. According to him, when it came time for Elizabeth to visit her mother, he went looking for her but couldn't find her anywhere. Finally, he discovered her "whimpering under a sofa, full of despair." The distraught child, he wrote, "had wanted to hide her heartache." He assured the sobbing little girl that her Mama loved her too.

"Mama *says* she loves me, but you *do* love me," Elizabeth responded.

Ernie candidly conceded that he remained silent and said nothing.

Ernie declared the child "the sunshine of my life"; lonely and neurotic, he couldn't bear to be parted from her for such a long time. And he was "worried that her character might be damaged" by the division of custody.

But what was damaged was the little princess's relationship with her mother.

When Elizabeth arrived at the Rosenau it took all of Ducky's efforts to induce the child to enjoy herself. And although she was somewhat successful, Ducky realized that Elizabeth's reserve indicated an emotional distance that would take a very long time to repair. No sooner would that reconciliation begin than Elizabeth would return to her father; Ducky would have to start all over again the following year.

Complicating matters further for Ducky was the continuing frustration of her relationship with Kirill. It seemed as if the entire Russian imperial family was closing ranks against them; Ducky's mother was the only Romanov not bitterly opposed to the affair.

Predictably, the Russian empress was the fountainhead of all opposition. Alix saw Ducky's romantic involvement with a Romanov cousin as a supreme affront to her husband and the Russian throne, and "an unforgiveable insult" to the empress herself. As in all things, the empress Alexandra enforced her views upon her husband, so Nicky and Alix were soon of one mind: Kirill must be kept clear of Victoria Melita. It was the duty of the emperor to take command of his foolish young cousin's destiny by whatever means and see to it that Kirill's path was diverted as far from Ducky's as could be arranged.

When Kirill arrived at Vladivostok, Russia's chief port on the Pacific, in the summer of 1902, he was immediately handed a telegram from the emperor. It tersely informed him that he was being commanded to stay on in the Far East; "for how long was not made clear."

It was "quite obvious" to Kirill that the empress had used her considerable influence to keep the lovers apart and to "ruin any chance" of their meeting in the future. He later remembered that "the Emperor's dispatch was followed by one from my father to the effect that I should submit for my own good. This made matters considerably worse. I was furious, not so much with the contents of these pronouncements as with the manner in which plots were being hatched behind my back."

Kirill's life seemed suddenly to have been cast into darkness. "My situation amounted to exile. I was desperate and great gloom fell on me, life seemed to have lost its purpose, there was nothing but a completely blank future bereft of all expectation of happiness and achievement. It was a dismal and sorry state to be in, made more unbearable because I had no means of knowing what stringent measures of suppression would be brought in my absence against the woman I cared for. Twelve thousand miles separated us."

But "to disobey the Emperor never entered my mind at any time." The grand duke was a man of honor, loyal to his naval command. He must somehow reconcile these conditions with his overpowering love for his cousin.

Just as he was wondering how strong a test his love could take, a solution appeared as if by magic. His easygoing uncle Alexis, who was also Ducky's maternal uncle, was the grand admiral of the Russian navy. With "a kindly and understanding heart," Alexis quietly arranged for his favorite nephew to be appointed lieutenant commander of the *Nahimov,* a cruiser of the Pacific Squadron which was scheduled to return to St. Petersburg soon—via the Mediterranean.

As the *Nahimov* slowly made her way south through the China Sea to Korea, and then to Singapore and Saigon, the captain suffered a stroke; he died three weeks later in a French hospital. After a long wait for a new captain, she finally resumed her course for Europe, stopping again at Singapore to spend the Christmas holiday. Kirill was surprised to receive a beautiful watch from Ducky as a Christmas present.

During the three-week stay at Singapore, Kirill made friends with a British sloop commander who had previously served with Ducky's father and knew her family quite well. As agreeable as the association proved to be, with games of golf every afternoon, the grand duke was made more lovesick than ever by the stories his new friend told him about Ducky and her parents. Visions of the beautiful woman "he had been forced to leave behind were destined to haunt him."

From Singapore the *Nahimov* sailed directly for Suez and on to Greece. An unpleasant surprise awaited Kirill at the port of Piraeus. His aunt Olga, the queen of Greece and a former Russian grand duchess, visited the ship, as she always did when any Romanov relative came floating by. This time she brought another visitor with her: Kirill's younger brother Boris.

Ordinarily, Kirill would have been overjoyed to see his brother. But the reason for Boris's surprise visit left him outraged. "I learnt, to my complete amazement and became thoroughly indignant as a result, that he had been sent there to prevent me from deserting ship, which the good people in St Petersburg verily believed I was certain to do."

Boris soon realized he was on a fool's errand; his brother was far too honorable to desert his duty. The two men quickly made peace and ignored the touchy purpose of the calculated reunion. But the interference and the lack of faith left Kirill embittered toward his relatives in St. Petersburg. They should have known, he believed, that "at no time had I intended to do anything rash." However, the grand duke admitted that "I had not the least intention of giving up the woman I cared for, and the more pressure was brought to bear on me, the more adamant I became in my attitude."

After a brief holiday in Athens, Kirill continued on to Naples where he again encountered the machinations of his imperial cousins. This time there was an official message notifying him that the *Nahimov* was to be put at the disposal of his father, Grand Duke Vladimir, when it docked at Villefranche in three days.

Just as Kirill had expected, his father immediately took his son aside and "tried, but by no means enthusiastically," to persuade him to abandon all hope of marrying the notorious former grand duchess of Hesse. But when Vladimir discovered that nothing could ever change his son's feelings, he "gave in with good grace."

Ducky, who had been staying in Switzerland, meanwhile boarded a train to Nice. Too impatient to wait for it, Kirill rushed to Ventimiglia on the Italian border and met her on board the express. It was a deliriously happy reunion "after this period of uncertainty and unbearable anxiety."

The couple spent "a delightful few days" together in Nice, her mother and his father leaving them alone as much as they could. There were also fancy luncheons and suppers, arranged for them by Vladimir. Before Kirill's father quite realized it, he was going out of his way to unite the two lovers, showing great "kindness and sympathy" toward them. All of this, of course, was "strictly contrary to the purpose for which he had come." Grand Duke Vladimir, though rigid and unyielding like the other Romanovs, loved his eldest son above all else, and was determined to be the very best friend possible to him.

And he was. Throughout his life, Kirill would "always remember Father's great sympathy in this matter and helping hand which he had stretched out to us during this difficult period of my life."

For Ducky and Kirill, these few days together in Nice at the Château Fabron almost erased the loneliness and pain of their long separation. When Kirill boarded the *Nahimov* and departed for Lisbon and then the last leg home of his twelve-thousand-mile voyage, he left Ducky with a new sense of hope. She went back to Coburg for the summer with her mother and Baby Bee, and there she waited for word from her beloved. Kirill had promised to plead their case to Emperor Nicholas.

The results of that interview were ambiguous at best. Though seeming sympathetic, Nicholas II didn't "give me any clear indication as to the future prospects of Ducky and myself, beyond that there was some hope that things would, possibly, straighten out." Kirill chose to hope that Nicholas's meaning was "Love conquers all." (In fact, though, the emperor merely expected that Kirill's ardor would eventually cool.) Kirill also took heart at being given permission to visit Coburg; since no member of the Russian imperial family could leave the country without the emperor's consent, by keeping Kirill in Russia, Nicholas could easily have prevented him from seeing Ducky.

Kirill went straight to the Rosenau and spent the rest of the summer in that idyllic setting with his beloved and her family.

Perhaps it was the strong sense of fantasy created by the enchanting little hillside castle that prompted Ducky and Kirill to indulge their imaginations, planning for the future. As Kirill later wisely admitted, "The making of such plans is one of the consoling things of life, because they are based on hope, and although they may never mature, the very making of them is a pleasant pastime."

Most of their time that summer was spent driving through the sur-rounding countryside in Kirill's two automobiles. He had brought his Panhard-Lavasseur from Nice, and also a large six-seat touring car from Russia that resembled "a clumsy kind of omnibus." Although it had a luxurious silver service for picnicking, the touring car was far less effi-cient and reliable than the Panhard-Lavasseur, "breaking down with an enervating regularity." In his memoirs Kirill remembered with some amusement:

> Motoring in those pioneering days was accompanied by continuous trouble either from frequent breakdowns or from people and animals which one met on the way. Besides, cars in those days were the "rich man's pleasure" and anyone having a car was naturally marked down as a capitalist, and there-fore as an enemy of the people. I often met with some who manifested their outraged feelings in various ways of indignant behaviour as I passed by them. Apart from offending people politically there was another side to the unpopularity of motor cars, one, indeed, which had a more reasonable cause. They terrified human beings and all manner of beasts. Chickens were scat-tered in all directions, dogs run over, horses shied, upsetting carts into ditches. There were claims for damages done; road tolls had to be paid. Fre-quently one was stopped by the police and things had to be explained. In my exasperation I had the number plate replaced by a crown and fixed a special flag on the bonnet which made things easier.

Driving from one end of the lush Thuringian Forest to the other, the couple explored the historic cities of Nuremberg, Bamberg, and Gotha, stopping off at old castles and picnicking in carefully chosen glades "far from the busy world." They were filled with "the joy of living which comes to one on such occasions with the whole vigour and entirely carefree spirit of youth." That summer was a very welcome "appease-ment after much anxiety and sorrow."

Only happy news intruded upon their idyll. On August 7 a telegram arrived from Romania announcing the birth of Missy's fourth child. It was a boy, a highly prized second son for the fledgling dynasty. The crown princess named her new son Nicholas in honor of the Russian emperor and flattered her cousin doubly by asking him to stand godfa-ther. Missy was "hoping to influence the Tsar in favor of Ducky and Kirill" so that he would grant permission for their marriage.

The emperor acknowledged the compliment and happily accepted the official spiritual stewardship of the new Romanian prince, but his attitude toward Ducky's involvement with Kirill remained unchanged. It seems incredible that even at this late date the two sisters could have believed Nicholas would ever allow Kirill to marry his first cousin, a divorced woman whose discarded husband was not only still living, but the brother of the empress.

A few months later, when Kirill had returned to Russia, Ducky was passing a lonely autumn in her mother's home. Little Elizabeth was living with her father in Hesse. At the beginning of November he took her to stay with Alix and Nicky at the imperial hunting lodge at Skierniewice in the dense forests of central Poland. With the emperor and empress were their four daughters; the eldest, Olga, was eight, the same age as Elizabeth. The girls became friends, enjoying picnics in the woods, walks around the estate, and games in the long corridors of the palace. The vacation had been a good one.

But one morning Elizabeth woke early, complaining of a dry throat and severe pains in her chest. Within a short time she was "in agony, panting feverishly for breath." A doctor was immediately called, but he could do nothing for the suffering child. More specialists arrived. Elizabeth failed to respond to their treatments. Alarmed, "the doctors warned the Tsarina that the child's mother should be called at once." Alix ignored their advice until Elizabeth's condition deteriorated so rapidly that the doctors insisted.

Ducky was having breakfast at the Rosenau when the message arrived announcing her daughter's illness. She immediately went upstairs and began packing her bags.

But another telegram arrived an hour and a half later, describing Elizabeth's condition as "grave."

Ducky became frantic. She stopped packing, quickly grabbed all she could carry, and ran to her carriage. But just as she was leaving for the train station, the postman came galloping up the road with a third telegram. It was cruelly brief.

Ducky's little daughter had just died.

It was a few minutes before noon.

There were rumors that Elizabeth "had eaten food from a poisoned dish intended for the Tsar," but an autopsy later confirmed that the child had died of typhoid, an unusually virulent case most likely contracted from a casual sip of unsanitary water.

Ducky, "heartbroken," disappeared into the Rosenau and quietly made plans to go, instead, to Darmstadt for the funeral. She had not set foot in Hesse since the divorce two years earlier.

Ernie was perhaps even more devastated than his ex-wife. He had based his whole life and his plans for the future on his little girl, so suddenly gone. And he had witnessed her horrible suffering and cruel death. His nerves completely shattered, the pathetic grand duke was unable to find words to express what he was feeling. In his memoirs he wrote, simply: "The return trip by special train with Elizabeth in her silver coffin, I will never forget."

The funeral was planned by Ernie. "Everything was in white": Four white horses pulled a white wagon up to the royal cemetery, the Rosenhohe, and even the coffin was wrapped in white cloth.

There was a profound national grief for Elizabeth. The Hessians had adored their beautiful, cheerful little princess with her huge, friendly eyes and long, dark, curly hair. They had waited for the sight of her happily "driving out with her father, or running through the streets with a dog at her heels." And now she had been stolen from them.

As the funeral procession slowly passed through the town, the grand duke was overwhelmed by the emotion shown by his subjects. "Thousands of mourners sobbed in unison so that I could hear it," he later remembered with some pride.

And although they had never really understood or liked the dead girl's mother, the people of Hesse greeted Ducky with sympathy and affection. The former grand duchess was received with "all honours" and was shown great respect as she participated in the funeral.

Elizabeth's death struck a final blow to any feelings Ducky still had toward Hesse. Having been reviled and shunned as an outcast for these last two dozen months, she was in no mood to accept this tardy attempt of her former subjects to conciliate.

At the funeral, she took her Hessian Order, an elaborate badgelike medallion, and placed it on Elizabeth's coffin to show to the world that "she had made a final break with her old home."

There could never be any going back now.

Count von Bülow witnessed her "melodramatic" action and harshly judged that it did "not reveal very good taste." However, the talented German diplomat, for all his accomplishments, did not comprehend the depth and intensity of this woman's heart.

Leaving her beloved little daughter behind in the Rosenhohe cemetery with an exquisite marble angel watching over her grave, Ducky
abruptly departed. At last, her ties to her past were completely severed.

The only whispers remaining in the streets of Darmstadt concerned
the Curse of Hesse, which apparently had struck again. Of hazy origin,
the curse was thought to have arisen several centuries earlier from the
evil incantations of a malicious monk seeking vengeance against a royal
house whose members had often placed ambition above faith, casually
changing their religion to make better dynastic matches.

Because the Hesse family had been faithfully followed by the cold
shadow of tragedy, the power of the curse had gradually gained credibility. In recent memory it had blighted the happiness of Ernie's parents,
killing his young mother and baby brother and sister and planting in his
surviving sisters the deadly seed of hemophilia, a time bomb that would
shatter the lives of their descendants.

There were many who still believed in the Curse of Hesse, and now
more than ever with the tragic death of the grand duchy's only royal
child.

Ducky may have thought that she was leaving such nonsense completely behind, but many of her former subjects sadly shook their heads.
They had no doubt that the beautiful Victoria Melita would not escape
the Curse of Hesse so easily.

CHAPTER TWENTY-SEVEN

Hearts in Darkness

T HE DEATH of her only child left Ducky feeling more determined than ever to make a new life for herself with the man she loved. Marriage still seemed impossible, with opposition in St. Petersburg stronger than ever. And without the consent of the Russian emperor, no wedding could take place.

The mood was somber at the Rosenau that winter of 1903. Kirill had been vacationing in Sicily when he heard the news. He left the tropical gardens of Palermo at once, and decided to stay in Coburg for Christmas rather than return to his own family in Russia as he had planned.

Hoping to raise Ducky's spirits, Kirill organized "a well-matched combination of the best features of the English, German, and Russian way of celebrating," thus creating a "thoroughly international Christmas." Thanks to his efforts, Ducky was able to smile and even laugh again for the first time since little Elizabeth's funeral.

On the night of February 8, 1904, as Ducky and Kirill were enjoying a peaceful dinner in the great hall of the Rosenau, the Japanese attacked the Russian fleet at Port Arthur. Japan had not declared war, and the sinking of seven of the Russian navy's finest ships rocked the empire "with all the shocking violence of surprise." The emperor received word of the disastrous attack that evening when he returned from the theater.

There was no mistaking the significance of what had happened: It meant war. Nicholas nervously wrote in his diary, "May God come to our aid."

Divine aid was certainly needed. Although "huge, patriotic crowds filled the streets of St. Petersburg" the next morning, eager at the prospect of war with the Japanese, those in command were not nearly so confident. Nicholas, in particular, feared that his empire was facing a potential debacle; he knew that the morale of his restless subjects would not survive an ignominious loss to the Japanese.

But the conflict had been unavoidable. Each nation had imperial ambitions in Asia and sought to establish dominance in China. When Russia began moving into Manchuria and Korea during the first few years of the century, Japan, after failing at diplomatic efforts, saw no other solution than war.

Japan might have seemed a feeble foe, but the Japanese were actually far better prepared than the Russians for battle at sea. Having acted first, Japan "seized the initiative and gained command of the sea."

The Russo-Japanese War completely altered the course of Ducky and Kirill's lives, plunging them suddenly into a morass of darkness and despair.

Being an officer in the Russian navy, Kirill immediately returned to St. Petersburg and reported for active service. While he eagerly prepared for war, Ducky and her mother went south to the Château Fabron to spend the rest of the winter. There, they waited anxiously for word from Russia. Quite unexpectedly, the emperor generously permitted Kirill to pay Ducky a farewell visit before journeying to the Far East and "plunging right into the midst of the witches' cauldron." They spent four days together at the Château Fabron.

It was more and more difficult to plan for the future, which seemed ever changing and increasingly elusive. When the hour of his departure finally came, Kirill and Ducky realized that they might never see each other again. Ducky was crying, and her lover later confessed that "it was hard to tear myself away—desperately hard."

Returning to St. Petersburg via Vienna, Kirill emotionally said farewell to his parents, took Holy Communion in the family chapel, then left for "the great unknown—for death maybe."

En route he spent a night in Moscow visiting his favorite uncle, Grand Duke Serge. It would be their last meeting. The next day Kirill boarded the Trans-Siberian Express for the five-thousand-mile journey to Port Arthur, passing through parts of Russia that he had barely known existed. It wasn't until early March that his train came steaming into Port Arthur. The trip had taken more than two weeks.

To the young grand duke, Port Arthur "looked like a human ant heap." The naval base had yet to be completed, and Kirill decided that "a more awkward place could not have been chosen" for such an operation. With its cramped harbor and tiny entrance passage, it resembled nothing more than "a death trap."

A week after his arrival Kirill was appointed to Admiral Stephen Makarov's staff aboard his flagship, the *Petropavlovsk*. This post put him in close touch with his superiors, so that he had good insight into what was really going on. The Russian fleet at Port Arthur was being blockaded by the Japanese so that they couldn't escape and join the rest of the fleet at Vladivostok. The Russian plan was to try to break the blockade with a surprise sortie by the entire squadron.

During the night of April 13 the admiral dispatched a number of his destroyers to search out the Japanese grand fleet. There was a violent blizzard raging that night; several of the destroyers became lost in the storm, and confusion quickly followed as the Japanese fleet advanced and the ships of both countries intermingled indistinguishably.

In a desperate attempt to save the trapped Russian squadron, the *Petropavlovsk* proceeded at full steam out of the little harbor of Port Arthur to engage the enemy. Kirill was standing on the bridge with the admiral when there was a terrific explosion "as though a typhoon had suddenly released all the pent-up forces of its violence."

As he later remembered, "Everything gave below my feet and I felt like one suspended by some uncanny force in mid air." His face severely burned and his body badly bruised by the force of the explosion, Kirill jumped from the bridge and clambered over the rolling turrets of the rapidly sinking ship. Everyone around him was dead. Instinctively he jumped into the freezing ocean, as far from the capsizing vessel as he could get. The suction of the sinking ship created a "fearful maelstrom." "Something struck me a violent and stunning blow in my back. There was the sound of a hurricane around me. Then I was seized by the uncanny force of a swirling whirlpool. It gripped me and dragged me into the black depth of its funnel. Round and round I went with a mad, corkscrew motion, rushing round in ever-narrowing spirals until all around me became dark as night. All seemed lost now. It is the end! I thought. There was a short prayer and a last thought for the woman I loved."

Prepared to die, Kirill nevertheless struggled violently against "the force that held me in its fearful grip." After what seemed an eternity, he felt the tension of the whirlpool suddenly decrease, and he "struggled madly" to the water's surface. A small piece of wood from the *Petropavlovsk* floated by; clutching it, Kirill bobbed up and down in the frigid sea until another Russian ship rescued him.

A Japanese mine, secretly laid the night before, had sunk the *Petropavlovsk*. Kirill was fortunate indeed: Of the ship's 711 men, only 80 survived. And in spite of the Russians' heroic efforts, Port Arthur still fell to the enemy.

Though he was badly burned and his back muscles were seriously damaged, Kirill suffered most from shell shock. In a state of collapse, he was, in his own words, "an absolute wreck." Since he was no longer fit for service, he was put on the next Trans-Siberian Express and sent home to recover. Along the way he received a string of letters and telegrams from an anxious Ducky.

At St. Petersburg he was greeted at the station by the members of the imperial family and "given an enthusiastic reception as befitted a war hero." A few days later he had another interview with the emperor. It was plain to see how overwrought Nicholas was by the dismal direction the war was taking. The men confined their conversation to the light topics of health and weather. The emperor never once asked his cousin about the *Petropavlovsk* disaster or anything regarding the war. He did, however, grant Kirill permission to go abroad when the doctors would allow it.

Of course, Nicholas had in mind a journey to the healing hot springs of a Swiss or Mediterranean spa, but to Kirill, leaving Russia meant traveling in only one direction: to Ducky in Coburg. Scarcely taking time to unpack his bags, the wounded hero set off immediately.

Ducky and her sister Sandra were waiting for him when he arrived at the station. They were both dressed in white, as if symbolically celebrating his joyful resurrection. It was a reunion he would never forget. On that spring day there was the sunshine of "spring in my heart. I felt like one who was returning from the land of the dead to new life."

There could have been no better medicine for Kirill than his stay at the Rosenau that spring and summer of 1904 with Ducky and her mother. This interlude was the most sublime the two lovers would ever enjoy, "one of those very intimate and lovely episodes of one's life which are part of that secret recess in one's memory that cannot be shared with the world."

Despite his shattered nerves, scarred face, and other injuries, Kirill took part in the rides and picnics and walks that were so much a part of the Rosenau's holiday atmosphere. He was gratified to find that "the good people of Coburg knew that I was courting their princess and treated me as one of their own wherever I went."

Most important, Kirill's brush with death had steeled his resolve to go after what he wanted and to refuse to compromise his happiness. And what he so desperately wanted was Ducky.

In his memoirs he confessed, "To those over whom the shadow of death has passed, life has a new meaning. It is like daylight. And I was now within visible reach of fulfillment of the dream of my life. Nothing would cheat me of it now. I had gone through much. Now, at last, the future lay radiant before me."

So marriage no longer seemed impossible, especially after August 12, when a telegram arrived from Tsarskoe Selo announcing that a baby boy had been born to the emperor and empress, which meant that Kirill was no longer a direct heir to the throne.

Until now, Nicholas and Alexandra had produced no male heir to their imperial legacy. To their bitter disappointment, during the last eight years one daughter after another had been born to them—four little grand duchesses in all—and it seemed probable that Kirill would one day succeed to the throne. This had been an important factor in Kirill's reluctance to disobey to the emperor. And his ambitious father, Grand Duke Vladimir, was particularly anxious that his eldest son not spoil his chances of succession.

However, the cannons at the Peter and Paul Fortress in St. Petersburg were now firing a three-hundred-gun salute in honor of a new czare-vich; it seemed to Ducky and Kirill that Alexis's birth eliminated Kirill from the imperial succession and so would allow them to pursue their own happiness.

What neither they nor anyone else yet knew was that the Curse of Hesse had struck again. Alix had passed hemophilia to her first and only son. Whatever emotional problems Ducky's former sister-in-law had before would pale in comparison to the complete collapse soon to come. The czarevich Alexis's hemophilia would not only mute the happiness of the imperial couple, but it would also help destroy the Romanov monarchy and the Russian empire.

Although things looked much brighter for Ducky and Kirill, they were still ostracized from royal society. And no matter how perfect a world they made for themselves in the forests of central Germany during that long summer of 1904, after four years of scandal, divorce, death, repudiation, and war, Ducky and Kirill felt as if they were sinking ever deeper. Kirill's injuries were far worse than he had first realized. Ducky had brought him back to life, watching over him and infusing his faltering spirit with her indomitable will. But when the rejuvenated grand duke left Ducky in Coburg and returned to Russia in the autumn of that year to begin working at the Admiralty, he suddenly appreciated how vital his lover's influence had been. Although his duties were confined primarily to advising the imperial navy on the construction of a new type of destroyer, something he found "neither exacting or interesting," the work sorely taxed his injured nervous system.

During that depressing autumn, while Kirill worked at the Admiralty and struggled to regain his health, the war with Japan was turning into a national disaster. The "grim prospect of a Russian defeat seemed more and more likely."

In the middle of October Kirill strengthened his ties with his cousin the emperor by accompanying him as his aide-de-camp to a naval conference on the flagship *Suvorov*. The cousins were closer than ever during this troubled time in their country's history; the emperor admired the heroism of his dashing young cousin. Kirill felt more confident that Nicholas would, if not grant official permission, then at least accept his marriage to Ducky.

Ducky, anxiously waiting back in Coburg, was more than ready for her lover's decision. Instead she got the alarming news that Kirill was returning to the front. It had always been his intention "to rejoin the Navy on active service in the Far East as soon as my health permitted."

But in late May 1905, as Kirill was on his way east, word arrived of a crushing naval defeat at the Straits of Tsushima. The war was over. Russia "no longer had the resources nor heart to prolong the hopeless conflict."

To the world's amazement, little Japan had won.

For Nicholas's discontented empire, it was a bitter humiliation. And it was the beginning of the end.

The war had already served to fire the revolutionary movement throughout Russia. In January, the workers of St. Petersburg had staged a peaceful march on the Winter Palace to petition the emperor for reform. Led by Father George Gapon, a much-respected Orthodox priest, the quiet demonstration had been dispersed by the savage gunfire of "panic-stricken police." More than a thousand people were slaughtered, earning the day its permanent name: Bloody Sunday.

One morning a few weeks later, Kirill's uncle Serge was driving away from his Kremlin palace when an assassin's bomb exploded right on top of him. His wife, the beautiful and saintly Ella, rushed to the scene, where she found "not her husband, but a hundred unrecognizable pieces of flesh, bleeding in the snow."

The brutal murder had severely shaken Kirill, as did the general unrest that swept the empire after the disastrous conclusion of the Japanese war. Deciding that Germany was a "considerably safer place for those of a nervous disposition in that ominous year of 1905," Kirill made immediate plans to return to Coburg for an indefinite stay.

However, before leaving St. Petersburg, he sought out Father Yanyshev, the empress's own confessor, to ask his advice about the religious aspects of marrying Ducky. The impatient grand duke had decided that "it would be easier for the Emperor to make a decision if he were confronted with a 'fait accompli.'" Father Yanyshev assured Kirill "that from the point of view of Canon Law there was not the slightest obstacle" to the marriage.

Perhaps Kirill heard what he wanted to hear. It is almost inconceivable that a leading Orthodox churchman, and especially the confessor of the empress, would sanction a marriage between first cousins, particularly when the bride was a divorced woman with her husband still living.

Poor Father Yanyshev may simply have been the confused victim of the persuasive young grand duke's enthusiasm.

Kirill spent the rest of the year in Coburg, interrupting his stay with occasional visits to a sanatorium near Munich; there he was receiving regular treatments for his nerves, which were still "very badly shaken" by his mishap at sea. For diversion, the lovers climbed into Kirill's car and drove through the countryside of central and southern Germany, paying a visit to the music festival at Bayreuth, where they met Cosima Wagner, the elderly widow of the great composer, and then journeying on to Schloss Langenburg near Lake Constance to stay with Ducky's younger sister Sandra.

Ducky and Kirill waited patiently to wed until the Russo-Japanese War officially came to an end. To wait was a patriotic gesture meant to placate the emperor by demonstrating their forbearance and goodwill. Finally, in the autumn of 1905, the Treaty of Portsmouth ended all hostilities between Russia and Japan.

At once, a very simple wedding was planned. To keep the ceremony as quiet and private as possible, it was to be held at the duchess of Coburg's new summer home on the Tegernsee, a beautiful lake in the foothills of the Alps. The date was set: October 8. At the last minute, to ensure even tighter security, the site of the wedding was moved to the nearby lakeside home of the duchess's friend Count Adlerberg. Because "no one could find a Russian priest who would risk disobeying the Tsar to perform the service," the religious ceremony was conducted by the duchess's loyal private confessor.

The guest list was kept to an absolute minimum; most of those attending didn't even know why they had been invited until the wedding ceremony began. Even Ducky and Kirill's dear uncle Alexis, the duchess's brother, was not told why he had been summoned so urgently to Tegernsee from his holiday stay in Munich. To Ducky's great distress, the short notice made it impossible for Missy to attend. Undoubtedly her presence would have completed her sister's happiness that special day.

On the afternoon of October 8, 1905, with "a blizzard raging outside," Grand Duke Kirill Vladimirovich and Princess Victoria Melita of Saxe-Coburg-Gotha were married by Father Smirov in the Orthodox chapel of Count Adlerberg's home. During the ceremony, the priest's hands visibly shook, for he "was very scared, as he feared the wrath of the Holy Synod and the Emperor."

Besides the bride and groom, the only ones present at the wedding were Marie, Beatrice, Count Adlerberg, the count's housekeeper, and three servants. Grand Duke Alexis did not arrive until later that evening, having been caught in the surprise blizzard. At first dumbfounded by what had taken place, he quickly regained his composure and laughed heartily, warmly embracing the newlyweds.

A modest wedding feast was held in the dining room of the count's home; then Ducky and Kirill quietly withdrew to the duchess's new house to spend their first night as husband and wife.

Kirill, never had the slightest regret for what he had dared to do. In the years to come his love for Ducky only increased. At the end of his life, he emotionally reflected on her: "There are few who in one person combine all that is best in soul, mind, and body. She had it all, and more. Few there are who are fortunate in having such a woman as the partner of their lives—I was one of these privileged."

When Missy received word of the marriage, her thoughts were only of her sister's future. She was not sanguine. As she confided to a close friend: "I hardly know to what sort of happiness it will lead."

CHAPTER TWENTY-EIGHT

The Czarina's Wrath

*I*F DUCKY AND KIRILL were hoping for the sympathy and forgiveness of the emperor and empress, they could not have chosen a worse time to get married. While their cousins were exchanging vows at the Tegernsee, Nicholas and Alexandra's antiquated empire was beginning to crumble.

The end of the war brought chaos and rebellion to Russia. For months, violence had spread to every corner of the country. "It makes me sick to read the news," complained Nicholas, "strikes in the schools and factories, murdered policemen, Cossacks, riots."

As Kirill and Ducky honeymooned in the cool Bavarian Alps during the second week of October 1905, all of the Russian empire was paralyzed by a general strike. From the streets of Warsaw to the shores of the Pacific, "trains stopped running, factories closed down, ships lay idle alongside piers. In St. Petersburg, food was no longer delivered, schools and hospitals closed, newspapers disappeared, and even the electric lights flickered out." Crowds marched through the city carrying red flags and shouting revolutionary slogans. And in the countryside, things were even more dangerous. Armies of angry peasants were raiding the large estates and stealing everything they could get their hands on. Across the dark landscape, "the flames of burning manor houses glowed through the night."

Surrounded by violent disobedience, the rulers of Russia had counted on the loyalty and cooperation of the other members of the imperial family. Nicholas was particularly sensitive at this time to misconduct by a Romanov; Kirill's "fait accompli" seemed to him nothing less than a flagrant defiance of imperial law and of Nicholas's own personal authority.

Blinded by their passion, Ducky and Kirill completely failed to understand their imperial cousin. They had counted on his generous nature to rescue them from their predicament, but they failed to appreciate the degree to which his ego could be injured. More important, they neglected to calculate how totally the emperor was under his wife's thumb.

Kirill knew that he must return to Russia as soon as possible to present to the emperor the fact of his marriage in hopes of gaining sympathy. When Kirill arrived in the capital, he went directly to the Vladimir Palace and informed his parents that the deed had been done. Kirill's father was delighted by the news and suggested that his son request an audience with the emperor the very next morning. Confident that all would go well, Kirill sat down to a game of bridge that evening. He was playing cards with his father and some friends when one of the household servants entered and announced that Count Frederiks, the minister of the court, had come to see him.

Immediately, Kirill realized that this late-night visit was "ill-omened." What happened next came as "a great blow" to the assured young grand duke. Count Frederiks soberly explained the nature of his mission. He was conveying commands from the emperor. Kirill was being ordered to leave Russia within forty-eight hours.

He was to be deprived of all of his honors and decorations.

He was to be stripped of all his titles and privileges.

His imperial allowance was to be discontinued.

He was expelled from the Russian navy.

He was to be "outlawed."

Kirill and his parents were "dumbfounded." Never had Nicholas "even vaguely hinted at such drastic steps." On the contrary; whenever Kirill had mentioned the proposed marriage to him, Nicholas seemed sympathetic and expressed his "sincere hope that things could be straightened out."

But it was also obvious who was really behind this extreme punishment. At last, the empress had her revenge. Ducky had exposed the family to public scandal, and now she had actually had "the temerity to marry a close relative of her own husband." As far as the empress was concerned, Ducky was an adulteress and unfit to be a member of the imperial family. Alexandra declared that nothing on earth could persuade her to receive either "a woman who had behaved so disgracefully," or the man who had criminally married her.

Kirill's parents were equally outraged. They had never liked Nicholas and Alexandra, regarding their childishness with contempt and thinking little of their abilities. Kirill's ambitious mother, Grand Duchess Marie Pavlovna, particularly resented the imperial couple's domination of her own, more talented family. Now, witnessing their wanton destruction of her son, Marie Pavlovna stalked back and forth across her drawing room floor, her contempt suddenly turned into "an abiding hatred."

In a long letter to her uncle Prince Henry VII of Reuss, Kirill's mother explained the complex events of the whole sordid affair:

The situation had become impossible and, since peace has come at last, Cyril [Kirill] was keeping his promise to wait till then. We have done all we could these last four years to hinder this marriage, but their love refused to be separated and so finally we considered it better both for Cyril's name and honour that the business should end with a wedding. We knew that the matter would not pass off very smoothly here, and were ready for some passing unpleasantness. But the blind vindictiveness and rage of the young Tsarina has, for sheer malice, exceeded everything the wildest imagination could conceive. She stormed and raged like a lunatic, dragging her weak husband along with her until he lent her his power and so made it possible for her to revenge herself on her ex-sister-in-law for marrying the man of her choice. The matter has been dealt with as though some terrible crime had been committed and judgement has been passed in this sense. Yet all these storms are directed against a Grand Duke, a war victim, a man who had made a name for himself at Port Arthur, who has chosen an equal for his wife, and who, instead of deserting like the others, came here at once to take his punishment from the Tsar. It is too much that the son of his eldest uncle, of the man who, for the last twenty-five years has been the true and indefatigable head of the Army, who has saved the Tsar a hundred times, should be treated in this way at such a moment. One unanimous cry of indignation has been raised by all classes of the people. Vladimir has resigned as a protest at the indignity of the treatment meted out to his son. Even he, the truest of the true, says he can no longer serve the Tsar with such anger against him in his heart. The troops are in a state of ferment at the loss of their beloved Chief, and I know the Tsar is being warned on all sides how dangerous it is to let his uncle go. That is why his answer has been delayed six days. But

I do not think that Vladimir will consent to stay, even at the Tsar's request, unless our son is rehabilitated. What puts the last straw upon our patience is that Cyril came here with the Tsar's sanction to announce his marriage, and yet this very appearance here has now been made his chief offence. You, my dear uncle will find this hard to believe; but, alas, here everything is possible; and when I add that this permission was given without the knowledge of the Empress you will be able perhaps to form a just idea of the position here. This is how it was done; scarcely had Cyril arrived when the House Minister came with an order that he must leave Russia at once. The Tsarina wanted him to go that very night but that would only have been possible in a balloon! Then he was dismissed from the Fleet and the Army, he was to lose all uniform and rank, to lose his regiment which was conferred on him at birth by his grandfather, to lose his appanage, his name, his title. He was to go into perpetual banishment. As far as his name was concerned the Tsar had to retract a few days later, since all the Ministers declared to him that this could simply not be done. And why all this? Because the Tsarina does not want her hated ex-sister-in-law in the family. All the other reasons given are mere formalities which could easily all have been arranged, since even if we did not desire this marriage there is nothing dishonourable about it. We have suffered much and still suffer, and in addition to it all I am worried about Vladimir's health. The Tsar knows that strong emotions are a danger to him. What does he care about that? Think of us.

It was, of course, a completely subjective view of what had occurred. While she vividly described her own family's feelings, she artfully neglected to concern herself with the fact of her son's deliberate defiance of the emperor and of imperial laws. The punishment was severe and unjust, as Marie Pavlovna stated—a cruel revenge, compliments of the empress, but Kirill was not an innocent victim.

As for Kirill's father, Grand Duke Vladimir possessed such a formidable temper that his family had good reason to be concerned about his health. For ten years his booming voice had terrorized his young nephew the emperor. At the message delivered by Count Fredricks, Vladimir flew into a monumental rage.

The very next morning he marched into the emperor's study at Tsarskoe Selo and shouted so violently at his nephew that the court chamberlain, waiting outside the door, feared for his master's safety and almost ran off to summon the imperial guards. Vladimir demanded that his son's punishment be rescinded at once. He conceded that to marry a divorced woman without the emperor's permission was "perhaps wrong," but to be banished and outlawed for such a minor transgression was an act of insanity. Certainly a verbal lashing was punishment enough. His voice trembling with fury, Vladimir pointed out that "no member of the family had ever been punished so heavily for such a trivial offense."

Nicholas sat calmly at his desk, looking at a pile of papers, and said nothing. He gave his uncle the impression that he was trying not to listen. Unfortunately for the emperor, this tactic only provoked Vladimir to greater fury; the grand duke screamed and shook his fist in the air until he finally ended the audience by "crashing his fist down on the desk in front of his nephew, tearing the decorations from his uniform and throwing them to the floor, and bounding out the room, slamming the great gold-studded door behind him." He slammed the door so hard he broke it.

Contrary to the impression he gave his uncle, Nicholas was considerably affected by the unpleasant scene. A few days later he decided to slightly soften Kirill's punishment. He wrote his mother: "I wonder whether it was wise to punish a man publicly to such an extent, especially when the family was against it. After much thought which in the end gave me a headache, I decided to take advantage of the name day of your grandson and I telegraphed to Uncle Vladimir that I would return to Cyril the title which he had lost."

Although Nicholas was the instrument of his wife's craving for revenge, he also had strong reasons of his own for reacting so strongly to his cousin's marriage. By 1905 the imperial family itself was crumbling. First, in 1891, Grand Duke Michael Mikhailovich "casually married a commoner" and moved to England to live the comfortable life of a country squire. Six years later Grand Duchess Anastasia divorced her Romanov husband, the duke of Leuchtenberg, to marry Grand Duke Nicholas Nicholaievich. Then in 1902 the emperor's youngest uncle, Grand Duke Paul, married a divorced commoner and set up housekeeping in Paris.

Kirill's transgression came on the heels of all these other indiscretions, which had already seriously "corroded the prestige of the dynasty." Many years later the emperor's younger sister, Grand Duchess Olga, bitterly blamed this last generation of Romanovs for bringing about the end of the empire. In her opinion, these members of the imperial family, "who should have been the staunchest supporters of the throne, did not live up to their standards or to the traditions of the family." Instead, they casually wandered off "to live in a world of self-interest where little mattered except the unending gratification of personal desire and ambition. Nothing proved it better than the appalling marital mess in which the last generation of my family involved themselves. That chain of domestic scandals could not but shock the nation."

Conscientious and devoted to duty, Nicholas was shocked by the behavior of his relatives. Writing to his mother—always sympathetic to his frustrations—he confessed: "In the end, I fear, a whole colony of members of the Russian Imperial family will be established in Paris with their semi-legitimate and illegitimate wives. God alone knows what times we are living in when undisguised selfishness stifles all feelings of conscience, duty, or even ordinary decency."

So Nicholas's punishment of Kirill was not only an expression of his wife's displeasure; it was also meant to make an example of the young grand duke.

Though, restoring Kirill's title, Nicholas retreated slightly, he held fast to most of his verdict. He quietly accepted Vladimir's resignation from his military offices and insisted that Kirill go into exile, banished and disgraced.

Kirill's fate created a great scandal in St. Petersburg. He was exceedingly popular, his looks and great charm having earned him a special status. He was also well liked by most of the nonaristocratic classes, enjoying a reputation as a war hero. His outlawing and forced exile elicited wide public sympathy.

Not only was Nicholas perceived as the heavy in this unhappy affair, but his actions served to establish what most had already suspected: that "he was a weakling under his hysterical wife's domination."

The result was that the Romanov family divided itself into two enemy camps. Chancellor von Bülow observed that from that moment on "the Grand Duchess Vladimir and her sons entertained towards the whole Court, the Tsarina, the Tsar, the sickly heir-apparent, those feelings which, from Philippe Egalité to Louis Philippe, the House of Orléans harboured towards the elder Bourbon line."

The Vladimirs would never forgive nor forget.

The day after he had so hopefully arrived home, Kirill climbed back on the train and left Russia.

CHAPTER TWENTY-NINE

Two Alone

D UCKY HAD BEEN WAITING at the Rosenau for news. When a telegram arrived from St. Petersburg the very night of her husband's arrival there, she realized that her worst fears had come true—her husband had lost everything by daring to marry her.

While the duchess of Coburg flew into a rage against the injustice and stupidity of her imperial nephew, Ducky numbly packed her bags and prepared to meet Kirill halfway on his sad journey into exile. How would this latest trauma affect his injured nervous system? She hurried to Berlin.

Ducky was pacing the platform of the Hauptbahnhof when Kirill's train slowly rolled in from Russia. The moment she saw his handsome, chiseled face she realized how severely the shock had struck him. Worn and almost dazed-looking, the humiliated man nearly collapsed in his wife's arms.

But Kirill's despair did not last long. As always, Ducky lifted his spirits and restored him to life. Together, they traveled by train back to Coburg, where they quietly took up their new lives as husband and wife. Determined to make the most of their diminished prospects, Ducky lent her resiliency to Kirill and filled him with optimism. Thanks to the strength of his wife's character, he could later claim that "the sudden vehemence of this storm did not mar our joy of being united at last, and life lay inviting and happy before us."

What distressed Kirill most was that since Nicholas refused to recognize the marriage, Ducky was denied the title of grand duchess of Russia. No doubt this was the most important part of the penalty as far as the empress was concerned.

Ducky's position was awkward and unsettled. The royals of Europe constantly debated her status and most often rejected her. Formally, she and Kirill were social outcasts. Few were willing to risk offending the Russian emperor, the most powerful sovereign of them all.

While the mighty Nicholas was stripping his cousin of all rights and privileges, the Russian people were doing exactly the same thing to him. Just after Kirill hastily departed for Berlin, conditions in St. Petersburg became even more catastrophic when a massive strike shut down the city. Day after horrible day, an unbearable standoff froze the city. The troops were ready to advance, just waiting for a signal, but the revolutionaries stood firm and refused to provoke them. Everyone was on edge.

For the meek and mild Nicholas, it was "the same feeling as before a thunder storm in summer."

Realizing that a continuation of the paralysis would destroy the country, the emperor saw "only two ways open: to find an energetic soldier to crush the rebellion by sheer force" or "to give the people their civil rights, freedom of speech and press, also to have the laws confirmed by a state Duma—that of course would be a constitution."

The first method meant cruelty and violence, which Nicholas absolutely could not abide. It "would mean rivers of blood and in the end we should be where we started," he moaned.

There was only one course of action open to him: He would have to give up his absolute powers.

Thus, less than two weeks after Kirill's banishment, Russia was transformed from an absolute autocracy into a semi–constitutional monarchy.

The Imperial Manifesto reluctantly signed by Nicholas II on October 30, 1905, promised his subjects "freedom of conscience, speech, assembly and association." It also established an elected parliament, known as the Duma, whose consent was required to pass any law.

Russia's new constitutional monarchy was not as liberal as England's, but it was a remarkable achievement, propelling Nicholas's empire "with great rapidity over difficult political terrain which it had taken Western Europe several centuries to travel." But no reform would have satisfied the hardcore revolutionaries fueling the drive for change. For them, nothing short of the abolition of the Romanov monarchy would do. The Imperial Manifesto made them more eager, like a splash of blood drawing sharks.

The immediate happiness of Ducky and Kirill's marriage more than compensated for the social slights they suffered. After a cozy Christmas holiday with the duchess at the Rosenau, they departed in January of 1906 for a long stay on the French Riviera. Marie went to the palatial Château Fabron, while the newlyweds, anxious for some privacy and not wishing to overtax the duchess's generosity proceeded to neighboring Cannes, where they stayed with the Mecklenburg-Strelitz family, relatives of Kirill's mother.

At this time, Cannes was the most elegant and fashionable resort on the Riviera. Using the warm days by the sea as a delayed honeymoon, Ducky and Kirill "spent a delightful winter" far from the icy imperial scorn of St. Petersburg and the snubs of the royal courts of Europe. It was during this sublime sojourn that the couple decided to make republican France home during their uncertain exile.

France, long established as a mecca for the more pleasure-loving members of the Romanov family, had been without a monarch for almost forty years. Always hospitable to the frolicking, free-spending crowned heads of Europe, the French loved and respected aristocratic titles without being troubled by questions of their legitimacy. France was the perfect place for people like Ducky and Kirill, exiles of dubious rank.

Here on the liberated soil of France they could style themselves Their Imperial Highnesses, the Grand Duke and Grand Duchess Kirill of Russia.

Paris it would be.

Having been brought up primarily on French culture, Kirill adored Paris above all other cities and was thrilled at the prospect of setting up housekeeping there.

Paris was an excellent choice for both spouses. A perfect place of exile for most of the world's more sophisticated dispossessed, it offered unsurpassed gaiety, beauty, and charm during that first decade of the twentieth century. With a climate far more inviting than St. Petersburg's, Paris drew a whole generation of transplanted Russian aristocrats. The large Russian community living in the City of Light had created a comfortable little slice of their homeland, establishing Orthodox churches, Russian restaurants, and various clubs and societies. For those who could afford it, the French capital had everything the heart could desire.

Money was Ducky and Kirill's chief problem. Having been deprived of his generous imperial allowance and all other sources of income, too, Kirill had very little money. Ducky had even less; having been the petitioner in her divorce, she had received an extremely modest settlement.

Luckily for the impoverished husband and wife, they had vastly wealthy parents. The duchess of Coburg, having been the only daughter of Emperor Alexander II—in his day, the world's richest man—had handled her immense dowry astutely; she was perhaps the wealthiest woman in Europe. And Kirill's parents were among the very richest of the Romanovs. Both sets of relatives "stepped in to support them."

As kind, energetic, and domineering as always, Ducky's mother provided the couple not only with unlimited financial assistance, but also with a pattern for their existence. To a large degree, her routine became theirs and they formed one family. Since her daughter and son-in-law were still newlyweds, requiring considerable privacy, the duchess shrewdly let them come and go without expectations or complaints.

Their decision to live chiefly in Paris helped assure this hands-off approach. For the puritanical duchess, *la vie parisienne* was anything but appealing. So Ducky and Kirill could visit her whenever they wished without having to worry about her venturing to Paris and intruding on their lives.

Soon, a regular routine was established. Kirill and Ducky bought a large, "charming" apartment near the Champs Elysées on the avenue Henri Martin, but spent several months each winter at the Château Fabron and usually passed most of the summer at the duchess's home on the Tegernsee. In between, long visits were made to two of Ducky's sisters, Sandra in tranquil Langenburg and Missy in colorful Romania.

It was a very pleasant life.

Returning from Cannes in that first spring of their exile, Ducky and Kirill drove up the valley of the Rhône to Strasbourg, where Sandra's father-in-law, Prince Hohenlohe-Langenburg, was serving as the viceroy of Alsace-Lorraine. Staying a night at his old castle, they explored the city, which, a pawn of Franco-German warfare and diplomatic caprice, "had witnessed so many dramas." Strasbourg must have seemed to the handsome young couple a fitting symbol for their own private little drama of radically changed fortune.

When the summer of 1906 arrived, Ducky and Kirill "emerged from discreet obscurity" to attend their first public function as husband and wife. The occasion was the Romanian International Exhibition in Bucharest, commemorating the first forty years of the reign of King Carol I. Making the most of her opportunity to show off her beautiful sister and publicly display her respect and support, Missy conspicuously attended the festive exhibition every evening for a week with Ducky and Kirill solidly at her side. Surrounded by the most important members of Europe's aristocracy, the crown princess and her sister, escorted by their husbands, dined in fashionable lakeside pavilions hung with bright flags and glowing Chinese lanterns. Afterward, they went "to drink champagne, eat caviar, dance to the music of gypsies, and watch fireworks."

By publicly recognizing Ducky and Kirill's status and acknowledging their position in the royal caste system, Missy hoped to persuade their other relatives to grant her sister and brother-in-law a similar reception.

The visit to Bucharest considerably lifted Ducky and Kirill's spirits. They were flattered by Missy's thoughtful attention and enjoyed being in the limelight again. The only thing that marred their visit was Ducky's health. She was two months pregnant at the time and experiencing the usual discomforts; toward the end of their stay she came down with a stomach flu, and was confined to bed with severe cramps and vomiting. She had never been ill before. Kirill, desperately worried, sat by her bed and supervised the doctors. Fortunately, Ducky recovered quickly; she and Kirill decided to return to the Rosenau so that she could enjoy a long rest.

Missy wrote her good friend Nancy Astor a few weeks later, in the middle of July:

> *My sister has left, the last part of the time she was not very well. She caught a mild form of cholera and was very weakened by it and as she too is in the same state as you [pregnant] I felt rather worried about her especially as she all the same stuck to the day she had fixed for starting. However they arrived safely at Coburg. I very much enjoyed their visit and felt very lost when she was gone. Towards the end all went very smoothly with the King and he even finally offered Kirill his highest decoration although Kirill is in disgrace with the Tsar. My sister and I knew how it must have cost him a great deal of thought and worry as above all he is a political man and always sacrifices any personal interest to his political views, that is what often makes life with him a very heavy business.*

The return to a quiet life left Ducky and Kirill feeling let down. In the festivities of Bucharest they had tasted all the sweetness and security they had forfeited by their forbidden marriage.

At home in Paris and the south of France, Kirill spent most of his day pursuing his favorite pastime, golf. An accomplished and avid golfer, he played as often as he could, regardless of where he was or what the weather was like. (The duchess of Coburg, unimpressed, remarked that he treated golf "as seriously as others would sitting in Parliament.")

In the evening Ducky and Kirill visited with friends, played cards, or went to the theater. Life was uneventful but satisfying. Ducky seemed "perfectly content for once"; as for Kirill, these first few years of his married life belonged "to those very intimate and happiest experiences of my life, and in spite of the loss of everything, of my career, my position, and all the rest that the world can give, I had kept what was dearest to me. These years passed quickly as all joy does."

The young couple "travelled much, generally by car, and saw a good deal of all that is interesting and beautiful." Ducky ventured to Romania often since Missy was so tightly controlled by the old king. Together they decorated the rooms of the Cotroceni Palace and the mountain palace at Sinaia. Neither age nor distance had diminished their close friendship; if anything, their devotion had grown. They would always remain best friends.

Now entering their thirties, Ducky and Missy were maturing and becoming more stable. Missy's hedonism was slowly being replaced by devotion to duty. Surprisingly, the beautiful crown princess of Romania was transforming herself into an astute political being. So skilled at affairs of state had Missy become that even King Carol was finally showing signs of respect and confidence in her judgment. "As the King came to know . . . [Missy] better, his admiration for her native intelligence increased, and a genuine affection sprang up between them."

Ducky was also a far different woman at thirty than she had been at twenty. Her spirit had been tamed by adversity, and she had learned patience and tact in dealing with the world. Ostracism and unhappiness had polished her character, and her marriage to Kirill had completely changed her disposition. Totally committing herself "to a man whom she loved, and for whom she had waited so long, had made Ducky a more placid, contented" woman than "the over-active young Grand

Duchess who had tried to forget her problems by riding recklessly in the woods around Wolfsgarten."

When Ducky retreated to Coburg in the fall of 1906 to await her confinement, she was satisfied to give up riding and other strenuous activities to prepare for the arrival of Kirill's child. And as 1907 began, Ducky joined the Russian Orthodox Church.

Her conversion deeply gratified Kirill and delighted her mother. Unfortunately, the duchess couldn't resist using this joyful occasion to contrast her two eldest daughters, praising her favorite, Ducky, and, as always, denigrating the disappointing Missy. "I had so hoped that you would also one day turn Orthodox," the Duchess wrote peevishly to Missy, "especially on account of the children! But no, it is better so, as one must take it seriously and your life is not like that."

On January 20, 1907, Ducky gave birth to a baby girl at the Edinburgh Palace in Coburg. Honoring both her devoted mother and older sister, Ducky named the child Marie.

Her unhappy former married life lay far behind Ducky now. And Ernie's life, too, had moved forward. Only a few months before little Marie's birth, he had again become a father. This child was the son and heir he had so desperately wanted.

Ernie had remarried in 1905. His second wife, Princess Eleanore of Solms-Hohensolms-Lich, was a frumpy, homely little woman five years older than Ducky. The marriage was considered by most to be a very poor match for the Hessian grand duke; Eleanore, who was from a minor princely family, ranked far below her husband. But few realized what the poor woman would have to put up with. However, Eleanore managed to adjust to her husband's sexual orientation and proved to be the placid, selfless mother substitute he had always searched for. Another son was born to this very odd couple in 1908, and they remained happily married until the end of their lives, in 1937, when the Curse of Hesse struck again.

Parenthood brought little change to Ducky and Kirill's leisurely but empty life. Like most exiles, they discovered that constant movement and diversion, even if aimless, created the illusion of substance and purpose.

In the autumn of 1908, little Marie, whom they called Masha, was approaching her second birthday; the family was preparing to retreat from the misty streets of Paris and journey to the Riviera when a telegram suddenly arrived from St. Petersburg announcing the death of their uncle Alexis. The huge, handsome bachelor grand duke, who had spent his life as a full-time bon vivant, chasing women and devouring prodigious quantities of vintage wine and gourmet food, had dropped dead of a heart attack at the age of fifty-eight. His death came as a great shock to the whole Romanov family. The jovial tease of Ducky's youth and her staunch ally during the last few stormy years, Alexis had done much to promote her happiness and that of her husband. Both of them were grief-stricken. Alexis's death somehow sharpened their feeling of abandonment by their homeland.

But, to their utter amazement, Kirill was granted permission by the emperor to return home briefly for the funeral. (Significantly, Ducky was not allowed to accompany him; she was still too touchy a subject at Tsarskoe Selo.) Kirill's brother Boris had been instrumental in obtaining the permission. He had also won the emperor's consent for Kirill to wear his official navy uniform during the formal ceremonies.

The grand duke was almost overwhelmed when he stepped off the express at St. Petersburg and fell into the arms of his awaiting family. But after only three days, he had to return to his life of exile in France. Still, Kirill optimistically interpreted the episode as "the first step on the way to my complete rehabilitation and justification." Even in death, the faithful and kindly Alexis had come to Kirill's aid, just "as he had always done during his life."

During the last few months of 1908 and the beginning of the new year, a climate of forgiveness and reconciliation was gathering in Russia. Kirill's family had been working long and hard for his "complete rehabilitation," and his devoted brother schemed and maneuvered like a Borgia to pressure Nicholas into retracting his decree of banishment. But there were other factors in the emperor's life that had far more to do with his eventual change of mind.

The year after Nicholas sent Kirill into exile, the emperor's only brother, the grand duke Michael, fell in love with a twice-divorced commoner. Nicholas predictably forbade Michael to marry this thoroughly objectionable woman, the younger man promptly went to live abroad with his mistress, soon fathering an illegitimate child.

Humiliated and grieved by his own brother's scandalous behavior, the emperor took another look at the way he had treated his gallant and honorable cousin. In comparison with the shameless behavior of the grand duke Michael, the conduct of Ducky and Kirill "had been virtually blameless."

Another powerful force also stirred the emperor's conscience. Although Ducky's Uncle Bertie, King Edward VII, had been enraged by her divorce, he was deeply fond of his niece and was willing to forget the past and do all he could to help her in her present life. Hating the family tensions and divisions promoted by his mother, Queen Victoria, King Edward tried to be a peacemaker. While visiting Nicholas and Alexandra at Reval during the summer of 1908, the British monarch used his considerable tact and charm to put in "a friendly word" about Kirill and his wife. Edward probably reminded his niece Alexandra of the importance of forgiveness and family feeling. And undoubtedly, he also suggested to the emperor, in his most diplomatic manner, that "the continued sentence of banishment on his cousins was unwise."

Nicholas was left with a lot to think about that Christmas of 1908. Regardless of his personal likes and dislikes, he had Russia to consider. His only son and heir, five-year-old Czarevich Alexis, suffered from hemophilia and was not expected to reach adulthood. The next in line for the throne was Grand Duke Michael, who was living in disgrace with his "totally ineligible mistress." The only promising successor to Emperor Nicholas was the candidate third in line: his exiled cousin, Kirill.

Nicholas now began to see Kirill's marriage to Ducky as a breach of etiquette rather than a criminal act. Divorced or not, Ducky was at least as royal as anyone could be. And Kirill began to look more and more like a courageous war hero, who had always shown himself to be totally devoted to his duty and who definitely had the skills and leadership abilities a good Russian emperor would need.

Perhaps meekly, Nicholas began sharing his new opinions with his strong-minded wife, hoping to overcome her bitter prejudices. At this point another event suddenly intervened.

In January 1909, the health of Kirill's sixty-one-year-old father, Grand Duke Vladimir, began to deteriorate rapidly. The potential loss of his last Romanov uncle was too much for Nicholas to face. In the sadly diminishing imperial family, there were few upright and capable males on whom the Emperor could depend. Certainly he could not rely on his delicate young son or his irresponsible brother. In February, when it seemed as if Vladimir would die at any time, Nicholas found that he could not bear the thought that Vladimir's eldest son, Kirill, should continue to be dispossessed. Although Kirill's brother Boris was loyal and helpful to Kirill, neither he nor the other brother, Andrei, otherwise amounted to more than a talentless idler and wastrel. Consequently, the emperor decided once and for all that Kirill must be fully restored to his former position for the sake of family harmony and the future of Russia.

And the empress, though still smoldering with righteous indignation, grudgingly agreed.

In that first week of February 1909, while the family anxiously gathered around the bedside of the ailing Vladimir, Kirill's mother suddenly fired off a brief and excited telegram to her exiled son.

It read simply: "Ta femme est grande duchesse."

"Your wife is a grand duchess." With these words, all had been forgiven. Ducky and Kirill's life in limbo was at an end.

CHAPTER THIRTY

Coming Home

ALL HIS LIFE Kirill would treasure that telegram. He carried it with him until the day he died. It was more than a sentimental memento; the message "meant that all had been restored to me and that I could now return."

On February 13, 1909, a few days after that telegram arrived, Kirill received word that Grand Duke Vladimir had died in St. Petersburg. For several reasons, including Ducky's advanced pregnancy, he traveled alone to the funeral. Because Vladimir had "not only been a loving father but also a kind friend and a source of strength," Kirill was profoundly grieved. Unexpectedly, his sorrow was mitigated by Nicholas and Alexandra, who "showed [him] the greatest kindness and sympathy."

During Kirill's short stay in Russia he was gratified to have his wife's new title politely confirmed by the emperor. Ducky would now be known as Her Imperial Highness, Grand Duchess Victoria Feodorovna.

It was a strict Romanov and Orthodox tradition that when a European princess wedded a grand duke of Russia, her name must be changed to a Russian one. Thus the current empress, who had been born Princess Alix of Hesse, became Alexandra after her marriage.

"Victoria" was certainly not a Russian name. But in an extraordinary break with custom, Ducky was allowed to keep it. This was a sign of both Nicholas II's great affection for his wife's late grandmother Queen Victoria, and his sensitivity to his cousins' injured feelings.

Her Imperial Highness, Grand Duchess Victoria Feodorovna of Russia!

At last, Ducky had an officially recognized married identity. It could not have come at a better time. With her next child due in only two months, Ducky desperately wanted her growing family to be given its proper place in society. But all this good news came with a somewhat discouraging footnote. Because of their past, his and Ducky's restoration would have to be gradual. A slow pace would ease tensions in the imperial family and help the emperor save face.

The first step had been Nicholas's formal recognition of their rank. The next would be Kirill's assignment to active naval duty. Last, husband and wife would return to Russia and join the imperial court. This was the most delicate step, and as it turned out, their exile was to continue for more than a year. Kirill was now permitted to pass in and out of Russia as his naval maneuvers required, but Ducky, still a thorn in the empress's side, was not allowed so much as a visit.

Ducky gave birth to their second child, in Paris, on April 26, 1909. They had hoped for a son but the child was another girl, whom they named Kira after her disappointed father.

Soon after, Kirill received his new commission in the Russian navy: He was to be second in command of the light cruiser *Oleg.* Leaving his wife and children in France, Kirill joined the *Oleg* in the Baltic Sea and began the usual routine of gunnery and fleet exercises. When the rest of the fleet returned to Kronstadt for the winter, Kirill's ship was ordered to the Mediterranean.

Traveling overland through Germany and France to Cannes, Kirill enjoyed a brief reunion with Ducky and the children on the Riviera, then went on to the Adriatic port of Brindisi, where he rejoined the *Oleg.* At her winter anchorage at Suda Bay on the island of Crete, Kirill passed several months of "uneventful service." He fell under the spell of the beautiful island, "rich in the treasures of an extraordinary and unique civilization of pre-classical days."

In April of 1910 Kirill was promoted to the rank of captain and proudly sailed the *Oleg* to Piraeus (the port of Athens) where Ducky had gone by herself to wait for him. Together they toured Athens and visited their relatives the Greek royal family, who were of Russian descent.

The long separation had been very hard on Ducky. She was passionately in love with her husband and he with her. For the first four years of their married life they had scarcely been apart for more than a day or two, and the resumption of Kirill's naval career was an emotional trial for which she had not been prepared. Even though she was surrounded by her family and her two daughters, Ducky had centered her life so completely upon her husband that she was intensely lonely whenever he was away. And Kirill had missed his wife as much as she had him.

Their reunion was joyous. Receiving the emperor's permission to bring Ducky on board the *Oleg* for the voyage to Toulon, in the south of France, Kirill proudly sailed west with his wife at his side.

Arriving at Toulon, they learned that their exile was finally over. On this fine May afternoon in 1910, "their rehabilitation was to be completed." After an emotional farewell, Ducky rushed off to Cannes, where she had left the children with their grandmother. While Kirill completed his voyage on the *Oleg,* slowly sailing to the Baltic port of Kronstadt, Ducky gathered up their household and packed everything on a train to St. Petersburg. In the middle of May, she and her husband simultaneously arrived in Russia. After a few days in Kronstadt, Kirill continued on to St. Petersburg, where his wife and children were waiting for him. "It was our first meeting on Russian soil and the beginning of our married life there."

They were given the use of the Kavalersky Dom—the Cavalier's House—at Tsarskoe Selo; it was an ornate mansion with spacious and comfortable rooms. Because of the delicacy of their reinstatement, the grand-ducal couple decided to keep a low profile at first, and "settled down to a quiet family life."

Just after they moved in, Ducky's uncle Bertie, King Edward VII of England, died at Buckingham Palace. At sixty-eight, the merry monarch had finally paid his dues for a lifetime of self-indulgence. Although she had known him well during the old Eastwell and Osborne days, Ducky had never really cared for her extroverted uncle. Being a devoted admirer of her aunt Alix, Queen Alexandra, Ducky always resented the king's marital neglect and grossly immoral behavior, which seemed to her to be needlessly cruel.

Writing to her sister in Bucharest, Ducky admitted: "I too profoundly did not care for him to feel sad now, except at all old traditions. The whole world seems to lift up its voice and cry for the loss of a great King. But do you not feel as if the greatness only consisted in the startling comparison with the frivolous and notorious emphasis of his life as Prince of Wales. It is curious how little May and George [Queen Mary and King George V, the new sovereigns] are known in general. No

Crown Prince and Princess have ever mounted a throne so entirely unknown to people abroad."

Missy shared Ducky's low opinion of their uncle.

Ducky's life now centered on her Russian heritage, and England lay in her past. Her mother, a grand duchess of Russia, had lost her title through an unhappy marriage; now Ducky had become a grand duchess of Russia through the happiest of marriages. Wanting to become a full-fledged Romanov, she embraced everything Russian, making a special effort to surround herself with the best of her adoptive land's art and literature.

And, writing to Missy, Ducky firmly stated her intention to learn Russian, if only because she "was missing so much of what went on around her." However, French was the preferred language of the Russian aristocracy, so except in order to communicate with the servants, the grand duchess Victoria Feodorovna had little opportunity or motivation to practice the new language. Consequently, although she did acquire some knowledge of Russian, she never became proficient.

Ducky and Kirill gradually entered society, attending more and more court functions and social activities. They were disappointed to find that the imperial agenda featured events "of a mild kind and nothing to compare with the brilliant occasions of Uncle Sasha's reign." Thanks to the restricted social lives of the emperor and empress and the lingering animosity between Ducky and her former sister-in-law, the two women rarely met. This was probably just as well.

To Ducky's great joy, her husband's naval career centered in St. Petersburg for the next few years, so they were no longer separated by lengthy sea voyages. In the autumn of 1910 Kirill entered the Russian Naval Academy, where officers were given advanced instruction in various special subjects, and prepared for work in the Admiralty. He remained a student for the next two years.

In their spare time Ducky and Kirill indulged their passion for touring the countryside in their automobile. An automobile club had been organized by the car-owning members of the Russian nobility. The grand duke became its patron and most avid enthusiast and motor rallies—called the Victoria Fahrt—"Victoria Drive"—in honor of Ducky —were held regularly. The rallies were very well organized affairs that featured visits to several of the famous old castles in the three Baltic provinces of Russia. The club's camaraderie and the gracious hospitality of the castle owners made the rallies a very happy experience for Ducky and Kirill—a rare opportunity for independence and freedom.

One of their favorite excursions was to the beautiful river valley of the Aa in Livonia, where they were guests of Prince Lieven at Cremon Castle. They were especially intrigued by the half-German, half-Scandinavian aspect of the neat country houses, farms, and churches of the region. On one of their trips to Latvia they visited the Hanseatic port city of Riga and marveled at the sixteenth- and seventeenth-century architecture; then they took a leisurely drive through northern Germany and visited Ducky's mother in Coburg.

In November of 1910 Ducky's old friend and ally from Darmstadt, Sir George Buchanan, became the British ambassador to the court of St. Petersburg. Having carefully kept up her correspondence with Lady Buchanan, Ducky arranged an immediate audience. They were overwhelmed by her delight at seeing them. Embracing the ambassador's wife and warmly kissing her on both cheeks, Ducky laughingly apologized for her "bad behavior" in the past and reminisced about the old days in Darmstadt. Having witnessed their friend's misery in Hesse, Sir George and his wife could not help but be impressed by Ducky's "radiant happiness in her second marriage."

Soon their friendship was stronger than ever. For the next several years the Buchanans would provide Ducky with unfailing kindness and understanding. They were, perhaps, the most loyal and devoted friends she would ever have. Admiring and liking Grand Duke Kirill almost as much as they did his wife, the Buchanans became their most intimate companions.

"Many were the pleasant evenings which we spent at their informal dinners and dances," Sir George wrote later in his memoirs. "One of the most attractive traits in the Russian character was its extreme simplicity; and all the members of the Imperial family were as simple and natural as could be. They never stood on their dignity and disliked being treated with too much ceremony. When they came to the Embassy it was always by preference to some informal entertainment, and what they liked the best of all was a 'diner dansant' at round tables, where they could talk unreservedly to their friends."

Ducky was so fond of the Buchanans' teenaged daughter, Meriel, that she later tried to make a match for her with an eligible Romanov cousin, Duke Alexander of Leuchtenberg, a great-grandson of Emperor Nicholas I. The two young people had danced together at a court ball and apparently had fallen in love. Ducky encouraged the handsome duke in his courtship of Meriel and helped to arrange meetings between them. Much to her delight, Alexander became a serious suitor. An incurable romantic, Ducky was liberal-minded enough to place love over position or politics.

Unfortunately, before things progressed very far, the duke's practical father refused his permission for the marriage, insisting that Alexander instead marry a young woman with a sizable private income. Lady Buchanan, believing that the young duke "had behaved like a cad," was glad to be rid of him. But when Ducky gently informed Meriel of the father's final veto, the young woman was crushed. To distract her, Ducky sent her into the next room to play with her young daughters, who were building a toy castle. When the castle collapsed, the crash struck Meriel as "the death-knell to all my dreams."

For consolation, Ducky gave the ambassador's unhappy daughter a beautiful Siamese cat named Fatima. With Fatima chattering endlessly and rubbing against her legs, Meriel was comfortably on her way to a quiet life of spinsterhood.

While Ducky was settling down to her new life in Russia, Missy was becoming a considerable political force in her adopted country; she sparklingly dominated every sphere she entered. Renowned for her beauty and flamboyance, the crown princess was also gaining a notorious reputation. Often misunderstood and victimized by gossip, Missy seemed always on the verge of scandal. Ironically, it was her immoral uncle King Edward VII who had understood Missy best. While the kaiser and many of Missy's other relatives reviled her as a "whore" behind her back, her understanding uncle Bertie accurately assessed her true character. "A little coquetry and a flirtation every now and then were surely permissible in a young and pretty woman," he observed with affection. It seems likely that most of Missy's love affairs were nonexistent.

In 1909 Missy had given birth to her fifth child, a little girl she named Ileana. The beautiful baby was exceptionally well-behaved, as if she had been "born with the law within her." She became Missy's favorite, "the child of my soul," and developed into a selfless woman who brought great solace to both her mother and her aunt Ducky in the troubled times to come.

Ducky's youngest sister, Baby Bee, had finally married at age twenty-five in 1908. Her husband was the Infante Alfonso of Bourbon-Orléans (known as Ali), a descendant of both the Spanish and French royal families. The marriage was a rare blending of the devoutly Catholic Spanish dynasty with the intricately intertwined Protestant royal houses of the north. Like Kirill and Ducky, Beatrice and Ali experienced "great difficulties about their marriage" and for a time were not allowed to return to Spain. They spent the first years of their married life living with the kindhearted duchess.

Ducky and her family found Baby Bee and Ali to be "a delightful and original couple, stimulating company, amusing, unconventional and always full of quaint principles and ideas." The charming Spanish prince quickly became Ducky and Missy's favorite brother-in-law. Missy later recalled that Ali "was quite one of the most perfect human beings I have ever met." He and Baby Bee possessed a variety of interests and talents, the primary ones being aviation and music. They were both passionate devotees of Wagner, and "there was not a note of music nor a word of the libretto[s] that they did not know by heart."

As for Sandra, Princess Alexandra of Hohenlohe-Langenburg, she continued living a placid country life in southern Germany with her husband. The least interesting and certainly the least attractive of the duchess's four daughters, Sandra was something of a hypochondriac, who suffered "from headaches and jealousy."

Thanks to their complex and busy lives, the sisters usually managed to meet only once a year, during their summer holiday at their mother's home on the Tegernsee. Being the site of Ducky and Kirill's marriage and honeymoon, the Bavarian resort naturally had a special meaning for them. At Tegernsee, the sisters were children again, living in a carefree paradise under the stern protection of their mother.

When the summer visits were over, Ducky and her family returned to St. Petersburg for the winter season. Here, in the full splendor of the world's most opulent court, the imperial family found itself being divided into two very separate and incompatible social groups. Because of the circumstance of her marriage, Ducky found herself at the center of this rivalry and dangerously at odds with her perennial enemy, the empress.

CHAPTER THIRTY-ONE

The Vladimir Circle

B Y THE TIME Ducky and Kirill had returned to Russia, Nicholas and Alexandra had virtually abdicated their social leadership of the imperial court. The empress was "totally unsuited by temperament and health to lead any sort of grand gathering." Loathing the "false glitter, indolence, love of pleasure, and scandalous loose living" of St. Petersburg society, the high-strung Alexandra "could not and would not conceal her contempt."

Queen Victoria had always worried about her granddaughter's "excessive shyness" and feared that Alexandra's sudden ascent from princess of Hesse to empress of Russia "had left no time for developing ease in society." Alix had immediately shown that these concerns were fully justified. Indeed, at her first public appearance in St. Petersburg, the young empress stood frozen with fright, staring mutely at the floor. Her subsequent appearances at court balls and receptions "were blighted by the same shyness." Taciturn, with a tight, unsmiling mouth and nervous eyes, Alexandra seemed stiff and cold. Most believed her to be disdainful and arrogant. And they weren't entirely wrong.

Having taken her grandmother's teachings to heart, Alix was priggish and narrowminded. Shocked by the sexual immorality of the Russian nobility, Alexandra showed her disapproval by striking the offenders' names off her invitation list. Soon the gatherings at the palace were very small affairs indeed.

In turn, the St. Petersburg aristocrats found the empress "a prude and a bore" and were embarrassed by her fanatical devotion to Russian Orthodoxy.

As unpopular as she could possibly be, Alexandra retaliated by withdrawing into her family and lavishing all of her time and attention on her husband and children. On her first Christmas in Russia, Ducky had reported to Missy: "Alix I haven't seen as she is laid up, or at least does not receive visits so once more there is no chance of court festivities this winter."

Ducky wasn't the only one who regretted the loss of these festivities. Her good friend Sir George Buchanan had the distinct impression that the emperor sorely missed having an active social life: "I remember how, at the diplomatic reception on New Year's Day, 1912, after speaking to me about some political question, he said: 'My sisters tell me that they are going to your house tonight. Are you giving a ball?' On my replying that it was not a regular ball, but that we were giving a dinner of about a hundred and fifty persons at round tables and were going to dance afterwards, His Majesty exclaimed: 'What fun that will be.' I longed to ask him to come too, but knew that it would be useless, as neither he nor the Empress ever went into society."

Adding to the empress's many social problems was the delicate state of her health. By the time Ducky and Kirill entered the Russian court, Alexandra was practically an invalid. Seemingly physically healthy, she "undoubtedly was suffering from psychosomatic anxiety symptoms brought on by worry over the health of her son." The constant emotional stress "took a terrible toll." Convincing herself that she had a bad heart, Alexandra kept to her bed, and out of it was usually seen in a wheelchair, looking pained and fatigued. But when the czarevich Alexis had a bout of dangerous internal bleeding, the empress sprung magically to life, her own ailments mysteriously disappearing as she kept vigil beside his bed day and night until her son was well again.

Nicholas despaired of his wife's precarious health and failed to realize that her illness was psychogenic. He reported to his mother: "She keeps to her bed most of the day, does not receive anyone, does not come out to lunches and remains on the balcony day after day. . . . It is very important for me to get better, for her own sake, and the children's and mine. I am completely run down mentally by worrying over her health."

The emperor's anxiety and exhaustion, the empress's declining health, and the czarevich's hemophilia all combined to isolate the sovereigns from their court. They could not even be objects of sympathy because Alexis's illness, the chief cause of all their distress, was kept absolutely secret. Nicholas and Alexandra were haunted by one ominous question: "What would be the fate of the boy, the dynasty and the nation if the Russian people knew that their future Tsar was an invalid living under the constant shadow of death?"

To keep the secret, even other members of the Imperial Family were kept at a distance. The Romanovs had always been a close-knit family; most of them "resented the way the Empress seemed to seal them off from the palace and the Tsar." There was great bitterness between Nicholas's family and the families of his uncles and cousins, and this private ill-feeling was played out in the dazzling arena of St. Petersburg society.

Although there were several rival social leaders, only two really counted: Nicholas's mother, the dowager empress, and Kirill's mother, Grand Duchess Vladimir.

The dowager empress, the cheerful and kind-hearted widow of Emperor Alexander III, was virtually without enemies. She had always remained a charming and effervescent young princess of Denmark, simple and unspoiled, with a childlike zest for life. The parties she threw at her home, the Anitchkov Palace, were famous for their brilliance and gaiety and featured "the best French food and wine to be tasted in Russia." Unfortunately, these do's were few and far between: The dowager empress was away for a large part of the year, at her villa in the south of France, in her Danish homeland, or in England visiting her favorite sister, the queen mother, Alexandra.

So the most active and ambitious hostess was Ducky's energetic mother-in-law, Grand Duchess Vladimir. After a proper term of mourning when her husband died in 1909, the grand duchess had begun to hold sumptuous dinner parties and soirées, "almost oriental in character," in her elegant palace at Ropsha on the Neva River, near the Peterhof Palace. And the great balls regularly given by the grand duchess were so magnificent that they even "eclipsed the splendour of the Winter Palace." (There, the emperor and empress half-heartedly gave a few balls during the season, because they saw it as their duty to do so.)

Society loved the grand duchess Vladimir as much as the dowager empress. Kirill's mother looked every inch an empress, as the real empress did not. Poised, exquisitely dressed, superbly cultured, the grand duchess was a charming extrovert who never took a wrong step. She was as vibrant and energetic as Alexandra was sickly and withdrawn, and far from sharing the empress's puritanism, she was a worldly woman devoted to gossip and intrigue.

Above all else, Kirill's mother was ambitious. She coveted wealth and power, and the more she had, the more she wanted, both for herself and for her three sons. Her only daughter, Helen, had already made an unimpressive match, marrying Prince Nicholas, one of the Greek king's numerous younger sons. Now the grand duchess was determined to see her boys as highly placed as possible. It was even possible that one of those sons would become emperor of Russia.

So it was only fitting that the glamorous widow had turned her "grand palace on the Neva into a glittering court which far outshone Tsarskoe Selo." At the dinner parties and gatherings given here, the lively conversations treated the ruling couple with amusement and scorn. Very soon the social orbit of the grand duchess became something of a counter-court, a collection of social and political critics of the emperor and empress. This group became known as the Vladimir Circle.

The Vladimir Circle gradually became an important political movement opposing the emperor's misrule and the empress's harmful influence and including almost all the other members of the Romanov family and most of the nobility and imperial court.

Ducky automatically entered this charmed and lively circle when she returned to Russia with her husband. Having much in common with her mother-in-law, Ducky got along unusually well with Marie Pavlovna. Instead of a rival hostess, Kirill's beautiful and vivacious wife became "a respected and valued participant" in the Vladimir Circle. The fact that Ducky had felt the empress's spite added to her appeal.

Although Ducky did not foster a feud with the imperial couple, she did find satisfaction and amusement in the clever criticisms voiced by the sharp-tongued Marie Pavlovna and her friends. And she was exceedingly popular. With the exception, of course, of the empress, Ducky seems to have been friends with nearly everyone in the imperial family. Although Marie Pavlovna and the dowager empress "never really liked or trusted each other," Ducky got along excellently with both of them and was especially fond of the dowager empress, her aunt Minnie, whom she "always found kind, delightful and attractive." Said Meriel Buchanan, "No party was considered complete without her, the lovely—and very often unusual—clothes she wore, were examined minutely, and sometimes copied, the colour and decorations of her rooms were discussed, admired, and envied, invitations to the entertainments she gave were angled for assiduously by everyone in society."

But balancing such a vigorous social life with her domestic duties was often quite a strain on Ducky's health, despite her natural robustness. In the first month of her return to Russia, Ducky was already complaining to Missy: "They keep such late hours here and as I stuck to getting up only because of the children I find it often very fatiguing; night after night to get to bed between one and two in the morning never did suit us, did it?"

There was much more than socializing keeping Ducky busy. Besides attending to her husband and children and running a large household and overseeing the maintenance of several elaborate homes, she painted, decorated, gardened, and rode. In addition, she was called upon by a variety of petitioners. Because Ducky was the granddaughter of both a Russian emperor and a queen of England, she held a unique place at the Russian court. The double relationship with her cousin-husband and his family only strengthened her position, giving her a complex web of intimate ties that strung together every royal house in Europe. Whether their purposes were personal or political, many found it useful to proceed to the door of the generous grand duchess Victoria Feodorovna.

Not the least of her services was that of matchmaker. Ducky had little interest in using her influence to create loveless unions of diplomatic advantage. When her support was enlisted for the planned marriage of her niece Elisabetha, Missy's eldest daughter, to the Duke of Montpensier, a grandson of Louis Philippe, the last king of France, she responded with little enthusiasm, warily writing Missy: "Yesterday I was officially asked to receive this gentleman whose letter I am sending you in the name of the Duke of Montpensier. They very, very dearly desire this marriage with Elisabetha. You know that I myself could see no charm in this fiancé. . . . He is full of French show-off which of course to our natures is abhorrent."

Simple and straightforward, Ducky was something of an anomaly in the Byzantine scheming of the upper echelon of St. Petersburg society. And, when the strong-willed, no-nonsense Victoria Feodorovna committed herself to a project, nothing could dissuade her or shake her loyalty.

Ducky and Kirill remained supremely happy in their marriage. They loved being together as much as possible and arranged their days to maximize their time together. A quiet home life seemed to bring the greatest gratification to both of them.

Traveling to their former residences in France, making winter trips to the Riviera and summer excursions to Coburg and the Tegernsee, the couple relaxed into a safe and secure existence. Since real love matches were so rare among early twentieth-century royalty, Kirill and his wife were quite a novelty. Great passion and dynastic unions seldom coincided.

Adding to their happiness was their close bond with Marie and Kira. According to their admiring aunt Missy, or Maddy, as they had come to call her, the girls "had everything on earth of which human children could dream." Missy called them "two splendid children, well-grown, solid, with lovely hair and perfect skin and as superlatively groomed as English ponies."

Ducky exercised her decorative talents by arranging her house beautifully and filling it with innumerable treasures, the most notable being several superb specimens of jade. In Missy's opinion, "Ducky had perfect taste and a passion for arranging her rooms in a rather unusual and uncommon way." But several elements of her new environment struck Ducky as less than ideal. It was the harsh northern climate that troubled her most. To Missy, she constantly complained of "the want of light and of the endlessness of the St. Petersburg winters, where the days are so cruelly short." Painting, still her favorite hobby, provided a distraction. Ducky had perfected her considerable talents, producing masterful watercolors of flowers in soft, pale tones.

One summer, while she was staying with her mother-in-law at Tsarskoe Selo, Ducky painted a dramatic portrait of Meriel Buchanan kneeling by a stone sarcophagus covered with white roses. There were black draperies around Meriel and her face was hidden in her arms. During the long posing sessions, Ducky chatted to Meriel and Lady Buchanan in a much freer and informal way than ever before. The beautiful grand duchess's violet eyes flashed as she shared her memories of "her former unhappiness" in her first marriage. Occasionally, she uttered heated "outbursts against the 'stuffiness' of her English relations, in particular the Queen who had refused to hear of her divorce."

Ducky emotionally told the Buchanans, "When I was young, Missy and I adored Grandmama Queen. We used to think it a great honour to

be invited to go and see her. We loved her bullfinch and all the photographs in her room, but we thought her spaniel was too fat. And, oh, how
solemn her Court was. How tired I got of the talk of 'Grandpapa in
Heaven,' and of the constant mourning. And how I later resented the
lectures she was giving me." It was apparently very difficult for Ducky to
completely forget the great injustice she believed had been done to her.

Now, however, she seemed profoundly contented. Surrounded by the
world's greatest luxury and enjoying one of royalty's most exalted ranks,
Ducky relaxed by the side of the man she loved, and proudly watched
their two beautiful daughters grow. She felt safe and secure and lucky. As
she flourished at the center of the Vladimir Circle and captured the admiration of St. Petersburg society, most observers could not help but
think that she "would have filled the imperial throne far better than its
actual occupants."

CHAPTER THIRTY-TWO

A Holy Devil

*I*N THE EARLY SPRING OF 1912 Kirill and Ducky's two-year idyll came to an end. Finishing his studies at the naval academy, the grand duke received command of his former ship the *Oleg*. He joined her at the Baltic port of Libau, where the entire fleet was still icebound thanks to the late-winter snows.

With a command at last, Kirill impatiently waited for the ice to break so he could put out to sea. His climb to command had been long and difficult. Like all naval cadets, he had faced labors, hardships, and perils, assuming only the responsibilities and privileges he had honestly earned. And now he "had reached the fulfillment of an ambition": He had a ship of his own. But he paid a great price.

Kirill's experiences at Port Arthur during the Russo-Japanese War "had impressed themselves with rather unfortunate results" on his psyche, leaving him with "a dread of the sea" that lasted for years and constantly impeded his career. Whenever Kirill was on water he "was haunted by the spectre of the disaster." At night his dreams were filled with "the vision of that gurgling maelstrom, the dark depth of the swirling whirlpools and the roaring blast of air issuing from the sinking ship as it pulled hundreds down with her while they were swarming about on the capsizing hull."

At first, Kirill could control his fear of the water. After participating in exercises with the Baltic fleet, he sailed the *Oleg* to Stockholm in July of 1912 to attend the Olympic Games, having been appointed by the emperor as Russia's official delegate. Ducky joined him, arriving on the yacht belonging to the Russian admiralty. They enjoyed a "thoroughly gay and delightful visit," attending many social events and yachting among the lovely pine-clad islands of the Swedish capital.

When the festivities were over Kirill sadly watched his wife sail back to St. Petersburg and then resumed his command of the *Oleg,* returning to the extensive fleet maneuvers and gunnery practice in the Gulf of Finland. In autumn he was ordered to take the *Oleg* to the Mediterranean for the winter. Kirill optimistically began the long voyage, but before he even reached the first port, Reval, he was suddenly attacked by what he called "the evil."

"The evil" was actually a paralyzing panic, the dread of the sea that had continuously pursued him in "ghastly and haunting" dreams. It was impossible for him to remain on the water; he had to abandon the *Oleg* at Reval. Ducky hurried to meet him there, and, carefully soothing his shattered nerves, took him to the country place of their friend Countess Orlov-Davidov. For two weeks they quietly strolled the grounds of the estate, enjoying the tranquil pleasures of the Estonian countryside.

Fully rested, Kirill made plans to rejoin his ship in the Mediterranean. With Ducky at his side, he set off by train for the south of France. Since the *Oleg* was at Port Said in Egypt, he planned to take a German steamer there from Marseilles. Just as he said good-bye to his wife and prepared to board the ship, he was seized again by his "holy terror" of the sea. As hard as he tried, it was absolutely impossible for him to set foot on the ship.

Ironically, at this same time Kirill was having a special motor yacht made for him in England. Desperate to conquer his fear of the water, he decided to take Ducky over to see it. They went directly to Paris to catch the boat train to London, but at the station Kirill was so overwhelmed by the thought of having to cross the narrow English Channel that he instantly abandoned the journey.

Ducky offered Kirill all her courage and moral strength, but he was powerless against his fear. The only solution was to give up his naval duties. As Kirill wrote in his memoirs, "The haunting spectre of the sea chased me mercilessly and brought my career afloat to a conclusion. I could do nothing whatever against it. I have faced death and much danger, but against this malady I could summon nothing to come to my aid." They returned to St. Petersburg and took up their quiet family life again. But soon Ducky and Kirill became aware that "a strange individual had entered into the close surroundings of the Imperial Family."

Gregory Rasputin, who had first appeared in several of St. Peters-burg's most elegant drawing rooms in 1905, was born in 1872 in a vil-lage in western Siberia. A dissolute man, he rejected the life of a hard-working peasant and quickly found that by assuming the role of a mystical holy man he could fully indulge his laziness and profligate ways. Drawing notoriety and many enemies, he wandered across Russia pre-senting himself as a *starets,* a man of God "who lived in poverty, asceti-cism and solitude, offering himself as a guide to other souls in moments of suffering and turmoil." But the gross lecher Rasputin was a fraudu-lent *starets.*

Arriving in the refined Russian capital, Rasputin quickly established himself as a holy man with extraordinary powers. With a deep, powerful voice, blazingly hypnotic eyes, and a strange psychic strength, the lusty Rasputin concentrated his attention on wealthy society women. Al-though much about him was "repulsive," he enjoyed an amazing success with some of the most elegant ladies of St. Petersburg. At first finding "him disgusting [they] discovered later that disgust was a new and thrilling sensation; that the rough and strong-smelling peasant was an al-luring change from a surfeit of perfumed and pomaded cavalry officers and society gentlemen." As for the more religious women who were willing to offer him money but not sex, to them his "coarse appearance was a sure sign of his spirituality" and humility.

Rasputin was nothing less than filthy. Rarely bothering to wash or change his clothes, he gave off a foul and sickening odor; his hands were grimy, his fingernails black, and his greasy beard and hair tangled and filled with scaly debris. The fake *starets*'s revolting appearance seemed to enhance his status.

Not only was Rasputin dirty but, according to Prince Felix Yous-soupoff, who would later play a critical role in his life, the broad-shouldered, muscular "*starets*" was ugly as well. His face was "a coarse oval, with large ugly features overgrown with a slovenly beard, and with a long nose." His eyes "were amazingly repulsive . . . small, almost colourless, and too closely set in large, exceptionally deep sockets; so that from a distance they were not visible—they seemed to get lost in the depths of their recesses."

Despite their appearance it was Rasputin's eyes that made his fortune. Compelling and magnetic, his gaze burned into his subjects, seeming to drain them of energy and willpower. Rasputin used his remarkable hyp-notic talents to seduce, manipulate, dominate, and control. He also used them to cure—usually nervous disorders and psychosomatic illnesses. It was this rare ability that brought him his greatest power and fame—and, eventually, his doom.

It was the grand duchess Militsa who first introduced Rasputin to the emperor and empress, in November of 1905. A daughter of the king of Montenegro, Militsa had married one of Ducky and Kirill's Romanov cousins. She and her family "were prominent practitioners of the pseudo-Oriental brand of mysticism then in vogue in many of the capital's most elegant drawing rooms" where the jaded aristocracy, "bored with the old church routines of traditional Orthodoxy, looked for meaning and sensation in the occult." Believing in all matters supernatural, Militsa was convinced that the amazing Rasputin could cure the hemophiliac czarevitch.

And it is a fact that this greasy, unkempt peasant from Siberia was able to stop Alexis's dreadful bleeding when all others had failed.

How he was able to do so is a question that has continued to plague modern science. The likeliest answer is that Rasputin was a naturally talented hypnotist. With his extraordinary eyes and overpowering will, he hypnotized the child until he was totally relaxed state and then planted the suggestion that the bleeding would stop. Recent scientific discoveries have established the great influence of the mind and the emotions on physical health; established under hypnosis a person can indeed be induced to constrict the small arteries and capillaries, significantly reducing the flow of blood.

This unique ability to save the Russian heir from bleeding to death was Rasputin's ticket to heaven. As long as he was able to deliver his magic cures, he was in an unrivaled position of power and authority at the imperial court. And because he cloaked his deeds in the unassailably holy garments of the church, to attack Rasputin was tantamount to attacking God. It was the perfect setup for a corrupt and unscrupulous man.

After insinuating himself into the imperial household as a divine messenger from God, Rasputin consolidated his power by "miraculously" saving the life of Nicholas and Alexandra's small son time and time again. In essence, "Rasputin took the empire by stopping the bleeding of the Tsarevich." His means were unimportant. All that mattered was that the empress "believed that Rasputin was able to stop Alexis's hemorrhages and she believed that he did it through the power of prayer.

Whenever Alexis began to recover from an illness, she attributed it exclusively to the prayers of the Man of God."

At first, Nicholas had reserved judgment on Rasputin's bold claims and uncanny abilities. Alexandra "was greatly troubled over this, and made it her most sacred duty to use all her influence to overcome her husband's distrust." She succeeded admirably. By the time Ducky and Kirill took up residence in St. Petersburg, the false *starets* was the most important person in the emperor and empress's life.

This would have been dangerous had Rasputin reigned only over Nicholas and Alexandra's domestic affairs. But the empress fell victim to Rasputin's political authority as well. She firmly believed that he had been "sent by Heaven to make the voice of the Russian people heard above the cowardice of the Court flunkeys."

Consequently, of course, Rasputin's voice was the only one the empress listened to; and the empress's voice seemed to be the only one the emperor listened to. The "holy man" from Siberia had stumbled onto a very simple formula for success: By controlling Alexandra, he controlled Russia.

Rasputin now became the man most in demand in the jaded, mannered world of Russian high society. After establishing his influence there, he commenced to satisfy his other desires. Maintaining his holy pose, he easily seduced the most elegant and beautiful women of the capital by convincing them that they could achieve salvation only by first committing a serious sin. Thus he could provide them with the entire process of purification: First, they would indulge together in the sins of the flesh; then they would pray together and reach the sacred state of redemption.

It didn't take long for the lascivious "*starets*" to gain a remarkable sexual reputation in the upper circles of St. Petersburg. Sleeping with Rasputin was considered the "supreme honor." Women boasted of doing so, and their husbands even publicized their holy cuckoldry. After all, to his worshipful disciples, "Rasputin was a reincarnation of the Lord, and intercourse with him, in particular, could not possibly be a sin." His sexual partners could experience pure pleasure without being bothered by their consciences.

But Rasputin eventually began to push his luck at Tsarskoe Selo a bit too far. Using the pretext of bedtime prayer, he hung around the bedrooms of Nicholas and Alexandra's four adolescent daughters while they changed into their long white nightgowns. The girls' governess was horrified by his leering presence, but when she tactfully mentioned the episode to the empress she was discharged. Returning to her family in Moscow, the governess visited Grand Duchess Elizabeth, Ducky's Aunt Ella, and implored her to speak with the empress, who was her younger sister.

Since her husband's brutal assassination in 1905, Ella had completely retreated from worldly life, becoming a nun in the Russian Orthodox Church. She founded her own abbey, the Convent of Mary and Martha, in Moscow and devoted herself to working with the poor. (For the rest of her life she wore a long, hooded robe of fine pearl-gray wool and a white veil.) However, Ella's piety had not eliminated her common sense. She saw Rasputin as nothing less than "a blasphemous and lascivious impostor." Worried about his growing influence over her sister, she used every opportunity she could to speak, "sometimes gently sometimes bitterly," to Alexandra about the fraudulent *"starets."* Tragically, the only effect of these talks was to gradually alienate the two sisters until "neither could touch the other."

The empress's sister was not the only member of the imperial family to condemn Rasputin. In fact, one by one, almost all of the Romanovs came to oppose him. By the time Ducky and Kirill were establishing their place at court, Rasputin was being repudiated even by the grand duchess Militsa. Militsa had gone directly to Tsarskoe Selo and confronted the empress with evidence of his sordid behavior. Refusing to discuss the matter, Alexandra coolly dismissed her.

The evidence of Rasputin's evil character began mounting higher and higher. The Church started an investigation, but when the first damning information was brought to the empress's attention, the theologians involved were quickly banished to remote posts. When close police surveillance of Rasputin's activities produced thick dispatches to the emperor detailing the most depraved and iniquitous conduct, the police themselves soon became the special enemies of the throne.

No matter what anyone said, "Alexandra refused to consider that there might be another side to her Man of God." Even in 1911, when he was caught by his fellow churchmen trying to rape a nun, Rasputin managed to exculpate himself by hurrying to the palace and convincing Alexandra that his version of what had happened was the truth. "Saints are always calumniated," she steadfastly repeated. "He is hated because we love him." Naive to the core, Alexandra simply couldn't conceive of

Rasputin's debauchery. "They accuse Rasputin of kissing women, etc.,"
she emotionally wrote to her husband. "Read the apostles; they kissed
everybody as a form of greeting."

No longer content to dominate the emperor and empress, Rasputin
took control of the Orthodox Church too, using his influence with the
throne to have his choices appointed to important positions, while those
who displeased him were removed or demoted. He dictated to Nicholas
and Alexandra who should fill what high office and what the government policy should be. The administrative structure of the Russian empire became, in effect, a giant chessboard upon which Rasputin moved
men back and forth for the mere pleasure of doing so.

The chain of command always remained the same: Rasputin directed
the empress, and the empress directed the emperor.

Meanwhile, it seemed as if the entire nation was becoming outraged
over the sovereigns' championing of a man so obviously evil. More than
any other factor during the last decade of the Romanov monarchy, the
presence of Rasputin beside the imperial throne divided the emperor
from his people. Each side had the unsettling impression that the other
was trying to pull it down into the darkness.

Perhaps the most precise evaluation of the tragic effect of Rasputin on
the imperial family was made by Pierre Gilliard, the children's Swiss
tutor, who closely witnessed these events. "The fatal influence of that
man was the principal cause of death of those who thought to find in
him their salvation."

Because of his extreme unpopularity with the Russian people and because of the scandals continually connected with his name, Rasputin
began to maintain a much lower profile in St. Petersburg society. After a
huge public uproar in 1911, he visited Tsarskoe Selo as secretly as possible. Few ever caught sight of him in the palace corridors. Even many of
the family servants never saw him.

Not surprisingly, therefore, few other members of the imperial family,
confirmed critics of Rasputin, ever actually met him. Ducky and Kirill,
for example, never did. Because of the growing animosity between their
branch of the family and the emperor's, they never entered the tightly
guarded circle around the latter.

But they were well aware of Rasputin's closeness to the throne and his
deleterious influence on the country's morale. They shared their aunt
Ella's view of Rasputin, seeing him as a dangerous fraud. As they saw
him, "he was neither a saint nor a monk, nor, indeed, mad . . . but quite

simply a very healthy and canny Russian peasant with an unusual gift for which science has hitherto found no explanation, but which is more frequently to be found among primitive peoples than among those who have been touched by civilization."

And they could clearly see that this clever and enterprising peasant was bringing disgrace to the imperial family. They saw that his sudden fame and authority "went to his head" and that he was being thoroughly "spoilt by the good things of life to which he was not used." To Ducky and Kirill's great alarm, several unscrupulous members of the Russian aristocracy were using the bogus *starets* to achieve results contrary to the true interests of the country.

Not having grown up in Russia, Ducky did not fully understand the mystical and fatalistic Russian spirit, so she was far more disturbed by Rasputin's domination of Nicholas and Alexandra than her husband was. The grand duchess was appalled by Rasputin's hypocrisy and posturing. In her opinion, he threatened not only the throne, but the entire Romanov family.

Visiting Missy in Romania, Ducky confessed to her sister her grave concerns about the phony *starets*. Tsarskoe Selo, she said, "was looked upon as a sick man refusing every doctor and every help." And, of course, at the very center of this problem was their unbalanced cousin Alix.

Rasputin was ever increasing his power over her. Although there was never any sexual involvement between them, rumors flourished for years that Rasputin and the empress were lovers. Unfortunately for Alexandra, her florid style of writing produced letters that were later used as evidence of the affair. In one such letter Alexandra effusively expressed her spiritual passion for Rasputin: "My beloved, unforgettable teacher, redeemer and mentor! How tiresome it is without you! My soul is quiet and I relax only when you, my teacher, are sitting beside me. I kiss your hands and lean my head on your blessed shoulder. Oh how light, how light do I feel then. I only wish one thing: to fall asleep, to fall asleep, forever on your shoulders and in your arms. What happiness to feel your presence near me. Where are you? Where have you gone? Oh, I am so sad and my heart is longing. . . . Will you soon be again close to me? Come quickly, I am waiting for you and I am tormenting myself for you. I am asking for your holy blessing and I am kissing your blessed hands. I love you forever."

In fact, realizing how great a risk such an indiscretion would have entailed, Rasputin never made romantic advances toward the empress. Besides, he was sexually occupied enough not to need yet another liaison. Every day a steady stream of women flowed in and out of Rasputin's St. Petersburg apartment to eat and drink with him while seeking his advice and holy company. Some came to gossip, others to find excitement and pleasure. The unkempt faux *starets* would sit at his dining room table surrounded by a large group of female admirers, stroking the arms and hair of the women next to him. Occasionally he "put down his glass of Madeira and took a young girl on his lap. When he felt inspired, he rose before everyone and openly led his choice to the bedroom, a sanctum that his adoring disciples referred to as 'The Holy of Holies.' " Once inside the darkened room, he would reassuringly whisper to them: "You think that I am polluting you, but I am not. I am purifying you."

Rasputin certainly would have been eager to make the acquaintance of so beautiful and high-ranking a member of the imperial family as Ducky. But she, like everyone else in her husband's immediate family, was so hostile to him that nothing could have convinced her to dignify him with her presence.

Nevertheless, curiosity remained. Ducky could never look at Nicholas and Alexandra without wondering whether they had just come from consulting in the shadows with the nefarious charlatan.

As time passed, national concerns about Rasputin grew urgent, and events proved that all fears had been fully justified.

CHAPTER THIRTY-THREE

The Last Waltz

T HE GOLDEN WORLD of European royalty was at its most magnificent in 1913, an intricate structure of ranks each of which ruled the one beneath it. It was a brilliantly detailed system of unquestioned values and inflexible rules. It was an elegant web too complexly spun to be maintained.

Ducky and Kirill, although not crowned sovereigns, were at the very center of this beautiful and privileged world. All over Europe they enjoyed a thrilling succession of glittering parties and balls and official galas. They had their palaces and town mansions in Russia, their apartment in Paris, a villa on the Riviera, a splendid yacht, and every luxury the earth could offer. And nowhere was life more spectacular than in St. Petersburg.

The winter season of 1913 was more brilliant than any in memory. It was almost "as if the participants and onlookers had some premonition of what was in store for them." Never had the celebrations been so numerous, colorful, and enthusiastic. The majestic palaces along the Neva River blazed with a thousand lights, and the streets and shops of the city were filled with happy, excited crowds. The Fabergé jewelry store, "with its heavy granite pillars and air of Byzantine opulence, was thronged with customers. In hair-dressing salons, ladies sat on blue-and-gold chairs, congratulating themselves on getting an appointment and exchanging the latest gossip." The hottest story concerned the appearance of the dancer Nijinsky at the Imperial Ballet in a revealing costume.

When he made his entrance onto the stage, "there was a commotion in the Imperial box. The Dowager Empress was seen to rise, fix the stage with a devastating glare and then sweep out of the theatre." Shortly after, Nijinsky was expelled from the ballet group.

From the tall, brightly lit windows of the ballrooms of the great houses of St. Petersburg, lilting dance music poured, mixing with the jingle of sleigh bells. Hostesses eagerly competed to throw original and exciting parties. One socialite gave a black and white ball. Another invited everyone to come to her party in ordinary evening dress, but wearing a wig. Meriel Buchanan, the British ambassador's daughter, arranged a series of picturesque tableaux at an embassy party; the guests impersonated thrilling figures such as Jack the Ripper and Bluebeard. The Princess Obolensky wrote the music for a ballet, which she had her friends perform; she followed this up with a Greek mythology party at which the guests dressed as Olympians.

Next to Ducky's mother-in-law, Grand Duchess Vladimir, the most sparkling leader of St. Petersburg society was "the highly rouged, sharp-tongued" Countess Kleinmichel. She gave the season's most spectacular social event, a ball at which the guests danced several set quadrilles in the costumes of different historical periods. The most magnificent dance was the Persian quadrille, which was led by Ducky and her brother-in-law Boris. Thanks to Ducky's influence, Meriel Buchanan was allowed to take part in the ball, which was officially closed to unmarried women.

These mansions and palaces were buried in snow, but inside they "were very hot and often filled with palm trees dispatched from the Crimea, or flowers sent by special train from the south of France." When it was time for the formal dinner, "strong powers of gastronomical endurance" were required. The elaborate meal always began with hors d'oeuvres served in a separate room and eaten standing up. Guests mingled and drank several glasses of vodka as they helped themselves to the expensive caviar, salted cucumbers, smoked salmon, gangfish from the Volga, hot mushrooms in cream sauce, and hundreds of other delicacies. Proceeding to the banquet table, the partygoers sat down to borscht with thick cream and hot pastries, followed by sturgeon or sterlets, partridge or venison. The meal concluded with a spectacular dessert served with great panache.

During these formal dinners, lively conversation flowed as freely as the sparkling wine. Between every course little yellow cigarettes would be handed around the table, and "through the blue haze of smoke the jewels on women's fingers would flash with some quick movement or the light would catch a thousand sparks in some decoration, or gleam on the golden aiguillettes swinging from the shoulder of some young Grand Duke."

A popular end-of-the-evening diversion was a midnight visit to the Gypsy quarter, Novaia Derevnia, on the outskirts of St. Petersburg. The fastest way to get there was in troikas, special carriages pulled by three horses, the center one trotting in a shaft while the loose outside ones galloped. It took great skill to drive a troika, for the driver had to stand up the entire way. Wearing a round cap adorned with peacock feathers, the driver would pass by the last suburbs of the capital and let his horses break into a furious gallop as he entered the forests of the frozen countryside. "The wild pace through the bitter-cold forest, under a starlit sky, was an excitement in itself."

Arriving at the crude Gypsy camps, the troika would stop before the low, hidden buildings and everyone would jump out and bang loudly on the doors. The sleepy Tatars who answered the door would soon be serving champagne and lighting candles while a Gypsy troupe of twenty to thirty performers played their instruments and sang in their curious metallic voices, "with a ring in it of something Eastern, barbaric and utterly strange to European ears, to the thrum of the guitars."

Not only was Russian society at its glittering peak in the winter of 1913, but the entire country was also experiencing a rare mood of optimism and hope. The nation was more prosperous than ever, the humiliating Japanese war was in the past, and, most important, the tercentenary of Romanov rule was being celebrated with a series of magnificent and patriotic ceremonies.

Exactly three hundred years before, Michael Romanov had become emperor of Russia and established his dynasty. Since that time the Romanovs had ruled. To stimulate the loyalty and patriotism of his people, Nicholas II had decided to celebrate in a grand fashion. He apparently succeeded very well, producing "a surge of enthusiasm for the ancient monarch." Everyone eagerly anticipated the official celebrations and even looked forward to a return to the tradition of sumptuous court balls.

But mantaining their complete withdrawal from society, Nicholas and Alexandra gave no court balls that season. However, they did abandon their solitude at Tsarskoe Selo in February, moving to the Winter Palace in the capital.

The festivities officially began on the morning of March 6, 1913, with a thirty-one-gun salute from the Peter and Paul Fortress. A great "Te Deum" was to be sung that afternoon in the Cathedral of Our Lady of Kazan. Early in the day, huge crowds began gathering; the Nevsky Prospect, along which the imperial procession would pass, was jammed with humanity. At noon the emperor and empress climbed into their carriage and began driving from the Winter Palace to the cathedral. The rest of the Romanov family, including Ducky and Kirill, followed. Despite the line of soldiers holding it back, excited crowds eventually managed to mob Nicholas and Alexandra's carriage.

The golden-domed cathedral was filled beyond capacity. Almost everyone crowded inside was standing, but special seats in front of the altar had been saved for members of the imperial family, foreign ambassadors, and government ministers. Ducky and her husband looked on in horror as Rasputin came in and sat down near them. Dressed in a crimson silk tunic and patent-leather top boots, he seemed more presentable than usual. No one quite knew what to do. At last Michael Rodzianko, the president of the Duma, marched up to Rasputin, began kicking him in the ribs, and finally grabbed him by the scruff of his neck and threw him bodily out of his seat. Defeated, Rasputin slunk away.

Several minutes later a hush fell over the assemblage and the sacred service began. The dark cathedral glowed with thousands of candles; hundreds of jeweled icons sparkled in the reflected light as old Patriarch Antiochus began conducting the religious ceremony. Every eye followed Nicholas and Alexandra, but the empress's perpetual look of somber disdain inspired "no feeling of warmth in the vast assembly, only cold curiosity."

There were other impressive ceremonies in the weeks that followed. Ducky and Kirill attended a grand ball given by the nobility of St. Petersburg in honor of the imperial family. Thousands of guests filled the ballroom—a dazzling, fairytale spectacle. There were receptions at the Winter Palace, where Nicholas and Alexandra stood for hours greeting a parade of delegates from every corner of their empire. Ducky could not help noticing how worn and remote her cousin Alix looked; she seemed to perform her duty grudgingly. Meriel Buchanan made the same observation. At two other major receptions, Alexandra did not even appear. Her mother-in-law, the popular dowager empress, happily filled in for her. The only real chance the people had to see their empress was at a gala performance of Glinka's *A Life for the Czar* at the Maryinsky Opera House. Meriel Buchanan, who attended, studied Alexandra at very close range:

> She was very pale when she came in, the pale blue ribbon of St Andrew that crossed her breast matching the turquoises in her magnificent tiara and parure, the soft folds of her white velvet dress setting off her stately figure. But her lovely tragic face was expressionless, almost austere as she stood by her husband's side during the playing of the National Anthem, her eyes enigmatical in their dark gravity, seeming fixed on some secret inward thought that was certainly far removed from the crowded theatre and the people who acclaimed her. Not once did a smile break the immobile sombreness of her expression when, the Anthem over, she bent her head in acknowledgement of the cheers that greeted its conclusion and sank down in the gold-backed arm-chair that had been provided for her.
>
> The Diplomatic Body had been given places all along the first tier and our box happened to be next to the Imperial one, and, sitting so close, we could see how a dull, unbecoming flush was stealing over her pallor, could almost hear the laboured breathing which made the diamonds which covered the bodice of her gown rise and fall, flashing and trembling with a thousand uneasy sparks of light. Presently it seemed that this emotion or distress mastered her completely, and with a few whispered words to the Emperor she rose and withdrew to the back of the box, to be no more seen that evening.
>
> A little wave of resentment rippled over the theatre, women glanced at each other and raised their shoulders expressively, men muttered despairingly below their breath. Was it not always the same story? The Empress hated St Petersburg, disliked its society, its people, anything to do with it; she refused to take her proper place by the Emperor's side, would not put her own personal feelings in the background and make herself pleasant. Later on I remember my mother and father asserted that whatever the reason for the Empress's sudden withdrawal had been, it was certainly a very real torment or affliction and no whim or fancy, but the disagreeable impression remained in people's minds and would not be conjured away by any argument or discussion.

Despite the warmth inspired by the tercentenary celebrations, Russians were offended by their aloof and sullen empress. Even later in the year, when Princess Catherine Radziwill daringly published a book that informed the public for the first time of the czarevich's tragic illness, Nicholas and Alexandra's subjects still withheld their sympathy. To their minds, Alexandra was simply refusing to play the game; her reasons weren't important.

The festivities finally ended in June of 1913 with a final procession. It began with Nicholas riding dramatically alone into the city of Moscow. The weather was hot and glorious, with a clear, sapphire sky. Sixty feet behind Nicholas came a massive squadron of Cossacks. At Red Square, the small, slender emperor dismounted and walked solemnly behind a line of chanting priests across the square and into the Kremlin. Behind him, in an open car, followed Alexandra and Alexis. They were supposed to have walked in procession after the emperor, but Alexis was ill from a recent dangerous hemorrhage; he had to be carried in the arms of a husky Cossack.

After attending the celebrations, Ducky and Kirill motored through their favorite holiday spots in the Baltic provinces, ending up at the duchess of Coburg's summer home on the Tegernsee. There, Ducky and her three sisters and their husbands gathered around Marie and spent sunny days sailing on the lake and laughing at the irrepressible antics of Missy's little boy Nicky, who infuriated his grandmother by putting water in the gas tank of her prized automobile. Evenings found the duchess reading aloud from the classics in her clear, crisp voice while her daughters sewed and knitted. Occasionally relatives came to visit, and there were happy excursions to Oberammergau and the Wagner Festival at Bayreuth.

This blissful summer of 1913 was the last time they would all be together.

While in Germany, Kirill was sent by the emperor Nicholas to unveil an elaborate memorial at Leipzig in honor of the Russian soldiers who had fought a hundred years ago in the Battle of the Nations, significant as the beginning of Napoleon's downfall. Ducky and their two daughters accompanied him. From Leipzig they returned to Tsarskoe Selo to spend the rest of the summer and the fall.

The greatest excitement toward the end of that year was the proposed marriage between Kirill's younger brother Boris and the emperor's eldest daughter, Olga. The proposal had been formally presented by Boris's mother, Grand Duchess Vladimir, who had placed great hope on easily achieving this most ambitious of matches, but Alexandra rejected it without a second thought. Even among the loose-living male Romanovs, the lazy and dissipated Boris was notorious. Alexandra was horrified at the prospect of this callous rake marrying her innocent young daughter.

"What an awful set his wife would be dragged into," she angrily wrote Nicholas. "Intrigues without end, fast manners and conversations . . . a half-worn, blasé man of 38 to a pure fresh girl of 18 and live in a house in which many a woman has 'shared' his life!! An inexperienced girl would suffer terribly to have her husband 4th-5th hand—or more!"

Grand Duchess Vladimir resented Alexandra's rejection for the rest of her life. It was the last nail in the family coffin as far as she was concerned. Now the Vladimir Circle condemned the throne more scornfully than ever.

In February of 1914 Ducky had the joy of hosting Missy and Nando for the first time in her new Russian home. The crown prince and princess of Romania had brought their eldest son, Carol, with them, so the purpose of their trip was obvious. Once again the elusive Olga was being sought out by a dissolute suitor, although this time a much younger one. Missy braved the frigid, off-putting personality of her cousin Alix to discuss the matrimonial fates of their firstborn children. As chilly as ever, Alexandra impressed Missy as having "no warm feeling for any of us and this was of course strongly felt in her attitude, which was never welcoming. Some of this was due to shyness, but the way she closed her narrow lips after the first rather forced greeting, gave you the feeling that this was all she was ready to concede and that she was finished with you then and there."

As Missy saw it, Alix "put an insuperable distance between her world and yours. . . . She made you, in fact, feel an intruding outsider. . . . The pinched, unwilling, patronizing smile with which she received all you said as if it were not worth while answering, was one of the most disheartening impressions I ever received." And when the empress finally did talk, "it was almost in a whisper and hardly moving her lips as though it were too much trouble to pronounce a word aloud." Missy was left with the disconcerting feeling that her cousin didn't even consider her to be grown up, although Missy was only three years Alexandra's junior.

As for Grand Duchess Olga, Missy was disappointed, finding her manner brusque and her appearance "not pretty, her face was too broad, her cheek-bones too high." Prince Carol evidently agreed; it was obvious to all that he was not attracted to the emperor's daughter. Nor, for that matter, was she impressed by him.

Missy now fully understood and sympathized with Ducky's difficult relations with Alix. Everything that her sister had said about their cousin was borne out. And Missy was also shocked to find that Ducky had hardly exaggerated her description of the strange and isolated lives Nicholas and Alexandra led, cut off almost completely from the real world. Missy's visits to Tsarskoe Selo left her with the impression that her cousins dwelt "in a sort of imperial mist."

Because her mother-in-law had recently died and she and Nando were still in mourning, Missy couldn't join Ducky in the brilliant social life of St. Petersburg, but the sisters did spend as much time as they could together, putting on high rubber boots and splashing about in the melting snow with their children. Alas, the visit was a short one, and soon Missy and her family returned to Bucharest.

However, to give Carol and Olga a proper chance to get to know each other before finally turning thumbs down on the match, their parents had decided to meet again in a few months. So in early June of 1914 the Russian imperial yacht, *Standart,* cruised from the Crimea down the western coast of the Black Sea to the Romanian port of Constantsa where, for one full day, the two families mingled and posed for group photos. At the lavish luncheon, Carol sat next to Olga and struggled with small talk, but it was no go; the two young people weren't attracted. And as the *Standart* carried the Romanovs back to Russia that night under a sky illuminated by fireworks, Olga confessed to her mother that she would never "make a marriage which would take her away from Russian soil."

But the Romanian visit had not been a total loss. After Nicholas and Alexandra returned home, Ducky reported to Missy that

the Majesties and daughters and suites all came back really thoroughly enchanted with their visit to you—Alix also admitted how nice and hearty it all was. I am so glad for you all. . . . We are all getting on nicely here. The weather has been monstrously stupendously hot, up to 47 degrees [118 degrees Fahrenheit] in town and it has been weeks without a drop of rain even. I've had a busy time through all this heat with official visits, the most amazing being that of the English fleet commanded by Beatty [Lord David Beatty (1871–1936)]. We had many a good talk of olden days and he asked much after you. He has rather a pretty wife who came on her own yacht with their little boys. Beatty is quite unchanged. We have a tiny little motor yacht of our own on which we made a trip of several days out in the Finnish waters amongst lovely islands, unhappily it can only contain us two so we are sending the children to the Finnish sea with the last remnants of

whooping cough. There we bathe daily and enjoy it. It is in fact the only
bearable time of the day.

Our maneuvers are late this year, last most of Russian August [Russia
used the Julian calendar until 1918] so that we will not get abroad till Eu-
ropean September but I do hope we'll meet then. Aunt Miechen [Grand
Duchess Vladimir] has her Dutch brother staying with her, a fat fair haired
creature, quite gemutlich [warmly agreeable] but very German, something
like "der Furst" but we don't allow anyone to develop their pomposity,
they are squashed in time. The life in Tsarskoie as you know 'est tout ce
que je n'aime pas' [is everything that I dislike] but the place is lovely and
sympathetic. I can't write more, I am too hot, dripping and sticking at all
angles. I've never known anything like it.

In fact none of Europe had ever known anything like it. The swelter-
ing weather covered the entire continent that June of 1914. The London
sidewalks actually steamed, and the canals of Venice seemed to boil
under the blazing sun. The heat was so extraordinary and oppressive that
people talked of nothing else—not even the assassination of archduke
Franz Ferdinand, the heir apparent to the Austro-Hungarian throne, and
his wife in the Serbian city of Sarajevo.

Ducky had just completed her letter to Missy and was enjoying the
cool waters of the Finnish coast with Kirill and their two little girls
when word arrived of the tragedy. It was, indeed, momentous news, but
it was not perceived as the critical event it in fact was. Although Austria
was reacting violently toward Serbia, blaming it for the murder of Emperor Franz Josef's heir, few Europeans expected the assassination to lead
to war. Nicholas and Alexandra, who were also vacationing on their
yacht in the Finnish fjords, did not even bother to return to the capital.
Besides, they had a personal crisis on their hands.

A few days before, Czarevich Alexis had accidently caught his foot on
the gangplank of the *Standart,* slightly twisting his ankle. The joint had
filled with blood from uncontrolled internal hemorrhaging. By now the
poor child was in excruciating pain, weeping and screaming night and
day as his suffering increased. At the same time, just as the frantic Alexandra desperately reached out for Rasputin and his miraculous cures, news
suddenly arrived that the monk had been the recent victim of an assassination attempt and lay mortally wounded in a Siberian hospital.

While visiting his village home, Rasputin had been stabbed in the
stomach by a fanatical follower of one of his many enemies. The culprit,

a woman named Khina Gusseva, had accosted him in the street, screaming "I have killed the Antichrist!" as she did the deed. The wound had
fully exposed Rasputin's entrails and for days he hovered between life
and death.

With both her son and her "savior" at death's door, Alexandra nearly
went mad. She prayed incessantly and silently waited. Alexis slowly
began to recover; then, after two weeks of doubt, Rasputin also passed
the crisis. Both would spend the rest of the summer convalescing in bed.

The faraway death of an Austrian archduke seemed the very least of
Nicholas and Alexandra's worries. Of course regicide, "that most monstrous of crimes," always appalled the courts of Europe; but there
seemed no reason for undue concern this glorious, clear-skied summer.

And as July continued, the weather throughout the continent became
even warmer. The whole world seemed to be on holiday, insouciantly
slumbering beneath the sun.

At the end of the month Kirill's magnificent new motor yacht finally
arrived from Southampton. An efficient English engineer came with it.
Fully staffed by a crew of Russian Imperial Naval Guards, the sleek,
streamlined vessel was the last word in opulence and nautical technology. Kirill was still struggling against his horror of the sea, but with
Ducky at his side he managed to control his fear and actually enjoy
cruising.

To begin with they took short voyages in the tranquil Gulf of Finland,
staying within sight of shore. Walking the decks and sitting in the sun,
Ducky relaxed and turned a deep golden brown. Unlike most other
ladies of her era, who scrupulously shielded their ivory complexions,
Ducky, inheriting her father's olive skin, never minded getting sunburnt
or tanned. Although careful of her appearance and appreciative of her
beauty, she was never vain. She enjoyed life too much and was far too
practical to waste time being obsessed by her looks the way her older sister had always been.

After "a little cruising" on their yacht, Ducky and Kirill decided not
to push his admirable progress too far; they returned to shore in early
August. Feeling calm and rested, they took part in the annual Victoria
Fahrt automobile rally in the Baltic provinces. To their delight, "that year
it was even a greater affair than usual." They traveled from castle to cas-
tle through Lithuania, Latvia, and Estonia, and ended their journey in
Riga, where they were honored with a banquet at the fashionable
Strandt Restaurant.

Ducky and Kirill planned to leave for Coburg immediately to visit the duchess. All the preparations having been made, the grand ducal couple sat down to dinner, surrounded by their good friends. There was much laughter and many jokes; stories were exchanged and toasts made. Ducky must have felt at this moment that, at last, she had everything a woman could ever want.

In the middle of the banquet Governor-General Zvegintzov of Latvia hurried to the front of the room and, his voice shaking, loudly read a telegram.

Germany had just declared war on Russia.

The announcement "produced the effect of a bomb" on the happy gathering. Numb and silent, everyone immediately scrambled from the room.

Ducky sat staring at her husband.

In ten seconds their world had completely shattered.

CHAPTER THIRTY-FOUR

Crowns Divided

Ducky and Kirill left Riga and headed home to Tsarskoe Selo at once.

Everywhere there was a "fearful commotion and chaos reigned on the roads, which were teeming with people, cattle, and horses." Russia's mobilization was in full swing, and swarms of excited reservists were traveling to their assembly points. It seemed that the entire country was suddenly in transit.

Ducky and Kirill rode in the automobile of Count Serge Shuvalov who, although an excellent driver, tended "to be reckless at times." But no matter how boldly the count drove, the roads were so crowded with traffic that it was impossible to get very far. At the town of Pskov the roads became so blocked that the trio decided to abandon the car and try to board a train. But the railways were in an even more chaotic state. At last Ducky and Kirill found space in the third-class carriage of a train headed for St. Petersburg.

Leaning back on the hard benches of the dusty, crowded compartment, Grand Duchess Victoria Feodorovna anxiously thought of her scattered family—her mother and sister Sandra in Germany; Missy in Romania; her aunts and uncles and cousins in all the capitals of Europe. What would the war bring to all of them? Would the family be divided between two enemy camps? The future had never been more frightening.

St. Petersburg was in a frenzied state. The entire population crowded out on the streets, "laughing, weeping, singing, cheering, kissing." A wave of passionate patriotism was sweeping the country, with striking workmen exchanging their "red flags of revolution for the icons of Holy Russia and portraits of the Tsar."

France, Russia's staunchest ally, had immediately joined the fight, much to Kirill's delight. Like most of the Russian aristocracy, he was passionately Francophile. What worried Ducky was the status of her homeland. It was bad enough to be at odds with Germany, the country of her parents' adoption, but to be fighting against England as well would have been too much for her. Although she had resented the domination of her grandmother and the English court, Ducky always considered herself an Englishwoman. The friends and relations who knew Ducky best always remarked that she was "passionately pro-English."

So nothing could have pleased her more than the announcement a few days later by her friend Sir George Buchanan that England had entered the war on the side of Russia. The cautious English had been reluctant to get involved, but because the German army had just invaded neutral Belgium, they were forced to join Russia and France in their fight.

After that, Europe's web of alliances and treaties brought almost every nation on the continent into the war. Germany's chief ally was the antiquated Austro-Hungarian empire. Also offering its support was the lackluster army of the kingdom of Italy. It seemed a woeful mismatch. England and Russia together could rule the world. Few doubted that Germany would be quickly defeated; the most pessimistic believed it would take six months, and many believed the war would be over in four or five weeks.

But Germany was far stronger than anyone had imagined. In the months to come, this fact would be slowly and painfully realized.

An agonizing aspect of the conflict that became known as the Great War was the cruelty with which it tore families apart and made bitter enemies out of loving relatives. This was particularly true for the royal houses of Europe, which had spent the previous two centuries weaving themselves into one large international family.

Now, in the private chambers of many a royal palace, one had only to look across the bed to see the enemy. King Albert, the popular ruler of ferociously anti-German Belgium, had a thoroughly German wife, the former Princess Elisabeth of Bavaria. Russia's Nicholas II was married to another German princess, Alix of Hesse, whose brother Ernie, Ducky's former husband, ruled the grand duchy. Even that most English of all

British monarchs, King George V, was married to a woman of predominantly German heritage, Princess Mary of Teck—the Tecks being the cadet branch of the royal house of Württemberg.

For many, the First World War would be remembered as "the war of cousins." The rulers of the major powers, England, Germany, and Russia, were all first cousins. King George V's father was the maternal uncle of both the kaiser and Empress Alexandra, while George's mother was Nicholas II's maternal aunt. The overlapping relationships made these cousins much closer than they would be in an ordinary family.

The resulting tensions and emotional problems can only be imagined. The war had, indeed, made strange bedfellows.

Not surprisingly, the kaiser had married within his own empire. But even though he had the comfort of a consort as rabidly German as himself, his own mother, Vicky, had been England's cherished princess royal, and his grandmother, Queen Victoria. Making matters worse, his sister Sophie was queen of Greece, a country soon to become one of Germany's foremost enemies.

These complexities were nowhere more vividly embodied than in Grand Duchess Victoria Feodorovna. Ducky alone was first cousin to all of the reigning monarchs—George, Wilhelm, and Nicholas and Alexandra. England, Germany, and Russia had all been home at various times in her life; she found it agonizing to watch these countries rip each other to shreds. And her Russian mother was living in Germany and passionately taking the German side.

As for Missy, Romania's royal family was a cadet branch of the Hohenzollerns; old King Carol was as German as the kaiser. He was aching to join his kinsman in battle, but geography dictated that Romania remain neutral for the time being. Missy, as pro-British as Nando and the king were German, was desperately campaigning for her country's immediate entrance into the war on the side of the Allies. However, given her very limited political power, she could do little but wait. And she hated neutrality, finding that it was "entirely out of keeping with my character."

It was even more unsuited to Ducky's temperament. She was outraged that Romania had not declared for Russia and the Allies. "Ducky is furious that we have not joined them," Missy wrote their sister Sandra in Germany, "and sends me insulting messages through the people who come here as only Ducky can produce in which she considers her rightful wrath against 'those cowards'!"

Missy also shared Ducky's worries about the fate of their family. She wrote Sandra, "Who knows what bitterness will remain and if we won't all have grey hair before we can peacefully come together once more. You and Ducky on opposite sides and each of you vibrant with your own country, each hoping for final victory."

During the first days of the war Russia scrambled to prepare itself for combat. One of the most important aspects of these preparations was the organization of a large and efficient ambulance service. Almost all of the traditional relief organizations in Russia, such as the hospitals and the Red Cross, were financed and supported by the imperial family and the other nobility; Ducky was one of the first to put together a modern ambulance outfit. All private motorcars throughout the empire were requisitioned for use as ambulances, and before long Ducky found herself the head of a huge mobile health-care system. She "threw herself wholeheartedly into nursing, and her motorized ambulance unit was one of the most efficiently run services in Russia."

"The task which she undertook required hard work and great thoroughness to make it function smoothly in the changing and difficult circumstances of the War," Kirill later wrote. "She helped in making her motorized ambulance work one of the best run auxiliary services in Russia. It worked with great regularity and was absolutely reliable, at a time when these characteristics, owing to our total unpreparedness, were, alas, conspicuously lacking in many of the various branches of our armies. . . . Unlike many others who were playing at Red Cross nurses, she had chosen hard and practical work, and on several occasions had carried out her duties under the enemy's fire."

At the front, near Warsaw, Ducky regularly visited the battle lines, often returning looking "worn and harassed, her eyes heavy with lack of sleep and overpowering weariness." She was constantly frustrated by Russia's pathetic fighting condition—the severe shortages of weapons, ammunition, and medical supplies. But she carried on. And everywhere she went, she won praise. When her Red Cross train arrived at the supreme commander's headquarters at the front, General Kondzerovsky watched her with admiration, remarking that he was "quite impressed by her energetic looks."

Kirill, too, was in Poland. He had been appointed to the naval department of Admiral Russin, a member of the staff of Grand Duke Nicholas, the commander in chief of the Russian military. The headquarters were at Baranovichi, a desolate place in the Belorussian forests. Kirill slept in

an old railway car and worked in a crude barracks whose previous occupants were railroad laborers. Kirill felt frustrated in his post, which
"was very lonely and distant from civilization and even war." Kirill
couldn't help observing that "there was little I could do in making myself useful in my capacity of naval officer."

The war had begun tragically for the Russians. They had launched an
all-out attack against East Prussia with a huge army of their very best
men. But after the five-day Battle of Tannenberg, the Germans "had
pulverized the Russians." More than 110,000 Russian soldiers had been
killed and another 90,000 taken prisoner. So devastating was the defeat
that the Russian commander, General Samsonov, committed suicide.
After Tannenberg, a great gloom settled over the Russian army. The
fallen men had been the best in the land and could not be replaced. And
with the supply system working poorly, one military disaster followed
another. The war now shifted onto Russian soil.

The carnage kept Ducky constantly busy. During the "appalling
slaughter the fleet of ambulance cars was plying to and fro from the front
to the rear full of wounded." Ducky worked day and night among the
wounded and the dead. The ordeal proved perfectly designed for her
iron will and courageous character. She toiled without reluctance or
complaint. Indeed, the very sight of the lively and smiling grand duchess
Victoria Feodorovna inspired her companions.

It was family matters that troubled Ducky most. Her sister Sandra's
husband, the hereditary prince of Hohenlohe-Langenburg, had just
been appointed Germany's ambassador to Constantinople and had made
frequent visits to Bucharest to persuade Missy and Nando to join the
German side. Missy considered her Langenburg brother-in-law to be "a
very sympathetic German agent," and feared that he was swaying her
husband.

Meanwhile, though, since Romania was still neutral, the family exchanged letters through Missy. It was difficult to keep politics out of
their personal correspondence. Missy managed to remain the epitome of
tact, but Ducky received Sandra's propagandistic letters with enraged
contempt, firing back scathing condemnations of Germany's behavior in
the war. But worst of all for Ducky were the bitter letters from her
mother.

The duchess of Coburg, though she was the daughter of a Russian emperor and had always been devoted to her homeland, had surprisingly
sided with her adopted country. She "become passionately pro-German,

and stoutly championed the cause of Germany." To have supported Russia, Ducky's mother would have had to abandon the life she had made for herself and moved back to her childhood home in St. Petersburg. To accept such failure and defeat was definitely not in the duchess's character. As stubborn and proud as ever, she found herself forced to turn her back on her homeland and cling desperately to where she was. So perhaps it was guilt that prompted Marie to barrage her two eldest daughters with letters fiercely defending the German empire and damning the Allies.

Ducky aggressively pressured Missy to bring Romania into the war on Russia's side, but Missy also remained her chief source of support and understanding. In 1915, when Ducky was concerned that the Germans were successfully propagandizing Romania, Missy wrote:

> *It is certainly difficult to discuss political questions today—they are too burning, too explosive—and each man becomes too passionate as every country's fate is in the balance. but I can only tell you one thing: here, in spite of German successes and the non-success of the Entente, our people still have absolute confidence in the Entente's victory. I am even astonished at this because it must be remembered that the Roumanians are "des Latins" and Latins adore success, but they are staunchly sticking to their sympathies and all the most clever and lavish propaganda has not made them change. . . . You cannot imagine with what a bleeding heart I follow your retreat, hardly daring to open a telegram. Luckily all those in my personal service, my ladies, Miss Milne, the children's governess, my A.D.C. [aide-de-camp], are completely "Entente" [i.e., they sided with Russia and England], only with Nando I must use tact always.*

Because Romania was squarely in Russia's orbit and completely at her mercy, it was eventually necessary to abandon neutrality and join Russia in battle. (The duchess sent Missy an eight-page diatribe blaming her for everything: "Oh! why, why did you begin this war? . . . The worst of all, is that they specially accuse 'you' of having been the chief element of bringing it about! . . . I can hardly believe in my old days, that a daughter of mine is at the head of such a movement, my former little beloved, peaceful, fair Missy, the sunshine in the house. . . . But all Germany says it was you, you who pushed on towards the war from insane, blind confidence in the Entente.")

Bucharest had held out just long enough to secure Russia's promise of a vast increase in Romanian territory in exchange for military support. The thoroughly German King Carol, proud of his Hohenzollern ancestry, had been crushed by his inability to bring Romania into the war as an ally of the Fatherland. He had died a few months later, at the end of 1914, a wretched and completely broken man.

It was Missy who now became the chief power in the land. Nando's crown did not sit on him well at all. As King Ferdinand, Missy's husband was even more painfully insecure and out of his depth than before. Timid and indecisive, Nando ruled only as a figurehead, receiving detailed guidance from his flamboyant and clever wife. As Missy later put it, Nando's "habit of counting upon me for his material comforts had been unconsciously extended also to brainwork." As Queen Marie, Missy would become not only the unofficial leader of her country, but also one of the most celebrated and dominant personalities of her era.

In February of 1916, when the German generals felt confident they could hold back the Russians, they moved a million of their soldiers to the western front to attack the pivotal French fortress of Verdun. The Russians seized upon the opportunity to initiate another campaign against East Prussia. Responding to the threat, the Germans abandoned the assault on Verdun and moved back to the Russian front. It was another disaster for Russia. The cost of the futile offensive was a terrible one: 1,200,000 men.

As the empire suffered more horribly with each passing month of war, the Russian people extended their hatred of the Germans to their unpopular empress. The fact that Alexandra had been born and bred on enemy territory was enough to excite the wrath of many of her subjects, even though her "allegiance was fervently Russian." "Twenty years have I spent in Russia," Alexandra would emotionally proclaim. "It is the country of my husband and my son. I have lived the life of a happy wife and mother in Russia. All my heart is bound to this country."

Still, she was vilified as "the German woman." Wild stories were spread about her activities as a German spy. Had Alexandra's coldness and remoteness not already alienated the Russian people to such an extreme degree, she might have survived the slander. But instead the gossip stuck. And, of course, there was still the matter of Rasputin. The war had only increased his influence over the court, much to the nation's bitter resentment.

And Rasputin engineered one of Russia's greatest wartime calamities.

Realizing that his power could be complete if Nicholas was out of the picture and Alexandra left entirely in his own hands, Rasputin plotted to have the emperor take command of the army at the front. The current commander, Grand Duke Nicholas Nicholaievich, was a skillful, popular, and courageous leader and also an enemy of Rasputin despite the latter's attempts to impress him. Rasputin's final effort to gain the grand duke's favor had been a humble telegram offering to come to headquarters to bless his icon. "Yes, do come," the grand duke quickly wired back. "I'll hang you."

If he succeeded in having the emperor take military command, Rasputin would weaken the grand duke as well, killing two birds with one stone. He began poisoning Alexandra's mind against a cousin she had never liked in the first place. Jealous of the grand duke's popularity and wary of his power, the empress needed little prompting to conclude that he must go. She began urging her husband to dump the commander in chief and take his place. Since this had always been the emperor's fondest dream, he took little convincing.

Against the desperate pleas of his advisers, Nicholas II took full command of the Russian army in August of 1915 and immediately left for the front. Not only was he completely unsuited to the job, but his absence from court created the perfect conditions for disaster.

"When the Emperor went to war, of course his wife governed instead of him," his brother-in-law Grand Duke Alexander later explained. There was nothing unusual about that; there was no formal regency, but merely a "domestic division of family duties," very much within the tradition of the Romanov monarchy: Whenever an emperor had gone to war, his wife stayed behind and assumed his administrative duties.

However well this arrangement had worked in the past, it was now the worst thing that could have happened to Russia. Rasputin's every wish became Alexandra's command, and the government began slowly to disintegrate.

Ducky watched with disgust as the empress filled the government exclusively with Rasputin's cronies and protégés. As corruption and incompetency strangled Russia's political structure, Ducky's anger toward her cousin "hardened into open hostility." But, putting her personal feelings aside, she went to see the empress and tried to reason with her, tactfully attempting to point out the harm being caused by Rasputin's instructions. Alexandra abruptly responded that Ducky was "meddling in matters which were not her concern." Ducky returned home "seething with exasperation," claiming that she "had been treated like an ignorant schoolgirl."

Alexandra's dislike of Ducky was aggravated by Ducky's close friendship with the Buchanans. Because of Sir George's plainspoken attempts to save the crumbling Russian monarchy, the empress was convinced that he, her widowed sister Ella, and Ducky were conspiring to get rid of Rasputin. She also (rightly) suspected that Ducky was criticizing her and stirring up ill-feeling toward Rasputin in her letters to their relatives.

During this chaotic period Ducky was almost constantly separated from her husband and children. Since their wedding—ten years ago—Ducky and Kirill had rarely been apart for more than a week or two at a time. Now, since she was running a large ambulance corps and he was on active duty with the navy, they hardly ever saw each other. The long separations were difficult for both of them.

In December of 1916 Ducky arranged a trip to Romania to visit Missy and bring her much-needed medical supplies and provisions. Missy and Ducky had been unable to communicate for the past few months; Ducky's sudden arrival was "indeed a blessed event." When the two sisters embraced again, "the joy was almost unbearably great." Surrounded by enemy nations on all sides, the Romanian queen had grown depressed by the "blind and almost hopeless struggle." She was in need of moral support, and there was no better source than Ducky.

"My sister's quiet, staunch, somewhat masculine personality was just what I needed beside me," Missy later wrote of Ducky's visit. "I could talk to her freely, ask her advice, lay my problems before her, discuss the situation and how best to meet the inflow of disaster. Besides, our love and understanding for each other was so great that to be together was in itself a supreme comfort and consolation."

Ducky arrived in Iaşi, Romania's wartime capital, the same morning Missy's husband was opening parliament. (As bad as the country's situation was, his speech was loudly applauded.) Not wanting to waste a moment, Ducky and her sister at once set out on the crude, muddy roads to the most remote military hospitals to distribute the medical supplies. Even the shortest trips took hours because of the impassable roads. Missy would proudly remember, "Ducky was as untiring as I was, even more so, being a real Spartan." During afternoons of pouring rain, the two sisters drove to the local station and "pottered about in unbelievable mud to look for railway carriages which could be turned into a Russian hospital train which Ducky hopes to arrange." Visiting the makeshift Russian hospital at Iaşi that was housed in a section of the Convent of Nôtre Dame de Sion, Ducky and Missy were confronted by the exasperated mother superior, who enraged Ducky by her insulting tirade against the Russians.

While Ducky was visiting Missy, their cousin Grand Duke George Mikhailovich, also arrived in Romania. A bluff, good-natured man who had once been one of Missy's suitors, George was also fond of Ducky and enjoyed testing her temper by picking fights, much to Missy's amusement. Most of the joking had to do with George's insatiable hunger and his habit of arriving much too early for every meal.

While in Romania Ducky formed a close friendship with her brother-in-law the king. She and Nando had always gotten on well together, but now more than ever the meek monarch appreciated his sister-in-law's courage and strength of character and "found it a comfort to talk to Ducky." He went out of his way to seek out his wife's sister and be around her as much as possible.

In the darkness of the long December evenings Ducky and Missy "wandered about endlessly" in the enormous Russian evacuation hospital near the train station, tending the wounded soldiers. They brought quantities of cigarettes, which they dispensed to everyone they met. Exhausted, the queen and her sister would return home late at night for a cup of hot tea and lengthy and serious conversations with Romania's premier, Ion Bratianu. Bratianu took pains to explain the Romanian situation to Ducky and requested her help in interceding with the Russian emperor, whose support was vital for the survival of Romania as a nation. He begged Ducky to make it clear to the emperor that Russian troops must hold their ground and respect the rights of the Romanian troops, instead of taking advantage of the situation by ransacking Romanian warehouses and stealing all of the best meat and bread. Ducky agreed to talk to her cousin back in St. Petersburg.

As Ducky's departure approached, both sisters realized how much Missy was going to miss her guidance and support. In her diary the night before her sister's departure, Missy wrote: "She has been a great help, encouragement and stimulant to me. I hate to let her go!" Watching her sister leave, Missy found it almost impossible "to crush down my sorrow."

Ducky took with her a "weighty letter to Emperor Nicky" in which Missy pleaded for assistance. But, when she arrived in St. Petersburg, she found the family in a far different situation than when she had left. Some of her relatives had taken the law in their own hands and done what many had been hoping for these past several years. And their bold action had set the stage for the downfall of their dynasty.

CHAPTER THIRTY-FIVE

The War
of the
Romanovs

*A*LTHOUGH THE EMPRESS was meant to be overseeing only internal affairs, she had soon expanded her authority to include Russia's military operations. This interest was inspired, of course, by Rasputin, who sought to control Russian military strategy. Whatever his motives and objectives were, he used all his considerable influence over Alexandra to see that things went exactly the way he wanted them to go, both in government and on the battlefield.

By October of 1916 Rasputin's domination was complete. His opponents had been replaced by his cronies—men who were either dishonest or incompetent or both. He had also succeeded in turning the operations at the front line into his own private chessboard. No longer under the spell of the bogus *starets*, Nicholas was affronted by these "clumsy intrusions" into his domain. But the emperor was forced to tolerate Rasputin because "he dared not weaken the Empress's faith in him—a faith that kept her alive." Nicholas could never risk sending the "holy man" away; if the czarevich then died, "in the eyes of the mother, he would have been the murderer of his own son."

Nicholas willingly shared Russia's secret military plans with his wife, but he did not want them passed on to anyone, especially Rasputin. Each time the emperor confided secret information to Alexandra, he carefully added: "I beg you, my love, do not communicate these details to anyone. I have written them only for you . . . I beg you, keep it to yourself, not a single soul must know of it." But Alexandra told Rasputin everything.

"He won't mention it to a soul," she tried to reassure Nicholas, "but I had to ask his blessing for your decision."

Needless to say, this arrangement provoked furious protest from all quarters of the empire. As 1916 approached its end, so, too, did imperial Russia. The country was beginning to disintegrate—corruption crippling the government, rebellion paralyzing the military, and decay breaking down the economy. As the Russian people angrily surveyed their blood-soaked, crumbling homeland, they targeted the sinister Rasputin the source of their despair.

And no one hated Rasputin more than the other members of the imperial family. With the exception of Nicholas and Alexandra and their young children, every member of the Romanov family violently opposed the *starets,* believing him a dangerous and malevolent fraud. They all agreed that something must be done.

As always, Ducky's husband's branch of the family were the strongest critics, and her mother-in-law, Grand Duchess Vladimir, was the loudest. Ducky had tried diplomatically to make the empress see reason, but the grand duchess actively organized and promoted a palace revolution. Her intent was to see Alexandra removed to a convent or Nicholas forced to abdicate. These schemes were far more original than practical; they never went beyond words.

Other, more pragmatic members of the Vladimir Circle were not satisfied by words, however strong. It may have been impossible to dethrone the emperor and empress, but it was within the realm of reason to plot the elimination of Rasputin. And given the "holy man's" fantastic powers, there could be only one effective method of disposal: death.

Grand Duke Dimitri, the twenty-six-year-old son of Ducky's last surviving Romanov uncle, the gentle grand duke Paul, was a charming, easygoing dandy, a favorite among all his cousins, but spoiled and dissipated. One of his friends was Prince Felix Youssoupoff—effeminate, homosexual, and fond of dressing in women's clothing. One of the richest and handsomest men in Europe, Felix pursued cruelty and pleasure rather like Oscar Wilde's Dorian Gray. As an added twist, Felix was happily married to the emperor's niece, Grand Duchess Irina, the only daughter of Nicholas's eldest sister.

It was Dimitri and Felix who boldly plotted Rasputin's murder. On the last day of 1916 they lured him to Youssoupoff's St. Petersburg home, the Moika Palace, under the pretext of meeting Irina, who was really in the Crimea.

Curiously, Rasputin had a premonition that his life was in danger; during that dark, feezing December he had taken long, lonely walks by the Neva, declaring afterward that he had seen the river filled with the blood of Romanov grand dukes. At his last meeting with the emperor, he refused to give Nicholas his usual blessing, insisting instead that "This time it is for you to bless me, not I you."

A week before he accepted Felix's invitation to midnight supper, Rasputin wrote this message, which he sealed and left with instructions that it be opened upon his death:

> *I feel that I shall leave life before January 1. I wish to make known to the Russian people, to Papa [Nicholas] to the Russian Mother [Alexandra] and to the Children, to the land of Russia, what they must understand. If I am killed by common assassins, and especially by my brothers the Russian peasants, you, Tsar of Russia, have nothing to fear, remain on your throne and govern, and . . . have nothing to fear for your children, they will reign for hundreds of years in Russia. But if I am murdered by "boyars," nobles, and if they shed my blood, their hands will remain soiled with my blood. . . . They will leave Russia. Brothers will kill brothers, and they will kill each other and hate each other. . . . Tsar of the land of Russia . . . if it was your relations who have wrought my death then no one of your family, that is to say, none of your children or relations will remain alive for more than two years. They will be killed by the Russian people. . . .*

Whatever he was, Rasputin wasn't a fool. He knew how much he was hated by the other members of the imperial family, and he realized that these privileged opponents were sufficiently powerful to undertake his murder. So it must have been with a fatalistic spirit that the "holy man" ventured to the opulent Youssoupoff house that New Year's Eve and accepted the dissolute young prince's hospitality.

Telling Rasputin that his wife was temporarily occupied by a party upstairs, Felix led him to an ornate and cozy room in the palace's cellar. Alone with his victim, the refined host offered Rasputin small cakes each of which had been stuffed with enough cyanide "to kill several men instantly." Rasputin gobbled up two of the cakes and smilingly requested some wine. Youssoupoff nervously poured him two tall glasses of Madeira, which had also been heavily poisoned. Rasputin drank and grinned with pleasure, asking for more. This went on for almost three hours.

Finally, the terrified Felix ran upstairs to where Dimitri and the other conspirators were waiting. Dimitri gave him his revolver and Youssoupoff slowly returned to the cellar. A few moments later, at the first opportunity, he shot Rasputin in the back. The monk collapsed to the floor. The other conspirators rushed down and pronounced him dead. But as they began celebrating their success, Rasputin slowly opened his eyes and suddenly jumped to his feet. His assailants were horrified and fled from the cellar with him following after them, "clambering on all fours, roaring with fury." Somehow Rasputin managed to get out into the palace courtyard, but before he could reach the gate, he was shot in the back again, and then in the head. Felix proceeded to club his body wildly.

The conspirators rolled Rasputin up in a blue curtain, bound it with rope, then took it to the river and pushed it through a hole in the ice. Three days later the corpse was found by the police. The autopsy revealed that Rasputin's lungs had been filled with water. Gregory Rasputin, "his bloodstream filled with poison, his body punctured by bullets, had died by drowning."

News of the murder was greeted with wild rejoicing. Grand Duke Dimitri, Prince Felix, and the other conspirators were hailed as heroes.

But, of course, the reaction at the Winter Palace was far different. As one would imagine, Alexandra was prostrate with grief. Her great sorrow was soon followed by an even greater rage when it was discovered that the murder had been committed by members of the imperial family. This fact made it especially difficult for Nicholas. "I am filled with shame," he said, "that the hands of my kinsmen are stained with the blood of a simple peasant."

However, he gave Dimitri and Felix received amazingly light sentences considering they had committed cold-blooded murder. Dimitri was simply ordered to leave the capital and join the Russian army in Persia, while Felix was banished to one of his magnificent country estates in the center of Russia. Ironically, in the near future these sentences would save their lives.

Rasputin's murder was the final blow to the unity of the Romanov family. After his death, Nicholas and Alexandra completely withdrew from the rest of the world and shunned their relatives. Retreating behind the well-guarded walls of Tsarskoe Selo, they seemed to be trying to escape reality. Both of them suffered a nervous collapse during this time and resigned themselves to what they saw as their unalterable fate.

Rather than freeing the occupants of the throne, Rasputin's death only succeeded in crushing their spirits.

A profound sense of doom descended upon the family—and, indeed, the whole country. Ducky and Kirill had "the feeling of being poised on the brink of a precipice or of standing on the uncertain surface of a swamp. The country was like a gradually sinking ship with a mutinous crew." Like most members of the imperial family, they were critical of the murder but were relieved that Rasputin was dead.

Alexandra "understood that she had been the real target of the assassins": The family had hoped that with Rasputin and his influence eliminated, Alexandra would stop interfering in the government and her husband would retake control again and save the monarchy. But the fact that Nicholas punished Grand Duke Dimitri and Prince Felix disappointed their hopes. In a daring and unprecedented move, the whole family wrote a collective letter to the emperor pleading for clemency for Dimitri and the immediate establishment of a responsible ministry. Ducky and Kirill's names appeared at the top of the list of signatures.

Nicholas was outraged by the letter, which seemed to indicate the family's support of the assassins and its disloyalty to him. He angrily replied: "I allow no one to give me advice. A murder is always a murder. In any case, I know that the consciences of several who signed that letter are not clear."

This response only antagonized Ducky and the rest of the family, who saw Nicholas as setting Russia's course toward suicide. A few days later the liberally inclined grand duke Nicholas Mikhailovich was observed in his St. Petersburg clubs berating the government and criticizing the emperor's leadership. Nicholas II retaliated by confining the grand duke to his country estate.

Even the amiable dowager empress failed to make her son see reason. "I am sure you are aware yourself how deeply you have offended all the family by your brusque reply, throwing at their heads a dreadful and entirely unjustified accusation," she wrote Nicholas from Kiev. "I hope that you will alleviate the fate of poor Dimitri by not leaving him in Persia. . . . Poor Uncle Paul wrote me in despair that he had not even been given a chance to say goodbye. . . . It is not like you to behave this way. . . . It upsets me very much."

Grand Duke Alexander Mikhailovich, the brother of the banished grand duke Nicholas and the husband of the dowager empress's eldest daughter, rushed from his home in Kiev to Tsarskoe Selo in a desperate attempt to make Nicholas and Alexandra realize the danger of their foolish path. The eloquent and level-headed grand duke was not only a very close relation, but also a dearly loved and highly respected friend who had provided Nicholas with fatherly support throughout his entire reign.

When Grand Duke Alexander entered the imperial suite, he found the empress lying languidly in the large bed wearing an elaborate white lace negligée. Nicholas sat quietly smoking on the other side of the bed. Immediately, the outspoken grand duke began pleading with Alexandra to stop tampering with Russian politics: "Your interference with affairs of state is causing harm. . . . I have been your faithful friend, Alix for twenty-four years . . . as a friend, I point out to you that all the classes of the population are opposed to your policies. . . . Please, Alix, leave the cares of state to your husband."

Alexandra responded by arguing the extent of her husband's autocratic powers.

The discussion ended with the grand duke in a rage: "Remember, Alix," he shouted at her, "I remained silent for thirty months. For thirty months I never said a word to you about the disgraceful goings on in our government, better to say in 'your' government. I realize that you are willing to perish and that your husband feels the same way, but what about us? You have no right to drag your relatives with you down a precipice!"

At this point, Nicholas interrupted his enraged cousin and quietly led him from the room. This passive and futile gesture convinced the grand duke once and for all that there was no hope for the dynasty's survival. Returning home to Kiev, he bitterly wrote, "One cannot govern a country without listening to the voice of the people. . . . Strange as it may appear, it is the Government which is preparing the Revolution. . . . We are watching an unprecedented spectacle, revolution coming from above and not from below."

January of 1917 was bringing all members of the imperial family into open conflict with the throne. And Nicholas and Alexandra made public statements tantamount to a declaration of war on their relatives.

Freshly returned from embattled Romania, Ducky was too worried about Missy's current ordeal to become deeply involved in the family's revolt against the emperor and empress. No sooner had Ducky returned to St. Petersburg than a letter arrived from Missy proposing an immediate visit to the Russian capital. It had been decided that the best chance of winning the emperor's support lay in a personal meeting. Missy asked Ducky if now would be an acceptable time to approach their cousin. But even before Ducky had a chance to telegraph her reply ("It is not a wise moment to come to Russia—the family situation is too strained") Missy heard rumors of the "serious trouble at the Russian Court . . . that the Imperial Family is in revolt against the Empress, clamouring that she should be sent to a convent."

On January 8 Missy wrote in her diary that Empress Alexandra "is extraordinarily hated and some event unknown to me must have brought this hatred to a climax. Anyhow, something uncanny and dreadful is going on there, so I hardly think it would be a propitious moment for me to arrive."

Ten days later Ducky was back in Romania, having stayed in St. Petersburg only long enough to assemble more of the supplies that her sister's country so desperately needed. Arriving at the besieged town of Iaşi on the eighteenth of January, Ducky found everyone greatly pleased that she had returned. Missy noticed with pride that her younger sister "is much liked, as all recognize her undeniable personality, her strength of character, and superior intelligence; besides, she is both agreeable and amusing and has a wonderful way of relating things, tersely, in a few words." Indeed, the Romanians were relieved, after the disturbing reports of Nicholas and Alexandra's bizarre behavior, to learn that "at least one of their Romanov allies had her fair share of common sense and leadership qualities."

As Missy's own country daily came nearer collapse and military annihilation, her feelings verged on despair. But the sudden return of her sister seemed to change all that. The joy of being with Ducky again worked miracles on Missy's morale. "To me," she confessed to her diary, "it means more than I can say to have her here again, it makes everything easier . . . even small things become pleasant."

Everyone in Iaşi must have thought Grand Duchess Victoria Feodorovna a tardy Santa Claus: It seemed she had brought something for each of them. There were splendid provisions for the Romanian soldiers and the local hospitals—"thousands and thousands of things." There were fur-lined leather jackets and watertight Russian boots, shirts, and trousers; gloves and sheets; bandages and dressing gowns; medicines, needles, and cotton. There were also wonderful things to eat—smoked fish and sweets and cherry brandy and teas and spices.

Princess Victoria Melita (nicknamed Ducky)
at her mother's home on Tegernsee in the Bavarian Alps
in 1901 after creating a scandal
that shocked the world.

Ducky's mother, the indomitable duchess of Edinburgh, in 1880. The spoiled daughter of the Russian emperor, she was the only person who could make Queen Victoria tremble.

Ducky's father, the self-absorbed duke of Edinburgh. The handsomest of all Queen Victoria's sons, he captured the heart of the world's wealthiest princess—and they lived unhappily ever after.

Princess Victoria Melita in 1886 at the age of ten.
She had an uncompromising belief in truth and
beauty—but unimagined cruelties would soon
crush her innocence.

Queen Victoria holds court at breakfast at her seaside summer palace, Osborne House. The duchess of Edinburgh sits with her back to the camera. Standing left to right are her three eldest daughters, Missy (the future Queen Marie of Romania), Ducky, and Alexandra.

The wedding of the century—Ducky marries her first cousin Grand Duke Ernst Ludwig of Hesse and the Rhine. Almost every member of European royalty came to Coburg to witness the uniting of this "ideal" couple.

*Ducky's husband, "Ernie," with their only child,
Princess Elizabeth. The grand duke centered his
entire world on his daughter.*

Grand Duke Vladimir of Russia, Ducky's future father-in-law. A dilettante but the most accomplished of all the Romanovs, he became Ducky's greatest champion when the world turned against her.

Vladimir's supremely ambitious wife, Grand Duchess Marie Pavlovna. After her schemes to become empress collapsed, she set her hopes on Ducky.

The children of Vladimir and Marie Pavlovna in 1886—left to right: Andrei, Kirill, Helen, and Boris.

Grand Duke Kirill at age ten. Bright, obedient and warmhearted, he was considered the best-looking member of the Russian imperial family.

*Grand Duke Kirill in 1896, about the time he fell in love
with Ducky, in the uniform of the fusiliers
of the imperial family.*

*A family gathering on the Riviera at Cannes, 1911. Standing left to right:
Grand Duke Andrei, Prince Nicholas of Greece (Grand Duchess Helen's husband),
Grand Duchess Marie Pavlovna, Grand Duke Kirill, Grand Duke Boris.
Seated left to right: Grand Duchess Helen with her three daughters, Marina
(the future duchess of Kent), Olga (Princess Paul of Yugoslavia), and Elisabeth
(Countess Toerring); and Ducky with her two daughters, Kira and Marie.
The strain of banishment and exile shows on Ducky's and Kirill's faces.*

Return to Russia—Ducky, now the grand duchess Victoria Feodorovna, with her two daughters, Kira and Marie.

Survivors of the Bolshevik reign of terror gather in Contrexéville, France, in 1920. Standing left to right: Princess Nicholas of Greece (Grand Duchess Helen), Grand Duke Andrei, Grand Duke Boris. Seated: Ducky and Kirill.

*Two who were once among the world's most celebrated
beauties: Ducky and her sister, Missy, the dowager queen
Marie of Romania, in 1931. The friendship between these
two sisters was the most meaningful relationship
in both their lives.*

Grand Duke Kirill of Russia in 1910.

Grand Duchess Victoria Feodorovna in 1910.

The duchess of Edinburgh, now the duchess of Coburg, with her four daughters and their husbands. Standing left to right: King Ferdinand of Romania, the duchess, Prince Ernest of Hohenlohe-Langenburg, Infanta Beatrice of Spain, Infante Alfonso of Spain, and Grand Duke Kirill. Seated left to right: Queen Marie of Romania, Princess Alexandra of Hohenlohe-Langenburg, Grand Duchess Victoria Feodorovna.

An emperor and empress in exile—Kirill and Ducky in front of their modest "imperial palace" at secluded St. Briac on the coast of Brittany in 1934. The final and greatest tragedy of Ducky's life has already begun to play out, as her face vividly shows.

Keeping up appearances—Ducky and Kirill pose with their children, Kira and Vladimir, at their home, Ker Argonid, in St. Briac, 1935.

A striking resemblance—Ducky's son, the grand duke Vladimir, alone in the world in 1941, sits at home in front of a portrait of his great-grandfather, Czar Alexander II of Russia. Vladimir carried on the imperial legacy until his death in 1992.

Ducky's garden, long neglected and gone to seed. Twilight often paints it with shadows of its former glory—a private kingdom once ruled by an extraordinary woman.

For the family, Ducky had brought along special presents—Orenburg shawls for Marie, a pair of rare rubber tires for fourteen-year-old Nicky's minature automobile "Bambino," and a fancy paintbox and much-desired toy horse and cart for her favorite niece, eight-year-old Ileana. Knowing how scarce goods were nowadays, Missy couldn't believe how much her sister had managed to bring. Ducky had truly saved the day. With tears in her eyes, Missy quietly repeated to herself over and over, "May my beloved Ducky be a thousand times blessed!"

After the excitement of their reunion had subsided, the two sisters sat down and talked endlessly of the serious situation in Russia. Ducky confided that things had become "very dangerous because of the prevailing hatred for the Empress, so that even the Emperor is looked on askance and there is actually talk about supressing them one way or another." After describing how the imperial couple were filling the government with "absolutely unknown and worthless people," Ducky confessed to her sister that what really worried her was Nicholas and Alexandra's growing habit of sending people into banishment until "no one is safe any more."

Threatened with an epidemic of typhus, Romania was grateful for the medical supplies Ducky delivered. After lunch each day, Ducky and Missy visited a different facility, trying to bring as much order as possible, supervising the setups and insisting upon improvements. One afternoon they went to the Convent of Frumoasa, on the outskirts of Iaşi, which had been turned into a hospital for soldiers with eye diseases. Although they knew ahead of time that the place was in terrible condition, they were thoroughly unprepared for the awful sight they encountered. In a barnlike building with mud floors and neither light nor ventilation, seven hundred men had been piled on top of one another in a space that couldn't have decently accommodated half that number.

Numbed with shock, these two carefully-brought-up granddaughters of Queen Victoria "wandered through these ghastly wards with the feeling that we were advancing into Hell, wondering how much misery human beings can bear without succumbing."

After this visit neither Ducky nor Missy was feeling well, but they forced themselves to put on their big Russian boots and go to the local train station, where they wearily walked miles through the yards, wading through snowdrifts and searching for empty railway carriages for another hospital train.

The next day they took a long drive in an open car to supervise the cutting and loading of wood for town. The weather was bright and sunny, but "deadly, cruelly cold." Because she was always "a martyr to poor circulation," Ducky hated the cold. Although she was dressed as warmly as she could possibly be, she "nearly perished."

Two months before, Ducky had celebrated her fortieth birthday, a milestone that few pass without a touch of regret and melancholy. Ducky, neither vain nor focused on the past, almost failed to take notice of the official departure of her youth. Her beautiful chestnut hair was now streaked with gray, and her porcelain complexion had been slightly lined by the sun, but her figure was as straight and slim as ever, and with her great joie de vivre, Grand Duchess Victoria Feodorovna still impressed most people as a dazzling young woman.

The unusually cold winter that year almost caused a breakdown of her celebrated indestructible health. Instead, however, it was Missy who suddenly fell ill. Overworked and harassed, the queen collapsed into her bed, so downhearted that she couldn't speak. Ducky had been scheduled to leave for home, but she refused to budge from her sister's bedside, angrily telling the visiting government ministers that they were illogically and unfairly placing every burden on Missy's shoulders while at the same time hampering her efforts. With an indignation that would have made her mother proud, Ducky condemned their actions as completely "unjustifiable" and demanded that they start treating their queen with more consideration and respect. She decided to stay on until she was certain that her sister was fully recovered. On February 12, Missy recorded in her diary that Ducky "is awfully kind and looks after me like a mother."

When Ducky returned to St. Petersburg in the middle of February 1917 she found things far worse than when she had left.

Kirill had just returned from the front, where the emperor had sent him to distribute decorations among the troops. Trying his best to lift their morale, he was disturbed to hear their revolutionary mutterings. As happy as he and Ducky were to be together, they were troubled: "The whole country was exhausted and in that state was like an ailing body at the mercy of any germ."

Kirill had just been appointed commander of the Naval Guards, who were currently quartered in St. Petersburg, so he and Ducky could remain together for the time being. With the situation in the country growing more desperate each day, they considered it a blessing to have the comfort of each other's presence.

Although opposed to Nicholas and Alexandra's misrule and concerned about its dangerous consequences, Ducky and Kirill were careful to remain publicly loyal to the throne. They began to meet privately with other members of the family, discussing how to save the monarchy. But what was being said in strict privacy, Kirill's mother was shouting from the rooftops. She invited Michael Rodzianko, the president of the Duma, to lunch at the Vladimir Palace and immediately launched a verbal attack on the general state of affairs and in particular on the empress. Rodzianko listened amazed as the grand duchess became "more and more excited, dwelling on Alexandra's nefarious influence and interference in everything, and said she was driving the country to destruction; that she was the cause of the danger which threatened the Emperor and the rest of the Imperial family; that such conditions could no longer be tolerated; that things must be changed, something done, removed, destroyed."

Trying to clarify Grand Duchess Vladimir's meaning, Rodzianko asked her, "What do you mean by 'removed'?"

"The Duma must do something," Marie Pavlovna exploded. "She must be annihilated!"

Who?"

"The empress!"

Rodzianko blinked with astonishment, then took a long, steady breath and carefully responded, "Your Highness, allow me to treat this conversation as if it had never taken place, because if you address me as the president of the Duma, my oath of allegiance compels me to wait at once on His Imperial Majesty and report to him that the grand duchess Marie Pavlovna has declared to me that the empress must be annihilated."

Rodzianko agreed, however, that the empress must be made politically powerless. Immediately calling on the emperor, he presented Nicholas with his last great warning of what was to come. But Nicholas said nothing and curtly dismissed him.

Rumors began circulating in St. Petersburg about a plot by the Vladimir Circle to depose the emperor and empress. Almost everyone in the capital knew the details: Four regiments of the guard were waiting to make a midnight march on Tsarskoe Selo and capture Nicholas and

Alexandra and their five children. They would apply the traditional Russian method of getting rid of an unwanted empress: Alexandra was to be imprisoned in an isolated convent. The emperor would be forced to abdicate in favor of his twelve-year-old son, and a regency would be created under Russia's popular ex–military leader Grand Duke Nicholas.

Kirill and his Romanov cousins were credited with this daring scheme, but in fact they never actually planned a palace revolution. It was, perhaps, something that most people wanted to see happen, so they found it easy to believe in. And anti-German sentiment was running so high that not only was Alexandra being vilified as an enemy spy but the German-sounding name of the capital, St. Petersburg, was changed to the more Slavic-sounding Petrograd. (In England, King George V dumped the German name of his dynasty, Saxe-Coburg-Gotha, and created the very British house of Windsor.)

But more than anything, it was the flagrant rebelliousness of the Romanovs that lent credibility to these fantastic stories. At a supper party given by Prince Gabriel Constantinovich and Kirill's brother Grand Duke Boris, the French ambassador, Maurice Paléologue, reported with amazement that "during the evening the only topic was the conspiracy—the regiments of the Guard which can be relied on, the most favorable moment for the outbreak, etc. And all this with the servants moving about, harlots looking on and listening, gypsies singing and the whole company bathed in the aroma of Moët and Chandon 'brut imperial' which flowed in streams."

Small wonder that Russia expected at any moment to see the imperial family topple the despised rulers from the throne. But before any decisive action could be taken by the Vladimir Circle, the Russian people themselves arose.

Ducky and Kirill huddled together in the window of their palace and helplesly watched their world begin to collapse.

CHAPTER THIRTY-SIX

Days of Blood and Fire

As March of 1917 began, the disorder in Russia dramatically increased. Food was scarce in the capital and bread was almost impossible to obtain. The war had crippled the railroad system and communications were chaotic. Ducky and Kirill vividly noted that "crime and violence increased daily and the police were frequently attacked by gangs of hooligans." Unsettling reports of barracks mutinies and violence against officers reached the capital, and there were strikes and demonstrations throughout Russia.

Ducky and Kirill saw that "the whole edifice of the exhausted Empire had begun to totter badly and that the collapse was imminent. If energetic measures had been taken to check the growing storm at that time all might yet have been saved. Nothing was done and everything, as if on purpose, was left to chance."

Finally, police in St. Petersburg were murdered en masse, and in the barracks soldiers started massacring their officers. Street fire broke out between rival gangs.

Ducky found it difficult to believe what was happening and expected the emperor would eventually take the drastic steps necessary to restore order. But he never did. And the revolution spread quickly, like a deadly epidemic.

Incredibly, in the midst of this pandemonium, the emperor decided to return to his military headquarters at the front. Kirill stayed in command of the Naval Guards in St. Petersburg; as mutiny spread through the na-

tion's barracks, he took pride in the fact that his men had remained totally loyal to him. In his opinion, the mob and the revolutionary soldiers
filling the streets of St. Petersburg were not particularly opposed to the
emperor; they simply wanted food and an end to the war. "Much of
what they shouted . . . they did not even understand. They had picked
up slogans and repeated them like parrots. The people as such were not
disloyal to the Emperor, as were those in the Ministries and in his entourage. As for the troops in the capital, they had enough of everything
and far too little to do."

On the morning of March 12 the city woke up to an eerie stillness.
At the British embassy, Meriel Buchanan stood at an upstairs window
and gazed out uneasily at "the same wide streets, the same great palaces,
the same gold spires and domes rising out of the pearl-colored morning
mists, and yet . . . everywhere emptiness, no lines of toiling carts, no
crowded scarlet trams, no little sledges . . . Only the waste of deserted
streets and ice-bound river . . . and on the opposite shore the low grim
walls of the Fortress and the Imperial flag of Russia that for the last time
fluttered against the winter sky."

A few months later, from his own window at the French embassy,
Maurice Paléologue saw a swarm of army troops confronting the revolutionary mob: "I looked out; there was no one on the bridge which
usually presents a busy scene. But almost immediately, a disorderly mob
carrying red flags appeared . . . on the right bank of the Neva and a regiment came towards them from the opposite side. It seemed as if there
would be a violent collision, but on the contrary, the two bodies coa-
lesced. The army was fraternizing with the revolution."

By noon frightened crowds were running through the streets, and
fires appeared everywhere as soldiers began helping civilians to erect
barricades. Suddenly, "the crack of machine-gun fire split the air." The
law courts were consumed by flames, as were the arsenal, the military
government building, the Ministry of the Interior, a score of police sta-
tions, and several other public buildings. The prisons had been opened
and the convicts liberated. The Peter and Paul Fortress had been overwhelmed and twenty-five thousand soldiers armed with heavy artillery
had joined the revolution.

Ducky and Kirill watched helplessly as the military commanders in
St. Petersburg, the only ones who could have "saved the situation,"
completely lost direction, issuing mutually contradictory orders that
rendered their efforts "useless."

It became so dangerous in the capital that Kirill ordered one of his Naval Guard battalions protecting the imperial family at Tsarskoe Selo to rejoin the rest of the guards in the city, because they were almost the only loyal troops left. Though the Duma quickly stepped in and seized political leadership of the revolution, chaos still dominated the streets. Each day brought an increase in mob violence and hooliganism.

Ducky and her husband later remembered: "There was continuous shooting at night and during the daytime, and it was hard to tell who waged war against whom. St. Petersburg was in the hands of rival gangs, which went about looting shops and stores. At night they encamped round bonfires at street corners where they had planted their machine-guns, and passed their time yelling and singing and shooting at anyone who ventured abroad along the deserted streets of the doomed city. Having plundered the wine cellars of private houses and hotels, anything could be expected from these armed gangs. Seeing that no measures were taken against the mutineers they became even bolder, as they realized that the real power was in their hands."

For Ducky, these days of violence and uncertainty were especially traumatic. She had just discovered why she had felt so tired and ill during her recent visit to Missy: She was pregnant. If all went well, she would be giving birth in less than six months.

Ducky took the news of her pregnancy with surprise and concern. She had a history of miscarriages and difficult pregnancies, and she was now forty-one. It had been eight years since the arrival of her last child; although both she and Kirill had desperately wanted a son, they had all but given up the idea. Now, worried for her family, Ducky took care of herself as well as she could.

One morning an armed mob crashed through the gates and into the courtyard of Ducky and Kirill's town palace. The leaders demanded to see the grand duke; he slowly walked out to confront them, expecting the worst. To his astonishment, they politely asked him to lend them his car so they could drive to the Duma. Kirill laughingly agreed, on condition that they not smash it up. They responded with cheers, shouting for him to lead them.

These early days of the revolution were "a time of extravagant rumours and there was a complete lack of reliable news." No one seemed to know what had become of the emperor or where he was, and there was a complete "absence of stability, of someone at the helm, of at least some semblance of direction."

Actually, Nicholas was five hundred miles west, at army headquarters near the front. Incredibly, he knew very little of what was happening in the capital. Until the moment when the city had almost completely fallen to the revolutionists, the emperor had merely been informed that St. Petersburg had been experiencing annoying "street disorders." Nicholas's response to these mild and ambiguous reports had been irritation at his subjects' lack of patriotism in the midst of the wartime emergency.

As news of the revolution spread across Europe, exaggerated reports alarmed Ducky and Kirill's royal relatives. In the remote countryside of Romania, where Missy and her court were in hiding from the invading German army, a message arrived informing the queen that her sister had been captured by the revolutionary mob. Missy immediately wired everyone she could think of in the Russian capital to get information about Ducky. While she nervously waited for news, Missy wrote in her diary: "The whole thing is mysterious and dreadful and I am horribly anxious for Ducky."

It was several months before Missy was able to get in touch with Ducky; during these days of anxiety, when vague and conflicting news arrived in "in little scraps," Missy was "torn to pieces with fear about what might be happening to my sister . . . tortured by a thousand visions of what she might be suffering, of the dangers she might encounter." The queen of Romania had reason to worry. Every hour brought greater danger to Ducky and her family. They were trapped in St. Petersburg, at the mercy of the rapidly changing whims of a brutal, bloodthirsty mob.

At last, in May 1917, Missy had the "tremendous joy" of receiving a letter Ducky had written in the middle of March; it was an "immense relief" to discover that, as of then, she was still safe. But the contents of the letter also filled Missy with dread. Ducky was in as much danger as Missy had imagined, if not more. The evening that the letter arrived, Missy emotionally wrote in her diary:

> She writes that they lived through days such as one reads of in history, days both of fear and danger, the mob crying and clamouring beneath their windows, shooting in the streets, no safety anywhere. She and Kyrill [sic] had been in sympathy with the movement for obtaining a freer government, their ideas were very liberal and the new government were friends; but the people having to make concessions to the mob, they will probably be sacri-

*ficed for the sake of keeping momentary peace in the interior. It was a brave
and noble letter, just as one would imagine she would write. She tells me
that Diamandi, our Minister [the Romanian ambassador], has been a brick
through thick and thin; defying all danger, he came to see them continually
whilst many closer friends foresook them in the hour of their distress.*

Abandoned by almost all their friends, Ducky and Kirill watched and
waited in their palace as the revolution exploded into full-blown anarchy, the wild celebrations becoming "mingled with violent outbursts of
mob fury." They were unofficially prisoners, chilled by the increasing
brutality of the rioters outside their front door. All over the city mansions and palaces were being "sacked by the mob from top to bottom,"
then set on fire, the blazes left burning as the firemen "were driven away
by soldiers and workmen who wanted to see the buildings burn." By
now the mob was frenzied. Death was no longer punishment enough for
their former leaders. The mob slaughtered only some, burying the others
alive, "side by side" with a rotting corpse.

One day an officer of the Naval Guards came to Ducky and Kirill's
palace and reported that the grand duke's sailors had locked up their officers. With no hesitation, Kirill hurried off to speak to his men. He
found them in "an ugly temper," but he managed to restore order because they were still personally loyal to him. To Kirill's surprise, they
even offered to provide a special guard around his palace.

So as the anarchy in the streets increased, Kirill's loyal men stood pro-
tectively at his door and ensured that the family was not molested. In the
evenings Ducky and Kirill's few remaining friends would drop by to see
how they were doing and discuss the growing crisis. These visits took
great courage, "for anyone who went into the streets of the city at night
was shot at indiscriminately."

Meanwhile, the Duma issued a formal order to all troops and their
commanding officers to show their allegiance to the new official government by publicly marching to the Duma and declaring their loyalty.
The Duma hoped that if the troops could be induced to carry out its
emergency measures in the capital, then normal conditions might be
brought about and "the rule of gangsterdom checked out for good
and all."

Since there had been no news of the emperor's whereabouts, it was
assumed that he was trying to return to the capital with the help of loyal
troops. Everyone waited and wondered.

In the absence of information concerning the monarch, Kirill was placed in an awkward position by the Duma's decree. As the commander of the Naval Guards, he was subject to the order; so he had to decide whether to obey the Duma or stay home, leave his men leaderless in this dangerous situation by resigning, and thus "let them drift on to the rocks of revolution with the rest."

Until now Kirill had been able to preserve his troops' loyalty and discipline. It "had not been an easy task to preserve them from the contamination of the revolutionary disease"; indeed, by this time they were the only reliable soldiers left in St. Petersburg. To deprive them of leadership at this critical time would only add to the enormity of the current disaster. From Kirill's point of view, his chief duty was to calm things in the capital "by every means at his disposal," even if it meant sacrificing his personal pride, so that the emperor might safely return. Seeing the authority of the Duma as "the last certain thing among the wreckage," Kirill hoped that Nicholas would return with loyal troops and immediately restore order; "all might yet be saved." To the Duma Kirill would go.

He embraced his wife and kissed her good-bye. Watching from her upstairs window as he disappeared down the street, Ducky, faint from worry and morning sickness, wondered if she would ever see him again.

Kirill went directly to the barracks of the Naval Guards, still hoping that it would not be necessary to "drink this bitter cup." But the men were determined to join the march to the Duma, and they wanted the grand duke, their commander, to lead them.

Thus, on this bright, cold Wednesday morning of March 14, 1917, Kirill and his Naval Guards joined the parade of troops to the Tauride Palace to pay mass obedience to the Duma. Watching from the French embassy, Ambassador Paléologue observed: "They marched in perfect order with their band at their head. A few officers came first, wearing a large red cockade in their caps, a knot of red ribbon on their shoulders and red stripes on their sleeves. The old regiment standard, covered with icons, was surrounded by red flags."

The most spectacular part of the long procession was the amazing appearance of Grand Duke Kirill leading the battalion of Naval Guards. Characteristically keeping his feelings to himself, Kirill marched proudly, holding his head high and his shoulders straight. Suddenly there came gunfire from some infantrymen. The attack left Kirill and his men unharmed, but it was decided that he would continue the rest of the way in the safety of an automobile.

Arriving at the Tauride Palace, Kirill found it "in absolute pandemonium," the atmosphere much more that of a "beer-garden" than
an orderly parliament. "Soldiers with unbuttoned tunics and their caps
pushed to the back of their heads were shouting themselves hoarse.
Deputies were yelling at the top of their voices. The place was in a state
of chaos and confusion. Cigarette smoke filled the air, the place was a
filthy mess, and torn paper littered the floor. Meanwhile officers were
driven up the stairs by their soldiers with the butts of rifles. They were
being insulted and bullied mercilessly. Among them were many whom
I knew well. That was what I found in the seat of the Liberal Government. Liberalism and Socialism expressed themselves in complete anarchy."

Guarded by his loyal men, the grand duke spent the entire afternoon
and evening in this painfully unpleasant arena. Finally, late at night, a
young student approached Kirill and politely informed him that a car
was waiting to take him home.

On the way back to Glinka Street the car was held up by an armed
gang demanding to know who they were. The student, sitting in the
front seat, shouted, "Students, comrades!" Miraculously, they were allowed to pass. They drove through a labyrinth of barricades past scores
of burning buildings that "lit up the night with their ghastly glare" as
"armed and shouting rabble went through the streets" and the terrifying
sound of "machine-gun and rifle firing could be heard quite near."

Kirill reached home in the early hours of the morning to find his wife
"in a state of great anxiety." Ducky had spent the day trying to keep
busy, forcing fearful thoughts from her mind. But when her husband's
"long absence" extended into the night, "she thought that all was over"
with him. As he entered the door of their home, she rushed to him and
collapsed in his arms, weeping.

Although Ducky understood how dangerous were her husband's actions that day, she never wavered in her conviction "that he was doing
the right thing." She knew that the power and authority of Nicholas
and Alexandra were at an end, and that the only chance for the survival
of imperial rule was the decisive leadership of another Romanov. And
Kirill was the best candidate, thanks to his proximity to the throne and
his forceful and liberal character. Thoroughly pragmatic and modern in
their thinking, Kirill and Ducky squarely faced reality, committing
themselves to the course best suited to saving their country and their
family's crown.

But the collapse of the empire was complete; at the end of this dangerous and farcical day Kirill and his wife knew they were witnessing "the triumph of the forces of disorder." "It was the end . . . the time for strong action had been missed . . . henceforth the country was being plunged headlong into anarchy, bloodshed, and complete dilapidation in the name of all the various human virtues."

A few days later Kirill wrote to his uncle Paul and tried to explain his actions: "These last few days, I have been alone in carrying out my duties to Nicky and the country and in saving the situation by my recognition of the Provisional Government."

But many saw Kirill's compliance with the new democratic government as nothing less than treason. Absolutists and hard-liners, loath to compromise an inch, condemned the grand duke's public support for the Duma's authority. Of course, it was these rigid and unyielding autocrats whose antiquated philosophies had brought about the bloody revolution. Surprisingly, even the liberal French ambassador, Maurice Paléologue, failed to appreciate the hopelessness of Nicholas II's position and the violence of the approaching storm. In his diary he disdainfully took Kirill to task for having "come out openly in favour of the revolution." Paléologue failed to recognize both the necessity and courageous intent of Kirill's action: "Forgetting the oath of fealty, and the office of aide-de-camp which bound him to the Emperor, he went off about one o'clock this afternoon to make obeisance to popular rule. In his naval captain's uniform he was seen leading the marines of the Guard, whose commander he is, and placing their services at the disposal of the mob!"

The next day was "the saddest moment" of Kirill's life: In his private railway coach near Pskov, several hundred miles west of the capital, Nicholas II abdicated his throne. Three hundred years of Romanov rule was at an end.

Appropriately, it was the afternoon of March 15—the Ides of March, on which Julius Caesar was assassinated.

Nicholas had also relinquished the rights of Czarevich Alexis, so the crown now passed, by default, to the next in line. This was Nicholas's prodigal younger brother, Grand Duke Michael. As irresponsible and immature as ever, Michael enjoyed a "ludicrously brief" reign. His first imperial action was to rush to the capital and abdicate.

To many, it must have seemed that the Romanovs no longer desired to sit on their uncomfortable throne.

After Michael's abdication, Kirill and Ducky were the rightful successors. But the idea of continuing the monarchy had now been entirely abandoned by the Provisional Government. "No more Romanovs! We want a Republic!" became the universal cry of the country.

And so it was.

Ducky and Kirill were thunderstruck by the news of the abdications. Until now they had remained somewhat optimistic, but everything suddenly appeared to be "futile and hopeless." They both wept as "the whole reality revealed itself mercilessly and like a lifeless vacuum before one. It was as though the very ground had given way beneath one's feet," Kirill later remembered. "All that one had worked, fought, and suffered for had been in vain."

Kirill was forced to resign his command of the Naval Guards. He immediately went to the barracks and addressed his men, explaining why he could no longer lead them and exhorting them to be loyal to their country, maintain their good discipline, and obey their superiors. Kirill had been with these men for twenty years; choked with emotion, he told them: "This is the hardest day in my life." With tears in their eyes, the men rushed up to him and seized him in their arms, lifting him up on their shoulders and shouting: "Where you are, sir, we will be!"

Several of the men continued to guard the palace on Glinka Street. On Easter Sunday a delegation of sailors arrived at Kirill's door and insisted that he attend the liturgy of Easter night with them. They hurried off together and, in the little chapel in the barracks, the sailors pointedly placed their former leader in a position of honor.

It was the last Easter Kirill would ever celebrate in Russia.

Plans had been made for the imperial family to leave the country and take up exile in England. As the revolution's hostility toward the dispossessed Romanovs increased, immediate departure from Russian soil was the only guarantee of their safety. The country's mood was becoming alarmingly similar to that during the Terror in France a century before.

Nicholas and Alexandra and their children were to be the first to depart. A British ship was headed to the Arctic port of Murmansk to pick them up. The Provisional Government had made all the arrangements. Bags were packed at Tsarskoe Selo and everything was ready. Then the Soviet Party in the capital discovered the plan and sharply asserted its growing power.

"The Republic must be safeguarded against the Romanovs returning to the historical arena," declared the chairman of the Petrograd Soviet. The Soviet gave immediate orders to the workers to block the passage of the imperial train from Tsarskoe Selo, then decreed that Nicholas and his family must be officially arrested and imprisoned in the Peter and Paul Fortress to await trial and execution.

On the question of the fate of the Romanovs there developed a stand-off between the radical Soviet Party and the relatively conservative Provisional Government, neither of which had enough power to dictate to the other. The plan for immediate exile was suspended, and a heated debate continued for several months, until the Soviets, finally having consolidated their power, began rounding up every member of the imperial family they could find and swiftly executing them as criminals.

During these chaotic months as the leadership of Russia teetered between madness and reason, Ducky and Kirill anxiously watched and waited from Glinka Street. Nearby, buildings burned every night; passersby were killed within view of their windows. The mansions of the aristocracy were especially prime targets. While the loyal Naval Guards protected Kirill and Ducky, others were not so lucky. Ducky's friend and rival social hostess Countess Kleinmichel, with only her quick wits to aid her, barred her doors, shuttered her windows, and placed a large bold sign on the front of the house: "No trespassing. This house is the property of the Petrograd Soviet. Countess Kleinmichel has been taken to the Fortress of St. Peter and Paul." The rabble read the sign, then went away. Inside, the countess was packing her bags and planning her escape.

Ducky herself was becoming desperate. Food was difficult to find. There were only a few persons left who could be relied upon. And the safety of her children preyed on her mind. Ducky did her best to comfort the little girls, who, traumatized by what was happening around them, couldn't sleep at night. She also worried about the child she was carrying. The terrible anxiety and meager diet had seriously undermined her health. She and Kirill came to one inescapable conclusion:

They would have to get away soon. They would have to leave Russia, or they would not survive.

CHAPTER THIRTY-SEVEN

Into the Night

"T HE WIND OF REVOLUTIONS is not tractable," Victor Hugo once observed. And certainly, during the spring of 1917, no one really knew where Russia was going or what would happen next.

Stripped of their titles and positions, he and Ducky lived in growing despair, their only solace the support of their few remaining friends. Chief among these were Sir George and Lady Buchanan, Ducky's oldest and most trusted companions. It had been Ducky's loving grandmama, Queen Victoria, who originally charged the Buchanans with safeguarding the rebellious young granddaughter when she was unhappily living in Darmstadt. After more than two decades of friendship the Buchanans were almost surrogate parents to Ducky.

But by now the Buchanans, too, were in a precarious position. The Provisional Government instructed Sir George to have no further communication with the imperial family; predictably, the ambassador replied that he would never abandon the grand duke and his wife, who had always been so kind to him. Indeed, if the grand duchess was in danger, he would offer her the protection of the British embassy, since she was an English princess by birth and "entitled to any help he could give her." The new Russian leaders received this statement coldly.

Lady Buchanan continued to visit Ducky, taking her out in the embassy carriage to visit her English nurse, who was hospitalized. When the leaders of the Provisional Government heard about this, they immediately sent for Sir George again and angrily informed him that they could not allow this fraternization to continue. It was explained to the ambassador that many people in the capital believed he was secretly plotting a counterrevolution with members of the imperial family. The continued association with Ducky and her husband was feeding these rumors, and the government leaders warned of a possible attack on the British embassy. They also threatened to have Buchanan recalled to London if he did not cooperate.

Because Great Britain had officially recognized the Provisional Government, Sir George now found himself in an awkward position. He was helpless to disobey the government's orders; he was also obliged to protect his wife and daughter and the embassy property. After painful discussion, Lady Buchanan sadly wrote to explain what had happened and why they could no longer visit.

Ducky responded graciously: "I quite understand and thank you both for all your niceness. Of course you must not think of coming to see me, if it can be misinterpreted. It is hard to be accused of being 'vieux régime' when all one's sufferings are due to mismanagement. Fondest love, and I hope we will meet again in happier days."

But despite these generous words, Ducky was wounded by the Buchanans' defection. Since she knew nothing of Sir George's impossible position—in addition to his personal danger, he was criticized by his homeland's liberals as a reactionary and condemned by its conservatives for not having done more to save the Russian monarchy—Ducky could only feel abandoned. She wrote Missy that the Buchanans "had deserted her in her hour of need, and had refused to help her." "Neither pride, nor hope, nor money, nor future, and the dear past blotted out by the frightful present; nothing is left, nothing!" she lamented.

Missy, disconsolate, wrote in her diary:

> At last a long letter from Ducky was brought me, a tragic letter, a heartbreaking, soul-torturing letter, a letter full of blackest despair, and deepest, most hopeless agony. I had always feared it would be thus with her and yet hoped against hope that it would not be. A dreadful letter of inconsolable grief, cruel and fearful in its desperate intensity.
>
> She could not suffer thus, because what is left? And I cannot go to her! I can be of no good, no aid, no relief. How can I, a queen, go now to Russia or send anyone of mine there? Poor, proud, great Ducky; why had her life to be as tragic as her face?

Missy was worried most about her sister's pregnancy, now advanced, and tried to find some way to send her the layette of her baby Mircea, who had died the year before. She also begged Romania's ambassador in St. Petersburg to see what he and his staff could do for her. The Romanian diplomats had always been "deeply impressed" by Ducky and were grieved to find "this proud, brave woman in such a cruel situation." But because the Russian government was making it impossible for anyone to see the members of the imperial family, there was very little that could be done.

After two months of bloody pandemonium that spring, a strange and eerie quiet had suddenly settled over the Russian capital. To the nervous Kirill, "it was not a natural calm"; he did not trust it any more than he "would have trusted one in Asiatic seas when the sky is ominously threatening before a typhoon." This mistrust was entirely appropriate, for the standoff between the Provisional Government and the rabid Soviets could not last much longer.

And it was no secret that the Soviets were determined to punish every member of the Romanov family as severely as possible. Throughout the capital the demand was becoming more strident that the emperor and empress be placed in prison and put on trial, the verdict being a foregone conclusion.

A spectral guillotine seemed to be rising in the square before the Winter Palace; it was impossible not to foresee the extermination of the Romanovs. The fact that they were still alive was remarkable in itself. And it was only because of Kirill's courageous march to the Duma and his public declaration of allegiance to the Provisional Government that he and his family had been spared. Had he not acted as he had, he would have risked death as a passive martyr for the imperial cause, "dragging his wife and children down with him to share the same fate." In any case, as has been recounted, Kirill saw the Provisional Government as Russia's last, best hope.

By comparison with Kirill and Ducky the other Romanovs were pampered parasites who lacked both the ability and the courage to act decisively. Unable to cope with the brutal challenge of the revolution, most of them would perish. But the ones who survived cursed their cousin for his quick-witted pragmatism while secretly admiring his strength and bravery.

In the navy, Kirill had learned the importance of swift, decisive action in the face of danger, "be it under enemy fire on board ship, or when revolutionary mobs stood within a stone's throw of his palace and family." He faced one of the most dangerous situations of his life. How would he get his family out of the capital and to a safe place?

It was decided that the remote and isolated Finnish countryside would be the best place to go. Though still a part of the Russian empire, Finland had an identity and sensibility of its own. It would provide a secure and relatively neutral haven for Ducky and the children while they waited to see how the storm in St. Petersburg would play itself out.

Besides isolating them from the impending disaster in the capital, Finland was a friendly and familiar retreat. Ducky and Kirill already had a standing invitation to move to the beautiful Haiko estate near Borgo (present-day Porvoo), a small town on the south coast of Finland near Helsinki. Haiko belonged to the von Etter family, who had played host to them several times in the past, notably during that sizzling summer of 1914 when only a constant immersion in the cool coastal waters brought Ducky relief from the torrid heat. (They had left Marie and Kira at Haiko when they had to return to St. Petersburg for a reception honoring French president Raymond Poincaré. The girls were still staying there when war was declared; Ducky had had great difficulty getting them home.)

Ducky had visited the Etter estate again in 1915 to escape the sultry weather. Now, as the summer of 1917 approached, with its more than merely physical heat, Ducky and her family were anxious to see Haiko again. But would they be able? They were, of course, not permitted to leave Russia; it was difficult even to get permission to travel within Russia or to change residence. To journey to Finland, a special permit from the Provisional Government was required. Such permits were rarely given, especially to members of the imperial family; to get one would entail months of frustrating delay and suffocating red tape.

Besides, to make the request would itself be perilous. Anyone who approached those in power was calling attention to himself or herself, inviting scrutiny and perhaps reassessment. The aristocracy, viewed as enemies of the new democratic Russian state, were in limbo, not knowing their legal status or what tomorrow would bring. Most of them, hoping for the best, tried to stand still, hold their breaths, and avoid drawing attention.

But it was not in Ducky and Kirill's nature to passively wait for others to act. They had always been the masters of their own fate, and now they were determined to move forward. With imprisonment or worse a strong possibility, Ducky and Kirill approached the Provisional Government and formally requested a special permit to leave the city for the Finnish countryside. Then they returned to the palace on Glinka Street and began to wait.

Days passed. No one knew how long it would take or what the response would be. Had they provoked the government? Had they foolishly signed their own death warrants?

The days crawled on.

Then, finally, after two weeks, a communication arrived.

It was from the a young official of the Provisional Government, Alexander Kerensky. Because the politically moderate Kerensky sympathized with the beleaguered imperial family and particularly admired Kirill's courage and patriotism, he had seen to it that the necessary documents were expedited. He had also swept aside the many obstacles that others had tried to place in Ducky and Kirill's way. By that evening the permits were in their hands.

They decided to leave as quickly as possible. So far, their house had not been ransacked by the revolutionary mob as most other aristocratic homes had been. It had not even been searched or otherwise disturbed by the soldiers of the Provisional Government. But now, as Ducky and Kirill prepared to depart, they were carefully watched by the authorities. They were forbidden to take "anything of value" with them. All they would be allowed to take was "such clothes as they could carry."

Ducky took her most precious diamond, ruby, emerald, and sapphire jewelry and concealed it in the family's clothing. She sewed jewels into hidden seams and stuffed them into underwear. Then she and Kirill held their breaths, hoping their treasure would remain undiscovered despite the endless inspections by overzealous authorities.

Kirill and Ducky's departure had been "very quietly arranged"; not even their closest friends knew they were leaving. At evening, they were taken downstairs and gathered in the courtyard of the palace. To avoid arousing public suspicion, Kirill left first, in a car with their two daughters, and took an indirect route to the train station. An hour later the heavily pregnant Ducky climbed into another car and was taken to the station by an entirely different route.

Had the Soviets learned of these Romanovs' departure, they would likely have insisted that Ducky and her family be instantly taken into custody—the frightening prelude to the firing squad. But the Soviets never knew what was happening.

One by one, military and bureaucratic officials carefully inspected the family's documents and special exit permits, then grudgingly passed them along, until finally Ducky, Kirill, and the two girls climbed nervously onto the rickety train and quietly took their seats. Eight-year-old Kira later remembered that their passes "were respected and we were not molested on the way." She also noticed their modest accommodations: "For the first time there were no royal trappings . . . i.e. red carpets, special comforts, etc."

As the train slowly moved out of the station, Ducky watched the last rays of the sun ignite the domes and spires of the city. As their train sped toward the Gulf of Finland and the veil of night descended upon them, neither she nor her husband realized that the vanishing crimson glow of St. Petersburg would be their last sight of their beloved home.

PART FOUR

The Shadow Empress

CHAPTER THIRTY-EIGHT

The Mortal Storm

ARRIVING AT THE SMALL TOWN OF Borgo on the secluded southern coast of Finland that first week of June 1917, Ducky and her family immediately proceeded to the safety of their friends' country estate, Haiko. They were accompanied by two Englishwomen, Miss Burgess and Miss Gregory, and a few servants. Kirill arranged to rent a large house in town that would serve as quarters for his equerry and the rest of the servants.

Ducky tried to relax in the serenity of the Etters' home while her husband began planning their future. Forty years old and seven months pregnant, she was suffering from severe cramps in her legs and "could hardly stand." She needed to stay as calm and rested as possible until the arrival of the baby.

She promptly wrote Missy to tell her where they were and that they were safe. Because of the chaos created by the continuing war in Europe, the letter took seven weeks to reach Missy, and when it did, it filled her with anxiety. "Her despair at the last events in Russia can find no expression," Missy sadly confided to her diary.

After two weeks at Haiko, Ducky and Kirill and their family moved to the rented house in Borgo, where they quietly passed the remainder of the summer. On August 30 Ducky gave birth to a boy. She and Kirill were overjoyed to have a son at last. With the abdication of Nicholas and his son and brother, Kirill was now the legitimate successor to the Russian throne. The existence of a male heir meant that Kirill's branch of the imperial family could claim the crown with confidence. The handsome and healthy baby was named Vladimir in honor of Kirill's late father.

In September, when Ducky was well enough to move, they accepted the invitation of the Etter family to resume their residence at Haiko, "hoping that it would be a safer place." Baby Vladimir was christened there on the eighteenth of September. Arriving from Russia to conduct the ceremony was the Very Reverend Protopresbyter Alexander Dernov, head of the court clergy and dean of the Cathedrals of the Winter Palace in St. Petersburg and of the Annunciation in the Kremlin. He was assisted by V. I. Ilyinsky, the psalmist of the Cathedral of Saints Peter and Paul. The godparents (by proxy) were Grand Duchess Marie and Grand Duke Boris. An intimate affair, the christening was attended by only a few fellow Russian exiles and some Finnish friends.

As winter approached, life in Finland became an ordeal. The Etters' pleasant summer home was no match for the severe winter of the Finnish wilderness. Ducky and Kirill suffered from the cold and there were serious food and fuel shortages. They had the added anxiety of not knowing what was happening or whether they would be captured and shot the next day. And they also feared for family members they had left behind in Russia.

For while Ducky and Kirill had expected that conditions in Russia would gradually improve so that they could return home, in fact they had gotten out of St. Petersburg just in time. In mid-August, while Ducky was preparing for the birth of her baby in rural Finland, Nicholas and Alexandra and their five children had been taken from Tsarskoe Selo and shipped off to Siberia. Imprisoned in a fortified house in a remote village, the former emperor and his family were being treated like criminals. One by one, the other members of the Romanov family were also being rounded up and placed under strict confinement or house arrest.

During that summer the moderate Provisional Government had been shaken by internal uprisings and had begun to crumble. The infant government was simply "too weak to resist the growing power of the Bolsheviks." (Ironically, the Bolshevik leader, Lenin, was hiding in Finland at the same time as Ducky and her family.) In October Lenin urged the radical Bolsheviks to make "an immediate lunge for supreme power," then, in disguise, slipped back to St. Petersburg and rallied his followers to revolt and overthrow the Kerensky regime.

It took only a single day.

On November 6, 1917, the Bolsheviks surrounded the Winter Palace. Almost effortlessly, they unseated the Provisional Government and seized control of the country. Kerensky immediately went into hiding and eventually fled to Europe and America. His sudden departure would prove disastrous, as "he carried with him the vanishing dream of a humane, liberal, democratic Russia."

Although local Soviet regimes were solidly established across most of the immense former empire, there was considerable opposition to this radical form of communism. Eventually, the clash of ideologies led to civil war between the Bolsheviks ("Reds") and their conservative, moderate, and royalist opponents, collectively known as the Whites.

With the revolution and civil war in full swing, the family "could not feel secure" even at remote Haiko. For one thing, the entire Russian fleet was stationed in the harbor of Helsinki, only thirty miles away. Although command was still in the hands of the officers, Kirill was uneasily aware that "their authority had suffered considerably from revolutionary disintegration." Finland itself was on the verge of seceding from Russia; tension was mounting and local fighting was about to break out.

As the brutal winter progressed, the family tried to fill the "long, dreary" hours with as many good friends and pleasant pastimes as they could, but even little Kira was conscious of "the hardship of bitter cold, hunger, privations of every sort, not to mention the constant danger of being murdered by the Reds and the terrible sadness of the political developments."

One of the few bright spots in these anxious and somber days was the unexpected arrival of one of Kirill's former sailors, who had made the long journey from Russia to find the grand ducal family. The sailor had brought provisions, including wine and cakes, and also delivered the latest news from home. Sickened by the ascendancy of the Bolsheviks, the man bluntly told Ducky and Kirill that the revolution was "a farce, which would end sadly."

Not all visitors to Haiko were so welcome.

One day a group of sailors appeared, declaring that that they had orders to search the house and ordering the inhabitants to gather together on the second floor.

Ducky and Kirill knew only too well "what a 'search' by sailors meant at that time": They had already heard that "the majority of the members of the Imperial Family had been arrested." They nervously "prepared for the worst." Gently taking the two girls and the baby, they went upstairs and quietly waited as the sailors rummaged below. For three hours they sat in agony. They had almost given in to panic when the sailor in command asked Kirill to come downstairs.

Kirill kissed his wife and then, very slowly, complied. As he left the room, Ducky collapsed in a chair and, fighting back tears, tried to comfort her daughters with a slightly trembling smile.

After what seemed an eternity, Kirill rushed back into the room. Happy and excited, he explained that the sailors had gone. They had decided not to proceed with the search or make any arrests after discovering who was in residence there. One of the sailors had served under Kirill on the cruiser *Oleg;* because the grand duke had been so popular with his crew, "in remembrance of that love the man persuaded the others not to disturb him."

At the end of 1917 a full-scale civil war broke out in Finland. Though a grand duchy of the Russian empire since 1809, Finland had enjoyed unusual autonomy, having its own constitutional government. But the last decade had been one of strife and repression by St. Petersburg; by the time of the Bolshevik revolution the Finns had had enough. Taking advantage of the radical climate, they declared their independence. There ensued a brutal struggle between the conservative Whites and the communist Reds to see who would control the new country.

Unfortunately for Ducky and her family, the first hostilities of the war took place near Haiko. Night and day they heard the firing of big guns. The winter weather was becoming terribly harsh, and obtaining food was a real problem. It was almost impossible to get even the most essential products, such as milk, bread, and meat. But Ducky kept up everyone's spirits by making sure that they all continued "enjoying their winter sports."

By the begining of 1918 the Reds began capturing the local landowners and executing them. A neighboring squire named Bjorkenheim was taken into the forest adjoining Haiko and shot. A few days later seven Finnish aristocrats took refuge in Ducky and Kirill's home and remained there three weeks until the Reds discovered their whereabouts and forced them to flee for their lives.

A week later, on February 9, fifteen Finnish Reds appeared at Haiko's front door looking for hidden arms. They proceeded to make a thorough search of the ground floor while Ducky waited nervously with the children on the floor above. The men behaved "very politely, and the way in which they put their questions suggested that they had orders not to touch anybody in Haiko." Again, Kirill's reputation saved the family from the fate that was befalling the rest of the Romanovs.

But the family was nevertheless in "a very precarious position." Haiko was almost entirely cut off from the rest of the world. Hearing "fantastic and contradictory" rumors about what was going on in Russia and what was happening to their relatives, Ducky and her husband didn't know what to believe. Life was more arduous than ever; food had become dangerously scarce and wood for the fireplaces more and more difficult to obtain.

Finally, on the last day of February, Kirill received news from Helsinki that the French government had been making inquiries about his and Ducky's safety and was seriously considering taking official steps for their immediate evacuation.

Ducky and Kirill agonized over how to reply to the offer. As grateful as they were for such consideration, they decided that they would have to decline. It was, of course, "very painful to go on living as we were," but they wished to remain within the empire. Leaving would be "too much like desertion."

As if to test their resolve, a few days after they conveyed their final decision to the French, another offer arrived from King Gustav V of neutral Sweden. Kirill thanked the king for his consideration and "admitted that he did not look upon the position of his family as safe, but replied that the moment had not yet come for an intervention." At that time both he and Ducky still believed that the Bolshevik regime could not last much longer and that some degree of reason and order would soon be restored.

Stockholm's hospitality was more than tempting. Life at Haiko was a nightmarish ordeal, and "not one they endured by choice." The health of baby Vladimir and the well-being of their daughters made any offer of foreign rescue seem heaven-sent. Also, the temptation of a return to a life of luxury and quiet safety was difficult to resist. But neither personal comfort nor the safety of her family could lure Ducky from the path that duty and honor compelled her to follow.

Because Ducky's first cousin the former Princess Margaret of Connaught was now the crown princess of Sweden, the Scandinavian monarch felt special concern for Ducky's safety. But even when the Swedish royal family persisted in trying to persuade the grand ducal couple to flee Finland to Stockholm, Ducky refused. At the end of January 1918, the anxious crown princess had written to a friend in England, Lady Egerton:

> *I feel so sorry for all Russians, I know several very nice ones here who feel so ashamed of their country. One I like very much is a Countess Orloff Davidoff who is a typical Russian, short, stout, magnificent pearls, ugly clothes, a deep voice and very downright, a little like Aunt Marie [Ducky's mother] in manner, she manages to get news from Russia some how and told me last night she had heard that the Empress Minny [the dowager empress] is better but she has been very ill a long time and has apparently grown so old. No wonder! This Countess Orloff brought me a letter from Ducky asking me to be kind to her, she is here with her only child and Princess Lieven who is expecting her first baby and whose husband is the Russian Red X's representative here in Sweden. Curiously enough they have not sent him flying yet altho' belonging to l'ancien régime. Ducky and Kyrill [sic] are staying with a Mme Etter in Finland, Ducky at last got a son last September, rather late in the day poor thing. Kyrill we hear has to go about and buy his own food at the market.*

Other friends were also showing concern for Ducky and her family. Lady Buchanan sent them a case of Red Cross supplies, canned milk, butter, cereals, jam, and clothes for the children. In response she received only a stiff letter from Ducky's English nurse "coldly acknowledging the gift's arrival." Lady Buchanan never received a personal message from Ducky, and in fact would never hear from her oldest and dearest friend again.

In the years to come both Ducky and Kirill publicly criticized Sir George and Lady Buchanan for turning their backs on them after the revolution. For someone as sensitive and loyal as Ducky, the Buchanans' withdrawal in St. Petersburg was unforgivable. It had been so crushing to Ducky's spirit and had caused her so much grief that she never attempted to understand her friends' behavior. As she saw it, the Buchanans had simply abandoned the emperor and his family to their fate and done nothing to save the Romanov monarchy.

Ducky and Kirill failed to appreciate the machinations of the British government. For the sake of international diplomacy and to help the Foreign Office in London save face, Sir George was made the scapegoat for his country's ineffectual and irresponsible policy toward the crumbling Russian monarchy. A gallant gentleman as devoted to honor and duty as Ducky herself was, Sir George made a perfect foil for the ruthless and unprincipled practices of world politics. It was not until his death two decades after the revolution that his daughter, Meriel, was able to reveal that he had been forced to abandon the Romanovs under the threat of ruin and disgrace and "the termination of his pension by the Foreign Office."

But even if Ducky had known the facts, she probably would have felt the same way. She always saw the world, and matters of right and wrong, in black and white. After all, when she had faced death time and time again to do what she knew was honorable and right, why shouldn't she expect those closest to her to do the same thing? If they didn't, they were not worthy to be her friends. They deserved only pity or contempt.

In the same situation, Missy would have found some way to understand the Buchanans, forgiving them and continuing the friendship. But Ducky could never yield. As if creating the mounting tragedy of her life, the fatally passionate grand duchess could neither forgive nor forget.

CHAPTER THIRTY-NINE

Alms for the Oblivion

I N M A R C H 1918, as spring slowly approached and the ice of coastal Finland began to melt, a huge German squadron floated menacingly into the harbors of Hangö and Helsinki and demanded that Russia return its Baltic fleet back to its home base at Kronstadt. Helpless to resist, the Russians complied. A week later the Bolshevik government signed a peace agreement with the Central Powers; the Treaty of Brest-Litovsk brought hostilities between Russia and Germany to an abrupt end.

In suing for peace, the new Soviet nation paid a terrible price, losing almost its entire foothold on the European continent. Gone were the formerly Russian holdings of Poland, Finland, the Baltic states, and most of Ukraine.

Ducky and Kirill were devastated by the terms of the peace treaty and their country's ignominious defeat. And their feelings about the German emancipation of Finland were mixed at best.

The kaiser's triumph had brought the final victory of the Finnish White army over the Reds and an immediate end to Finland's civil war. So Ducky and her family were now safe from the bloodthirsty Bolsheviks—but they hardly knew how to behave toward the Germans. Once the country of Ducky's own sovereign rule and that of her parents, Germany had been a hated enemy for the last four years. Now, suddenly, Germany had come to her family's rescue—while at the same time, recognizing the legitimacy of the savage mob that had recently dispossessed them. Ducky was never able to resolve her violently conflicting feelings for Germany.

Although they were now safe, the family continued to suffer. Life at Haiko was still as primitive as ever, and food and fuel shortages were just as severe. Even the arrival of summer did not improve conditions. Ducky's concerned cousin the crown princess of Sweden wrote to her friend Lady Egerton again at the end of July, vividly describing the grand duchess's plight: "I had a letter from Ducky from Finland two days ago begging me to send her some baby food for her 8 months old boy, they can get nothing to give him, doesn't it sound rather awful. I shall do my best to help her of course."

As Ducky struggled to keep her family going, "homesickness, shortages, cold weather and boredom hung over them like a pall." At the end of May, her younger daughter, nine-year-old Kira, wrote her aunt Missy: "How I wish I could see you. Here it is quite cold though it ought to be summer. Boy [the baby Vladimir] is so sweet. When he is hungry and Nana is preparing his lunch, the tears simply stream down his cheeks with hunger. We go for long walks and hunt for mushrooms in the woods. There are many wild flowers in bloom. Each Friday we go to the cinema. On Saturday evening we have games. . . . I often wonder if we will ever go away from here. We are getting so dreadfully homesick but I suppose we are better off here. When there is no more sugar I think we will miss it very much. Our lessons keep us occupied, otherwise we are rather bored sometimes."

Meanwhile, the vicious civil war still raged in Russia. Unknown to Ducky and Kirill, the Bolsheviks were winning. Because the grand ducal couple "were not content to look impassively," they did everything they could do from their Finnish exile to keep the Reds from tearing their country to shreds. Although they were personally powerless to stop the Bolsheviks, they looked to those who had the strength to do so. The natural choice of allies was Ducky's homeland, Great Britain.

England had already sent troops to Russia earlier in the year, before the Treaty of Brest-Litovsk, to create an eastern front against the Central Powers and prevent arms and ammunition from falling into German hands. After the Bolshevik government had pulled out of the war and made peace with the enemy, Britain felt betrayed, considering the new rulers of Russia traitors who had deserted the Allied cause. Feeling was now running very high, especially in the War Office, that England "should help the anti-Bolshevik Russians to destroy Lenin and his regime." But any such action would have to wait until a successful completion of the world war.

Then, like a violent thunderbolt out of a clear sky, came the Bolsheviks' announcement in late July 1918 that they had executed Emperor Nicholas II.

A universal sense of shock and horror greeted the news.

Ducky and Kirill collapsed in the upstairs room at Haiko and stared at each other with agonized disbelief at the thought of their gentle cousin's horrible and unjust fate. Though they had taken care to protect themselves and their children, they had never really thought that the revolution would come to this.

Ducky now realized her family's situation was far more terrifying than she had ever believed. And had she known what had just been officially decided by the Central Executive Committee of the new Russian government, her nerve might have totally failed her. Lenin had adopted the simple philosophy of not leaving the Whites "a live banner to rally around, especially under the present circumstances." This meant the extermination of the entire imperial family. To begin with, along with Nicholas, his wife, the empress Alexandra, and their five children had been slaughtered in the dark basement of the "House of Special Purpose" in Ekaterinburg, where they had been imprisoned. So appalling was this crime that it had been kept secret; the news of the Romanovs' gruesome demise would not become known to the outside world until the following year.

With the emperor and his immediate family out of the way, "the same ruthless logic dictated the murder of every member of the Romanov family on whom the Bolsheviks could lay their hands." This merciless drive to make the ruling family of Russia extinct was, in the eyes of the Bolshevik leaders, "not only expedient but necessary." There was no turning back for them now, and ahead lay either "complete victory or complete ruin."

On July 10, six days before the massacre at Ekaterinburg, Nicholas's younger brother, Grand Duke Michael, had been executed at Perm. On July 16 Ducky's beloved Aunt Ella—the saintly grand duchess Elizabeth—Grand Duke Serge Mikhailovich, three sons of Grand Duke Constantine, and a son of Grand Duke Paul were brutally murdered in a forest near the Ural Mountains. They were thrown alive down a deep mine shaft, and hand grenades were tossed in after them to complete the job.

The bloodletting continued for the rest of the year. In January of 1919 four more grand dukes, including Ducky's uncle Paul, her mother's favorite brother, were executed in the Peter and Paul Fortress in St. Petersburg. Grand Duke Nicholas Mikhailovich, an acclaimed historian famous for his liberal beliefs, was also murdered. The writer Maxim Gorky had pleaded with his friend Lenin for the grand duke's life, but Lenin refused, coldly declaring: "The Revolution does not need historians."

As Ducky and Kirill gradually heard of their relatives' cruel and savage deaths, they were overwhelmed by revulsion and guilt. They were also galvanized into fighting the Bolsheviks and reclaiming their suffering country.

Now, more than ever, England was their only hope. But unfortunately, after the world war finally ended in November of 1918, England was battle weary, with no "stomach for further fighting." In addition, the British prime minister, David Lloyd George, firmly opposed intervention. Sending British troops to Russia to fight the Reds would only solidify Bolshevik rule, he believed. And he feared that it would ignite a dangerous movement of Lenin supporters in England.

Ducky was stunned when she learned that her homeland had turned its back on the helpless Russian people. After conferring with Kirill, she decided the best course of action—perhaps the only possible one— would be an impassioned letter to her cousin Georgie, now King George V of England. Devoted friends since the long-ago Malta days, these two first cousins respected each other for their unflinching honesty. On January 29, 1919, Ducky sat down at her desk in Finland and began writing the English king a sixteen-page letter. She was fully confident that he would heed it.

My dear George:

Though neither Kirill nor I have the slightest wish or intention of playing a political part, I have been asked to lay before you once more the feelings of all true Russians and to give you an exact picture of the desperate conditions in Petersburg. I undertook to do so, having the possibility of writing to you unofficially in the hope that it may accelerate the sending of help so urgently needed. That this cry for help should remain unanswered we still refuse to believe in spite of the news that has just reached us that England, ignoring France's willingness to assist us, has definitely refused all help to her former true ally, Russia. Also the news that England has invited the Bolsheviks to the peace conference is considered by Russia a crime such as

*history has never known. A crime before which the abomination and base-
ness of the Brest-Litovsk peace (an everlasting shame to both sides that
signed it, and which logically ended in bringing about Germany's downfall)
pales into insignificance, being a crime towards the world at large.*

*Is it possible that England does not see that she is courting the same dis-
aster that overtook Germany, in her attempts at recognizing the Bolsheviks
as a respectable and legitimate government? Is it possible that great political
men such as England has at the head of her government fail to realize that
the Bolsheviks do not represent the democracy of Russia and that they are
not socialist, even in the remotest sense of the word; that they are nothing
but the scum of the earth profiting of a momentary madness to maintain
their power by a reign of terror against which all humanity and civilization
cry aloud. This proposal of dealing with the Bolsheviks will inevitably lead
to one of the largest political mistakes ever made by any country, as only we
who have lived, through and under their regime are fearfully and terribly
competent to judge—in a way that none of you, not even the greatest politicians amongst you, can hope to be. Excuse this plain language, but those
who have been through this have a right to speak.*

*This letter is to ask for help to destroy the source itself from which this
contamination of Bolshevism spreads over the world. In the coming struggle
for freedom from the Bolsheviks, struggle which even Lloyd George will not
be able to stem by temporising with them, Petersburg remains the chief object of military operations. In spite of this, General Judenitch, the head of
the Russian military formations on the coast of the Finnish gulf, has not
been able to equip his army, nor has he received an answer to his appeal to
the Allies, sent end of December. Yet his forces will be called on to play a
most important part when our northern, eastern, and southern armies will
be approaching Petersburg, as the only means of preventing the retreating
Bolsheviks from invading Finland and the Baltic provinces. As all the
above mentioned armies, with Admiral Kolchak at the head, are receiving
ample support from the Allies, officially or unofficially, we implore the same
help for this western army without which its further formation becomes
hardly possible. Every week's delay makes the position more serious. Petersburg is dying of hunger, and though this army which is now in formation is geographically and therefore strategically in the most advantageous
position for the decisive blow to the stronghold of Bolshevism, we dare not
deal it without an ample supply of food for the starving population. If you
could but send us sufficient food transports to feed this army and the population of Petersburg for a few weeks, the military operations could start im-*

*mediately, even though the army were insufficiently equipped in other re-
spects, very little assistance being feared. Independent of nationality, Russians, Finns and Balts are ready, all to march together against the enemies
of humanity and civilization, but without food we can do nothing. Petersburg at the present moment has reached the limit of human endurance, the
population reduced to some seven hundred thousand souls who are dying of
starvation and want. The remaining supplies of food are entirely in the
hands of the Bolsheviks and not allowed to reach any of the population not
belonging to the Bolshevik organizations—all the bourgeoisie and higher
classes and a great part of the working classes, not employed by the Bolsheviks are literally dying daily by thousands for want of food, clothing and
warmth. Their lodgings are taken from them—all former officers and officials are thrown into prison and forced into Bolshevik service by drastic
measures such as the shooting of their entire families, wives and children.
The cruelties increase daily the crimes and horrors committed are such that
they cannot be put down on paper. Is England who has ever been the first
to raise an indignant protest against cruelty, oppression and tyranny, now
going to remain, not only an impassive onlooker, but by her trying to recognize the bolsheviks as a government, a partaker in the most heinous and
monstrous enterprise that ever the world has known.*

*Please forgive anything in this letter which may sound uncourteous or
presumptuous and remember that I am only the mouthpiece of real Russia,
trying to make itself heard in the midst of the world's tumult. Not the voice
of one or another political party—but the voice of all the parties united in
one great endeavour to save their country from anarchy and murder.*

Ducky's rambling, impassioned letter, written in a bold, swirling, almost illegible scrawl, reflects the emotional turmoil she was going
through at the time. Her feverish emotions dominated her literary style
as well as her logic.

King George received the letter several weeks later, "with feelings of
the deepest concern." On March 13, 1919, he wrote Ducky from Buckingham Palace:

*. . . Together with my Ministers I have given careful consideration to the
points which it raised.*

*There is no truth in the news which reached you—that while France
was willing, England refused to assist Russia. On the contrary, we have
been anxious to do our utmost to help, so long as we could be certain that
we were giving assistance to the right people. Equally it is untrue that En-*

gland wished the Bolsheviks to be represented at the Peace Conference. We fully recognise who, and what they are. We are appalled at and outraged by their revolting crimes, and realize that they are daily becoming an international danger—a danger from which it behooves us to defend our own land.

Our desire and intention is to send food and munitions to those who are resistant to the Bolsheviks, and before your letter was written, effect had been given, to a certain degree, to carry out those intentions. For, on the 1st of December, four light cruisers and six destroyers arrived at Libau with a large consignment of arms, some of which were supplied to Esthonia and to the Latvian Government in Libau, and the light cruisers actively assisted in the operations against the Bolsheviks.

By this time a force of light cruisers and destroyers must have reached Libau with more war materials, including 20,000 rifles, six 6″ howitzers, twelve 18-pounder guns and 20 motor lorries. No assistance has been asked for from the Admiralty by General Judenitch. In December, when he was in Finland, an unofficial application for arms and ammunition to assist the formation of a new Russian Army was made to the War Office, but no request came through diplomatic channels. However, the above mentioned supply of munitions was dispatched, and arrangements have also been made for an early supply of coal to the Esthonian Government.

I recognise and sympathise profoundly with the terrible condition into which the people at Petersburg and Moscow have been brought under Bolshevik domination, and also can understand what you say—that if Petersburg were occupied, order restored and the starving population supplied with food and clothing, an important step would have been taken in the regeneration of Russia.

There is unfortunately a serious obstacle in the deficiency of ships, which increases the difficulty in carrying out our wishes. To this end I am exerting my utmost endeavours, but please remember that nothing can be done except through concerted action of the Entente powers which, in itself, constitutes a serious element of delay, and I must add that the lack of any united action of the Russian people themselves, adds to the complexity of a problem which seems to be almost insoluble.

Ducky was unsure how to take this reply. Although she found George's pledges of support reassuring, she also could see how the unsympathetic political and military factions of the immensely complex British empire were attempting to use bureaucratic slow motion to stall. Ducky knew, of course, that strong anti-Romanov sentiment ran through all the classes of England. The Russian monarchy had been always perceived by the relatively democratic English as a ruthlessly autocratic institution that worked against the interests of its own people. Even Ducky's own grandmother Queen Victoria had held the Romanov family in contempt as despotic barbarians who were courting disaster by their repressive rule.

The bloody debacle of the Russian revolution had been vividly foreseen by the wise old queen. She had dreaded her grandchildren becoming members of the doomed Imperial family, and time had proved her fears sadly well placed. Two of her favorite granddaughters, Alix—Alexandra—and Ella of Hesse, had already been slaughtered, and Ducky had just barely escaped the same horrible fate.

Many powerful leaders in London were even whispering that the Romanovs were only getting what they so richly deserved. Ducky's cousin George, far from being an autocratic ruler himself, could only do so much. Although his feelings for the Russian imperial family prompted him to do everything he could to help, he could not completely ignore the strong public and political opinion of his own country.

In April of 1919, the English monarch at least had the satisfaction of being able to save the life of his mother's favorite sister, his aunt Minnie, the dowager empress of Russia. Held captive in her villa near Yalta on the Crimean coast of the Black Sea, the seventy-two-year-old dowager empress had defiantly refused all previous offers of help. But, now, as the Red Army quickly approached from the north, her nephew insisted on her immediate evacuation from Russian soil. The king sent the battleship *Marlborough* to Yalta to fetch her; even so, she consented to leave only at "the insistent urging of her sister Queen Alexandra."

Anxious as George V was to rescue his Romanov relatives, his hands were tied when it came to taking Russia by force from the Bolsheviks, as Ducky had urged. At the end of July, Ducky wrote to him again:

Dear George,

Once more I have been asked by our leading men to give you a brief account of the present situation here. The kindness with which you answered my last letter enables me to do so. We are fully aware of the reasons and difficulties of the allied governments which are inducing them to withdraw from us their help at the most urgent moment. We see however that our representatives have failed to give you the impression of the imminent danger such a course is creating, and of the European disaster it is conjuring up.

The present situation is as follows. Admiral Kolchak's retreat, caused by the want of ammunition etc. on which it had counted, has endangered General Denikin's successful advance. His right flank is exposed to the full forces which the Bolsheviks have been enabled to withdraw from the Eastern front and which they are now throwing against him and our moth-eaten army. Should Denikin in consequence meet with the slightest defeat, then now Finland, the last buffer state between Northern Europe and Bolshevism, must unavoidably succumb. To prevent such a contingency all our energies must be concentrated on the immediate taking and retaining of St Petersburg by our North-Western army. This can only be done with the help of Finland. All questions as to the participation of Finland in this undertaking have been clearly settled and accepted between General Judenitch and General Mannerheim. General Mannerheim can march any moment if he receives from England the declaration that she will give Finland her full moral and material support without which he is not in a position to propose such a step to his government though he is backed by the whole of his country. Finland is naturally too weak to support such an undertaking on her own. Therefore we ask that England should insist on Finland's immediate advance on Petersburg. Should, however, the English government find it impossible for her own reasons to put this pressure on the present Finnish ministry, she could achieve the same result by fully supporting General Judenitch, by supplying him with all necessary material support with which to supply Finland. As Gen. Mannerheim and Judenitch are working in complete understanding and similar interests of their countries, it is of the greatest urgency that the English government should not lose a moment in doing this and that Petersburg should be taken in the next few weeks before the Bolsheviks have time to concentrate their forces, taken from the Eastern and Southern fronts (which they have already started doing) to throw them over Finland and the Scandinavian countries, by which England herself would be threatened. We press the full particulars of this Bolshevik plan.

Great Russia with Petersburg and Moscow, have so reached the limit of human endurance, under the despotic rule of the Bolsheviks, that they are now ready even to accept help and salvation at the hands of Germany. German agents are already fully at work all over Russia offering with true German precision, point by point, all help for present and future—in fact are preparing themselves an alliance with Russia, which, if the Allies continued in their present unreliable politics towards us, will eventually be accepted by all anti-Bolshevik parties independent of their political views and feelings.

Such a result would ultimately enable Germany to throw off and annul the obligations of the treaty of Versailles.

Russia, once liberated from the Bolsheviks and more or less in working order has sufficient food supplies to feed herself and Germany for years to come, thereby rendering any future blockade of Germany ineffective. I have been asked to express the necessity that all the above mentioned negotiations with Gen. Mannerheim and his ministry should be kept absolutely secret. The present moment is of vital importance especially from all points of view of the League of Nations. Bolshevism puts an end to all true democracy, not to talk of the unrealizable socialistic ideal. In asking for assistance against Bolshevism one cannot sufficiently insist on the fact that the allied governments are not asked to help retrograde imperialism but are fighting for the people and for true democracy independent of their future form of government. It is all important that such countries which still have sound governments themselves should not reach that state of dissolution which hands over the power to the rabble as happened in Russia.

General Gough at the head of the English military mission here is fully acquainted with the military and political situation in Finland and has inspired all parties here with full confidence.

Perhaps embarrassed by his inability to do anything for his cousin's lost cause, King George never responded to this letter.

As the summer of 1919 progressed and the Bolsheviks rapidly tightened their death grip on the former Russian empire, Ducky and Kirill learned with horror of atrocity after atrocity befalling their country, their friends, and their relatives. With overwhelming grief, Ducky was forced to finally give up her great hopes for redemption and confront the sad fact that her cousin George "was powerless to act further." England would not be coming to Russia's rescue. Despite George's best efforts, England provided only token support for the anti-Bolshevik forces. The Bolsheviks would destroy the old order and enslave the nation.

Bitterly disappointed, Ducky was permanently alienated from England.

CHAPTER FORTY

A Searching Wind

B Y THE END OF the summer of 1919, imperial Russia had been shattered. With the victories of the Bolsheviks and their systematic slaughter of all the remaining Romanovs, Ducky and her husband had to accept that their country had been lost and that it would be a very long time before they could return.

Although the Finnish government had formally granted Kirill and his family permission to stay in Finland until the beginning of the following year, he and Ducky decided not to renew their application to remain. Unable to be permanent house guests, they had recently left Haiko and returned to the house in Borgo. Finland had been "most hospitable" to them, but they "were naturally tired of living in the modest provincial town of Borgo, especially in conditions so primitive and trying." Since the world war was now over, they were free to travel wherever they wished. Rather than face another Finnish winter, they started making plans to pack up and leave by the end of autumn.

Their decision was also prompted by a sudden personal tragedy. Spanish influenza had recently broken out locally and had killed many people. One of the victims was the family's beloved English governess, whose death "was a severe blow" to both parents and children alike. Ducky felt the loss keenly. She had relied on the woman for friendship and emotional support as well as for the education of her daughters, and the death also brought back memories of the painful loss of her Nana Pitcathly when she was a child of six. Luckily, the rest of the family escaped the flu, a highly contagious and particularly severe form that soon spread throughout the world and claimed more victims than had the previous five years of war.

Thus, when birches began shedding their small leaves, Ducky and her family gathered together their scant belongings and headed south, toward Switzerland. In Berlin they stayed with Ducky's younger sister Sandra, the princess of Hohenlohe-Langenburg, for an uncomfortable two days; then they went to Munich, where the duchess of Coburg was waiting for them.

Ducky was shocked by the sight of her mother, whom she had not seen in five years, since the summer before the Great War began. In the meantime the haughty duchess had lost almost everything she had. The war had not only torn her family apart but completely destroyed the order of her world, and what little remained had been obliterated by the social revolutions that followed the fighting. The Bolsheviks had stolen her vast Russian fortune and banished her from her homeland; the duchy of Coburg had followed suit. Reviled by the world, the humiliated kaiser had been tossed off his throne and sent into exile to the tranquil Dutch countryside. When the empire collapsed, so did the entire delicately balanced network of German royal states. Each and every one had sent its rulers packing.

Ducky's mother no longer had a home. And the defiant old woman had not adapted well to the change. She had not only lost a great deal of weight, but was almost bent double. She walked with uncertainty; "her once plump hands were now thin and trembling." The frailty of her once physically powerful mother brought tears to Ducky's eyes. But it was soon evident that Marie Alexandrovna had lost none of her domineering character. She might have lost her fortune, most of her Russian family, and her rank and titles, but she was still the exalted person she knew herself to be. And she still ruled the lives of her daughters, if nothing else.

Arriving in Zurich at the end of September, Ducky and Kirill arranged for the duchess to take up residence in the Waldhaus, a rustic and slightly shabby annex of the luxurious Dolder Grand Hotel. Far from the gilt and marble palaces of her youth, the Waldhaus was "an awful little pension—very refugee-like," as her granddaughter Ileana later remembered. But, sadly, it was all they could afford.

Ducky and Kirill had very little money, only the jewelry they had managed to sneak out of Russia. The duchess too had only the personal jewelry she had taken from Germany. These fabulous pieces were worth a small fortune, but they were all loath to sell, hoping to use the jewelry as security against an unknown future. They still believed that their plight was only temporary; to begin selling their most cherished possessions would have been an admission of the hopelessness of their fate.

In Zurich Ducky experienced her greatest joy in years. Missy was there to meet her.

Ducky had last seen her beloved sister during that horrible winter of 1917, in the bloody and beleaguered Romanian countryside where they toiled together in the makeshift military hospitals, tending the wounded soldiers until they had both dropped from sickness and exhaustion. Ducky's whole world had collapsed since then. At the sudden ending of the longest separation they had ever endured, they fell into each other's arms and wept.

The differences between the two sisters could not have been more dramatic. As always, they presented a striking contrast of light and dark, velvet and steel; but now they were also a sad study in divergent destinies. Missy had gone through fire and come out a dazzling winner, almost more beautiful and youthful-looking than ever. Ducky, a year younger than her sister, had ended up on the losing side; she was lined from hardship, worn and gray from worry. Missy had joined in England's victory and had almost single-handedly placed her small country on the map by giving it a glamorous and charming face at the Versailles Peace Conference and winning enough territory to more than double its size. She was now a celebrated, almost legendary figure, famous enough to provide Dorothy Parker with a figure of speech:

> *Oh, life is a glorious cycle of song,*
> *A medley of extemporanea;*
> *And love is a thing that will never go wrong;*
> *And I am Marie of Roumania.*

But the sisters' divergent fortunes did not push them apart. In fact, it accomplished the exact opposite; it brought them closer together than ever before. In the uncertain future, Missy would continually come to Ducky's emotional and financial rescue, and their mutual love and devotion would endure beyond all else.

Unfortunately, relations with the duchess were not to be so happy. Their mother's abrupt descent in life had brought about an equally abrupt change in her temperament. Unsurprisingly, the change was not for the better. Stripped of her wealth and her titles, banished from her two adored homelands, the duchess had no outlet for her autocratic personality. The only realm remaining to her was that of motherhood. Her daughters became her obedient subjects, and over them she ruled with an almost desperate tyranny.

Of the four daughters, Ducky fared best under the new maternal regime. Still her mother's favorite, she rose even higher in the duchess's affections because of the tragedy of her recent circumstances. Having suffered and lost more than her mother and sisters, she was given whatever sympathy the duchess had left and very little of her sharp, critical tongue. The fact that Ducky was beginning to lose her great beauty helped endear her to her unattractive mother.

It was Missy who evoked most of the duchess's bitter wrath. Her eldest daughter's abundant feminine charm and beauty had always inspired a strange maternal resentment. The duchess's consistent disapproval of Missy's frivolous and glamorous persona now turned to frank hostility to the great success it had apparently won her. Angrily focusing on Missy's pro-English role in the war, the duchess accused her of "rejoicing over the devastating peace terms" forced on the Germans by the Versailles Peace Conference. When Missy silently accepted this because she felt sorry for her mother, the duchess's abusiveness only increased. Marie produced a painfully personal critique of imagined failings.

"She continues to bicker, bicker about quite forgotten things I did or left undone," Missy later sadly complained to a friend. "She never admitted that I had any intelligence, only a certain good nature and a sunny face that bamboozled the world."

Ducky did her best to comfort Missy and protect her from their mother's emotional blows, but she had other serious family problems to deal with too. Her mother-in-law, Grand Duchess Vladimir, was in even more pitiful condition than Ducky's own mother. She had last been heard of in March 1917, when she was at her Red Cross hospital in the Caucasus mountains in the south of Russia. The revolution had stranded her there along with her youngest son, Andrei, and his mistress, the prima ballerina Mathilde Kschessinska, who had also once been the mistress of Nicholas II. Disguised, the grand duchess had made her way in a peasant cart to the Black Sea port of Novorossisk, where the occupying White army had managed to book passage for her on an Italian ship taking refugees to Constantinople. There she was eventually able to board a boat for Venice, from where she finally made her way to Switzerland.

When Kirill met his mother at the station in Lausanne he didn't recognize her. Although only in her mid-fifties, the once regal and superbly dressed leader of Russian society was now a haggard scarecrow of a woman, "bowed and broken, lean, and white-haired." Her health and spirits completely shattered by her long ordeal, she was sent by her family to recuperate at the spa of Contrexéville near Nancy in the north of France.

Restless and not knowing how to plan their future, Ducky and Kirill drifted across the continent looking for prospects. They visited Missy in Romania and went to the south of France in the winter, returning to Switzerland in the spring of 1920. Money was a constant problem. Having no income, they relied on the modest sum they had managed to take out of Russia, but that was dwindling very quickly. Missy, true to her generous nature, had been sending them money and gifts. When she returned to Zurich to visit her mother again that summer, she took Ducky with her to Paris and treated her to a luxurious vacation. They happily visited with their youngest sister, Baby Bee, and went to see the premiere performance of a ballet, *The Lily of Life,* based on a fairy tale by Missy.

At the beginning of August news arrived that Kirill's mother was sinking rapidly. He and Ducky rushed to Contrexéville, where the grand duchess Vladimir died two weeks later. Only two months later, on October 22, Ducky's stubborn and indomitable mother died in her sleep in the shabby little annex of the Dolder Grand Hotel. Although the duchess's legendary vitality had been recently failing, there had been no sign of serious illness; her sudden, totally unexpected death was a great shock to Ducky and her sisters. (The duchess had had a heart attack in her sleep, but stories quickly began circulating that she had dropped dead upon "receiving a letter addressed bluntly to 'Frau Coburg.' ")

Missy immediately left Romania to join her sisters in Switzerland, but when she arrived she discovered that she could not travel with Ducky to Coburg for the burial without "provoking an international incident." Equally disappointed, Ducky left her sister behind at the station in Zurich as she and Baby Bee traveled with their mother's coffin back to Coburg, where Sandra was waiting. On a cold and gray October morning Ducky stood with her two younger sisters and watched their mother be placed in the family crypt next to their father.

Ducky's difficult mamma, who had always supported and stood by her, defying the world's opinion in defending her passionate and misunderstood child—Mamma, who had loved Ducky more than anything in life, was gone, forever. After so many tragic losses during the last few years, it must have overwhelmed Ducky to have to say such an unexpected farewell to a woman who had always been her greatest source of strength.

Only the sad circumstances of her mother's last years made her passing seem bearable. Perhaps Missy spoke for all the sisters when she prayed, "I hope God will not disappoint her as most things and beings did in this life."

When Ducky and Baby Bee returned to Zurich three days later, they sat down with Missy and began reading their mother's diaries. At last, confronting their rigid and unbending parent as an equal, they laughed and cried over the revelations of her well-hidden feelings. For the first time they saw the duchess as a sensitive, sulky child "at the mercy of her tormenting governess" and as a shy, bewildered bride coping with a new country and an impossible mother-in-law. Perhaps at this moment Ducky felt closer to her mother than ever before.

The only positive aspect of the duchess's passing was the lavish legacy she left for her daughters. Unbeknownst to them, she had managed to salvage all of her fabulous jewelry, which she had smuggled from Germany deposited in a bank vault in Zurich. In her will their meticulous mother had divided up her precious gems among her four daughters. Since Ducky was not only her favorite but also in far greater need than the others, she got the lion's share of the treasures. While Missy got pearls, Ducky received diamonds and sapphires.

However, mere ownership of magnificent jewels was no guarantee of usable wealth in 1920s Europe. Because major buyers across the continent were all well aware of the financial plight of the dispossessed Habsburgs, Hohenzollerns, and Romanovs, they shrewdly entered into a gentlemen's agreement to buy royal jewels at a fraction of their true value. Given the sellers' desperate need for cash, these buyers succeeded more often than not in having their meager offers accepted.

Ducky's cousin and the late emperor's brother-in-law, clever Grand Duke Alexander, had been one of the first to discover this calculated collapse of the jewel market. Escaping to Paris with a fortune in Romanov gems, he was dismayed to find that no one would offer him even a fraction of their value. Jewelry that he thought would easily keep him and his family in luxury for at least a decade sold for a sum that hardly lasted them a year. This crushing disappointment eventually helped to shatter his marriage.

So Ducky's priceless inheritance had very limited market potential. Fortunately, she and Missy realized that they could exchange assets to their mutual benefit. Ducky had lavish jewels, which she really didn't need. What she needed was cash. Missy was cash rich—and, as the glamorous queen of Romania, she was eager to establish an impressive collection of crown jewels. It was decided that, as her budget allowed, Missy would buy Ducky's incomparable collection piece by piece, both the magnificent gems the duchess had left her and the treasures she had managed to smuggle out of St. Petersburg.

To Ducky's everlasting gratitude, Missy not only provided her with a reliable and dignified market, but also paid a premium for each piece of jewelry. The first item the wealthy Romanian queen bought, just two months after their mother's death, was a dazzling chain of large diamonds with a huge sapphire pendant. (It was to be a wedding present for Missy's eldest daughter, the glacially beautiful Princess Elisabetha, when she married Crown Prince George of Greece in February.)

Now, instead of looking forward to a life of well-adorned poverty, Ducky and her family could relax in the expectation of having, at least, comfort and security.

But the future continued to haunt them. Where would they live? What would they do? How would they occupy themselves?

They didn't want to continue living in Switzerland. It was a picturesque limbo, tranquil and safe, but best suited to those who aspired to be perpetual tourists or resigned themselves to a cozy and aimless suspension of time. Ducky and Kirill were looking squarely toward the future, and they wanted to raise their children in an environment that reflected their heritage as fully as possible. Therefore, they fell back on the places that had given them their fondest memories: Germany and France.

Paris had become the great magnet for aristocratic émigrés from imperial Russia. Because the City of Light had always been a second home and favorite playground for Russian high society, it was the obvious choice of residence after the revolution. Already possessing a sizable czarist community, the French capital quickly established itself as something of a resurrected St. Petersburg during the 1920s and 1930s.

But Ducky and Kirill found Paris émigré society indolent and self-indulgent, with an undignified exploitation of fallen thrones. They both loved the city—especially Kirill, who delighted in the cafés and the numerous golf courses—but they no longer had their luxurious apartment on the avenue Henri Martin.

Besides, there were financial issues to consider—and they already owned two homes, for the duchess had left Ducky her Riviera villa and her house in Coburg. So she and Kirill divided their time between the Château Fabron in Nice and the Edinburgh Palace in Germany, where they had spent their courtship and the first years of their marriage.

Her sister's permanent safe settlement was a great relief to Missy. Since Ducky and her family had left Finland and brought the duchess to Zurich, they had roamed Europe, often traveling for months without a word. Only nine months before, in March of 1920, Missy had anxiously written England's Queen Mary: "I have had no more news from her for several months although I have also tried to send her things through our Roumanian Minister in Holland."

But when Ducky and Kirill finally returned to Coburg to take up residence, their nostalgia was tempered by the reality of present German politics. Everything in the quaint town "reminded them of the best part of their lives—the first few years after their marriage," and the Edinburgh Palace had not changed at all, the interior decoration and every piece of furniture being "exactly in the same place where it had been twenty years before."

But Coburg was no longer a royal duchy with an obedient populace. Instead, it was now a *Land,* or state, of the new socialist Weimar Republic. With characteristic speed and efficiency, Germany had reorganized its entire political structure in a year. While avoiding a bloodbath like the Russian Revolution, the Germans had also managed to rid themselves of kings and crowns.

The toppling *en masse* of Germany's numerous minor monarchs affected many of Ducky's closest relatives. Her mother suffered most, perhaps, but Sandra also lost her realm, Hohenlohe-Langenburg, and Ducky's cousin Charles Edward had to forfeit Coburg. Several other cousins, aunts, and uncles lost their realms as well. One who made the best of an unhappy fate was her first husband, Ernie.

Ernie had lost much more than a kingdom: He had lost most of his family. His two favorite sisters, Alix and Ella, had been slaughtered in Russia along with the rest of their families. Because of his pacifist principles and his close personal ties to England and Russia, the Hessian grand duke had been excused from active service in the German army during the war. As a result, he had been accused by his countrymen of siding with the enemy and passing them secret information. Trying to dispel these suspicions, Ernie devoted his energy to caring for the wounded, visiting hospitals and traveling on the ambulance trains. Although he had been deposed at the end of the war and lost his throne, he decided to stay on in Darmstadt, remaining "a popular and well loved figure on the Hessian scene." His chief interest in life was now the rehabilitation of men whose minds and bodies had been shattered by the war. He brought them to live in his own home and devoted himself to nursing them back to health. Imitating his mother's rare kindness and charity, Ernie had finally resolved the emotional conflicts of his unusual nature in a selfless and bittersweet way.

Ducky must have envied her ex-husband's productive new life. At least he had not been separated from his homeland and his people, and could work on a daily basis for their welfare. In Coburg she and Kirill were far removed from events in Russia. Such isolation was lonely and frustrating. By now, the Red Army had won a complete and resounding victory over the Whites, and the fighting in Russia had come to an end. But Ducky and Kirill still had hopes that some international intervention might take place; they refused to give up their struggle against the new Soviet state.

In a world that had been totally turned upside down, the spirited grand duchess Victoria Feodorovna unfalteringly searched for a solution to her family's problems. As despair threatened to consume her husband, she inspired him to fight on and believe in the future.

CHAPTER FORTY-ONE

The Phantom Throne

T HE EARLY 1920s were tumultuous and challenging times for all of Europe, and especially so for the new German republic. Living in Coburg, Ducky and her husband were vulnerable to the chaos and suffering of the defeated nation. Economically devastated and spiritually crushed and humiliated by the harsh peace terms of Versailles, Germany mirrored Ducky and Kirill's own plight. In their eyes, the floundering German attempt at democracy was a dangerous though pale imitation of the disastrous experiment with socialism that had resulted in Bolshevik tyranny. Mourning the demise of the imperial regime, they passed their first year in Coburg alternately trying to adapt to and resist the radical political changes.

After living at the center of the world's most lavish and glamorous court, Ducky and Kirill now found Coburg, once such a haven, "pleasant [only] in small doses." It was "neat and tidy and rather dull, as every small provincial town should be . . . but boring to stay for any length of time." At first, Ducky and her family led a very cloistered life, having almost no local friends except for the families of Duke Karl of Saxe-Coburg-Gotha and King Ferdinand of Bulgaria, an outrageously effeminate old cousin who had recently lost his Balkan throne and returned to his childhood home to live in exile.

To fill the long days they fell back on their favorite former pastime, touring the countryside by automobile. With Kirill happily behind the wheel, "there was hardly a day when we did not drive out into the beautiful environs of the town." He also played golf whenever the weather permitted and went hunting in the forest.

With all these diversions, Ducky was struggling with secret problems. Despite her mother's lessons in successful adaptation to any circumstance, "she was never quite able to resign herself to the loss of power and position." As her former friend Meriel Buchanan later observed, "After years of unhappiness she had married the man she loved, and, having at last got all she wanted, saw it destroyed, and herself faced a future of despair and bitterness, an exile in poverty and humiliation." Ducky may have let it show only rarely, but it was painful for so proud a woman to watch everything beautiful in her life fade so completely.

And as she approached her forty-fifth birthday in the fall of 1921, it was obvious that the ordeals of the past few years had aged her prematurely. The sudden loss of her great beauty may have caused her husband to search for it elsewhere. According to local gossip, Kirill "indulged his passion for . . . beautiful women." If these Coburg infidelities happened, Ducky heard nothing of them. She was still in love with her husband—as much as she had ever been—and her devotion to him was as unquestioning as it was limitless.

Ironically, Kirill, who was the same age as his wife and had suffered alongside her, was more handsome than ever. The parched, lined skin and gray hair brought about by worry and exposure to the elements gave the exiled grand duke a distinguished and mature look that he had never had before. Kirill's once almost too-perfect good looks were now made even more appealing by the implications of substance and character produced by age.

While Ducky and Kirill quietly settled down to a domestic life of austere obscurity in the not at all notable *Residenz-Stadt* of Coburg, they still closely followed developments in Russia. Intensely political, Kirill immediately began surrounding himself with sympathetic supporters. Although "his circle of followers was said to be small and isolated," they were enthusiastic and loyal. However, without the intricate structure of the old imperial court, numerous exploiters and opportunists sought to use Kirill's name and gain his support for various selfish and nefarious schemes. It soon became apparent to Ducky that someone would have to protect her husband, so she and her friends very firmly and efficiently "formed a barrier to keep out any unwanted visitors."

After five years of chaos, Ducky and Kirill, like most of Europe, finally seemed to be adjusting to the great changes that had taken place. For a long time, they had been consumed by worry over their safety and that of their children. When their security had finally been guaranteed, they were troubled by the practical aspects of day-to-day life. Now, comfortable and secure in Ducky's childhood home, they had the luxury of focusing their minds on other matters.

Elation and gratitude at having survived were beginning to wear thin; Ducky and Kirill began thinking of all they had lost and mourning its passing.

And desperately planning for its retrieval.

While Kirill and Ducky struggled to establish their identity in the postwar world, so did all of Germany. The old rules had been set aside, the kings and courts had been discarded, and nothing had yet taken their place. Everything that was now happening seemed to be an experiment whose proponents hoped for miraculous results. Perhaps because need and expectations were so high, those results were always disappointing.

To many, what seemed most needed was a source of unquestioned authority. After centuries of monarchical rule, the ex-kingdoms of Europe found it impossible to immediately abandon the habit of absolute power and relax into the uncertainty and intricate demands of democracy.

Russia was totally unsuited to proceed as a democratic state. The czars' despotic rule could only be overthrown and replaced by another form of authoritarian leadership. In proving this, the Bolsheviks had shown themselves to be more ruthless than the czars. But in Germany, the pressure for a radical political solution had not been as great. The Weimar Republic had effectively steered the German people toward the self-rule of democracy, but there remained several serious problems.

Foremost was the German character. The kaiser had left behind him an incredibly rigid and unyielding national sensibility. Power and authority, exalted and unchallenged, was a need very basic to the German spirit. This dangerously handicapped the republic and made the nation perilously vulnerable to dictatorial movements like Russian Bolshevism. Communism was threatening to devour Germany just as it had Kirill's homeland, and to many it seemed to find a form of government strong enough to satisfy the German people and crush the radical opposition.

Eager for the perfect autocratic solution to its problems, Germany in the early 1920s embraced whatever came along that looked shining and promising. What shined brightest and promised the most at this time was the National Socialist German Workers' Party, also known as the Nazi Party. Its leader, Adolf Hitler, began to mesmerize the nation with a thrilling vision of a regenerated and glorious Germany. Hitler's party was also offering the extreme authority needed to protect Germany from the growing menace of communism.

It was the National Socialists' rabid anti-Bolshevik stance that captured Ducky's enthusiasm. Given the current circumstances, it was logical that any political movement that offered Europe salvation from the spread of communism "would provoke interest, if not active support, on her part." Much of Europe's royalty and most of the German nobility were guardedly pro-Nazi during the party's first years. It wasn't until the more sinister aims of Hitler's philosophy were put into practice that Ducky and her royal relatives, embarrassed, withdrew their support.

Meanwhile, Ducky and her younger sister Sandra were openly enthusiastic about the Nazis. The extent of Ducky's partisanship is unknown, but there were those who claimed that Ducky had gone as far as to hand over to the party "some of her remaining valuables to be sold to raise funds for them." Far off in Romania, Missy was impressed by Ducky's admiration for Hitler, but, more open-minded and considerably less passionate in her opinions, the shrewd Romanian queen couldn't decide on the merits of the man. As late as 1934 she still didn't know what to make of the charismatic German leader, writing to an American friend: "What a curious figure Hitler is. I withhold every judgement, but most everybody is virulent against him abroad."

While Missy cautiously pondered Hitler's ominous character until the very end, Ducky followed her emotions, blinded by her hatred for the Bolsheviks and willing to believe anyone or anything that could bring order and sanity back to her disintegrated world.

Apparently, Kirill was more cautious and skeptical than his politically inexperienced wife. He was also attracted to the party's potential as a bulwark against the Bolsheviks, but its undercurrent of fanaticism made him uneasy. However, in Coburg both members of the couple became best friends with Max Scheubner-Richter and his wife, Mathilde, two of Hitler's most fervent supporters. Ducky and Mathilde "would sometimes watch the stormtroopers drilling in a Munich suburb, and attend Nazi meetings and parades together." Ducky and Kirill were also seen at a Nazi rally in Coburg in 1922. Many people believed that Ducky was convinced "that support for the movement could further . . . [Kirill's] imperial aspirations, and also assist in a restoration of the German monarchy."

For Kirill's political future was Ducky's most urgent concern. As the years passed and a continuous stream of dismal news arrived from Russia, she sadly watched her husband sink deeper and deeper into despair. There no longer seemed to be any hope that the Soviet government would ever allow Kirill and his family to return to their homeland. Nor would there be any financial settlements, any reparations, any recognition of personal rights.

Ducky's husband found himself staring at a life without purpose. In the beginning of 1923 he suffered a complete nervous breakdown. His recovery was to be very long and very slow.

At first, Kirill was so totally "shattered" that he was "unable to cross the street without holding Ducky's hand or sleep unless she sat up next to him." It was pitiful to see the handsome, towering grand duke being taken by the hand and escorted around town like a child. Like a tender mother, Ducky patiently cared for him for all the world to see. Literally leading him one step at a time, Ducky took him out into the world again and began restoring his courage and his confidence. Her devotion was infinite.

After Kirill had progressed enough, he and Ducky and the children temporarily moved to the cool and peaceful north coast of Brittany. Here, in the tiny fishing village of St. Briac, Ducky rented a modest house near some of their English and Russian friends and Kirill rested next to the soothing sea.

When Missy came to visit in the summer of 1924 she found Ducky "badly lined, overworked, and too tired to think about her personal appearance." Shocked by her sister's condition, Missy felt that Ducky was sacrificing herself for the sake of her husband's recovery. And Missy liked Kirill no better than she had before. As far as she was concerned, he was the same "Marble Man" he had always been, a living statue that demanded admiration and attention but gave little in return.

While the two sisters worked together in the garden and became carefree girls again, Kirill busied himself in his study with grandiose schemes for the future. His manner had gradually become even more regal and self-important than before; Missy realized that Ducky was encouraging his imperial dreams "as a means of his regaining confidence." But the queen had little enthusiasm for what was happening at St. Briac. Describing Ducky's situation to a friend, she wrote: "No home, no fortune . . . no hope—trying to keep things together, to make both ends meet, with a family accustomed to live in utmost luxury."

And though Missy would have liked to solve Ducky's problems, she had serious trouble of her own in Bucharest. The flamboyant Romanian queen was being undone by her own progeny. A doting mother, Missy could never bear to discipline her children, so they grew up selfish, amoral, and irresponsible in a dissolute society. The two youngest girls, Mignon and Ileana, were the exception, having their mother's idealistic and generous character, but the two boys and their eldest sister were monsters. Crown Prince Carol was causing his mother the most grief. Having been sexually abused by his pedophiliac tutor, Carol grew up to be an angry, emotionally unbalanced young man who placed his own pleasure above all else.

Missy had been continually horrified by the behavior of her heir. First, Carol had deserted from the Romanian army during the war. Missy had to intercede to save him from the firing squad. Then the crown prince had turned around and secretly married a commoner—an act specifically forbidden by Romanian law. The ensuing mess involved a confusing annulment, the birth of a son, and a succession of mistresses. Missy had just managed to marry Carol off to a daughter of the king of Greece and see the dynasty secured by the birth of their son when her unstable offspring deserted his wife and went off with his mistress, the calculating daughter of a Jewish junk dealer.

So Missy had to rush back to Bucharest to deal with the crumbling future of the Romanian monarchy, while Ducky encouraged her husband to devote his life to the resurrection of the Russian.

Both Ducky and Kirill firmly believed that monarchy was the only form of government that suited the unique character of Russia's people. It was absolutely clear to them that the upheaval of the revolution and its eventual descent into communism had "brought only suffering to the Russian people." So Ducky decided to provide her husband with the strength to confront the world. He would assume what remained of the imperial throne—the title, though nothing else—and lead the fight to restore the Romanov monarchy. By doing so, he would "save his country from suffering and misfortune." And by passionately encouraging her husband, Ducky would save him from madness.

The recent collapse of many of the world's great monarchies seemed to confirm the popular opinion that the time of kings and courts had passed. The Romanov throne seemed to be the most lost cause of all. Even in the Russian émigré community the prevalent mood was one of defeatism. There were only a few who sincerely believed that a restoration could ever take place, and Kirill and Ducky were in the vanguard of those few. They had faith in each other, in the nobility of their cause, and in the traditional unpredictability of history.

Having decided to live for the future, they moved dangerously close to living in the future.

Kirill officially assumed leadership of the imperial cause and proclaimed his rights to the Romanov throne. On August 8, 1924, at his small rented house in St. Briac, he issued his first "Manifesto," in which he declared himself "Guardian of the Throne." A month later he issued a more lengthy proclamation, which began with the moving words "There are no limits to the suffering of the Russian people" and went on to express Kirill's great regret for the horrible famine that had recently befallen his country. The proclamation encouraged the Romanov's former subjects to "rise together with the army and recall . . . [the] lawful Tsar." And the identity of the current lawful Russian ruler was established once and for all. Kirill's manifesto decisively concluded:

> *Our hope that the most valued life of the Lord Emperor Nicholas Alexandrovich or of the Heir and Czarevich Alexis Nicolaevich or of the Grand Duke Michael Alexandrovich had been spared, has not been fulfilled. . . .*
>
> *The Russian laws of Succession to the Throne do not permit the Imperial Throne to remain vacant after the death of the previous Emperor and His nearest Heirs has been established. Also in accordance with our laws the new Emperor becomes such on the strength of the Law of Succession.*
>
> *The terrible hunger and the cries for help which again are heard from Russia strongly demand that the work of the rescue of Russia should be headed by a legal supreme authority which is above classes and parties. And in accordance with this I, the senior member of the Czarist House and sole legal Heir of the Russian Imperial Throne, take the title of Emperor of all the Russians which without possible doubt is mine.*
>
> *I proclaim My Son, Prince Vladimir Kirillovich, as Heir to the Throne with the title of Grand Duke Heir and Czarevich.*
>
> *I promise and swear sacredly to observe the Orthodox Faith and the Russian Fundamental Laws of Succession to the throne, and engage to protect at all times the rights of other faiths. The Russian people are great and have many gifts of mind and heart, but have fallen into terrible misfortune and disaster. May the great tests which have been sent them by God purify them and bring them to a bright future, having renewed and strengthened before the Almighty the sacred union between the Czar and the People.*

After tossing this bold and controversial statement out into the world, Kirill and Ducky anxiously held their breaths and waited.

The Manifesto created an instant and violent sensation in the Russian émigré community throughout Europe. Kirill's assumption of the Romanov crown "was bitterly contested by most of the aristocratic survivors of the revolution." Foremost amongst his critics was his cousin Grand Duke Nicholas, the former commander in chief of the Russian army. The towering and grim-faced Nicholas had previously assumed unofficial leadership of the exiled Russians who had settled in western Europe. With his stolid personality, military record, and seniority in age, Nicholas was the favorite candidate of most émigrés. And because many of them believed that the invasion of Russia by a powerful army was the only possible way to regain their homeland, they clustered around the former commander in chief, crediting him with "sufficient authority to bring about such an intervention."

Kirill was also faced with rejection of his claims by the Supreme Monarchist Council, which held the leadership of all monarchist organizations in exile.

In consequence, the Russian émigré community was deeply split. But as time passed, Kirill gradually became the more popular choice. His policy of waiting for an internal rebellion rather than inflicting an invasion and a long and bloody war on his homeland became accepted as the most positive and realistic approach to the tyranny of the Soviet state. The closest in line of descent to the throne, Kirill was also perceived to be far more liberal and "less reactionary in outlook" than Grand Duke Nicholas.

The controversy might have been easily resolved at the very beginning, for there existed someone who was universally revered and respected, someone who was above all politics and intrigue: the late emperor's mother. The dowager empress was the highest-ranking living member of the imperial family. Although not eligible to succeed her son, she carried perhaps as much influence as any ruling sovereign possibly could. Having escaped the Bolsheviks in the nick of time via the Crimea, "Minnie" had returned to her childhood home in Denmark and become a recluse. She might well have supported Kirill's claim to the throne, but as far as she was concerned "there was no such dynastic issue to consider." For the dowager empress maintained that her son and his family were still alive somewhere and apt to return at any moment.

To the end of her life, she refused to accept any evidence of her children's and grandchildren's murder.

Their aunt Minnie's desperate delusion was not only pathetic, but also, for Ducky and Kirill, unfortunate. Her adamant rejection of her nephew's imperial claims set the tone for almost the entire Romanov family. Most of the other members, with the exception of Kirill's dissolute younger brothers, Boris and Andrei, were unwilling to recognize his new status. Even his only sister, Helen, married to Prince Nicholas of Greece, did not support his claims. Helen was fond of Ducky and sympathized with her difficult position, but her affection for her sister-in-law did not prevent her from being critical of what she viewed as her brother's foolish pretensions.

The chief issue raised by most members of the family was Kirill's declaration of loyalty to the Provisional Government in the spring of 1917, which to them was nothing less than treason and disqualified Kirill's claim to the throne. Since these same Romanov relatives, however, were freely compromising on the fine points of other imperial rules, particularly as applied to their own lives, it was obvious that their complaints about Kirill were primarily inspired by guilt and jealousy.

Adding a bizarre and almost comical aspect to the family opposition was a woman claiming to be the late emperor's youngest daughter, Grand Duchess Anastasia. Maintaining that she was the sole survivor of the Ekaterinburg massacre and had secretly escaped from Russia, she denounced Kirill as a "pretender" guilty of high treason to the Romanov crown. She suggested that if Kirill really wanted to restore the laws of the old imperial order, "he should begin by hanging himself." The "resurrected" Anastasia was equally scornful of Kirill's wife. She contemptuously referred to Ducky as "that Coburg." When confronted with the news of Kirill's manifesto, she declared, "If he and his wife come into my parents' place, then there is no God!"

In response, Ducky and Kirill found themselves agreeing for once with most of their family: They all viewed this volatile "Anastasia" as a fraud. During the years to come, both Ducky and her husband "steadfastly refused to have anything to do with her, let alone meet her."

Writing to his cousin Grand Duchess Xenia, the sister of Nicholas II, Kirill painted a very dark future for himself: "Nothing can be compared with what I shall now have to endure on this account, and I know full well that I can expect no mercy from all the malicious attacks and accusations of vanity." However, ignoring the roars of his critics, Kirill returned to Coburg with his family in late 1924 and proceeded to act the part of an emperor.

One of his first acts was to elevate his immediate family to conform to his own new status. His seven-year-old son became Grand Duke Vladimir Kirillovich of Russia, and his teenaged daughters became Grand Duchess Marie and Grand Duchess Kira.

And Ducky, his consort, became Empress Victoria Feodorovna of Russia.

CHAPTER FORTY-TWO

An
Empress
Without a Crown

I F ONE HAD CAREFULLY SEARCHED the continent of Europe
in the fall of 1924, it would have been difficult to have found a more
determined woman than the new empress of Russia. As she prepared to
celebrate her forty-eighth birthday that November, Ducky burned with
a purpose more passionate than any she had ever known.

Although she was merely the consort of the actual inheritor of the
throne, she gave the unmistakable impression of being the driving power
behind the imperial cause. Like her sister and several of her cousins, who
were also married to gentle, weak-willed men, Ducky was widely "credited with all the ambition which Queen Victoria imparted to her granddaughters." Most of Ducky's distant relatives admired her husband's
profile and his charm, but it was her they saw as "a very strong character, rather stiff and proud, even military in her manner." Always in control of any situation, she "did nothing to dispel the impression that her
personal ambition and pride had spurred her husband on to making his
claims, and that she was responsible for keeping pressure on him to play
the part of the Tsar."

Ducky was every inch the empress, playing her part with grace, dignity, and confident authority. She appeared to be very happy in her new
regal status and gave everyone "the impression that she believed they
would eventually return to Russia and claim their rightful inheritance."
One night at a banquet when Kirill laughed too long and too loudly at

an amusing remark, Ducky chided him: "Remember, Kirill, you will be Emperor one day!"

Ducky may have been the more fiery of the pair, but the easygoing claimant to the Romanov throne was as enthusiastic about his new role. Rising every morning at daybreak, Kirill worked in his study for hours, writing letters, issuing orders, examining communiqués, signing promotions, and sending out imperial directives. Many of the recipients were waiters, taxi drivers, and titled gigolos, so all these directives were of dubious importance. But no doctor could have provided Ducky's husband with a better cure.

Suddenly, the Edinburgh Palace became a lively and stimulating ersatz court. All kinds of political workers came to visit Ducky and Kirill from every corner of the world. They brought "reports on the internal situation in Russia, on the life of the Russian exiles in the countries in which they lived and worked, and on their own efforts to bring about a united front." Politics now dominated the lives of the entire family. Even seven-year-old Vladimir "lived in the world of political events." He later remembered: "I often saw troubled looks on the faces of my parents, and I knew what those looks meant. They were always caused by some new events which had taken place in Russia, or some fresh development of the Russian question in general."

Realizing that the New World now held the key to the future of the Old, the imperial couple looked toward the American continent.

In October of 1924 the U.S. press devoted "considerable space" to the forthcoming visit of Empress Victoria Feodorovna of Russia. The exact motives for her trip were unknown, and her imminent arrival gave rise to "much excited rumour and some confusion." At first it had been stated in the papers that Ducky was coming to New York to give lectures concerning her work for Russian relief, under the patronage of Mrs. Henry P. Loomis, a member of the advisory committee of the Monday Opera Supper Club, an organization devoted to collecting funds for the starving people of Russia. But no sooner had the story appeared than it was quickly denied by the committee, which announced that the empress was coming to America "simply in recognition of the efforts made by the club to aid her suffering compatriots in Europe."

This announcement seems to have provoked the American press to make a stinging denunciation of Kirill and "an outspoken attack on virtually everything he had ever done during his life." Seizing upon the rumor that Kirill was preparing to sail to New York with his aide-de-camp, General Sipoupski, to meet with wealthy American capitalists who were anxious to restore the Russian monarchy in order to resume the once-profitable trade between the United States and Russia, the press went out of its way to emphasize "the peculiar position of this particular action of the imperial family."

At the beginning of November, an article in *The New York Times* asserted that the Soviet government was pleased by Kirill's current activities and "was fostering his role as self-proclaimed Tsar in order to promote dissension in the monarchist ranks and render united action impossible, as most of the family strongly supported Grand Duke Nicholas." Colonel Balashev, a former secret agent of the last czar, was credited with having inspired Kirill's imperial pretensions. Balashev had defected to the Bolshevik cause during the revolution, but, having apparently changed his mind, had fled to Paris in 1923, convincing Kirill that he wished to work for the Romanov restoration. The implication was that Balashev was a double agent and that Kirill was the dupe of secret Soviet manipulations.

The article went on to say that Kirill had earned himself great unpopularity and the derisive nickname "Cyril Egalité" for having taken an active part in the intrigues leading to the downfall of Nicholas II and for giving support to the revolutionary government. It stated that Kirill had publicly professed republican beliefs and "had always opposed the policies of his sovereign and cousin." Giving Kirill's actions the most negative interpretation possible, the paper claimed that he had demanded to be known as "Citizen Cyril Romanov" and, in return, had been left unmolested in the Russian capital while all of his relations were being rounded up, imprisoned, and eventually executed. However, when the Communist regime took over, Kirill "became alarmed for his own safety, for which he has always had a great regard."

It seemed more than a little bizarre that a leading American newspaper would be attacking the Romanov grand duke who had most vocally opposed czarist despotism and supported republicanism and liberal reform. Almost as if deliberately misinterpreting the facts of his life, the paper condemned Kirill's service in the Russo-Japanese War, saying he had suffered from nothing more serious than shock, had resented the fact that he had not been the first to be rescued from his sinking ship, and had resigned his command and "under the pretext of peremptory orders of his physicians retired to the south of France to convalesce." It criticized him for being the only member of his family to fail to do his duty and take an active part in the recent world war, and scrambled the facts of his escape into exile by claiming that he had lived in a luxurious villa in Finland and had easily made his way to Paris via Sweden "while his wife was helping to nurse the wounded and cholera-stricken at Jassy [Iaşi]."

To make sure readers understood that Kirill was a bona fide social outcast, the article concluded by stating that his presence at St. Briac had been very coolly received by the French government and that "he was given plainly to understand that his presence would not be welcomed in Great Britain."

This article, along with a series of other inaccurate and prejudiced diatribes appearing in the American press, seriously damaged Kirill's prestige and quickly put an end to any hopes he might have had of visiting the United States.

It was up to the perennially popular Ducky to carry the standard of imperial Russia to the suspicious New World. She kissed her husband and children good-bye and set sail from Le Havre on the luxury liner *Paris* on Saturday, November 29, 1924. Accompanied by two ladies-in-waiting, Countess Orlov and Madame Makarov (the widow of Admiral Makarov, who had died in the sinking of the *Petropavlovsk* in 1904), Ducky immediately found herself on a diplomatic tightrope. Measuring each and every word, the empress without a crown sent ahead an official message to the women of the United States: "Tell them of my joy at meeting them and how happy I will be to thank them for all they have done for us."

After a stormy six-day crossing, Ducky and her retinue arrived in New York harbor on the morning of December 6 and instantly became the center of intense public interest. A squadron of American journalists swarmed onto the ship and besieged "the possible future Czarina," as they tactfully called Ducky, firing their flash bulbs in her face and shouting a hundred simultaneous questions. Every inch her mother's daughter, Ducky maintained her calm and serenely dealt with the shipboard chaos. The press's only victory was a candid photo of the titular Empress baring all of her teeth in a broad smile. Because Ducky was "always self-conscious about her teeth, she rarely smiled for the camera."

Since Russian politics was a very touchy issue, Ducky's visit was being conducted with the strictest security. Fearing a possible Bolshevik attack, the police commissioner of New York City had posted dozens of officers on the pier and provided Ducky's car with an escort of ten motorcycle policemen to take her to her hotel, the Waldorf-Astoria on Park Avenue.

When questioned by reporters, "the possible future Czarina" firmly denied that there was any political motive involved in her visit to the United States. It was "purely social and had been decided on before her husband issued his manifesto proclaiming himself Tsar." She said that rumors that Kirill intended to come to America himself were untrue and that newspaper reports that he had been denied an entry visa were "absolutely without foundation." She very smoothly avoided controversy when a reporter asked her if she thought the old Russian nobility would be returning to power in the near future. "I am here simply as a grateful woman to thank the American people for their kindness," she gently replied, "and I do not wish to talk of political matters at all."

Then, to make certain there was no misunderstanding, she read the reporters a prepared statement saying that she wished "to invoke the courtesy of the newspapers in publishing a complete and unequivocal denial of all reports that my visit is for political purposes, to help restore the Russian monarchy, or to sell property."

But, of course, nothing could have been further from the truth. The monarchist cause was exactly the reason for her trip.

Since neither England nor the rest of Europe would act to get the Communists out of Russia, the only remaining hope seemed to be the United States, the world's emerging colossus. When the decaying monarchies of Europe had hopelessly languished on the battlefield during World War I, America had finally come to the rescue and swiftly ended the stalemate. In 1924, the United States had the money, the military might, and the political influence to kick the Soviets out of Russia and put Kirill and Ducky on the throne.

Most important, the United States was rabidly anticommunist. Fearful to the point of paranoia, the country dreaded the spread of communism to its own shores and anxiously sought its extermination whenever and wherever it could be found.

Ducky and her husband were banking on using this American antipathy to produce gold for their cause. But, like most of their European contemporaries, they failed to appreciate how deeply isolationism ran in the American consciousness in the 1920s. Thoroughly resenting its costly involvement in the last war, the United States wanted nothing to do with the political developments on the other side of the Atlantic. The Red Menace may have been lurking beneath every American bed, but until the Soviet army marched up Madison Avenue, the reclusive and practical-minded Americans were not interested in taking any definite action.

Ducky at least had the good sense to recognize America's reluctance to get involved and its natural antipathy toward royalist causes. Shrewdly determining that an oblique approach would work best, she continued to deny the political motives for her visit. But no one could have been fooled. Even her son, the grand duke Vladimir, later confessed: "In accepting this invitation my mother had one end in view—to further my father's cause in America."

And if anyone could carry it off, it was Ducky—"an exceptional woman in every sense," according to her son. "Her brilliant intellect, her profound knowledge of life, and her great presence never failed to win the hearts of all with whom she came in contact." With her regal dignity and warm, gracious manner, Empress Victoria Feodorovna immediately fascinated the American public. From her first appearance on the deck of the *Paris,* patiently posing for photographers, Ducky was closely scrutinized. Reporters described in detail how she looked and what she wore, taking special note of her elegant, "close-fitting" blue dress, her turquoise coat trimmed with sable, and her large black felt hat and suède slippers. They even described the beauty of the three pearl rings on the fingers of her right hand, her pearl earrings, her jade bracelet, and her striking dagger pin crafted from Russian amethyst. *The New York Times* observed that she spoke her native language, English, with only a slight Russian accent, but went on more tactlessly to say, that she was "tall, rather thin and has keen gray eyes, with fair hair turning gray. She is younger and not so attractive looking as her sister, the Queen of Rumania."

Overwhelmed by what was then the world's largest city, Ducky marveled at the vibrant crush of humanity filling New York's canyonlike streets and was awestruck by the towering skyline. She admired the city's modernity and great energy, and she especially fell in love with the sleek luxury of Park Avenue, later describing the rows of apartment houses to her cousin, Grand Duke Alexander, with rapture and "suggesting that all of us move there."

Comfortably ensconced in the tower of the Waldorf-Astoria, Ducky answered press questions concerning one sensational rumor after another. The current talk of the town was that the late Nicholas II had "made large personal investments in the United States, said to be about $60,000,000, held in the National City Bank." When queried about this phantom fortune, Ducky replied with a tolerant smile that she knew nothing of its existence. Asked her impressions of New York, she enthusiastically responded: "I am immensely surprised at the size of the place. And everything is in such beautiful order. Your traffic police are perfectly amazing and those motorcycle men who have been accompanying me do the most extraordinary things in getting through traffic. And the Broadway lights: There is nothing like them in the world. They make your nights a charming and beautiful thing."

She raved about a performance of Sigmund Romberg's *The Student Prince,* which she had attended the night before at the Jolson Theater: "The singing was as good as any I have heard. You Americans do things up in a most extraordinary way." Ducky praised the police and confessed herself to be quite "in love" with them, declaring that "they are a fine body of men."

As determined as this very determined woman was to avoid politics, it was inevitable that the relentless hammering of the reporters would eventually push her into a comment on the current situation in Russia. On December 9, when a journalist from *The New York Times* asked her whether the Russians wanted their monarch back or were satisfied with the new regime, she exploded, "Every sane person knows they are dissatisfied with the present government. Just read their statistics and you will find out why."

But, quickly catching herself, Ducky turned the rest of the interview into a light-hearted discussion of innocent subjects.

What did Her Imperial Majesty think of New York's elegant stores?

"Shopping? They don't give me time for that."

Had she done anything with her free time?

"I have been introduced to your crossword puzzles," Ducky said with a laugh. "I have tried three already but have not solved even one."

Did she think crossword puzzles might catch on in Russia?

"Yes, I do." She smiled, then wistfully added: "But then the whole world is a puzzle just now."

When asked if New Yorkers seemed as rushed and busy as they were reputed to be, Ducky found herself echoing her late mother's fondest sentiments: "Yes, I do, and I enjoy seeing it. I like to see people who get a move on."

What about careers for women?

"I believe in women having careers if they want them. In Russia women are independent to a large degree, and very serious."

After the nonstop hoopla of the city that never sleeps, Ducky caught her breath and traveled to Washington, D.C., on December 11. In contrast to her gala reception in New York, her arrival in the nation's capital was marked by a complete lack of official honors. The State Department had decided to ignore her visit, refusing to recognize her status or grant her any honors apart from a small corps of uniformed policemen to protect her. When the admiring wife of a minor official telephoned the State Department to request that a Russian imperial flag be sent to the Empress Victoria Feodorovna's suite at the Willard Hotel on Pennsylvania Avenue oposite the White House—the flag was needed so that it could be draped over the empress's chair when she formally received "the homage of her admirers"—the department quickly replied that this would be impossible, and firmly reprimanded the woman for having "misjudged the intricate diplomatic requirements of the occasion."

Struggling to decide how to deal with the new Soviet state, the United States was cautious in addressing political legitimacy and imperial claims. Any sign of governmental friendship toward Ducky might well be interpreted as a declaration of official policy. Hence the cold shoulder.

Undaunted, Ducky decided to make the most of her stay by pursuing her extensive private social contacts. It was announced that she would be the guest of honor at several gala functions given by the leaders of Washington society. The highlight was to be a large ball held for the benefit of the Russian relief fund. (Awkwardly, no plans had been made for her presentation to President Coolidge. As for the first lady, she had conveniently left town the morning of Ducky's arrival and would not be returning until after she had departed, so there was no possibility that embarrassing questions of protocol would arise. Whether Mrs. Coolidge was absent "by coincidence or design, to avoid being upstaged, was left to the citizens of Washington to decide for themselves.")

Unfortunately, as much as Ducky loved Washington and privately enjoyed her stay, a pall was cast over it by the attitude the capital's leading newspapers took toward her husband. Obviously inspired by the numerous Russian émigrés in America who supported the candidacy of Kirill's elderly rival Grand Duke Nicholas, they denounced Kirill and his imperial pretensions.

Used, from her earliest days in Darmstadt, to being an outcast and the subject of condemnation, Ducky didn't flinch when these attacks began.

Confidently, she looked her husband's critics in the eye and gave them the impression that she couldn't care less about their opinions. However, behind this façade, Ducky was angry and badly shaken. For the first time, she was coming face to face with the magnitude of her husband's unpopularity. Unfortunately, she didn't learn to take a more objective, and thus perceptive, view of Kirill's complex nature. But she did put "a brave face on" the situation, refusing to be provoked into "any statements that might be construed as retaliation." She smiled ambiguously at her more impertinent interviewers and referred them to her secretary, Captain George Djamjarov. When asked by a reporter whether Kirill had been popular with the other members of the Romanov family, the captain shrugged and remarked noncommittally that "a Grand Duke is always a Grand Duke, you know."

At this point in Ducky's struggle against the political hostility to her cause, *The New York Times* printed an editorial that fixed American public opinion and doomed her efforts once and for all. The *Times* argued that all the talk of restoring the Russian monarchy, even if it went no further than the public debate between two rival royal candidates, was not easing the grip of communism. On the contrary, said the editorialist: At this critical time, when the communist movement was making headway in the vulnerable countries of western Europe, Kirill's imperial crusade was actually helping his enemies, the Soviet regime being "bolstered up effectively by inviting the Russian people to consider the alternative of the Czar and the landlords coming back." The *Times* maintained that "the leaders of Soviet Russia prefer to utilize the fear of Czarism for the maintenance of their own unimpaired dictatorship. . . . The fact that the Russian people today has less work, less food, and less education than it had under the Czar will be overridden by the fear of relapse into still worse conditions and the prospect of reprisals."

Ducky's Atlantic crossing was rendered totally useless. She might as well have stayed at home. It certainly would have saved her a great deal of frustration and embarrassment.

To add insult to injury, the Washington press began making scathing attacks on Ducky herself. "Soft murmurs of adoration, happy bleatings," one prominent paper sneered, "greeted the Empress who was on exhibition to those worthy of the vision." Other articles commented derisively on her appearance and even made fun of her husband's name, "which makes some of us think of Offenbach and champagne and all the lost delights of our frivolous ancestors." But Ducky shrugged off these attacks, making the most of her Washington society contacts before returning to New York and preparing for her trip home.

Despite its severe disappointments, the American visit had provided a refreshing change from the tragic gloom of the past ten years. The social diversion and excitement must have done Ducky a great deal of good, for reporters remarked on her departure that she "looked much better in health and spirits than she had on her arrival."

Just before Ducky left New York harbor aboard the French liner *France,* she held a farewell press conference at her Waldorf-Astoria suite, where she graciously told reporters that she was very sorry to be leaving, for "Americans everywhere have been so kind to me."

"And how do the American people compare to the Europeans?" a journalist inquired.

"I have found the Americans to be extraordinarily well-informed," Ducky responded.

In fact, perhaps too well-informed for her tastes.

On the afternoon of December 16, Ducky began the long, cold voyage through the wintry waters of the north Atlantic. She had faithfully written to Kirill every day, reporting exactly what was going on. On several different levels, her trip had been "a cause of great anxiety" to him, and "he eagerly awaited news from her all the time."

When Ducky arrived in Paris two days before Christmas, she was still exhilarated. Interviewed by the press, she was even more enthusiastic about her Yankee hosts: "If everybody copied the American's upright common sense," she declared, "there would be less trouble in the world. It was my first visit to the United States, but I hope to go again. I think my American friends will continue to help Russian refugees as they have done in the past."

Asked if she had brought back any funds for the imperial cause, she replied that she had not, adding that she "had not asked for any" and was returning with only "thanks for the reception she had received." And she emphasized that "everywhere I went I found great sympathy for Russia and the hope of seeing her in order again."

Toward the end of the interview a journalist asked if she had said that America needed royalty.

"America needs nothing," Ducky smilingly replied. "She is getting along beautifully. Prohibition? It didn't interfere with me."

Unfortunately, no matter how appreciative and complimentary she tried to be, Ducky just wasn't popular or influential enough to carry any weight with U.S. public opinion. There was no support for the Romanovs in the Land of the Free, and all Ducky's professed admiration netted her little more than a handful of wealthy, social-climbing American friends.

Even after she had returned home to Europe, the hostility and suspicion of the American public continued to grow. Many began to question the financing of her tour. Accused of funding Ducky's trip, her hosts at the Monday Opera Supper Club had to issue a public denial. Likewise, the Waldorf-Astoria and the steamship company were forced to make similar official disclaimers that they had provided free services to their imperial visitor.

As the months passed by, it became all too apparent that Ducky's cleverness and charm had not worked a miracle. The brave New World was not going to be rushing over to resurrect the Old and help it rebuild on its dubious and dated foundations.

It was a bitter lesson for Ducky. The absurd futility of her uncrowned status was never so apparent as during her American adventure. In the first few months of her "reign," Empress Victoria Feodorovna had quickly and painfully discovered how humiliating and frustrating it was to be a sovereign without the benefit of a coronation.

CHAPTER FORTY-THREE

Sea of Dreams

W HEN DUCKY ARRIVED in Coburg on Christmas Eve, she kept her disappointment and discouragement to herself. Knowing how fragile her husband's good spirits were, she put the most optimistic face on the facts of her failed American tour. With great skill and care, she gave Kirill a feeling of renewed hope in their cause and faith in the future.

Actually, there was no reason to believe that 1925 would be any better for the imperial exiles than the previous bleak years had been. As time passed and the Soviets consolidated their control over Russia, dreams of recapturing Kirill's homeland receded further and further, toward a distant horizon.

But the new emperor and empress of Russia were not disheartened. Seemingly with more energy than ever, Ducky used her charm and leadership abilities to solicit and inspire new supporters and solidify her husband's position. Bolstered by her confidence and zeal, Kirill spent less and less time hunting in the Thuringian forests and more at his study desk, receiving visitors and corresponding with his scattered loyal subjects.

At this time, there were "some five hundred thousand exiled Russian monarchists who were making their precarious living in thirty-odd countries, east and west of Suez." Although their allegiance to the Romanov crown was divided among several imperial claimants, most were supporting Grand Duke Nicholas. Thus, activity at the Edinburgh Palace was primarily aimed at inducing this fickle and weary multitude to unanimously accept Ducky's husband as Emperor Kirill I of All the Russias, "the legitimate successor to the throne of the Romanovs relinquished by his cousin Czar Nicholas II on March 15, 1917."

Ducky and Kirill devoted their lives to working day by day, step by step, to establish the legitimacy of their claims, win universal recognition of their status and rights, and resurrect their fallen empire. Although their successes may have been almost imperceptible, they never abandoned their great faith or enthusiasm.

Without Ducky, none of this would have been happening. She singlehandedly provided her husband and the monarchist movement with a passionate resolve that no one else could have contributed. It was her irreproachable character, iron will, and discipline that propelled the Romanov cause and gave it hope. And for the first time in her life, Ducky was the center of something grand and spectacular. No longer the middle child overshadowed by her glamorous older sister, or the neglected wife of an eccentric and insignificant sovereign, or a snubbed satellite in a glorious imperial court, Victoria Melita was, at last, the one in the spotlight, the one in control.

America had opened Ducky's eyes in more ways than one. She had never before received so much undivided attention and adoration. The world had sought her out and listened carefully to everything she had to say. It was a heady experience, and it helped erase the horrors and tragedies of the past eight years. Having lost almost everything but her life, Ducky was regenerated by the respect and recognition, albeit unofficial, given her by her vibrant and dynamic hosts. If she hadn't felt like an important woman—a full-fledged empress—before, she certainly did now.

When summer arrived, the family traveled to Brittany again and spent several months in St. Briac, where the fresh sea breezes and the company of friends considerably raised their spirits. Also adding to the excitement of their stay was the recent engagement of their eldest daughter, Marie, to Friedrich Karl, the hereditary prince of Leiningen. Although Ducky and Kirill were happy that their daughter was truly in love, they were acutely disappointed in her choice of a husband.

Leiningen was a tiny German principality at the extreme western edge of Bavaria—not far from Hesse-Darmstadt, where Ducky had once been so unhappy. The princes of Leiningen held modest (almost nonexistent) court in a pleasant, unpretentious manor house in the remote and sleepy little village of Amorbach. It was all very warm and cozy and gemütlich—something Grandmama Queen would have adored, but the Leiningens were about as unimportant as royalty came. In fact, they weren't even "royal highnesses"; they were "serene highnesses," one step below.

For the elder daughter of a couple proclaiming themselves the emperor and empress of Russia, it was almost an unacceptable match, one that would not have been allowed before the fall of the Romanov monarchy. But times had changed; the strictness of royal hierarchy and dynastic protocol had been among the revolutionary casualties. It was now permissible for a Romanov grand duchess to make a vastly inferior marriage. Ducky and Kirill could at least take heart in the fact that their future son-in-law was a legitimate prince with his own realm, tiny though it was. So they approved the match.

Eighteen-year-old Marie was a shy and easygoing girl loved by both her parents. With her blond hair, blue eyes, and broad, full face, she looked far more like her namesake aunt Missy than her dark and slender mother. In the turmoil of the past few years, Ducky had almost lost sight of her eldest daughter's advancement into womanhood. Marie had still seemed like a child when she went to visit her aunt Sandra in 1924 and fell in love with her handsome young prince at a house party in Langenburg.

Ducky must have contemplated the impending marriage of her daughter with conflicting emotions. For whatever its merits and liabilities, Marie's wedding was a reminder that Ducky had reached another milestone in her life: She was approaching the threshold of old age.

Returning to Coburg in the fall, Ducky and Kirill began planning the wedding, which took place on Wednesday, November 25, 1925. Significantly, it was Ducky's forty-ninth birthday.

As was customary when a match between dynasties involved two religions, there were two wedding ceremonies. The first and most impressive was the Russian Orthodox ritual, which was conducted in the family's private chapel in the Edinburgh Palace. The chapel had been Ducky's mother's pride and joy, the vestments and decorations having been given to her by her father, Emperor Alexander II, and having originally belonged to the movable military chapel attached to his headquarters during the Russo-Turkish War of 1877–78.

Bittersweet memories must have arisen; celebrating her birthday by watching her daughter getting married in her own girlhood home,

Ducky couldn't avoid glancing across the Schlossplatz at the stately Residenz, where her marriage to Ernie had begun.

After the solemn Orthodox ceremony, a Lutheran service was celebrated in the local church.

Because almost all of Ducky and Kirill's surviving relatives attended the wedding, it was a notable royal event. Besides the two impressive religious ceremonies, "a number of merry festivities" amused the illustrious guests. Although the parents of the bride were unfailingly gracious and led everyone to believe that they "were very pleased with the match," they remained disappointed in their daughter's humble choice and the poor future that awaited her.

Ducky and her husband spent that winter quietly with their two other children in the Edinburgh Palace. But beneath the heavy Coburg snows that season the political situation in Bavaria was heating up. Suddenly, their environment was not as friendly as it used to be. Shortly after Kirill had proclaimed himself emperor in 1924, the powerful Communist Party in Bavaria had demanded his expulsion. Other political groups had also complained about his presence, arguing that "the republic could not permit an alleged court to function within its borders." *The New York Times* noted that "unemployed royalty, it appears, has become a serious problem in Bavaria."

When Germany established friendly relations with Moscow in the mid-1920s, the Bavarian Communists stepped up their campaign against Kirill. They began demanding that he take his imperial court "to some place where monarchies are more popular." Although the Bavarian government rejected all demands for Kirill's expulsion—officially, it found his behavior compatible with the rules covering political asylum—it was becoming much cooler toward him and certainly did nothing to encourage his continued residence. There were even rumors that "the Bavarian ministers had asked him to leave after he refused to sign a statement promising to desist from further political activity."

Since their presence in Coburg was obviously an embarrassment for the Bavarian government, Ducky and Kirill decided in the spring of 1926 to establish a permanent residence in France at their favorite summer resort, St. Briac. Over the past few summers they had fallen in love with the tiny, picturesque fishing village and the surrounding area. It was an ideal choice for a year-round home, offering them almost everything they needed. The remoteness of the Breton coast provided both privacy and security. The mild maritime climate was cool in summer and agreeable in winter, which suited it to Ducky and Kirill's health problems. She had always had a hypersensitivity to the cold weather and suffered terribly during the winter snows of Russia and Central Europe, while her husband's war injuries made him "a martyr to circulatory trouble." Sometimes Kirill was so incapacitated in freezing weather that he had difficulty walking.

But St. Briac had much more to offer than warmth and seclusion; it also provided a wealth of social and recreational activities. Kirill, an almost fanatical golfer, was delighted by the gorgeous championship golf course at the edge of the village, overlooking the sea. He could enjoy this magnificent facility every day of the year, wearing his favorite London-made hat, a rumpled, well-worn piece that he faithfully kept on his head until the day he died. And when he wasn't out on the links and Ducky wasn't tending her precious garden, the imperial couple could join the bright social scene of the neighboring town of Dinard, a fashionable spa where the international set gathered to play at the palatial casino and mingle at fancy dress balls and dinner parties.

St. Briac also had the added attraction of having become home to a large colony of White Russian exiles and retired English people, many of them former officers living on their comfortable pensions. Likewise, the much larger town of Dinard had a sizable English population and a constant stream of wealthy and cosmopolitan visitors from around the world. Too, Paris was only four hours away by train, so frequent trips to Ducky and Kirill's favorite city could easily relieve the boredom of small-town life.

And, most important, the tolerant French republic was far more hospitable to a shadow emperor and empress than the radical air of unstable and increasingly fanatical Germany. As political and social chaos spread throughout Europe in the latter half of the 1920s, Ducky and her husband would feel secure in the distant tranquillity of the north coast of Brittany, in a village for which they "had all developed a great fondness."

So in the summer of 1926 the family returned to St. Briac with the intention of buying a permanent home. Because houses were usually passed by inheritance for centuries, the real estate market in northern Brittany was rather limited. But Ducky finally found something that would suit perfectly: a large, modest-looking house about a mile south of the village. Originally built by a retired captain in the 1880s, the villa was a simple three-story rectangle of coarse Breton stone with granite masonry and stained-pine woodwork. Ducky and Kirill gave it a

Breton name, Ker Argonid, which can be translated into English as Villa Victoria.

Immediately, Ducky took charge of making Ker Argonid a comfortable and beautiful home, using her color sense and talent for interior decoration to create an exquisite environment. For a sentimental touch, Ducky arranged that the furniture from their prewar Paris flat be brought out of storage and sent to St. Briac.

But before the family could permanently settle in to their new life in Brittany, it was necessary to put their Coburg affairs in order and prepare for the move. Back in Germany, Ducky went straight to Amorbach, where she sat patiently at her daughter's side. Marie was expecting her first baby. On October 18, 1926, she gave birth to a son, Emich Kirill.

Ducky was now a grandmother. She quietly celebrated her fiftieth birthday in Coburg that November.

Most of the following year was spent packing up their possessions and moving them to Brittany. Finally, in the late fall of 1927, just before the heavy winter snows began, Ducky gathered up her family and departed for good.

At Ker Argonid they continued to live a secluded country life, but found it "far more lively than at Coburg." Ducky, perhaps feeling an urge to return to her roots, quickly established "the friendliest relations" with the English population of St. Briac and neighboring Dinard. She and Kirill effortlessly became the leaders of the local social scene. No matter how their sophisticated English and French acquaintances felt about the couple's imperial pretensions—some of them didn't recognize them as emperor and empress of Russia—they were at least impressed by the fact that the couple were a bona fide grand duke and grand duchess, especially since Ducky was an English princess and a granddaughter of Queen Victoria.

Their first year at St. Briac was filled with simple pleasures and diversions. Kirill played golf almost every day, and his health improved noticeably. He and Ducky joined their friends for picnics in the forest and on the beautiful rocky seacoast, a gemlike range of deep, twisting coves and tiny, pine-ringed bays nicknamed Le Balcon d'Emeraude, the Emerald Balcony. Group excursions were made to nearby points of interest such as the walled medieval city of St. Malo, six miles away, and the spectacular island abbey of Mont St. Michel, a huge spired monolith rising from the distant flatlands of the Norman coast and often eerily visible from the heights of Dinard.

As in Russia, the game of bridge played a large role in their evening social life; parties were frequent, as were festive dinners, amateur theatricals and the quaint and time-honored pastime of tableaux vivants. Large numbers of local residents were also invited to these parties. Although Ducky and Kirill mixed freely and were a democratic host and hostess, it was considered good manners in their circle to let them win at their favorite game, Murder, and anyone who "dared to beat them was left in no doubt as to their displeasure."

After the "drudgery of post-war Coburg," that first year at St. Briac was a much-needed and well-deserved escape.

A more serious issue was that this perennial holiday had to be paid for. Money was still a desperate worry, for the family finances were precariously balanced. Far more clever, enterprising, and talented than her husband, Ducky shouldered the burden by devoting herself to her art. She painted exquisite watercolors of the flowers from her beloved garden and illuminated old books and Bibles, selling these "works of an accomplished artist" for a respectable profit. Ducky used her modest earnings "to keep the household going, and to pay for the education of their children."

The children's schooling posed a particular problem. Eighteen-year-old Kira was a raven-haired beauty who was more or less finishing her formal education with private tutors, but ten-year-old Vladimir was just at the threshold of his education. Since he was the couple's only son and the heir to the Romanov throne, his complete and proper education was of the utmost importance. Ducky didn't want him to learn a trade or be trained for a profession, insisting, instead, that he be brought up "as if he was to inherit the position and wealth of his ancestors."

But what concerned her most was her son's safety. Living "in constant dread that Vladimir might be kidnapped by their enemies," she was reluctant to let him out of her sight. She even refused to send him to the fine public schools of St. Briac and instead decided to have him educated at home by an expensive private tutor. When Vladimir was offered a scholarship to the prestigious Winchester School in southern England, Ducky vetoed the plan because of her concerns for his safety (and also because "the experience might transform him into an Englishman").

Not that Ducky was anti-British. On the contrary, she still treasured her heritage, but as fine as it might be to be an Englishman, Vladimir's destiny lay in his Romanov blood. In preparation for becoming the future emperor of Russia, he must be made a Russian.

Ducky and Kirill's placid and unpretentious new life may have suited them perfectly, but it alarmed many of their relatives. Missy paid another visit to St. Briac and afterward wrote to their cousin King George V with characteristic theatricality: "Ducky is in very sad circumstances, but both she and Kirill are magnificently resigned and uncomplaining, bearing nobly almost unbearable misfortunes."

It was true, however, that even the children were impressed by the strain their parents, particularly their mother, placed on themselves in the attempt to maintain imperial pretentions on a very limited budget. Kira wrote her aunt Missy, "Mummie is as usual dreadfully overworked; it never stops, only gets more and more. If at least she had some capable secretary but she hasn't found one and done most of the work herself. Her tiny room is simply littered with papers and letters; as she says she soon won't be able to turn around in it. . . . She looks so tired and worried again and when she came back from America she was looking decidedly fresh and not so harassed."

In the summer of 1927, Ducky had visited Romania, where her glamorous sister had woes of her own. In 1926, Missy, too, had made an American tour, which had been highly publicized, but had ended in an even more embarrassing fiasco than Ducky's. Still recovering from her humiliating treatment by the American press, Missy now was keeping vigil at her husband's deathbed. Nando had been slowly dying of cancer for the past two years, and now his suffering was nearing an end. Ducky had rushed across Europe to be at Missy's side, arriving at the summer palace at Sinaia in the Transylvanian Alps just after Nando passed away on the morning of July 20. Sandra and Baby Bee arrived a few days later, and the four sisters, stylishly dressed in black mourning, sat together for the first time in years and talked of the happier times of the past.

Though she brought grieving Missy warmth and emotional support, Ducky could do nothing to resolve her sister's other problems. All Missy's hard work for her adopted homeland was coming undone. Her eldest son, Crown Prince Carol, had given up his right to the throne and fled in disgrace to Paris with his mistress. He had left his son Michael to take his place, and now a six-year-old boy sat on the Romanian throne. Tiny King Michael was no match for the Machiavellian character of his nation's politics. Praying for a miracle, Missy watched her former realm slowly descend into chaos.

Perhaps focusing on problems other than her own helped to refresh Ducky and revitalize her spirits. When she returned to St. Briac in early

August, she seemed so improved that Kira appreciatively wrote to her aunt Missy to say how much good the trip had done her mother and how she hoped that "this may be the beginning of more visits in the future." Of their new French home, Kira wrote: "This is a little hidden-away corner, full of peace and quiet which I think you would like as much as we do. It has been the source of much trouble and work but now certainly repays it."

There were other quiet comforts in Ducky's life. At the beginning of 1928 Marie made her a grandmother again with the birth of a second son, Karl. When Ducky wasn't occupied with her art or her family, or spending long hours "taming the wilderness" behind Ker Argonid and turning it into a magnificent garden, she lavished her attention on interesting new friends.

One of these was a young Englishman named Edward Voules who was spending a short holiday at Dinard that summer. He had gone to a Russian wedding, and at the reception that followed, searched all the tables in vain for his place card. Observing "this forlorn stranger slinking around," Ducky called him over to her table and inquired what the problem was. She was so delighted to discover "a raw young man from England" that she instructed the waiter to squeeze in an additional chair next to her so that they could spend the rest of the afternoon talking about their native land.

The chance meeting led to a long friendship, and Voules came to know Ducky and her family very well. Whenever he visited Dinard he was invited to their parties, where he frequently partnered Kira on the dance floor. They kept up an active correspondence, and met whenever Ducky came to London. (She stayed at Kings Cottage in Chiswick, a grace and favor residence that cousin King George had leased permanently without charge to Baby Bee and her husband, the Infante Alfonso of Spain.) A few years later, Kira and Vladimir went to London without their parents, and the three young people attended fashionable parties together.

Voules's most vivid memories of the titular emperor and empress of Russia concerned the striking contrast in their personalities. He found Kirill "a quiet, austere man who spoke very little, leaving conversation to his vivacious and ebullient wife." The perceptive young Englishman remarked that the taciturn emperor led a surprisingly "unobtrusive" life and was scrupulously polite to everyone he met. Voules greatly admired

Ducky, who, he said, was "as talkative as was said to be her sister, Queen Marie."

Voules was well aware of the imperial family's impoverished state and sympathized with their constant struggle to make ends meet. During his very first meeting with Ducky at the wedding reception in Dinard, she was wearing a magnificent ring with a huge pearl in the center; with a wistful smile, she casually remarked that this would be the next piece of jewelry for which she would be "looking for a buyer in order to help meet their living expenses."

The work of locating to a new home and the myriad social diversions of a popular resort had diverted Ducky and Kirill's finances, time, and attention from the creation of an imperial court in exile. With Ducky busy painting and gardening while her husband golfed, by the fall of 1928 it must have appeared that the monarchist cause had peacefully drifted into quiet domesticity. The dissension in the royalist ranks must have been discouraging to Ducky and Kirill, and their new home and pleasant way of life were a tempting alternative.

But just as their dreams and ambitions seemed to have been lulled into extinction by the sparkling Breton sea, two events happened that totally changed their prospects for the future in the space of a few months.

CHAPTER FORTY-FOUR

Kirill's New Clothes

O N THE EVENING OF October 13, 1928, a telegram arrived at Ker Argonid announcing the sudden death of Dowager Empress Marie Feodorovna at her home, Hvidore, near Copenhagen. Ducky and Kirill's aunt Minnie had just turned eighty and had ruled supreme as the matriarch of the Romanov clan. As a crowned empress, she was considered by most Russians "to be the highest authority in the Imperial Family." Her refusal to the very end to accept the irrefutable evidence that her son and his family were dead had made her withhold support from Kirill's dynastic claims. Now that she was dead, Kirill was the most prominent of the Romanovs, and his place on the nonexistent Russian throne was more secure than ever.

Because Marie Feodorovna had been the daughter of a Danish king, she was honored with an elaborate state funeral at Roskilde Cathedral, the burial place of the monarchs of Denmark. Feeling obliged to attend the ceremony on account of his new position in the family and his "great love and respect for the deceased Empress," Kirill left Ducky behind with the children at St. Briac and took the Nord Express from Paris to Copenhagen. He was received at the Danish court "with all of the honours due to the Head of the Imperial House of Russia," and stayed at the palace as the special guest of King Christian X and Queen Alexandrine.

The funeral was the first great gathering of the Romanov family since the revolution, and Kirill encountered many relatives he had not seen since their abrupt departure from Russia eleven years earlier. Thousands of other Russian exiles also flocked to Denmark, as did members of all of Europe's royal houses, to pay tribute to the woman who had been the last surviving crowned head of the once-grand Romanov empire. So the pageantry of imperial Russia was momentarily revived.

Witnessing this fleeting vision of his spectacular legacy, Kirill must have been struck by renewed determination and dedication. "Taking it upon himself to act the leader," he left his seat of honor in the cathedral and ceremoniously conducted the arriving Danish royalty to their seats. The deceased empress's youngest daughter, Grand Duchess Olga, as hostile to Kirill as her mother had been, bluntly announced that he "should have had the sense to stay away." It must have angered her to see that the Danish press respectfully called him "Tsar Kyrill, Keeper of the Throne."

But whether they liked Kirill or not, it was clear to most of his royal relatives that he was now the head of the Romanov family. The kaiser's only daughter, Princess Viktoria Luise, had written to her father in Holland after the funeral: "For the poor Russians, it means the end of an era; Aunt Maria [the dowager empress] held them all together. Now it is Kyrill who is in charge."

Had there been any doubt concerning this, it vanished less than three months later, on January 5, 1929, when Grand Duke Nicholas died at his home in Antibes on the French Riviera. He was seventy-two and his authority had been on the wane for some time because prolonged illness had prevented him from taking part in public affairs. Since the majority of Russian émigrés had looked upon Nicholas as their leader, his death was "an event of great significance" for the monarchist movement. Kirill was now the senior surviving member of the family, and his position as emperor-in-exile was, at last, unassailable.

Although Ducky and her husband had always acknowledged Nicholas's authority as the eldest male member of the family and sincerely respected his great military service to Russia, they had resented his relentless hostility and his refusal to abide by "the Fundamental Laws" which, they believed, established Kirill as head of the dynasty. They had never had a close relationship with him and once in exile had never even met again. Recognizing the importance of his late cousin's support, Kirill had continually tried to establish friendly relations with him, but had always failed.

After Grand Duke Nicholas's death, the pro-Kirill wing of the monarchist movement began to flourish. Kirill's opponents quickly dropped out of the political area and "Legitimist" groups supporting his claim to the throne were established in every country where Russians had settled. Ducky and Kirill organized a "general secretariat" head-quartered in Paris, which zealously kept in touch with Russian exiles across the globe and gathered a comprehensive file of information on monarchist developments.

Kirill and Ducky's hopes were thus reborn. He interpreted every world event as confirmation of his political forecasts and felt that each passing day was only ensuring "the success of his cause."

But this confidence in the future was hardly justified by the reality of the present. There was still many Russian émigrés, particularly in Paris and London, who regarded Kirill as "just another Russian Grand Duke with absurdly-inflated ambitions." Many others were outwardly con-temptuous of the way St. Briac was becoming a make-believe imperial court. To them it seemed that Kirill had returned from the dowager em-press's funeral inspired more by Hans Christian Andersen than by Ro-manov Russia. The "emperor" was donning gorgeous new clothes, but they simply couldn't be seen.

Transferring his "general secretariat" to St. Briac in the spring of 1929, Kirill established his home as "the phantom capital of an invisible empire." Immediately resurrecting his Coburg routine of officially re-ceiving his secretary-general every morning and devoting hours to cor-respondence and paperwork, Kirill ruled daily from nine to six in his cramped ground-floor study. According to his sympathetic cousin Grand Duke Alexander, this "Shadow Emperor" lived a life of "sus-tained pathos."

During long visits to St. Briac, Alexander closely observed his cousin at work. He considered Kirill's position as Russian emperor "highly overrated at best and nothing short of a nightmare when one is obliged to rule over an Empire that is no more, with one's subjects driving taxis in Paris, serving as waiters in Berlin, dancing in the picture houses on Broadway, providing atmosphere in Hollywood, unloading coal in Montevideo or dying for Good Old China in the shattered suburbs of Shanghai."

His subjects' dispersion necessitated that Kirill's sovereignty "be en-forced solely by mail." In his memoirs, published in the early 1930s, Alexander vividly described the daily routine at Kirill's phantom court at Ker Argonid:

Each morning, the robust sunburned postman of St. Briac appears on the
threshold of the improvised Imperial Palace, puffing and panting under the
weight of batches of letters which carry the stamps of almost every country
under the sun. The foreign representatives of the Shadow Emperor of Rus-
sia keep him posted daily on the physical welfare and the morale of his far-
away subjects, although they would be the first to admit that it would take
a super-Moses to solve the infinitely involved problems of the Russian ex-
iles . . . dreaming sages and scheming cranks, heartbroken heroes and un-
abashed cowards, candidates for the Hall of Fame and full-fledged patients
of Dr. Sigmund Freud.

These scattered Russians continually begged Kirill for his time and
attention. From Yugoslavia came a desperate plea that only a "Personal
Letter from His Majesty" could restore the faith of the Russian community there, which was dangerously besieged by Red agitators. Another letter, from New York, was marked "extremely important";
Kirill opened it to discover that the unemployment crisis in America
was rapidly growing and "a word or two of Monarchical Encouragement would be greatly appreciated by the impoverished Russian
colony in Harlem." A letter from China asked Emperor Kirill's advice
on the wisdom of former Russian officers lending their military services to the local warlords. A group of Cossacks who had settled in
Paraguay, and a gallant Russian general living in India asked for similar
imperial guidance.

And there is that brilliant cavalryman in Chile, a whole-hearted royalist if
ever there was one, who has suddenly discovered the socialistic tendencies of
the government that is employing him. . . .

Then comes a batch of complaints. The passing of the last eighteen years
has failed to impress their authors. Their clocks stopped on July 31, 1914.

A former Supreme Court Justice of Moscow—he is still using his full
title although he is working at present as a factory hand in Canada—wants
it to be distinctly understood in St. Briac that a young Russian employed
in a bakery in Montreal is a very dangerous radical who should not be per-
mitted to return to Russia when the monarchy is restored.

A former Captain of the Guards—now a dishwasher in a self-service
cafeteria somewhere in the Middle West—feels deeply hurt because his
name has not been included in the latest "list of promotions." He is con-
vinced that his age and merits entitle him to the rank of Colonel. "I hap-

pen to know," he adds with considerable resentment, "that several friends of mine have already been made Colonels although they left Russia as mere Lieutenants." Come what may, he wishes to be "promoted" . . . even if he is never able to wear a Colonel's epaulettes or collect the "back salary" due him since 1917.

To Alexander and most other reasonable observers, this world of make-believe was a delicate and pathetic mixture of absurdity with blind loyalty and hope. "Nothing is real," Kirill's cousin wrote; "everything is a prop. Promotions and demotions, orders and counter-orders, citations and reprimands, promises and threats, salaries and bonuses—all being done on a 'when, if and as' basis, subject to the ultimate decision of History."

While Alexander was skeptical of Kirill's imperial status, he admired both the man himself and his remarkable wife. Describing his cousin as "a very tall, extremely handsome man who bears the weight of his middle-fifties with a quiet dignity seldom observed in the case of an actual occupant of a throne," Alexander thought Kirill "so thoroughly czar-like" in appearance that he was always surprised not to find him surrounded by a stately squadron of chevalier-guards on casual strolls through the dusty and unpaved streets of St. Briac.

As for Ducky, she impressed her cousin as a beautiful woman still, with all the charm, royal bearing, and poise to be "expected from the granddaughter of Queen Victoria." Alexander noticed that Ducky's natural dignity and strong character inspired her many admirers to address her as "Your Imperial Majesty." Awed by her self-discipline and quiet tenacity, he noted that the Shadow Empress woke every morning at sunrise and was out working in her large and impressive garden before seven o'clock. It was easy to see that Ducky was creating her own perfect empire ("vaguely suggestive of the English countryside") behind the crumbling stone walls of her yard.

Visitors found the routine at Ker Argonid relatively simple. Rising early, the family had breakfast together, then quietly passed the day in different pursuits. While Kirill spent most of his morning and afternoon attending to "affairs of state," Ducky gardened and painted. Young Vladimir, "a huge and handsome boy looking like an image of his grand-uncle Emperor Alexander III," spent most of the day preparing his lessons with his tutor, while Kira usually read and sometimes joined her mother in the garden. Evenings were spent together at the dinner table, unless there was a party when they enjoyed a game of contract bridge with their guests. The only break in this placid routine was an occasional short trip to Paris to visit friends and go shopping.

Despite all this tranquil domesticity, Kirill continued to see himself as fulfilling his duty to lead the Russian royalists and to revise "the age-worn monarchistic precepts in a manner that would make them acceptable to the Russians in Russia." He was determined that nothing, "not even the fear of ridicule, should interfere with the fulfillment of our duties."

Speaking fluently and sonorously, Kirill often sounded like "a wisely disillusioned Heir Apparent" when he explained his cause:

> I am working for the salvation of our country. I know enough about the cardinal laws of mechanics to understand that each forceful swing of the pendulum to the left is bound to be followed by an equally forceful swing to the right. It is my duty, the duty of every sensible statesman, to be prepared for the moment of that counter-swing and to do all in my power to limit its scope and arrest its potential destructiveness. There is no way of accomplishing this except by creating a new set of healthy national ideals which in themselves would carry both the ability to prevent another deluge of blood and a powerful appeal to the constructive elements of our country.
>
> I know no parties. I am making commitments to no classes. Mine is the task of interpreting the inarticulate groans of the now disfranchised majority of the Russian people, the majority that is not permitted to send its representatives to the Soviets, the majority that is utterly tired of the revolution and its so-called conquests, the majority that is clamoring for a simple life of peace and personal happiness. I am doing my duty and I am teaching my son to follow in my steps.

Of course, few could deny Kirill's good intentions and high ideals, but the question remained how he could possibly carry them out from a little fishing village fourteen hundred miles from the Russian border. Yet as impractical as his political ambitions may have been, the Shadow Emperor was fulfilling a very important need by carrying out his imperial duties and preserving the authority of the Romanov throne. Many of his supporters were destitute and beleaguered, struggling against despair; their "implicit confidence in the miracle-working talents" of their illustrious sovereign in St. Briac gave them hope and courage. To them he symbolized the possibility of a better future and a free Russia.

However, most of Kirill's nonsupporters saw the Romanov court on the windswept coast of northern Brittany as a pretentious absurdity. This was certainly Missy's view. The dowager queen of Romania, who "managed to spend part of every summer bathing at the seaside home of her favorite sister," enjoyed Brittany, where she played something of a Lady Bountiful to the simple villagers. And of course she adored her sister, her niece, and her handsome nephew. But Missy still disliked her brother-in-law, whom she considered the same "extraordinary cold and selfish man" he had always been. And now added to her personal dislike was the fact that she "was not particularly enthusiastic about Kirill's new status" as Russian emperor. To Missy's mind, this St. Petersburg in miniature was produced at Ducky's physical and emotional expense.

Perhaps Missy was feeling the victim herself at this time and was projecting those feelings onto her younger sister. After all her struggles to hold her country together, Missy was very soon to become a prisoner in her own home. It's no wonder that she perceived tragedy where none existed.

At least, not yet.

CHAPTER FORTY-FIVE

The
Betrayed

O CTOBER 3, 1930, was Ducky and Kirill's silver wedding anniversary. A great celebration was held at Ker Argonid, to which most of their far-flung relatives came, bearing greetings and gifts. Their daughter Marie came from Amorbach with her three-month-old baby, Kira. (Ducky's third grandchild, Kira would one day marry one of Missy's grandsons, Prince Andrei of Yugoslavia, thus rejoining the bloodlines of these two devoted sisters.)

Ducky and Kirill were honored at a large, formal banquet on Wednesday, October 8, to which members of the imperial entourage and all of their friends in St. Briac and Dinard were invited. At the end of the evening a series of old-fashioned tableaux vivants were staged, "with great success." An elaborate luncheon party the following Sunday was attended by representatives of monarchist organizations from all over Europe, paying homage to their emperor and empress's twenty-five years of happy marriage. In the evening a reception was held in Dinard at the beautiful harborside home of some good friends from America. The celebrations continued, less formally, for another week.

Everyone recognized the fact that the marriage of Ducky and Kirill had not simply *survived* for a quarter of a century, it had flourished as an extraordinary pairing of two perfectly matched people. Their happiness was apparent to all who knew them; everything they had suffered as a result of their decision to defy the world and marry seemed to have been more than worth it. To their children, Ducky and Kirill seemed an ideal

couple as well as flawless parents. Their son, Vladimir, later wrote glowingly of their relationship: "It was a marriage which was based entirely on
the mutual love of my parents, and which took place in spite of the circumstances in which they found themselves. For twenty-five years they
lived together with one heart and mind, and our family could well be an
example to all. We adored our parents and their love for us was infinite.
All the hardships and bitterness we had to endure in the years were fully
covered by our mutual love. We were proud of our parents, and the celebration of their Silver Wedding had a special significance for all of us."

The hardness and bitterness of exile was perhaps what made the family such a close and devoted one. Having been deprived of everything
else in life, they had only each other. And grand and legitimate as their
imperial heritage might have been, it was becoming more apparent all
the time that royalty and the concept of divinely ordained sovereignty
were as passé as the horse-and-buggy.

Ducky and Kirill were hardly alone. The last war had toppled many of
the world's mightiest monarchs. Besides Russia's, two other dynasties
had fallen: the Hohenzollerns of Germany and the Austrian Habsburgs.
Widowed in 1922, the dowager empress Zita of Austria was in even
graver circumstances than the Romanovs. With almost a dozen young
children to care for, the penniless Zita had to shuffle back and forth
among her relatives and rely upon their generosity. Surprisingly, Ducky's
manic and bellicose cousin the German kaiser had adjusted to his ignominious fate far better than his fellow ex-monarchs. The theatrical Wilhelm II, who had once thrived on pomp and circumstance, was now
living quietly and contentedly in a modest and secluded country house
in Holland, with his nose buried in archaeological research. He chopped
wood for exercise and laughed over the comic stories of P. G. Wode-
house. He had finally not only joined the enemy, but had actually become him: The kaiser was now nothing less than an English country
gentleman.

Ducky's former sister-in-law, Princess Victoria of Hesse, now the
widowed marchioness of Milford Haven, was probably speaking for several of her princely relatives when she confessed in her famous
forthright manner: "I dare say Royalty is nonsense and it may be better
if it is swept away. But as long as it exists, we must have certain rules to
guide us." And with so many of the rules swept away by war and revolution, exiled royals found it exceedingly difficult to make their way
through the new and unfamiliar world. These once-exalted beings now

seemed to be damned whatever course they chose to follow. If they tried
to live according to the realities of their former lives, and to uphold their
illustrious traditions, they were ridiculed and even had their sanity questioned. But if, trying to adapt to the democratic circumstances of their
new lives, they conformed to the relaxed and casual style of the modern
world, they were sneered at as undignified and incongruous.

More than most of her dispossessed relatives, Ducky found it difficult
to adapt. After the splendors of St. Petersburg, she must have found life
in Brittany rather dispiriting. Forced to keep the family on a strict budget, and reduced to the drudgery of running a household, Ducky was
also plagued by the fear that she or her husband and children might at
any time "fall prey to Bolshevik vengeance." But—gallant, uncomplaining, and facing her "uneasy and none too happy existence" with a brave,
resigned smile—Ducky, as always, drew strength and solace from her
great love for her husband. Kirill's happiness was, simply, the meaning
and purpose of her life.

Just as the emperor and empress of Russia were celebrating their twenty-
fifth anniversary, Missy was suddenly struck by an action so treacherous
that it finally drove her to a nervous breakdown. Crown Prince Carol,
having come to regret giving up his right to the Romanian throne, had
plotted with some wily politicians in Bucharest to return from exile and
take the crown from his now eight-year-old son. With great speed and
slippery efficiency, Carol accomplished the deed. Everyone, including his
mother, was willing to believe his sworn promises and give him a second
chance.

But Carol had not changed. As dissolute and sociopathic as ever,
Missy's boy began his reign by refusing to reconcile with his divorced
wife, the docile and angelic Helen of Greece. Instead, he sneaked his
universally detested mistress into the country and installed her in the
master bedroom of the royal palace. Next, he forced Helen to give up
custody of the son he had deserted, and then proceeded to persecute her
and the other members of his family as if they were political prisoners.
Far from being spared her son's paranoid wrath, Missy was its prime target. Carol humiliated his mother in every way he could, taking away her
honors and privileges and banning her from all court functions. "I often
feel I must awake from some torturing dream," Missy said. "I feel that
this cannot be reality, that we are losing ourselves in some dark maze."

But this was no mere nightmare, and it was to get much worse. Carol appropriated his mother's money, her inheritance, and her property. He had his spies surround her in her own home and report on her every word and movement. By the beginning of 1931, Carol's domination over his mother was almost complete. Missy wrote to an American friend: "Never, even in wartime, have we lived in quite such an atmosphere. It makes us sad, anxious, depressed. It breaks our wings and weighs down our hearts. No one any more feels joyful or free, and each day hope becomes less. That your own nearest and dearest should have been able to bring this about seems incredible."

His love for his mother now having turned to hate, Carol's twisted soul reveled in this triumph of childish spite.

Ducky went to Romania to comfort her sister while Kirill toured Italy and then went on a Mediterranean cruise, visiting Lebanon, Palestine, Egypt, Yugoslavia, and Greece. In Romania the sisters retreated to the isolated beauty of Missy's home on the Black Sea, a romantic fantasy of Turkish architecture, cascading gardens, and hidden waterfalls she aptly named Tenya-Yuvah, the Solitary Nest. Here Ducky and Missy quietly passed the days and nights, sitting above the sea and strolling through the splendidly landscaped terraces, sharing memories of many years and escaping into their unshakable childhood love.

Returning to St. Briac, Ducky rejoined Kirill and resumed the placid routine of their pretend court. In May of 1932 Marie made them grandparents for a fourth time with the birth of her daughter Margarita. A break in St. Briac's bucolic routine came five months later, when Ducky went alone to a family wedding in Coburg. Princess Sibylle of Saxe-Coburg-Gotha, the daughter of Ducky's cousin Charlie, who had succeded her father to the dukedom, was marrying the strikingly handsome Prince Gustav Adolf, the son and heir of the crown prince of Sweden. The sumptuous ceremony was held at the church of St. Moritz, where Ducky had worshiped as a child. Witnessed by almost two hundred princely guests, it was one of the last great royal weddings in Europe before the Second World War.

In a rare moment of limelit triumph, when Ducky was to be presented, the *Oberhofmarschall,* or court chamberlain, announced in his loud, Prussian drill-sergeant voice: *"Die Kaiserin aller Russen, handküssen und rückwärts treten!"*—"The Empress of Russia, hand-kissing and step backwards!"

When the procession of royalty emerged from the church after the wedding ceremony, Ducky suddenly found her exalted rank being challenged by a cousin, the dethroned King Ferdinand of Bulgaria. His touchy dignity seriously threatened, the "gouty septuagenarian did not hesitate to wield his stick—something between a sceptre and a field-marshal's baton—to brush aside anyone who dared to try and take precedence over him, 'Die Kaiserin aller Russen' included." The other guests must have been amused by the sight of the equally unyielding Ducky glaring at Ferdinand with a look "expressing anger and dignified contempt at the same time."

Ducky brought back to St. Briac happy memories of her cousin's wedding and thoughts of her cozy childhood in Coburg, her first wedding there, almost forty years ago, and her years of exile there with her second husband, both before and after the war. Celebrating her fifty-sixth birthday that November probably made her feel even more nostalgic about her golden-tinged past, and an unusually harsh winter of heavy coastal snows no doubt turned her mind inward more than ever. So when spring finally arrived Ducky was probably in an exceptionally vulnerable state. But vulnerable or not during these first few months of 1933, she was certainly unprepared for the blow she now received.

It came in the form of a revelation, which sent a feverish Ducky to her sickbed. She sent urgently to Romania for Missy, but the dowager queen was touring Morocco as a guest of the French government. A wire eventually reached her there, and she rushed directly to St. Briac.

What exactly necessitated this "errand of mercy" will never be known. Ducky wouldn't confide even in Missy at first. Eventually, she did open up, but Missy gave her sacred promise that she would never divulge Ducky's secret to another soul. And Missy kept her word; no one else ever found out just what horrible thing had happened.

However, Missy's extensive correspondence with her numerous friends does provide some clues. The terrible revelation concerned Kirill; and until she died, Ducky refused to have any further physical contact with him. In June of that year Missy wrote a close friend, Lavinia Small, that Ducky had "had an overwhelming soulgrief which has shattered her conception of life and humanity." It has been assumed that this grief involved a love affair of Kirill's, but "it would seem that a case of simple infidelity, particularly on the part of a Russian Grand Duke, would not justify the violence" of Ducky's reaction. Perhaps more plausibly, there has been speculation that Kirill was involved in behavior or relationships far more sensational and unorthodox than a simple and casual affair with another woman.

Whatever the dark discovery was, Ducky was totally crushed by it. According to Missy, she began dying "by inches." After thirty years of sacrificing everything for her husband and worshiping and supporting him to the exclusion of all other concerns, she had been betrayed.

Those closest to Ducky thought she seemed to take "some sort of perverse pleasure in her misery." Alarmed at her descent into melancholia and self-pity, Missy stayed on at St. Briac for several weeks, trying to convince her younger sister to return with her to Tenya-Yuvah. Ducky finally agreed, and the two sisters shut themselves off from the rest of the world for more than a month.

Ducky's soul didn't heal as quickly as Missy had hoped, and her permanent state of "anger and sadness" greatly concerned her sister. When the Romanian dowager queen finally sent her sister home to France in July 1933 to face her contrite and imperfect husband, she was still worried enough to ask her good friends Waldorf and Nancy Astor "to keep an eye on her from England."

No one knows what happened when Ducky reappeared at Ker Argonid. Whatever arrangement she made with her husband, outwardly their life together continued as usual. Neither their children nor their close friends ever suspected that anything had changed between the two. It was a precise and artful charade, one that Kirill refused to put aside even on his deathbed; his final memoirs fail to mention the estrangement and, indeed, portray the marriage as perfectly harmonious, adoring, and blissful to the very end.

The dark secret of her sister's sorrow weighed heavily upon Missy. Her premonitions of disaster had, at last, come true. Now, she could only watch helplessly as Ducky's passion turned inward and slowly destroyed her. As Missy had often observed, Ducky was "the most unforgiving of us all."

CHAPTER FORTY-SIX

Among
the Ruins

*A*FTER RETURNING from her Romanian retreat in July of 1933, Ducky put on a brave face so that she could celebrate an important family event the following month. Her only son, Vladimir, the heir to the throne, had reached the age of sixteen. According to the fundamental laws of the Russian empire, he could now exercise all the prerogatives that belonged to him by virtue of his birth. To mark the occasion officially, Kirill issued a special "Imperial Manifesto" addressed to the Russian people, and sent a circular letter to all the royal houses of Europe informing them of the event.

On August 30 a large party was held at Ker Argonid to proclaim Vladimir's majority. His uncles Grand Dukes Andrei and Dimitri came from Paris with several representatives of monarchist organizations. As Vladimir took his sacred oath to uphold the Romanov throne, Ducky watched proudly, with tears in her eyes. There was no denying that her boy was now a man.

Perhaps the elaborate affair seemed little more than "a meaningless pantomime to contemporary observers," but it provided desperately needed symbolism and gave brightness to the family's drab lives. With her health beginning to deteriorate as she moved through late middle age, the uncrowned empress of Russia found less and less relief from her hollow and unhappy existence.

The following autumn Ducky and her family received an invitation from King George V and Queen Mary to attend the London wedding of their youngest son, the Duke of Kent, to Princess Marina of Greece. Because the beautiful Marina was the daughter of Kirill's sister, Helen, the marriage was particularly significant for the imperial Russian couple. And the invitation marked an end to the rather strained and touchy relations that the English royal house had had with the Romanovs since the revolution.

Delighted by the prospect of a grand and festive occasion in her homeland, Ducky immediately wrote to accept the invitation. But her letter, dated October 12, 1934, shows that her pleasure was dimmed by grief. For, just three days earlier, her nephew King Alexander of Yugoslavia had been assassinated in Marseilles. The popular Alexander had been married to Missy's docile daughter Mignon, and his violent death affected the entire family. Ducky wrote to Queen Mary: "It is a very long time since anything has given us so much pleasure as this delightful invitation of yours. . . . These last few days we have all been so dreadfully upset by the horrid death of Sandro of Serbia. The meeting of Missy and Mignon in Paris was heartrending. What a terribly hard task poor kind Mignon has ahead of her. It must have caused you all great sorrow and anxiety—pray God it will give rise to no more complications."

Although Ducky had been paying frequent visits to London, which she "thoroughly enjoyed," Kirill hadn't been in England since the beginning of the war twenty years ago. This would be the first official and public visit they made as personal guests of the English king and queen. Deciding to take the children with them, Ducky and Kirill sailed for England in the middle of November.

They first took up residence at Kew Green, then moved to Buckingham Palace. On the eve of the wedding there was a magnificent reception at the palace for the monarch's relatives and the members of the diplomatic corps. In a scene that might have been taken from Jacques Deval's comic play *Tovarich,* Kirill found himself seated near Ivan Maisky, the Soviet ambassador. Obviously, "no conversations passed between them."

It had been a long time since Ducky and Kirill had attended a court function on so vast a scale, and it made an overwhelming impression on them and the children. King George was as kindly and gentle as Ducky remembered him from the old Malta days, and she was pleased to see that her children also "conceived an immense liking" for him. In turn, the British monarch had "always had a soft spot" for Ducky since those carefree days when they madly raced their ponies with Missy across their paradisiacal Mediterranean island. Very likely feeling guilty at not having been able to do more to save Nicholas II and his family during the Russian Revolution, George seemed determined to shower Ducky and her family with every possible kindness. This "royal treatment" did wonders for Ducky's spirits. She came really alive for the first time in more than a year, and her obvious enjoyment of all that was happening almost distracted her from Kirill's betrayal. But that misery was always with her.

There were so many royal relatives present that the "abundance of kin" became a running joke. It was hard to remember names and titles, especially for Vladimir and Kira, and the many family dinners were so huge that they lacked any semblance of domestic intimacy. One such "private" supper party was attended by no fewer than seventy-four people.

While casually inspecting the vast collection of wedding presents on display at the reception, Kirill received a great shock: Turning at one of the tables, he found himself face to face with his childhood nurse, Miss Crofts. The old lady was as astonished as he was, and they spent a long time sitting and reminiscing about the distant past.

Ducky was happy to be back home in England. The resentment of her English relatives fostered by her frustrated mother and the Anglophobic German imperial family had now completely disappeared. Consumed by grief, Ducky had turned away from everything in her life except her innocent origins. These days, it meant far more to her to have been born a princess of Great Britain than to be the titular empress of Russia. She saw the country of her birth as a "bastion of stability" in a world where everything else had collapsed. If only because nothing else had lasted, Ducky was "proud to remember her English blood."

Besides recovering her heritage, she also took advantage of the royal wedding to reconcile with her sister-in-law, Princess Helen of Greece, the mother of the bride. Kirill and his sister had been alienated for the past few years, Helen finding his assumed role of emperor embarrassing and ridiculous. Now, because the bride had always been devoted to her aunt Ducky and uncle Kirill, all ill-feeling was put aside.

A sad note was Missy's absence. Helen spoke for Ducky as well as herself when she wrote the dowager queen of Romania from Buckingham Palace on the twenty-fifth of November: "If only you could have been here to share it all with us, what a joy it would have been. One longs for one's own generation in such moments, those with whom one has shared moments in the past and who remember and understand. For us it is like a dream finding ourselves in these surroundings again after all these last sad, drab years of exile—it is a mixed blessing of intense joy and sadness."

The wedding took place at Westminster Abbey on November 29. Kira was one of the bridesmaids, a distinction she shared with the duchess of York, England's future queen and now its popular queen mother. Vladimir was also given a special place of honor, serving as one of the groomsmen at the Greek Orthodox ceremony, which took place in the chapel at Buckingham Palace.

The day after the wedding Ducky and her family went to stay for a few days with their good friends Lord and Lady Howard de Walden. Ducky spent hours preparing herself for a party in their honor, putting on her finest evening clothes. When the party was in full swing she confidently came downstairs and began mixing with the guests. A little later she casually glanced down and was shocked to see that she was still wearing her bedroom slippers. Always a good sport, Ducky told this story on herself.

After a thoroughly enjoyable visit with the Waldens, the Russian imperial family moved on to Lord and Lady Astor's palatial estate, Cliveden, on the banks of the upper Thames. The Astors had been very close friends of Missy's for more than thirty years, and while Nancy Astor, a strident and flamboyant Conservative member of Parliament, sat down with Ducky to tea and gossip, quiet and kindly Waldorf Astor led Kirill and Vladimir on a personal tour of London, showing them the Tower, the British Museum, the Battersea Power Station, and the London Zoo. Afterward, Ducky and her family were honored at two luncheons, one at the Astors' London house and the other at the German embassy.

It may be recalled that Missy had asked the Astors to keep a close eye on her grieving sister. Although Ducky and her husband gave the impression that nothing was wrong with their marriage, those closest to them could plainly see that Ducky was extremely unhappy (although, as has been mentioned, she seemed almost to enjoy her martyrdom). Missy wrote Nancy Astor another emotional plea on December 13, while Ducky was at Cliveden:

> I am so glad you and Waldorf are looking after my poor sister. She needs helping and yet no one on earth is more difficult to help—all in her is overflowing bitterness and despair. . . . I bless you for every kindness towards her, I am glad you understand her mental distress and how she needs to be

helped in spite of herself—and he, poor ruin—it is all so sad and pa-
thetic—and yet she is a great human being for all her mistaken ideas. She
finds a sort of dreadful satisfaction in torment, she will not lift herself above
her own misery nor will she ever admit that anybody else's point of view is
right or even possible. She is the creature I love best in the world, I help her
all I can but there is no help if she will not help herself. A really good,
happy, comfortable, consoling time, could however do her good, because she
is so starved of all good things—her life is fearfully melancholy, isolated and
depressing, and as you can see he is poor company! The boy [Vladimir] is
delightful and Kira can be awfully nice, but because of their humiliating po-
sition, she is always on her defensive—God bless you for being kind and
helpful for these dear ones and I can never do enough for them, being so far.

Perhaps realizing that it would be her last chance to visit the pleasant-
est scenes of her English youth, Ducky accompanied Nancy and Waldorf
to Plymouth on December 14 and stayed for the weekend, sentimentally
exploring the places she and her sisters "had known so well nearly half a
century earlier." She was surprised to find that, while everywhere else in
Europe had changed almost beyond recognition, southern Devonshire
seemed frozen in time. Admiralty House, Cotehele House, Mount
Edgcumbe, the Devonport waterfront—all had hardly been altered since
the long-gone days when "the daughters of Devonport's Commander-
in-Chief had played, walked and swam there." Seeing these sights again
must have made Ducky wish more than ever that she could have escaped
into the past.

After her visit to Plymouth, Ducky spent another two days in London
and then went home with her family to St. Briac. Throughout the following somber winter she continued to act as if nothing were wrong,
but beneath her calm surface the storm was still raging. In fact, her misery threatened to consume her.

In the late spring of 1935 Ducky went to visit Missy at her daughter
Ileana's home near Vienna. After this reunion with her sister, Missy sadly
wrote Waldorf Astor in early June:

We were very happy together and we talked much, as much as we dared as
neither of us wanted to break down, and certain depths cannot be touched
without burning tears searing her already tired eyes.

Her misery, both physical, mental, and financial is so great that it has
sapped her will power, she confessed this. Her problems and difficulties are
occasionally so devastatingly crushing, and no one near to turn to, no one to

advise her, to stop in and help—to help her carry her burden, no one effi-
cient to discuss things, to move, to act, only she herself, always, and never any
recognition and never any joy, that finally that magnificent strong nature of
yore, is tamed, overcome, done with—This fills me with grief. She never
complains, it is only by short sentences torn from her soul, in spite of herself,
that I piece things together—She needs a change, but it is no good offering
her a change or a holiday unless one gets at her herself and arranges it for
her. She is neither financially nor mentally able to start, if you understand
my meaning. . . . She lives with such hopeless people, her husband being at
the head of the list, that she cannot move herself. Her strength has run out,
a sort of grey despair sets in, a feeling that only death could liberate her from
the intolerable, crushing, overwhelming burden.

As it is by what I give her that she lives, she has the feeling that she
won't ask more of me, even when all gives out. Now I have made her
swear, that if she feels at the end of her tether that she should send out a cry,
that she should simply telegraph "Try and come." . . . Through the hor-
ror of what happened to her in her married life, she has learnt to doubt of
all men; let us three at least teach her that this is wrong and let us try, by
continual effort, to show her that there are some who feel and mean what
they say.

Although Missy's impressions may have been colored by her legendary theatricality, there was no mistaking the tragedy that her sister's
life had become. And when Missy wrote that Ducky might be looking
toward death as a welcome liberation, she had no idea how very right
she was.

CHAPTER FORTY-SEVEN

Lilies at Amorbach

A SENSE OF DOOM swept Europe during the latter half of 1935. One political crisis followed another and the seemingly endless depression was in full swing. When Mussolini attacked Ethiopia, and Hitler began arming Germany and rattling his sword, it was clear to everyone that fascism was on the rise and that the continent was drifting toward another cataclysmic war.

Watching these developments from St. Briac, Ducky must have felt her sorrow to be perfectly justified. All during that summer and autumn she sank even deeper into depression, spending more and more time in her garden and avoiding her husband as much as she could. Seeing herself as most cruelly victimized, she fed on her husband's betrayal and ignored every occasion for happiness.

Although many tragedies had struck Ducky in the past, there was much in her present existence to provide her with hope and even joy. She had three fine children and four beautiful grandchildren. Certainly they could have comforted her suffering soul, had she let them. And while most mothers of her age had long since seen their offspring leave home, Ducky still had Kira and Vladimir to herself. Her adoring older sister was faithfully providing emotional and financial support, and she had a wide circle of devoted and sympathetic friends as well.

Somehow, none of these things mattered. Ducky stubbornly refused to count her blessings. Perhaps her nature made it impossible. Always having felt life more deeply and fully than most, she was now the victim of that same remarkable passion.

After Ducky's fifty-ninth birthday, Kirill took Vladimir to Paris, where he was to be coached for his final academic tests. When they arrived on December 8, Vladimir immediately fell seriously ill with whooping cough. His condition worsened, "causing great anxiety" for Kirill; on December 19 Ducky arrived from Brittany. She was not well herself; her son, rather than being encouraged by her presence, had "quite a shock to see how ill she looked."

Ducky was planning on leaving the next day for Germany to spend the Christmas holidays with Marie, who was about to give birth to her fifth child. She "felt very nervous" and hated the idea of leaving Vladimir while he was still so sick, but the doctors convinced her that he was rapidly improving and would do best to return to St. Briac. So Kirill took Vladimir home and Ducky went on alone to Germany.

Arriving at Würzburg, Ducky found Marie also confined to bed. Instead of attending to her own precarious health, Ducky insisted on tending her daughter; she contracted a chill and became even sicker than before. On January 2, Marie had her baby—a girl, whom they named Matilda—with no complications. Both Matilda's mother and grandmother then rested, and by mid-January they felt well enough to return to Schloss Amorbach.

At Amorbach a message was waiting that King George V was seriously ill at Sandringham. A few days later, on January 20, 1936, word came that the English monarch had quietly passed away in his sleep. Ducky took her cousin Georgie's death very hard. Illness and death seemed to be surrounding her and closing in. "I'm so sorry for the dear King," she sadly remarked to a friend. "You know, we have rights on the Russian throne and some on the English; how splendid it would be if our two Empires could be joined, we would dominate the world."

It seemed that dreams of past grandeur were all that Ducky had left. Her condition deteriorated again and she steadily got weaker. The doctors warned that her situation was serious, but, not wanting "to spoil the festive atmosphere," Ducky "summoned up all her will" and attended Matilda's christening at the local church. The effort severely taxed her strength and she became yet worse.

A day later she suffered a major stroke. One side of her body was paralyzed, and she could barely speak.

An immediate call went out to the family. Kira arrived at Amorbach on February 5 and found that her mother's condition was rapidly worsening. Back at St. Briac, Kirill and Vladimir were sent daily bulletins. For a brief while it seemed that Ducky might be improving, but on February 18 her husband and son received an urgent message informing them that she "had taken a distinct turn for the worse." The following day they left for Germany.

By the time her husband and son reached her bedside, Ducky was semiconscious and so weak that she could hardly move or speak. Occasionally she muttered a few barely understandable words. But she showed signs of recognizing the members of her family when they spoke to her. Vladimir later remembered: "The days that followed were one long nightmare for all of us. Mother was getting weaker and weaker, the doctors could do nothing, and we were expecting the end at any moment."

Ducky's sisters were sent for. Sandra was the first to arrive; then Baby Bee joined the sad gathering, and Missy's daugher Ileana came from Vienna. Missy herself was the last to arrive. Almost a prisoner in Bucharest, where she helplessly watched her son "dance his mad dance," Missy was lucky to get permission to come at all. As it was, she arrived just in time. She later wrote a friend, "When told by my sisters that I was there, she immediately connected the thought of me with flowers and murmured something about lilies. We both loved our gardens."

When Ducky was asked if she was pleased that Missy had come, Missy had the great consolation of hearing her struggle to say, "It makes all the difference."

Now there was nothing else to be done.

Missy sat up night and day holding her sister's hand and speaking tenderly to her of the past. Finally, in the evening of March 1, 1936, the doctors noticed a sudden and swift weakening of Ducky's pulse. Everyone gathered around her bed and began praying that she would not be further tormented by a lingering death.

The clock in the hall chimed midnight. Fifteen minutes later Ducky slowly breathed her last breath and died.

Russia's last empress had finally found peace.

Missy wrote an emotional letter to Nancy Astor two days later:

The whole thing was tragic beyond imagination, a tragic end to a tragic life. She carried tragedy within her—she had tragic eyes—always—even as a little girl— But we loved her enormously, there was something mighty about her—she was our Conscience.

But when he betrayed her, she did not know how to forgive, so she allowed him to murder her soul. From then onwards, her strength became her weakness, her undoing—she was too absolute, she could not overcome herself. And now she had to die, unforgiving! Her lips were sealed because of the stroke which had felled her to the ground—but although she knew we were there and the first day she found a murmur of recognition for each of us in turn, she shuddered away from his touch— Whilst we sat, in turns holding her hand, he stood like an outcast on the threshold of her door not daring to enter her room—

It took 11 long days before she was released. The last five she lay in a sort of coma—and suddenly it was all over, as she lay there grey, gaunt, the mask of grief . . . it was torture—but I am calm, I know it is better thus— she could not have lived as a cripple—But with their egoism, those she loved killed her. They left her too lonely and she cried continually for three long years and nothing brought her comfort nor resignation, except occasionally her garden or her painting. She would not let us help her. Her faith in humanity was dead.

I know how much both you and Waldorf tried to help her—she was deeply grateful, I know she was, only her dreadful habit of never answering made her case hopeless—In spite of our tremendous love for each other, because of her silence, I was never able to keep in touch with her, nor to really help her— There is an unbearable tragedy in it all.

To another friend, Missy wrote: "She died at midnight. The next morning I went to see her for a last time alone. We had wrapped her in a long soft white silk robe. We had few flowers at Amorbach, but I had some white lilies which I laid round her head and shoulders, and Sandra put a bunch of freesia in her hands. I had not many tears, but I talked to her. I told her how sad it was to see her go and how lonely it would be."

On March 5 Ducky's coffin was taken to Coburg and placed in the family vault of the dukes of Saxe-Coburg-Gotha. The funeral, a simple family affair, took place the next day during a winter storm of rain and snow. Although there were no official representatives from the royal houses of Europe, a great many of Ducky's relatives attended. Besides her three surviving sisters, there were Missy's daughters—Ileana, Archduchess Anton of Austria, and Elisabetha, now the queen of Greece— plus the present ducal family of Saxe-Coburg, ex-King Ferdinand of

Bulgaria, the grand duke of Mecklenburg, and Grand Dukes Andrei and Dmitri.

As the mourners followed the coffin through the streets of Coburg to the royal mausoleum, a large crowd of people lined the way, paying their last respects to the pretty young princess who had become an empress.

Ducky was laid alongside her mother and father and her brother Alfred.

It was the final curtain of a great tragedy.

Her old friend Meriel Buchanan would later conclude that the uncrowned empress Victoria Feodorovna had died "a bitter, disappointed woman, whose brilliant personality had been warped by failure and frustration." But that day Missy could think only of that "passionate, often misunderstood child" who had never learned to compromise. After everyone else had gone, Missy still remained at the graveside. It was hard for her to leave: Ducky had "always hated being alone."

CHAPTER FORTY-EIGHT

Sunset at St. Briac

A FTER DUCKY'S FUNERAL, Kirill and the children returned to
St. Briac. They found it "terrible to enter the house for the first
time," for Ker Argonid was a place "where her spirit seemed always to
be present."

His wife's sudden death came as a severe shock to Kirill. Perhaps because of a guilty conscience, he was never able to reconcile himself to
the fact that she was gone. He spent his days reading over her old letters
and looking at her photographs, and he spoke of her constantly, never of
anything else.

Time passed very slowly now for Emperor Kirill I of Russia. Vladimir
and Kira left home, he for London University and she for Germany,
there to be courted by the kaiser's grandson. Sitting by himself in his
study filled with memories, Kirill was "acutely lonely."

He was also very sick. Having developed arteriosclerosis, he was suffering serious problems with his circulation and eyesight. Soon he was
struck by a partial paralysis of his left leg and the fingers of his right
hand. Within a year of his wife's death, Kirill was beginning to die.

The one bright spot of his remaining years was Kira's marriage to
Prince Louis Ferdinand of Germany, the kaiser's grandson and eventual
heir. Kirill saw the match as the brilliant joining of two imperial dynasties, and his "joy knew no bounds."

At the beginning of April 1938, the Russian colony in Paris organized
a reception to honor Kira and celebrate her engagement. Kirill traveled

to the capital, but by the time he arrived he was too sick to attend and had to remain alone in his hotel room. Nevertheless, seeing his last chance for glory, he insisted on going to Potsdam the following month to attend the first magnificent wedding ceremony; he then went on to Doorn, the place of the kaiser's exile, for the second. The celebrations took a heavy toll on his health, and he returned to St. Briac in exceedingly poor condition.

That summer he lingered on at Ker Argonid, "a virtual skeleton with bedsores, surrounded by memories of his married life." Though he showed some enthusiasm for dictating his memoirs, it was obvious to his family that he had lost the will to live. In September, he developed gangrene and had to be moved to the American Hospital in Paris. Because he was terribly weak and the gangrene was extensive, surgery was impossible. The family was called to his bedside and, after a month of intense suffering, Kirill died. It was early afternoon on October 12, 1938. He was only sixty-two, but he had been a very old man. At Ducky's death two and a half years earlier, he had lost heart.

To most Russian exiles around the world, Kirill's death came as a "national sorrow." Requiem services were held everywhere, and a large memorial ceremony took place in Paris. The actual funeral, like Ducky's, was at Coburg; he was laid to rest in the family vault, next to her. So bitterly estranged in life, they were now united forever in death.

Missy had died three months earlier, in July 1938. Mercifully, she was spared seeing the Romanian monarchy under Hitler and then Stalin. She had developed a serious liver disease but, persecuted by her son until the very end, was prevented from getting the correct and necessary treatment. Only when it was too late was she allowed to seek the help of experts in Dresden; seeing that her condition was hopeless, they sent her back home to die. Lying semiconscious and in great pain in her private railway car, Missy lasted just long enough to pass quietly from life in her beloved adopted homeland.

Ernie, Grand Duke of Hesse and the Rhine, died peacefully in October 1937, surviving his volatile first wife by a year and a half. His demise was most fortunately timed, for it saved his gentle soul from the horrors of the Second World War and from a family tragedy to rival that of Ekaterinburg. For just a month after his death, the Curse of Hesse struck again.

Ernie's younger son, Louis, was about to be married in London, and the entire remaining Hesse family was flying from Frankfurt to England to attend the wedding. On board the chartered Junker plane were Ernie's widow, the patient Eleanore; their eldest son, George Donatus, the current grand duke; George's wife, Cecile of Greece, the sister of England's Prince Philip; and their two small sons. As the small plane flew over Ostend and toward the Channel, a thick fog blew in from the sea. The pilot decided it would be safer to circle back and land in the city until the weather cleared. Approaching the airport in the sudden fog, the plane dipped too low; a wing was torn off by the tall brick chimney of a nearby factory. The aircraft fell to earth in a ball of flame, killing everyone on board.

The wedding in London took place as planned, but in private. The devastated bride and groom were dressed in black.

Early death seemed to be a pattern in Ducky's family. Her eldest daughter, Marie, endured the misery of the Nazi regime, her husband, Prince Charles of Leiningen, being forced to join the German army. Charles served on the Russian front and was taken captive by the Soviets at the end of the war, dying a year later of starvation at the age of forty-eight. The widowed Marie, with little money, struggled to provide for her six children. After a very hard life, she died in October of 1951, only five years after her husband, of a heart attack. She was forty-four.

Kira fared far better. Prince Louis Ferdinand, became the heir to the German throne when his older brother, Wilhelm, died on a French battlefield in 1940. Hitler, jealous of the continuing popularity of the Hohenzollerns, prevented them from becoming war heroes by forcing them to retire from military service. So Louis Ferdinand was discharged in 1941, a few months after his grandfather the kaiser had died peacefully in exile. The prince then proceeded to work with the underground against the Nazi regime; he and his family were forced to stay on the move to avoid capture. Eventually, Kira and her husband settled in a comfortable home in a village near Bremen and raised a family of four sons and two daughters.

In 1951, upon the death of his father, Crown Prince Wilhelm, Louis Ferdinand became the head of the House of Hohenzollern and the titular emperor of Germany. Kira was now the empress, which would have greatly pleased her parents. A straightforward and high-spirited woman, she concentrated her attention on her home and had a happy life. But it, too, was short. Visiting her brother, Vladimir, at Ker Argonid in September 1967, she died in her sleep of a heart attack at the age of fifty-eight.

Vladimir inherited his father's claim to the Romanov throne. He attended the London School of Economics and for a brief spell in 1939 was employed as a mechanic in Peterborough. (Perhaps in playful homage, he used the name Mikhailov, the same one used by his ancestor Peter the Great when working incognito as a laborer in England's Deptford shipyard over two hundred years before.) And despite Ducky's careful precautions, Vladimir ended up becoming a perfect English gentleman both in dress and manner.

Returning to Ker Argonid, the heir to the Russian throne carried on the traditions of his inheritance and faithfully continued his father's work towards upholding his imperial claims and regaining the Romanov crown. But Vladimir avoided calling himself the emperor; instead, he used the rank of grand duke. Solitary in his remote stone house in St. Briac, the grand duke must have led a very lonely life, especially during the Second World War, when the Germans occupied Brittany and kept him a virtual prisoner in his home.

Though they kept him under house arrest, Nazis also courted Vladimir, perhaps remembering his parents' early enthusiasm for the movement. He remained thoroughly anti-Nazi—so, fearing he would fall into the hands of the Allies, the Germans forced him to move from St. Briac in 1944, allowing him to settle wherever he wished in the "Fatherland." Vladimir passed the rest of the war at Schloss Amorbach with his sister Marie.

With the defeat of Germany, Vladimir returned to St. Briac. In 1948, at the age of thirty, he married Princess Leonida of Bagration-Moukhransky. Three years his senior, Leonida was descended from the former royal family of Georgia, one of Russia's southernmost provinces, and by tradition traced her origins back to the biblical King David. She was the widow of Sumner Moore Kirby, a Jewish American killed by the Nazis. In 1953 Vladimir and Leonida had their only child, Grand Duchess Maria. The family established its main residence in Madrid, but continued to spend summers at Ker Argonid.

A quietly conscientious and intelligent man, Vladimir took a realistic view of monarchical restoration. He especially disliked the words "pretender" and "restoration," being critical of their imaginative and retrogressive associations. In the late 1970s, Vladimir modestly admitted that "the only way of justifying our existence lies in being ready to serve our country and to do our duty if one day called upon to do so. . . . While in my opinion all non-reigning European monarchs have equally remote chances, it must be said that monarchy is holding its own in Europe. It is a most convenient form of government, infinitely adaptable. It can accommodate every system, from complete dictatorial absolutism to complete democracy."

For the first seventy-four years of his life, Grand Duke Vladimir never set foot in Russia. Conceived in St. Petersburg, he was born in exile and never really expected to see his homeland. Then, after the sudden changes in Soviet politics, the impossible became possible; he visited the Soviet Union in November of 1991. Ironically, he had been officially invited to St. Petersburg to mark the seventy-fourth anniversary of the Bolshevik revolution.

The visit created a sensation in monarchist circles, where it was anticipated that Vladimir would now play a significant role in Russian politics. But tragically, just as he was becoming thoroughly involved with his homeland for the first time in his life, he dropped dead of a heart attack at a news conference in Miami on April 21, 1992.

To the world's amazement, Vladimir was given a magnificent funeral at Petersburg's St. Isaac's Cathedral and was buried next to his imperial ancestors in the Peter and Paul Fortress.

The throne now passed to his only child, the thirty-nine-year-old grand duchess Maria. A vibrant and exotically beautiful woman of exceptional intelligence, Maria was educated in England at Oxford University and worked for a while at the noted couture house of Grès in Paris. In 1976 she married Prince Franz Wilhelm of Prussia, a great-grandson of the kaiser. As heiress to the throne, she retained her title and her husband officially became her consort, receiving Russian grand ducal rank and taking the name Michael. Their child, Grand Duke George, was born in 1981. Unhappily, the marriage was eventually dissolved.

Today Maria lives with her mother and son in an elegant top-floor apartment in Paris, a block from the Place de la Concorde. Occupying herself with the uncertain future of the country of her ancestors, this dynamic and conscientious woman who would be empress of Russia divides her time between her villa in Madrid and the family home in St. Briac.

If the history of the last century has taught us a lesson, it is that no one can predict the destiny of the Russian nation. While Kirill and Ducky endured the scorn of their contemporaries during their phantom reign, they very effectively maintained a tradition of duty and leadership and successfully maintained the Romanov heritage. Today, as the citizens of Russia long nostalgically for the security of their imperial past, few laugh at Grand Duchess Maria's cause.

Far from the busy salon in Paris, the weather-worn walls of Ker Argonid in the holiday village of St. Briac shelter a somber-looking house that now stands empty for most of the year. At the back of that lonely house is a large garden that has gone to seed, untended for years, overgrown with vines and weeds. The garden is now a sad and haunted place. But on certain afternoons at sunset the mist drifts in from the sea, and then, suddenly, as if by magic, the garden again becomes a wonderland of beauty and color—the special realm of a passionate young princess who became an empress.

Notes

PAGE

Monday, June 4, 1917

xiii "it was not a natural": Kirill of Russia, *My Life in Russia's Service,* p. 213.

xv "arrogant and false . . .": St. Aubyn, *Edward VII,* pp. 290–93.

ONE: *The Golden Crust*

3 "from duty": Tuchman, *The Proud Tower,* p. 3.

5 "How stifling": Massie, *Nicholas and Alexandra,* p. 21.

5 "I never": Longford, *Queen Victoria,* p. 116.

5 "They will": St. Aubyn, *Edward VII,* p. 293.

6 "half-Oriental": ibid., p. 290.

6 "The murder": Van der Kiste, *Princess Victoria Melita,* p. 9.

TWO: *A Daughter of Two Empires*

8 "the world's": Longford, *Queen Victoria,* p. 404.

9 "by education": Massie, *Nicholas and Alexandra,* pp. 230–31.

9 "traveled in private": ibid., p. 231.

9 "as guests": ibid.

10 "Ladies and gentlemen": ibid., p. 229.

10 "melancholy": Custine, *Empire of the Czar,* p. 474.

11 "he has": ibid., p. 137.

11 "attentions and": Queen Victoria, *Letters,* vol. 2, pp. 12–16.

12 "studied long": Elsberry, *Marie of Roumania,* p. 5.

PAGE

13   "something of": ibid.

13   "she loved": Marie, Queen of Roumania, *The Story of My Life*, vol.
         1, p. 3.

13   "Dear Marie": Elsberry, op. cit., p. 6.

15   "Elephant and": Kroll and Lindsey, *Europe's Royal Families*, p. 41.

16   "the harmony": ibid., p. 43.

16   "he has": Bennett, *King Without a Crown*, p. 17.

17   "a caricature": Kroll and Lindsey, p. 43.

18   "a very": Royal Windsor Archives, M 13/79, Lady Lyttelton to
         Queen Victoria, December 11, 1845.

18   "one is": Woodham-Smith, *Queen Victoria*, p. 231.

18   "uncommon abilities": Royal Windsor Archives, M 13/95, Lady
         Lyttelton to Queen Victoria, March 7, 1849.

19   "if we": Bolitho, *The Prince Consort and His Brother*, p. 170.

20   "she had": St. Aubyn, *Edward VII*, p. 74.

20   "heartless and . . .": Van der Kiste, *Princess Victoria Melita*, p. 4.

20   "heavy blow": Fulford, *Dearest Mama*, p. 107.

21   "He is": ibid., p. 213.

21   "it would": St. Aubyn, op. cit., p. 75.

21   "possibly the": Pakula, *The Last Romantic*, p. 24.

21   "very plain": Fulford, *Dearest Mama*, pp. 177–78.

21   "so odd . . . ladylike": Fulford, *Dearest Child*, pp. 311, 290, 224.

22   "much . . . Affie": Pakula, *The Last Romantic*, p. 25.

23   "that the": Fulford, *Your Dear Letter*, p. 120.

23   "with reluctance": Van der Kiste, *Princess Victoria Melita*, p. 4.

23   "ovations as": Fulford, *Your Dear Letter*, p. 200.

23   "If he": ibid., p. 147.

23   "amounted to": Van der Kiste, *Princess Victoria Melita*, p. 8.

24   "a pampered": Vorres, *The Last Grand Duchess*, p. 54.

24   "is still . . . them": Corti, *The Downfall of Three Dynasties*, p. 212.

24   "half-Oriental . . . false": St. Aubyn, *Edward VII*, p. 290.

24   "bourgeoisie": Vorres, *The Last Grand Duchess*, p. 54.

24   "absolute autocracy": Van der Kiste, *Princess Victoria Melita*, p. 8.

24   "would be . . . Stuarts.": St. Aubyn, *Edward VII*, p. 290.

25   "a dispensation": Pakula, *The Last Romantic*, p. 29.

       THREE: *A Royal War at Windsor*

26   "permanent scowl": Pakula, *The Last Romantic*, p. 29.

27   "has always . . .": Dean of Windsor and Bolitho, *Latter Letters of
         Lady Augusta Stanley*, p. 229.

PAGE

27   "silly old fool": Corti, *Downfall of Three Dynasties,* p. 214.

27   "the Doyenne . . . Russians": Longford, p. 395.

27   "I have . . . better": St. Aubyn, *Edward VII,* p. 291.

28   "most pleasing": Fulford, *Dearest Child,* p. 132.

28   "not a bit . . .": Van der Kiste, *Princess Victoria Melita,* p. 10.

28   "an abominable": Morris and Halstead, *The Life and Reign of Queen Victoria,* p. 268.

28   "ungracious, reserved": St. Aubyn, op. cit., p. 291.

28   "treasure": Elsberry, *Marie of Roumania,* p. 8.

28   "thoroughly English": Pakula, *The Last Romantic,* p. 33.

29   "good and": Elsberry, op. cit., p. 8.

29   "London hideous": Corti, op. cit., p. 216.

30   "Like an": Elsberry, op. cit., p. 8.

30   "shrugging her": Meriel Buchanan, *Queen Victoria's Relations,* p. 115.

30   "in no . . . impatient.": Van der Kiste, *Princess Victoria Melita,* p. 12.

31   "rare intelligence": Cornwallis-West, *The Recollections of Lady Randolph Churchill,* p. 238.

31   "Who comes": Van der Kiste, *Princess Victoria Melita,* p. 10.

32   "any reason": Buckle, *The Letters of Queen Victoria,* vol 2., p. 338.

32   "The insulting": Corti, op. cit., p. 244.

33   "avoided discusing": Morris and Halstead, op. cit., p. 267.

33   "You only": Corti, op. cit., p. 243

33   "the sole": Morris and Halstead, op. cit., p. 267.

33   "no-one likes": St. Aubyn, op. cit., p. 291.

33   "Rude, touchy": ibid.

33   "I am grieved": ibid., pp. 291–92.

33   "driven into": Pakula, op. cit., p. 33.

34   "legitimate . . . degrading": Windsor Royal Archives, RA V, 1787/1895, Duchess of Coburg to Crown Princess Marie of Roumania, December 10, 1895.

34   "said she": Queen Marie, *Story of My Life,* vol 1, p. 3.

34   "She made": ibid., p. 15.

34   "dissatisfied": ibid.

34   "oppressive influence . . . her": ibid.

34   "My mother": ibid.

35   "rare . . . children.": ibid., p. 11.

35   "exceedingly good-looking . . . stranger": ibid., p. 4.

35   "entirely in": Pakula, op. cit., p. 32.

35   "red-lettered": Queen Marie, *Story of My Life,* vol. 1, p. 4.

PAGE

35   "discover us": ibid., p. 11.

35   "easy being": ibid., p. 14.

FOUR: *The Passionate Princess*

37   "difficult child": Queen Marie, *Story of My Life,* vol. 1, p. 5.

37   "passionate child": ibid.

37   "I took things": ibid.

37   "true daughter": ibid., p. 60.

37   "Ducky usually": ibid., p. 64.

37   "There was": ibid.

38   "whatever hurts": interview with Mother Alexandra, the former Princess Ileana of Romania, at Ellwood City, Pa., July 1982.

38   "Ducky and": Queen Marie, *Story of My Life*, vol. 1, p. 5.

38   "Mamma loved": ibid., p. 4.

38   "comrade nor": ibid.

38   "power over": ibid., p. 5.

39   "There is": Pakula, *The Last Romantic,* p. 42.

39   "amounted to": Queen Marie, *Story of My Life*, vol. 1, p. 43.

39   "Try as": ibid.

39   "But if . . . there": Elsberry, *Marie of Roumania,* p. 9.

40   "Children, don't": Pakula, op. cit., p. 42.

40   "A headache": ibid.

40   "People who": interview with Mother Alexandra.

40   "We were": Elsberry, op. cit., p. 9.

41   "All of ": ibid.

41   "born leaders . . . disappointed.": Bolitho, *A Biographer's Notebook,* p. 44.

41   "We were": ibid.

41   "funny-shaped . . . alike": Pakula, *The Last Romantic,* p. 42.

41   "she ruled": Queen Marie, *Story of My Life*, vol. 1, p. 55.

42   "a warning": ibid., p. 56.

42   "groomed and . . . misunderstood": ibid., p. 5.

42   "curious sensation": ibid., p. 21.

42   "a sort": ibid.

42   "felt the": ibid.

42   "the indescribable": ibid., p. 22.

FIVE: *Wonderful Eastwell*

44   "not grand": Queen Marie, *Story of My Life,* vol 1, p. 3.

44   "no place": ibid., p. 9.

44   "very terrifying": ibid.

PAGE

44   "to descend": ibid., p. 10.

45   "extraordinary": ibid., p. 9.

45   "fearful creature": ibid.

45   "a wonderful": ibid., p. 8.

45   "the stirring": Elsberry, *Marie of Roumania*, p. 11.

45   "delicious fragrance": Queen Marie, *Story of My Life*, vol. 1, p. 13.

46   "naughty farce": ibid., p. 44.

46   "a bit": ibid.

47   "enchanting vision . . . away": Pakula, *The Last Romantic*, p. 43.

47   "magnificent creature": ibid.

47   "speechless adoration": Queen Marie, *Story of My Life*, vol. 1, p. 6.

47   "simply looked": Pakula, p. 43.

47   "supremely delicious": Queen Marie, *Story of My Life*, vol. 1, p. 35.

47   "Somehow Aunt . . . teeth": ibid.

47   "like a . . . side.": ibid., p. 18.

48   "with the": Van der Kiste, *Princess Victoria Melita*, p. 18.

48   "her shy": Queen Marie, *Story of My Life*, vol. 1, p. 18.

48   "shocked and": ibid.

48   "secretly relieved": ibid.

48   "Grandpapa in": ibid., p. 19.

49   "mysterious photographs": ibid.

49   "an aunt": ibid., p. 20.

49   "all smiles": ibid., p. 21.

49   "through the": ibid.

49   "considered healthy": ibid., p. 31.

49   "it was": Queen Marie, *Story of My Life*, vol 1, p. 28.

49   "stocking-knitting": ibid., p. 31.

49   "We children hated": Elsberry, *Marie of Roumania*, p. 9.

50   "would chuck": ibid., p. 39.

51   "that wonderful": Van der Kiste, *Princess Victoria Melita*, p. 18.

51   "somewhat haphazard": Queen Marie, *Story of My Life*, vol. 1, p. 48.

51   "up and": ibid., p. 45.

52   "inconsolable for . . . loss": ibid.

SIX: *London "Smuts" and Russian Delights*

53   "meant great . . . greasiness": Queen Marie, *Story of My Life*, vol. 1,
           p. 49.

53   "was the . . . bushes.": ibid.

54   "it was . . . room": ibid., p. 51.

54   "a huge": ibid., p. 53.

54   "curios Papa . . . grey": ibid.

PAGE

54   "those 'objets'": Pakula, *The Last Romantic,* p. 40.

55   "fearfully correct . . . bliss": Queen Marie, *Story of My Life*, vol. 1,
        p. 61.

55   "made us": ibid., p. 62.

55   "a certain": ibid., p. 64.

56   "exquisitely soft": ibid., p. 65.

56   "although she": ibid., p. 66.

56   "beloved, big-hearted": ibid.

56   "need not . . . thing.": ibid.

57   "heady incense . . . Holies": Pakula, op. cit., p. 41.

57   "with grey": Van der Kiste, *Princess Victoria Melita,* p. 19.

57   "a pale": Pakula, op. cit., p. 45.

58   "an overwhelming": Queen Marie, *Story of My Life*, vol. 1, p. 80.

58   "sheet of": Massie, *Nicholas and Alexandra,* p. 16

58   "uniquely picturesque . . . gorgeousness": Queen Marie, *Story of
        My Life*, vol. 1, p. 87.

58   "over-life-sized halls . . . ice": ibid., p. 78.

58   "wild-looking . . . real": ibid.

59   "wonderful and": ibid., p. 79.

59   "never looked": ibid., p. 83.

59   "loved you . . . hands": ibid., p. 79.

59   "a game": Pakula, op. cit., p. 44.

60   "deliciously amiable": Queen Marie, *Story of My Life*, vol 1, pp.
        83–84.

60   "gentle charm": ibid., p. 84.

60   "The most": ibid.

61   "superb specimen": ibid.

61   "His was": Alexander, *Once a Grand Duke,* p. 139.

61   "as tall": Queen Marie, *Story of My Life*, vol. 1, p. 85.

61   "by far": ibid.

61   "unhealthy curiosity": Alexander, op. cit., p. 140.

62   "her purity": Queen Marie, *Story of My Life*, vol. 1, p. 87.

62   "almost menacing": ibid., p. 86.

SEVEN: *Return to Paradise*

64   "as if": Queen Marie, *Story of My Life,* vol. 1, p. 97.

64   "Papa at": ibid.

64   "with spacious": ibid., p. 100.

64   "everything grew": ibid., p. 98.

65   "its perfect": ibid.

65   "glorious and": Elsberry, *Marie of Roumania,* p. 16.

PAGE

65 “Mamma knew”: Queen Marie, *Story of My Life*, vol. 1, p. 101.

65 “insane passion”: Elsberry, op. cit., p. 16.

65 “legs of”: ibid., p. 103.

65 “Our ideas . . . ground”: Van der Kiste, *Princess Victoria Melita*, p. 22.

66 “who could . . . turn”: Queen Marie, *Story of My Life*, vol. 1, p. 103.

66 “little savages”: Elsberry, op. cit., p. 16.

66 “that strange”: ibid.

66 “an ocean”: Queen Marie, *Story of My Life*, vol. 1, p. 130.

66 “No tree”: ibid., p. 108.

66 “like a troop”: ibid., p. 109.

67 “blessed days”: ibid., p. 109.

67 “in floods . . . bones”: ibid., pp. 128–29.

68 “*My dear*”: Windsor Royal Archives, RA Z82/73.

69 “nearly as”: Buckle, *Letters of Queen Victoria,* vol. 1, p. 498.

70 “somewhat farouche”: Hough, *Advice to My Granddaughter,* p. 36.

70 “We did”: Queen Marie, *Story of My Life*, vol. 1, p. 112.

70 “a delicious”: ibid., p. 111.

70 “would have”: ibid., p. 112.

71 “not a bit”: ibid., p. 127.

71 “kind, honest”: Nicolson, *King George V: His Life and Reign,* p. 37.

71 “like a”: Windsor Royal Archives, RA V 1005/1920, King George to Queen Marie, December 12, 1920.

71 “just between”: Queen Marie, *Story of My Life*, vol. 1, pp. 135–36.

72 “paradise one”: ibid., p. 136.

EIGHT: *A Kingdom All Their Own*

73 “unbearable sadness”: Queen Marie, *Story of My Life,* vol. 1, p. 137.

73 “beloved haunts”: ibid.

73 “hearts were . . . note.”: ibid., pp. 137–38.

74 “Good bye, little”: ibid., p. 139.

74 “entirely according”: ibid., p. 144.

74 “social climate . . . loyal”: Pakula, *The Last Romantic,* p. 47.

75 “sole arbiter . . . wished.”: Queen Marie, vol. 1, p. 144.

75 “omnipotent”: ibid.

76 “a collection”: Elsberry, *Marie of Roumania,* p. 22.

76 “ogre in”: Queen Marie, *Story of My Life*, vol. 1, p. 153.

76 “fearful excitement”: ibid., p. 154.

76 “the jaw”: Pakula, op. cit., p. 49.

76 “dear, sweet”: Queen Marie, *Story of My Life*, vol. 1, p. 154.

76 “drooping, sad-looking”: Pakula, op. cit., p. 49.

76 “der liebe”: ibid.

PAGE

76   "treated her": Queen Marie, *Story of My Life*, vol. 1, p. 156.

76   "it was": Pakula, op. cit., p. 50.

77   "that clown": Corti, *The Downfall of Three Dynasties*, p. 145.

77   "simple and easy . . . charm": Queen Marie, *Story of My Life*, vol. 1,
        p. 147.

77   "the real love": ibid.

77   "the same startling": Bennett, *King Without a Crown*, p. xiii.

78   "If I were": Longford, *Queen Victoria*, p. 178.

79   "high, shadow-filled": Queen Marie, *Story of My Life*, vol. 1, p. 148.

79   "self-righteous little": Pakula, op. cit., p. 49.

79   "*Christenvervolgung*": Elsberry, op. cit., p. 22.

      NINE: *Rebellion at Coburg*

80   "wormed themselves": Queen Marie, *Story of My Life,* vol. 1,
        p. 144.

80   "word became law": ibid.

80   "was to uproot": ibid.

81   "we resisted this": ibid, pp. 144–45.

81   "steel-like rectitude": Van der Kiste, *Princess Victoria Melita*, p. 30.

81   "German 'Kultur' ": Queen Marie, *Story of My Life*, vol. 1, p. 144.

81   "eager, blundering": Pakula, *The Last Romantic,* p. 48.

81   "a heart of gold": Queen Marie, *Story of My Life*, vol. 1, p. 183.

81   "liked to ridicule": ibid., p. 145.

81   "all the feelings . . . him": ibid.

81   "honeyed language": ibid.

81   "how perfectly . . . ways": Pakula, op. cit., p. 48.

82   "she had wormed": Queen Marie, *Story of My Life*, vol. 1, p. 146.

82   "organically treacherous": Ibid.

82   "silk underwear": Pakula, *The Last Romantic,* p. 48.

82   "humiliatingly ugly": Queen Marie, *Story of My Life*, vol. 1, p. 166.

82   "acute torture": ibid.

83   "to ask questions": Elsberry, *Marie of Roumania*, p. 21.

83   "encouraged and stimulated": Van der Kiste, *Princess Victoria Melita*,
        p. 29.

83   "Her eye was": Queen Marie, *Story of My Life*, vol. 1, pp. 150–51.

83   "deliciously amusing . . . world.": ibid., p. 151.

83   "she treated . . . Nature": ibid.

83   "autocratic, conservative . . . rebuke": ibid., p. 152.

84   "cut off her . . . understand.": ibid., pp. 152–53.

84   "always had herself . . . life.": ibid., pp. 178–79.

PAGE

85   "sick": ibid., p. 175.

85   "an irrepressible eccentric": Van der Kiste, *Princess Victoria Melita*, p.
        30.

85   "roomy, worm-eaten": ibid.

85   "a somewhat": Queen Marie, *Story of My Life*, vol. 1, p. 181.

85   "bosom friends": ibid.

86   "the authorities": ibid.

86   "imbibe": ibid., p. 158.

86   "the better pupil": Van der Kiste, *Princess Victoria Melita*, p. 27.

86   "less ready": ibid.

86   "Ducky seldom": Queen Marie, *Story of My Life*, vol. 1, p. 159.

86   "complicated theological . . . thrill": ibid., p. 163.

86   "mooning": ibid., p. 167.

87   "in that . . . pot": ibid., pp. 167–68.

87   "an event . . . was over": ibid., p. 168.

TEN: *Missy's Farewell*

89   "Princesses must . . . matters": Queen Marie, *Story of My Life,* vol.
        1, p. 188.

90   "It is a pity . . . church": Pope-Hennessy, *Queen Mary,* p. 240.

90   "like most things": Pakula, *The Last Romantic*, p. 53.

91   "Papa dreaded": Queen Marie, *Story of My Life*, vol. 1, p. 192.

91   "Sister Ducky": Van der Kiste, *Princess Victoria Melita,* p. 30.

92   "sweet young . . . thunderbolt": Queen Marie, *Story of My Life,*
        vol. 1, p. 196.

92   "side by side": ibid. p. 196.

92   "slashed . . . bride": ibid., p. 197.

93   "stared at . . . too much": ibid., p. 199.

93   "Don't you know": Elsberry, *Marie of Roumania,* p. 24.

93   "blending of": Queen Marie, *Story of My Life*, vol. 1, p. 200.

93   "We too . . . persuasion": ibid.

94   "no matter": ibid., p. 201.

94   "an extraordinary . . . possessed": ibid., p. 202.

95   "could make ourselves": ibid.

95   "put your back up": ibid., p. 203.

95   "brave and impersonal": ibid., p. 204.

95   "moved with": Pakula, op. cit., p. 56.

96   "one of the": Queen Marie, op. cit., p. 207.

96   "There was love": ibid., p. 58.

96   "that she": ibid., p. 57.

PAGE

96   "Missy herself": Pope-Hennessy, op. cit., p. 241.

97   "a great victim": Romanian Archives, RA V 1740/1893, Duchess
        of Coburg to Crown Princess Marie of Romania, June 28.

97   "with something": Queen Marie, *Story of My Life*, vol. 1, p. 210.

97   "And above all": ibid.

97   "half of me": ibid., p. 224.

98   "To be entirely happy": ibid., p. 241.

98   *"My dear Grand Mama"*: Windsor Royal Archives, RA Z84/108,
        Victoria Melita to Queen Victoria, November 26, 1892.

98   "A risqué book": Queen Marie, *Story of My Life*, vol. 1, p. 243.

99   "inseparable companion . . . grief": ibid., p. 269.

ELEVEN: *The Poet Prince*

100   "princesses should": Van der Kiste, *Princess Victoria Melita,* p. 32.

101   "very handsome . . . day": Hough, *Advice to My Granddaughter,* p.
        107.

101   "seemed to rush": Van der Kiste, *Princess Victoria Melita,* p. 34.

101   "Victoria and Ernie": Hough, op. cit., p. 113.

102   "rugged mountains": Hatch, *The Mountbattens*, p. 8.

102   "I shall not": Benson, *Queen Victoria's Daughters,* p. 56.

103   "good, amiable . . . high spirits": ibid., p. 62.

103   "Beauty I don't": Longford, *Queen Victoria,* p. 285.

103   "too sentimental": ibid.

104   "He wears a": Hough, op. cit., pp. 17–18.

105   "in a sun-filled": Massie, *Nicholas and Alexandra,* p. 28.

106   "the prettiest": Hough, op. cit., p. 36.

106   "I trust": ibid.

107   "I don't like . . . my hand": Alice, Grand Duchess of Hesse and the
        Rhine, *Biographical Sketch and Letters,* pp. 327, 342.

108   "swept through": Hough, op. cit., p. 46.

108   "draughty chill": ibid., p. 47.

108   "Poor dear Ernie": ibid., p. 32.

109   "I must say": ibid., p. 33.

109   "Dear Ernie": ibid., p. 105.

TWELVE: *The Queen Commands*

111   "no Guard of Honour": Duff, *Hessian Tapestry,* p. 226.

112   "an eternal": ibid., p. 227.

112   "Spoilt and pampered": Hough, *The Mountbattens,* p. 155.

112   "the old ones": Duff, op. cit., p. 227.

112   "a wish that": ibid., p. 232.

PAGE

113   "When Dr. Jenner": Hough, *Advice to My Granddaughter,* pp. 116–17.

113   "hint . . . wishes": Hough, *The Mountbattens,* p. 156.

113   "beloved chum": Van der Kiste, *Princess Victoria Melita,* p. 37.

113   "to help her": ibid.

114   "Uneasy about": Hough, *The Mountbattens,* p. 156.

114   "one particularly": Van der Kiste, *Princess Victoria Melita,* p. 37.

114   "preferred male company": ibid.

114   *"I still worry"*: Hough, *The Mountbattens,* p. 156.

115   "the same blood": Duff, op. cit., p. 233.

115   "a tall, dark . . . Darmstadt": ibid.

115   "spritely, mercurial": Hough, *The Mountbattens,* p. 156.

115   *"Please forgive me"*: Windsor Royal Archives, RA Z90/44.

117   "Aunt Marie will": Duff, op. cit., p. 232.

117   "I have had it out": Hough, *Advice to My Granddaughter,* pp. 120–21.

117   "I have not": Windsor Royal Archives, RA Z90/55.

118   "will no longer": Hough, *Advice to My Granddaughter,* p. 120.

118   *"I have just"*: Windsor Royal Archives, RA Z90/64.

118   "in all Royal": Queen Marie, *Story of My Life,* vol. 1, p. 201.

119   "In a way": ibid., pp. 68–69.

119   "so shut away . . . fetish-like": ibid., p. 69.

119   "Your and my": Buckle, *The Letters of Queen Victoria,* vol. 2, p. 372.

THIRTEEN: *The Wedding of the Century*

123   "my interest in . . . wisely": Hough, *Advice to My Granddaughter,* p.
       120.

124   *"My dearest Grandmama"*: Windsor Royal Archives, RA Z90/69.

125   "is a charming . . . nicer": Lee, *Empress Frederick Writes to Sophie,* p.
       159.

125   "the English family . . . adore her": Romanian Archives, RA V
       1764/1894, Duchess of Coburg to Crown Princess Marie of
       Romania, March 8 and March 20, 1894.

125   "still catch my": Queen Marie, *Story of My Life,* vol. 1, p. 311.

126   "a pleasant": ibid., pp. 325–26.

126   *"The wedding at Coburg"*: The *[London] Times,* April 19, 1894.

127   "heart . . . full": Duff, *Hessian Tapestry,* p. 234.

127   "she was received": *Annual Register—1894,* p. 23.

127   "I am not": Longford, *Queen Victoria,* p. 532.

128   "I never saw": Pakula, *The Last Romantic,* p. 100.

128   "hung from pillar": Van der Kiste, *Princess Victoria Melita,* p. 43.

129   "Ducky looked": Lee, p. 170.

129   "the venerable": The *[London] Times,* April 20, 1894.

PAGE

129   "During the service": Lee, op. cit., p. 170.

129   "but I like": Longford, op. cit., p. 532.

130   "decorated liberally": Van der Kiste, p. 44.

FOURTEEN: *Stolen Thunder, Vanquished Dreams*

131   "Alicky and Nicky": Duff, *Hessian Tapestry,* p. 234.

131   "had been thoroughly": Massie, *Nicholas and Alexandra,* p. 33.

131   "took everything": ibid., p. 31.

131   "a direct affront": ibid.

132   "She says": Longford, *Queen Victoria,* p. 512.

132   "this must *not*": Hough, *Advice to My Granddaughter,* p. 110.

133   "Only with great": Van der Kiste, *Princess Victoria Melita,* p. 46.

133   "caused a stormy": ibid.

133   "his marriage was": ibid.

134   "She cried": Massie, op. cit., p. 32.

134   "not really so": ibid., p. 33.

134   "At that moment": ibid., p. 33.

134   "the whole family": ibid.

134   "Alix is very": Radziwill, *The Intimate Life of the Last Tsarina,* pp.
       18–19.

135   "filled with happy": Van der Kiste, *Princess Victoria Melita,* p. 45.

136   "sexually incompatible": interview with Mother Alexandra.

136   "an adequate husband": Hough, *The Mountbattens,* p. 156.

136   "was not attracted": Van der Kiste, *Princess Victoria Melita,* p. 37.

136   "completely shattered": interview with Mother Alexandra.

136   "things pertaining to": Queen Marie, *Story of My Life,* vol. 1, p. 178.

136   "Crushingly disappointed": interview with Mother Alexandra.

137   "already there are": Hough, op. cit., p. 157.

137   "merry and colorful": ibid.

FIFTEEN: *God's Gracious Gift*

138   "a certain regal": Buchanan, *Queen Victoria's Relations,* p. 193.

138   "every inch": Pakula, *The Last Romantic,* p. 104.

138   "more like": Van der Kiste, *Princess Victoria Melita,* p. 48.

139   "my duty to": Massie, *Nicholas and Alexandra,* p. 39.

140   "show your own": ibid., p. 41.

140   "Sandro, what am": Alexander, p. 169.

140   "Never did I": Massie, op. cit., p. 45.

141   "Down there in": Queen Marie, *Story of My Life,* vol. 1, p. 327.

141   "everything I did": ibid., pp. 327–28.

PAGE

142   "with a pang": ibid., p. 326.

142   "lovely, but very": Lee, *Empress Frederick Writes to Sophie,* p. 180.

143   "she made happy": Ernst Ludwig, *Erinnertes,* p. 56.

SIXTEEN: *Babylon on the Rhine*

144   "brutally struck": interview with Mother Alexandra.

145   "the sun-warmed woods": ibid.

145   "it was pure": ibid.

145   "exquisite delight": ibid.

145   "alongside the": Van der Kiste, *Princess Victoria Melita,* p. 53.

145   "was full of": Queen Marie, *Story of My Life,* vol. 1, p. 449.

146   "almost too good": ibid., p. 450.

146   "old and out": Duff, *Hessian Tapestry,* p. 257.

146   "sipping tea": ibid.

147   "hated frauds": Queen Marie, *Story of My Life,* vol. 1, p. 64.

148   "much to the": ibid., p. 49.

148   "schoolchildren": Van der Kiste, *Princess Victoria Melita,* p. 49.

148   "the jolliest": Nicholas, Prince of Greece, *My Fifty Years,* p. 117.

148   "the most informal": Van der Kiste, *Princess Victoria Melita,* p. 49.

148   "a wonderful place": Queen Marie, *Story of My Life,* vol. 1, p. 450.

149   "cheeky, impertinent": Duff, op. cit., p. 257.

149   "new and very": ibid., p. 258.

149   "a limp, black": ibid.

150   "both helpless": Van der Kiste, *Princess Victoria Melita,* p. 50.

150   "with scant respect": Duff, op. cit., p. 258.

150   "Why does . . . best?": ibid.

SEVENTEEN: *The Little Spitfire*

151   "strong and rebellious": Queen Marie, *Story of My Life,* vol. 1, p. 64.

151   "kept progress": Duff, *Hessian Tapestry,* pp. 259–60.

151   "a highly volatile": ibid., p. 260.

152   "forgot to answer": ibid.

152   "had been well": ibid.

152   "ungovernable temper": ibid.

152   "a wonderful collection": Queen Marie, *Story of My Life,* vol. 1, pp. 450–51.

152   "their first-rate": ibid., p. 450.

153   "was a splendid . . . road": ibid.

153   "a means of": Van der Kiste, *Princess Victoria Melita,* p. 51.

153   "made others fear": ibid.

PAGE

153 "as he bolted": Duff, op. cit., p. 260.

153 "Ducky's laughter": Van der Kiste, *Princess Victoria Melita*, p. 52.

153 "harnessed Hungarian-wise": Queen Marie, *Story of My Life*, vol. 1, p. 451.

153 "we were considered": ibid.

153 "whatever we did": ibid.

153 "which has remained": ibid.

153 "passion for horses": ibid.

154 "in grand style": ibid.

154 "with as much": ibid.

154 "simple but striking": ibid.

154 "It was this": ibid., p. 452.

154 "reaped all . . . occasion": ibid.

154 "sinful love . . . princesses": ibid.

154 "the Little Spitfire": Duff, op. cit., p. 261.

154 "the Fighting Grand Duchess": ibid., pp. 260–61.

155 "I envy him": Lee, *Empress Frederick Writes to Sophie*, p. 221.

155 "suits her wonderfully": Van der Kiste, *Princess Victoria Melita*, p. 52.

155 "is wonderfully": Duff, op. cit., p. 261.

155 "had great sympathy": Van der Kiste, *Princess Victoria Melita*, p. 53.

156 "a sack of": ibid.

156 "the most uninteresting": Romanian Archives, RA V 1836/1898, Duchess of Coburg to Crown Princess Marie of Romania, October 22, 1898.

EIGHTEEN: *Journey to Moscow*

157 "the past and": Kirill, *My Life in Russia's Service*, p. 65.

157 "belonged to the": Queen Marie, *Story of My Life*, vol. 1, p. 338.

158 "to come . . . life": ibid.

158 "of all the": Kirill, op. cit., p. 65.

158 "a large following": Queen Marie, *Story of My Life*, vol. 1, p. 338.

158 "her eye was": ibid., p. 341.

158 "her withering criticism": Van der Kiste, *Princess Victoria Melita*, p. 55.

158 "tendency towards . . . affectation": Queen Marie, *Story of My Life*, vol. 1, p. 342.

158 "when we knew": Van der Kiste, *Princess Victoria Melita*, p. 55.

158 "Let the children": Queen Marie, *Story of My Life*, vol. 1, p. 342.

159 "so as to": ibid., p. 330.

159 "wearing long": Massie, *Nicholas and Alexandra*, p. 50.

159 "gold braid": ibid.

159 "not clad in": Queen Marie, *Story of My Life*, vol. 1, p. 330.

PAGE

167 "was the most kindly": ibid.

167 "strict conservative . . . erudition": Kirill, op. cit., p. 12.

167 "my dearest friend": ibid., p. 13.

168 "an incomparably": Massie, op. cit., p. 370.

168 "she could spend . . . children.": ibid., pp. 475–76.

168 "everyone who": ibid., p. 476.

168 "my first": Kirill, op. cit., p. 12.

169 "which were": ibid., p. 14.

169 "were Grandpapa's . . . other": ibid.

169 "shrouded in black": ibid., p. 16.

169 "You are to": ibid., p. 23.

170 "all my life": ibid., p. 25.

170 "virgin soil": ibid., p. 33.

170 "to divide the": ibid.

171 "examinations were": ibid., p. 34.

171 "necessary equipments": ibid.

171 "was a rude . . . period": ibid., p. 35.

171 "a monument to": ibid., p. 38.

171 "a pestilent . . . devil": ibid., p. 39.

171 "savage outbursts": ibid.

171 "who had . . . filth": ibid.

171 "like a little": ibid., p. 42.

172 "it was a rude": ibid., p. 43.

172 "antediluvian design . . . addicted": ibid., p. 46.

172 "luxuriant and": ibid., p. 52.

172 "His death was . . . peace": ibid., p. 55.

172 "never again was": ibid., p. 56.

173 "was very proud": ibid., p. 69.

174 "an ardent supporter": Van der Kiste, *Princess Victoria Melita*, p. 56.

174 "a very favorable . . . acquaintance": Kirill, op. cit., p. 69.

174 "built like . . . well": Alexander, *Always a Grand Duke*, p. 144.

174 "We, the elders": ibid.

174 "the idol of . . . towering": ibid.

174 "I don't think": Astor Papers, Reading University, Lady Bowes-Lyon, *Letters*, Crown Princess Marie of Romania to Pauline Astor, November 6, 1903.

175 "with an expression": Pakula, *The Last Romantic*, p. 129.

TWENTY: *The Awful Truth*

176 "Travellers, like poets": Sir Richard Burton, *Narrative of a Trip to Harar*, p. 25.

PAGE

176   "joy at being": ibid.

176   "we were probably": ibid.

177   "would never dare": ibid., p. 367.

177   "Having visitors": ibid.

177   "with 'the fighting' ": Pakula, *The Last Romantic,* p. 113.

177   "broke through": ibid.

177   "to have Ducky": Queen Marie, *Story of My Life,* vol. 1, p. 367.

177   "temper their": Pakula, *The Last Romantic,* p. 114.

177   "the term and": Callimachi, *Yesterday Was Mine,* p. 48.

177   "life was not": ibid.

178   "till our feet": Queen Marie, *Story of My Life,* vol. 1, p. 369.

178   "the gayest of . . . degree": ibid., p. 366.

178   "large pearly": Van der Kiste, *Princess Victoria Melita,* p. 58.

178   "were in the": ibid.

179   "now that I": ibid., p. 373.

179   "penetrate undismayed": Pakula, op. cit., p. 116.

179   "Bewildered, dazed": Queen Marie, *Story of My Life,* vol. 1, p. 373.

179   "Crouching above": Pakula, op. cit., p. 117.

179   "so as to": Van der Kiste, *Princess Victoria Melita,* p. 59.

179   "would dress up . . . attire": Pakula, op. cit., p. 116.

179   "liked being as": ibid.

179   "very tight-fitting": Queen Marie, *Story of My Life,* vol. 1, p. 370.

179   "Empress Eugénies": Van der Kiste, *Princess Victoria Melita,* p. 59.

180   "a prettier picture . . .": Bülow, *Memoirs: 1897–1903,* vol. 2, p. 482.

180   "answered with": Van der Kiste, *Princess Victoria Melita,* p. 59.

180   "had to content": ibid., p. 60.

180   "giddy and frivolously . . . than ours.": Queen Marie, *Story of My Life,* vol. 1, p. 371.

180   "was not honouring": Van der Kiste, *Princess Victoria Melita,* p. 60.

180   "the horrified look": ibid.

181   "so happy": Queen Marie, vol. 1, p. 369.

181   "could not bear": Van der Kiste, *Princess Victoria Melita,* p. 61.

181   "locally-produced": ibid., p. 60.

181   "piled high": ibid.

181   "We sisters": Queen Marie, *Story of My Life,* vol. 1, p. 369.

181   "only too ready": Romanian Archives, RA V 1796/1897, Duchess of Coburg to Crown Princess Marie of Roumania, March 21, 1897.

181   "who had a": Queen Marie, *Story of My Life,* vol. 1, p. 376.

182   "awkward and strange": interview with Mother Alexandra.

182   "No boy was": Elsberry, *Marie of Roumania,* p. 62.

PAGE

182   "homosexuality lay": Rohl and Sombart, *Kaiser Wilhelm II: New Interpretations,* p. 48.

182   "went through his . . . empire.": ibid.

182   "was the vilest . . . criminal": Manchester, *The Arms of Krupp,* p. 221.

183   "Wilhelm never resolved": Rohl and Sombart, op. cit., p. 48.

183   "was in love": Manchester, op. cit., p. 222.

183   "most virile": ibid.

183   "disgusting nature.": interview with Mother Alexandra, July 1982.

184   "in urgent need": Manchester, op. cit., p. 225.

184   "a wild-eyed and": ibid.

TWENTY-ONE: *A Royal Scandal*

185   "could not prevent": Queen Marie, *Story of My Life,* vol. 1, p. 386.

185   "Several times he": Queen Marie, ibid., p. 384.

185   "injections of salt": ibid.

185   "long and wearisome . . . stranger.": Pakula, *The Last Romantic,* p. 118.

185   "gaunt waxen face": Bibesco, "Ferdinand of Roumania," p. 6.

185   "a rather touching": Pakula, *The Last Romantic,* p. 118.

186   "in a sombre": Van der Kiste, *Princess Victoria Melita,* p. 62.

186   "a masterpiece of": St. Aubyn, *Edward VII,* p. 251.

186   "as if Grandma": Van der Kiste, *Princess Victoria Melita,* p. 62.

186   "gorgeous procession": *Annual Register,* 1897, p. 34.

187   "After sixty years": St. Aubyn, op. cit., p. 252.

187   "they had with": Kirill, *My Life in Russia's Service,* p. 71.

187   "very ancient piano": ibid.

187   "a continuous series . . . fever": ibid., p. 72.

187   "excellently": ibid.

188   "Ducky's flirtations": Pakula, op. cit., p. 118.

188   "some measure of": Van der Kiste, *Princess Victoria Melita,* p. 63.

188   "the English camp": ibid.

188   "Your account of": Hough, *Advice to My Granddaughter,* p. 138.

188   "my own darling . . . wishes": Van der Kiste, *Princess Victoria Melita,* p. 62.

188   "May I present": Kirill, op. cit., p. 73.

188   "very distinctive and": ibid.

189   "it was impossible": Van der Kiste, *Princess Victoria Melita,* p. 65.

189   "showed a marked": ibid.

189   "old ladies . . . wild": Duff, *Hessian Tapestry,* p. 262.

189   "all was not . . . grandchildren": Van der Kiste, *Princess Victoria Melita,* p. 65.

189   "he chose his": ibid.

PAGE

189   "I arranged that": Duff, op. cit., p. 262.

190   "implored . . . proposition": ibid.

190   "my precious . . . Gran": ibid.

190   "very odd . . . before": Kirill, op. cit., p. 77.

191   "all of a sudden": ibid., p. 77.

191   "had been let": ibid., p. 78.

TWENTY-TWO: *Death and Reconciliation*

192   "had fallen apart": Van der Kiste, *Princess Victoria Melita,* p. 66.

192   "If you only": Romanian Archives, RA V 1821/1898, Duchess of
       Coburg to Crown Princess Marie of Romania, February 15,
       1898.

192   "suffering from": Van der Kiste, *Princess Victoria Melita,* p. 66.

193   "It is true": Lee, *Empress Frederick Writes to Sophie,* p. 156.

193   "life of debauchery": Van der Kiste, *Princess Victoria Melita,* p. 66.

193   "still shrouded in . . . decision": ibid., p. 67.

193   "was suffering": Van der Kiste, op. cit., p. 67.

193   "pale and . . . away": Queen Marie, *Story of My Life,* vol. 1, p. 404.

193   "He hardly recognizes": Pakula, *The Last Romantic,* p. 121.

194   "would die within": Van der Kiste, *Princess Victoria Melita,* p. 67.

194   "heavy drinking and": ibid.

194   "it was unbearable": Queen Marie, *Story of My Life,* vol. 1, p. 404.

194   "We were all": ibid.

194   "All of a sudden": ibid.

195   "an overwhelming sight . . . hearts": ibid., p. 405.

195   "racked by guilt": Van der Kiste, *Princess Victoria Melita,* p. 67.

195   "as far away": ibid., pp. 67–68.

195   "Germanized": Pakula, op. cit., p. 121.

195   "a determined attempt": Van der Kiste, *Princess Victoria Melita,* p. 68.

196   "special attention": ibid.

196   "Granny Gran": Buchanan, *Queen Victoria's Relations,* p. 3.

196   "immersed herself": Van der Kiste, *Princess Victoria Melita,* p. 68.

196   "extremely critical": ibid., p. 69.

196   "She draws unerringly": Mallet, *Life with Queen Victoria,* p. 167.

196   "she could make": Van der Kiste, *Princess Victoria Melita,* p. 69.

196   "of Royal manufacture": ibid.

196   "loathing of Germans": Mallet, op. cit., p. 167.

197   "adores England with": ibid.

197   "Most heartfelt thanks": Windsor Royal Archives, RA Z90/91,
       Grand Duke Ernest of Hesse and the Rhine to Queen Victo-
       ria, June 9, 1899.

197   "quite homesick for": ibid., Victoria Melita to Queen Victoria, June 10, 1899.

197   "leaving straight for": ibid.

197   "every precaution taken": ibid., June 11, 1899.

197   "Ernie still doing": ibid., June 12, 1899.

197   "Condition very": ibid., June 13, 1899.

197   "Ernie getting": ibid., June 14, 1899.

198   "making rapid progress": ibid., June 15, 1899.

198   "saw Ernie today": ibid., June 17, 1899.

198   "We are so": ibid., Ernest and Victoria Melita to Queen Victoria, June 27, 1899.

TWENTY-THREE: *The End of Two Eras*

200   "happiest recollections": Kirill, *My Life in Russia's Service,* p. 104.

200   "great sin . . . woman": Romanian Archives, RA V 1867/1899, Duchess of Coburg to Crown Princess Marie of Roumania, December 7, 1899.

200   "his laziness . . . passions": ibid., RA V 2716/1899, Duchess of Coburg to King Carol I of Roumania, November 15, 1899.

200   "the whole truth . . . behavior": ibid., RA V 1862/1899, Duchess of Coburg to Crown Princess Marie of Roumania, November 17, 1899.

200   "get herself as": Pakula, *The Last Romantic,* p. 124.

201   "mostly at . . . harmonious": Queen Marie, *Story of My Life,* vol. 1, p. 404.

201   "a very quiet": Van der Kiste, *Princess Victoria Melita,* p. 71.

201   "to play the": ibid., p. 70.

201   "The Grand Duke": Windsor Royal Archives, RA Z90/97, Sir George Buchanan to Sir Arthur Bigge, May 15, 1900.

201   "the disappointment at . . . blow": Hough, *Advice to My Granddaughter,* p. 147.

202   "beginning to give": Van der Kiste, *Princess Victoria Melita,* p. 71.

202   "fed from a": Pakula, op. cit., p. 127.

202   "would only excite": Romanian Archives, RA V 2431/1900, Crown Princess Marie of Roumania to the Duchess of Coburg, July 7, 1900.

202   "Oh, God . . . eighty-one": Longford, *Queen Victoria,* p. 558.

202   "very seedy": ibid.

203   "the three weeks": Kirill, op. cit., p. 112.

203   "to meet": ibid.

203   "enormously in the": ibid.

PAGE

203   "Another year begun": Longford, op. cit., pp. 559–60.

203   "monotonous procession . . . coming": ibid.

203   "made all the": Van der Kiste, *Princess Victoria Melita*, p. 72.

204   "But I don't": Longford, *The Royal House of Windsor*, p. 45.

204   "Sweet little David": Windsor Royal Archives, RA GV CC45/229,
          Princess Charles of Denmark to the Duchess of York, Febru-
          ary 3, 1901.

204   "The thought of": Pope-Hennessy, *Queen Mary*, p. 353.

204   "A sense of": Longford, op. cit., p. 562.

TWENTY-FOUR: *Divorce Most Shocking*

206   "dangerous brakes . . . noises": Kirill, *My Life in Russia's Service*, p.
          113.

207   "stiff and unfriendly": Van der Kiste, *Princess Victoria Melita,* p. 73.

207   "After what you": Pope-Hennessy, *Queen Mary*, pp. 363–364.

207   "Your old Mama": Romanian Archives, RA V 1861/1899,
          Duchess of Coburg to Crown Princess Marie of Roumania,
          November 9, 1899.

208   "no patience": Queen Marie, *Story of My Life,* vol. I, p. 64.

208   "a living hell": Van der Kiste, *Princess Victoria Melita*, p. 73.

208   "Now that I am": Hough, *Louis and Victoria,* p. 209.

208   "*In October*": Hough, *Advice to My Granddaughter,* p. 97.

209   "*I must inform*": Bing, *The Letters of Tsar Nicholas and the Empress
          Marie,* pp. 157–58.

209   "What truth is": Windsor Royal Archives, RA CC 29/40, Grand
          Duchess Augusta of Mecklenburg-Strelitz to the Duchess of
          York, November 4, 1901.

209   "invincible mutual": Van der Kiste, *Princess Victoria Melita*, p. 75.

210   "God had moulded . . . this": Pakula, *The Last Romantic,* pp.
          128–29.

TWENTY-FIVE: *Tide Against Tempest*

213   "a virtual outcast": Van der Kiste, *Princess Victoria Melita,* p. 76.

213   "found something": Pakula, *The Last Romantic,* p. 128.

213   "was benign compared": ibid.

214   "uncharitable treatment": Van der Kiste, *Princess Victoria Melita,* p. 76.

214   "shed tears of": Pakula, op. cit., p. 146.

214   "always been a": Queen Marie, *Story of My Life,* vol. 1, p. 316.

214   "generally outwitted . . . way": ibid.

215   "It is ridiculous . . . all": ibid., p. 390.

215   "she was particularly": Kirill, *My Life in Russia's Service,* p. 123.

PAGE

215   "as this was": ibid.

215   "She was in exile": ibid.

216   "feeling that this . . . courage": ibid.

216   "we were casting": ibid., pp. 123–24.

216   "left to fight": ibid.

TWENTY-SIX: *The Curse of Hesse*

217   "immense bitterness": Van der Kiste, *Princess Victoria Melita,* p. 76.

217   "sad, anxious eyes": ibid.

217   "deep sensitivity and": Ernst Ludwig, *Erinnertes,* p. 56.

217   "I never knew . . . love me": ibid.

218   "the sunshine . . . be damaged": ibid.

218   "an unforgivable insult": Van der Kiste, *Princess Victoria Melita,* p. 80.

219   "for how long": Kirill, *My Life in Russia's Service,* p. 137.

219   "quite obvious . . . any chance": ibid.

219   "the Emperor's dispatch": ibid.

219   "My situation": ibid.

219   "to disobey": ibid.

219   "a kindly and": ibid., p. 138.

220   "he had been": Van der Kiste, *Princess Victoria Melita,* p. 82.

220   "I learnt, to": Kirill, op. cit., p. 148.

220   "at no time": ibid.

220   "I had not": ibid.

220   "tried, but by": ibid.

220   "gave in with": Van der Kiste, *Princess Victoria Melita,* p. 83.

221   "after this period": Kirill, op. cit., p. 149.

221   "a delightful few . . . come": ibid.

221   "always remember": ibid.

221   "give me": ibid., p. 152.

221   "The making of": ibid., p. 152.

222   "a clumsy kind": ibid., p. 153.

222   "breaking down with": ibid.

222   "*Motoring in those*": ibid.

222   "far from the": ibid.

222   "the joy of": ibid.

222   "appeasement after": ibid.

222   "hoping to influence": Pakula, *The Last Romantic,* p. 136.

223   "in agony": Van der Kiste, *Princess Victoria Melita,* p. 77.

223   "the doctors warned . . . late": Pakula, op. cit., p. 136.

223   "grave": Van der Kiste, *Princess Victoria Melita,* p. 77.

PAGE

223 "had eaten food": ibid.

224 "heartbroken": ibid.

224 "The return trip": Ernst Ludwig, op. cit., p. 56.

224 "Everything was in": ibid.

224 "driving out with": Van der Kiste, *Princess Victoria Melita*, p. 77.

224 "Thousands of mourners": Ernst Ludwig, op. cit., p. 56.

224 "all honours": Bülow, *Memoirs,* vol. 1, p. 483.

224 "she had made": Van der Kiste, *Princess Victoria Melita*, p. 78.

224 "melodramatic . . . taste": Bülow, op. cit., vol. 1, p. 483.

TWENTY-SEVEN: *Hearts in Darkness*

226 "a well-matched . . . Christmas.": Kirill, *My Life in Russia's Service,*
     p. 154.

226 "with all the": ibid.

227 "May God come": Massie, *Nicholas and Alexandra,* p. 86.

227 "huge, patriotic crowds": ibid.

227 "seized the initiative": ibid., p. 87.

227 "plunging right into": Kirill, op. cit., p. 159.

227 "it was hard": ibid.

227 "the great unknown": ibid.

228 "looked like a": ibid., p. 161.

228 "a more awkward . . . trap": ibid., p. 162.

228 "as though a": ibid., p. 168.

228 "Everything gave below": ibid.

228 "fearful maelstorm . . . loved": ibid.

229 "the force that . . . madly": ibid. p. 169.

229 "an absolute wreck": ibid., p. 173.

229 "given an enthusiastic": Van der Kiste, *Princess Victoria Melita,* p. 85.

229 "spring in my": Kirill, op. cit., p. 174.

230 "one of those": ibid.

230 "the good people": ibid.

230 "To those over": ibid.

231 "neither exacting or": ibid., p. 175.

231 "grim prospect of": Massie, op. cit., p. 88.

231 "to rejoin": Kirill, op. cit., p. 179.

231 "no longer had": Van der Kiste, *Princess Victoria Melita,* p. 87.

232 "panic-stricken police.": ibid.

232 "not her husband": Massie, op. cit., p. 99.

232 "considerably safer": Kirill, op. cit., p. 180.

232 "it would be . . . obstacle": ibid.

PAGE

232 "very badly shaken": ibid., p. 181.

233 "no one could": Pakula, *The Last Romantic,* p. 143.

233 "a blizzard": Kirill, op. cit., p. 182.

233 "was very scared": ibid.

233 "There are few": ibid.

234 "I hardly know": Pakula, op. cit., p. 143.

TWENTY-EIGHT: *The Czarina's Wrath*

235 "It makes me": Bing, *The Letters of Tsar Nicholas and Empress Marie,*
        p. 183.

235 "trains stopped running": Massie, *Nicholas and Alexandra,* p. 100.

235 "the flames of": ibid.

236 "ill-omened.": Kirill, *My Life in Russia's Service,* p. 183.

236 "a great blow . . . steps": ibid.

236 "sincere hope that": ibid.

236 "the temerity to": Van der Kiste, *Princess Victoria Melita,* p. 89.

237 "a woman who": ibid.

237 "an abiding hatred": ibid., p. 90.

237 *"The situation had"*: Bülow, *Memoirs,* vol. 2, pp. 168–70.

239 "perhaps wrong": Van der Kiste, *Princess Victoria Melita,* p. 92.

239 "no member of": ibid.

239 "crashing his fist": ibid.

239 "I wonder whether": Massie, op. cit., p. 232.

239 "casually married a": ibid., p. 231.

239 "corroded the prestige": ibid.

239 "who should have . . . nation": Vorres, *The Last Grand Duchess,* pp.
        114–15.

240 "In the end": Massie, op. cit., p. 232.

240 "he was a": Van der Kiste, *Princess Victoria Melita,* p. 92.

240 "the Grand Duchess": ibid., p. 93.

TWENTY-NINE: *Two Alone*

241 "the sudden vehemence": Kirill, *My Life in Russia's Service,* p. 184.

242 "the same feeling": Massie, *Nicholas and Alexandra,* p. 100.

242 "only two ways . . . constitution": ibid., pp. 100–101.

242 "would mean": ibid., p. 101.

242 "freedom of conscience": ibid., p. 103.

242 "with great rapidity": ibid.

243 "spent a delightful": Kirill, op. cit., p. 184.

244 "stepped in to": Pakula, *The Last Romantic,* p. 144.

PAGE

244   "charming": Queen Marie, *Story of My Life,* vol. 1, p. 546.

244   "had witnessed": Kirill, op. cit., p. 184.

245   "emerged from discreet": Pakula, *The Last Romantic,* p. 144.

245   "to drink champagne": ibid.

245   *"My sister has"*: Astor Archives, Crown Princess Marie of Rouma-
       nia to Nancy Astor, July 12, 1906.

246   "as seriously as": Romanian Archives, RA V 2039/1907, Duchess
       of Coburg to Crown Princess Marie of Roumania, March 10,
       1907.

246   "perfectly content": Van der Kiste, *Princess Victoria Melita,* p. 94.

246   "to those very": Kirill, op. cit., p. 184.

246   "travelled much": ibid.

246   "As the King": Pakula, op. cit., p. 146.

246   "to a man . . . Wolfsgarten": Van der Kiste, *Princess Victoria Melita,*
       p. 95.

247   "I had so": Romanian Archives, RA V 2038/1907, Duchess of
       Coburg to Marie of Roumania, February 2, 1907.

248   "the first step": Kirill, op. cit., p. 185.

248   "as he had": ibid., p. 184.

248   "complete rehabilitation": ibid., p. 185.

248   "had been virtually": Van der Kiste, *Princess Victoria Melita,* p. 97.

249   "friendly word": ibid.

249   "the continued sentence": ibid.

249   "totally ineligible": ibid.

250   "Ta femme est": Kirill, op. cit., p. 185.

THIRTY: *Coming Home*

251   "meant that all": Kirill, *My Life in Russia's Service,* p. 185.

251   "not only been . . . sympathy": ibid.

252   "uneventful service . . . days": ibid., p. 186.

253   "their rehabilitation": Van der Kiste, *Princess Victoria Melita,* p. 98.

253   "It was our": Kirill, op. cit., p. 186.

253   "settled down to": ibid., p. 187.

253   "I too profoundly": Romanian Archives, Victoria Melita to Marie
       of Roumania, June 22, 1910.

254   "was missing so": Van der Kiste, *Princess Victoria Melita,* p. 99.

254   "of a mild": Kirill, op. cit., p. 187.

255   "bad behavior . . . marriage": Van der Kiste, *Princess Victoria Melita,*
       p. 100.

255   "Many were the": Buchanan, *My Mission to Russia,* vol. 1, pp. 176–77.

256   "had behaved like": Van der Kiste, *Princess Victoria Melita*, p. 103.

256   "the death-knell": Meriel Buchanan, *Queen Victoria's Relations,* p. 199.

256   "A little coquetry": Bülow, *Memoirs,* vol. 2, p. 28.

256   "born with the": Queen Marie, *Story of My Life,* vol. 1, p. 521.

256   "the child of": Pakula, *The Last Romantic,* p. 157.

257   "great difficulties": Queen Marie, *Story of My Life,* p. 457.

257   "a delightful": ibid.

257   "was quite one": ibid.

257   "there was not": ibid.

257   "from headaches and": Pakula, op. cit., p. 105.

THIRTY-ONE: *The Vladimir Circle*

258   "totally unsuited by . . . contempt": Van der Kiste, *Princess Victoria Melita,* p. 100.

258   "excessive shyness . . . society": Massie, *Nicholas and Alexandra,* p. 68.

258   "were blighted by": ibid.

259   "a prude and": ibid., p. 69.

259   "Alix I haven't": Romanian Archives, Victoria Melita to Marie of Roumania, December 25, 1910.

259   "I remember how": Buchanan, *My Mission to Russia,* vol. 1, p. 177.

259   "undoubtedly was suffering": ibid., p. 153.

259   "took a terrible": ibid., p. 152.

259   "She keeps to": ibid., p. 153.

260   "What would be": ibid., p. 155.

260   "resented the way": ibid., p. 69.

260   "the best French": Van der Kiste, *Princess Victoria Melita,* p. 101.

260   "almost oriental . . . Palace": ibid.

261   "grand palace on": Massie, op. cit., p. 370.

261   "a respected and": Van der Kiste, *Princess Victoria Melita,* p. 101.

261   "never really liked": Van der Kiste, *Princess Victoria Melita,* p. 102.

261   "always found kind": ibid.

261   "No party was": Meriel Buchanan, *Queen Victoria's Relations,* p. 199.

262   "They keep such": Romanian Archives, Victoria Melita to Marie of Roumania, June 12, 1910.

262   "Yesterday I was": ibid., Victoria Melita to Marie of Roumania, May 10, 1913.

263   "had everything on . . . ponies": Queen Marie, *Story of My Life,* vol. I, p. 577.

263   "Ducky had perfect": Queen Marie, *Story of My Life,* vol. 1, p. 577.

263   "the want of": ibid.

PAGE

263 "her former unhappiness . . . divorce": Van der Kiste, *Princess Victoria Melita*, p. 104.

263 "When I was": Meriel Buchanan, op. cit., pp. 200–201.

264 "would have filled": Van der Kiste, *Princess Victoria Melita*, p. 108.

THIRTY-TWO: *A Holy Devil*

265 "had reached the": Kirill, *My Life in Russia's Service*, pp. 188–89.

265 "had impressed themselves": ibid., p. 189.

265 "a dread of": ibid.

265 "was haunted by": ibid.

265 "the vision of": ibid.

266 "a thoroughly gay": ibid., p. 190.

266 "The evil . . . haunting": ibid.

266 "holy terror": ibid.

266 "The haunting spectre": ibid., p. 191.

266 "a strange individual": ibid.

267 "who lived in": Massie, *Nicholas and Alexandra*, p. 183.

267 "repulsive . . . spirituality": ibid., p. 180.

267 "a coarse oval . . . recesses": Yousoupoff, *Rasputin*, pp. 48–50.

268 "were prominent practitioners . . . occult": Massie, op. cit., p. 187.

268 "Rasputin took the": Haldane, *Heredity and Politics*, p. 39.

268 "believed that Rasputin": Massie, op. cit., p. 193.

269 "was greatly troubled": Fulop-Miller, *The Holy Devil*, p. 157.

269 "sent by Heaven": ibid.

269 "supreme honor": Massie, op. cit., p. 196.

269 "Rasputin was a": Fulop-Miller, op. cit., p. 207.

270 "a blasphemous and . . . other": Massie, op. cit., p. 197.

270 "Saints are always . . . him": ibid., p. 202.

271 "They accuse Rasputin . . . greeting": ibid.

271 "The fatal influence": ibid., p. 203.

271 "he was neither": Kirill, op. cit., p. 192.

272 "went to his . . . used": ibid.

272 "was looked upon": Queen Marie, *Story of My Life,* vol. 1, p. 574.

272 "My beloved, unforgettable": Moorehead, *The Russian Revolution,* p. 72.

273 "put down his . . . you": Massie, op. cit., p. 196.

THIRTY-THREE: *The Last Waltz*

274 "as if the": Van der Kiste, *Princess Victoria Melita*, p. 105.

274 "with its heavy . . . theatre": Massie, *Nicholas and Alexander,* p. 235.

275 "the highly rouged": Cowles, *1913,* p. 111.

PAGE

275   "were very hot . . . endurance": ibid., p. 112.

275   "through the blue": Meriel Buchanan, *Ambassador's Daughter,* p. 128.

276   "the wild pace": Cowles, op. cit., p. 112.

276   "with a ring": ibid.

276   "a surge of": Massie, op. cit., p. 235.

277   "no feeling of": Cowles, op. cit., p. 103.

278   "*She was very*": Meriel Buchanan, *The Dissolution of an Empire,* pp. 35–37.

280   "What an awful": Pares, *Letters of the Tsaritsa to the Tsar,* p. 23.

280   "no warm feeling": Queen Marie, *Story of My Life,* vol. 1, p. 573.

280   "put an insuperable": ibid.

280   "not pretty": ibid., p. 574.

281   "in a sort of": Pakula, *The Last Romantic,* p. 170.

281   "make a marriage": Van der Kiste, p. 106.

281   "*the Majesties and*": Romanian Archives, Victoria Melita to Marie of Roumania, June 29, 1914.

283   "I have killed": Massie, op. cit., p. 245.

283   "that most monstrous": ibid., p. 244.

283   "a little cruising": Kirill, *My Life in Russia's Service,* p. 194.

283   "that year it": ibid.

284   "produced the effect": ibid.

THIRTY-FOUR: *Crowns Divided*

285   "fearful commotion and": Kirill, *My Life in Russia's Service,* p. 195.

285   "to be reckless": ibid.

285   "laughing, weeping . . . Tsar": Massie, *Nicholas and Alexandra,* p. 264.

286   "passionately pro-English": Van der Kiste, *Princess Victoria Melita,* p. 105.

287   "entirely out of": Pakula, *The Last Romantic,* p. 186.

287   "Ducky is furious": ibid., p. 188.

288   "Who knows": ibid.

288   "threw herself": Van der Kiste, *Princess Victoria Melita,* p. 110.

288   "The task which . . . fire": Kirill, op. cit., pp. 196–98.

288   "worn and harassed": Van der Kiste, *Princess Victoria Melita,* p. 110.

288   "quite impressed by": ibid.

289   "was very lonely": Kirill, op. cit., p. 197.

289   "there was little": ibid.

289   "had pulverized the": Whittle, *The Last Kaiser,* p. 275.

289   "appalling slaughter the": Kirill, op. cit., p. 199.

289   "a very sympathetic": Queen Marie, *Story of My Life,* vol. 2, p. 21.

290   "*It is certainly*": Queen Marie, *Story of My Life,* vol. 2, pp. 29–30.

PAGE

290   "Oh! why, why": Romanian Royal Archives, RA V 2180/1916,
        Duchess of Coburg to Queen Marie, November 4, 1916.

291   "habit of counting": Pakula, op. cit., p. 191.

291   "allegiance was fervently": Massie, op. cit., p. 314.

291   "Twenty years have": Buxhoeveden, *The Life and Tragedy of Alexan-
        dra Feodorovna*, p. 186.

292   "Yes, do come": Knox, *With the Russian Army*, p. 334.

292   "When the Emperor": Pares, *The Fall of the Russian Empire*, p. 280.

292   "domestic division of": Massie, op. cit., p. 327.

292   "hardened into open . . . concern": Van der Kiste, *Princess Victoria
        Melita*, p. 111.

293   "seething with . . . schoolgirl": Meriel Buchanan, *Queen Victoria's
        Relations*, p. 201.

293   "indeed a blessed . . . struggle": Queen Marie, *Story of My Life*, vol.
        2, p. 103.

293   "My sister's": ibid.

293   "Ducky was as": ibid., p. 104.

293   "pottered about in": ibid., p. 106.

294   "found it a": ibid., p. 105.

294   "wandered about endlessly": ibid., p. 107.

294   "She has been . . . sorrow": ibid.

295   "weighty letter to": ibid.

THIRTY-FIVE: *The War of the Romanovs*

296   "clumsy intrusions": Massie, *Nicholas and Alexandra*, p. 362.

296   "he dared not . . . son": Gilliard, *Thirteen Years at the Russian Court*,
        p. 177.

296   "I beg you . . . decision": Massie, op. cit., p. 339.

298   "This time it": Viroubova, *Memories of the Russian Court*, p. 174.

298   "*I feel that*": Pares, *The Fall of the Russian Empire*, p. 399.

298   "to kill several": Yousoupoff, *Lost Splendor*, p. 220.

299   "clambering on all": Massie, op. cit., p. 358.

299   "his bloodstream filled": ibid.

299   "I am filled with": Viroubova, op. cit., p. 183.

300   "the feeling of": Kirill, *My Life in Russia's Service*, p. 202.

300   "understood that she": Massie, op. cit., p. 366.

300   "I allow no one": Paléologue, *An Ambassador's Memoirs*, vol. 3, p. 167.

300   "I am sure": Bing, *Secret Letters of the Last Tsar*, p. 302.

301   "Your interference with": Alexander, *Once a Grand Duke*, p. 283.

301   "Remember, Alix": ibid.

301   "One cannot govern": ibid., p. 184.

PAGE

302 "it is not": Queen Marie, *Story of My Life,* vol. 2, p. 113.

302 "serious trouble at": ibid., p. 112.

302 "is extraordinarily": ibid.

302 "is much liked": ibid., p. 123.

302 "at least one": Van der Kiste, *Princess Victoria Melita,* pp. 114–15.

302 "To me": Queen Marie, *Story of My Life,* vol. 2, p. 124.

302 "thousands and thousands": ibid.

303 "May my beloved": ibid.

303 "very dangerous because . . . any more": ibid.

303 "wandered through these": ibid., p. 126.

304 "deadly, cruelly": ibid., p. 125.

304 "a martyr to": Van der Kiste, *Princess Victoria Melita,* p. 115.

304 "nearly perished": ibid.

304 "unjustifiable": Queen Marie, *Story of My Life,* vol. 2, p. 130.

304 "is awfully kind": ibid., p. 131.

304 "the whole country": Kirill, op. cit., p. 203.

305 "more and more . . . annihilated": Rodzianko, *The Reign of Rasputin,*
        p. 246.

306 "during the evening": Paléologue, op. cit., vol. 3, p. 157.

THIRTY-SIX: *Days of Blood and Fire*

307 "crime and violence": Kirill, *My Life in Russia's Service,* p. 204.

307 "the whole edifice": ibid.

308 "Much of what": ibid., p. 205.

308 "the same wide": Massie, *Nicholas and Alexandra,* pp. 382–83.

308 "I looked out,": Paléologue, *An Ambassador's Memoirs,* vol. 3, p. 221.

308 "the crack of": ibid., p. 222.

308 "saved the situation . . . useless": Kirill, op. cit., p. 206.

309 "There was continuous": ibid., pp. 206–7.

309 "a time of": ibid., p. 208.

310 "The whole thing": Queen Marie, *Story of My Life,* vol. 2, p. 144.

310 "in little scraps . . . encounter": ibid., pp. 145–47.

310 "tremendous joy . . . relief": ibid., p. 150.

310 "*She writes that*": ibid.

311 "mingled with violent . . . burn": Massie, op. cit., p. 387.

311 "side by side": ibid.

311 "an ugly temper": Kirill, op. cit., p. 208.

311 "for anyone": ibid.

311 "the rule of": ibid.

312 "let them": ibid., p. 209.

312 "had not been": ibid.

PAGE

312   "by every means": Van der Kiste, *Princess Victoria Melita*, p. 121.

312   "the last certain thing . . . wreckage": Kirill, op. cit., p. 209.

312   "drink this": ibid., p. 210.

312   "They marched in": Paléologue, op. cit., Vol. 3, p. 232.

313   "in absolute . . . beer-garden": Kirill, op. cit., p. 209.

313   "Soldier with unbuttoned": ibid., pp. 209–210.

313   "Students, comrades! . . . near": ibid., p. 210.

313   "in a state of . . . over": ibid.

313   "that he was": Van der Kiste, *Princess Victoria Melita*, p. 122.

314   "the triumph of . . . virtues": Kirill, op. cit., p. 210.

314   "These last few": Kerensky, *The Murder of the Romanovs*, p. 89.

314   "come out openly . . . mob": Paléologue, op. cit., Vol. 3, p. 232.

314   "the saddest moment": Kirill, op. cit., p. 211.

314   "ludicrously brief": Massie, op. cit., p. 400.

315   "No more Romanovs": ibid., p. 401.

315   "futile and hopeless . . . vain": Kirill, op. cit., p. 211.

315   "This is the": ibid.

315   "Where you are": ibid., p. 212.

316   "The Republic must": Massie, op. cit., p. 438.

316   "No trespassing": ibid., p. 387.

THIRTY-SEVEN: *Into the Night*

317   "The wind of": Victor Hugo, *Les Miserables*, p. 104.

317   "entitled to any": Van der Kiste, *Princess Victoria Melita*, p. 124.

318   "I quite understand": Meriel Buchanan, *Queen Victoria's Relations*,
        p. 203.

318   "had deserted her": Van der Kiste, *Princess Victoria Melita*, p. 125.

318   "Neither pride, nor": ibid.

318   "*At last a*": Queen Marie, *Story of My Life*, vol. 2, p. 175.

319   "deeply impressed . . . situation": ibid., p. 176.

319   "it was not . . . typhoon": Kirill, *My Life in Russia's Service*, p. 213.

319   "dragging his wife": Van der Kiste, *Princess Victoria Melita*, p. 125.

319   "be it under": ibid., p. 126.

321   "anything of value . . . carry": ibid., p. 128.

321   "very quietly arranged": Kirill, op. cit., p. 213.

322   "were respected and": McNaughton, *The Flight of the Romanovs*, p. 131.

322   "For the first": ibid.

THIRTY-EIGHT: *The Mortal Storm*

325   "could hardly stand": Van der Kiste, *Princess Victoria Melita*, p. 129.

325   "Her despair at": Queen Marie, *Story of My Life*, vol. 2, p. 213.

PAGE

326   "hoping that it": Kirill, *My Life in Russia's Service,* p. 216.

326   "too weak to": Massie, *Nicholas and Alexandra,* p. 454.

326   "an immediate lunge": ibid., p. 455.

327   "he carried with": ibid., p. 456.

327   "could not feel": Kirill, op. cit., p. 216.

327   "their authority had": ibid.

327   "long, dreary": McNaughton, *The Flight of the Romanovs,* p. 131.

327   "the hardship of": ibid.

327   "a farce, which": Van der Kiste, *Princess Victoria Melita,* p. 131.

327   "what a 'search' ": Kirill, op. cit., p. 216.

327   "the majority of . . . worst": ibid.

328   "in remembrance of": ibid., p. 217.

328   "enjoying their winter": ibid.

328   "very politely, and": ibid.

329   "a very precarious": Van der Kiste, *Princess Victoria Melita,* p. 133.

329   "fantastic and contradictory": Kirill, op. cit., p. 217.

329   "very painful to . . . desertion": ibid., p. 218.

329   "admitted that he": ibid.

329   "not one they": Van der Kiste, *Princess Victoria Melita,* p. 133.

330   "*I feel so*": Windsor Royal Archives, RA Add C22/206, Crown
          Princess Margaret of Sweden to Lady Egerton, January 24,
          1918.

330   "coldly acknowledging the": Van der Kiste, *Princess Victoria Melita,*
          p. 130.

331   "the termination of": Summers and Mangold, *The File on the Tsar,*
          p. 252.

THIRTY-NINE: *Alms for the Oblivion*

333   "I had a": Windsor Royal Archives, RA Add C22/210, Crown
          Princess Margaret of Sweden to Lady Egerton, July 28, 1918.

333   "homesickness, shortages": Van der Kiste, *Princess Victoria Melita,* p.
          135.

333   "How I wish": Romanian Archives, Princess Kira to Queen Marie,
          May 28, 1918.

333   "were not content": Van der Kiste, *Princess Victoria Melita,* p. 135.

334   "should help the": ibid., p. 136.

334   "a live banner": Trotsky, *Diary in Exile,* p. 81.

334   "the same ruthless": Massie, *Nicholas and Alexandra,* p. 497.

334   "not only expedient . . . ruin": Trotsky, op. cit., p. 81.

335   "The Revolution does": Massie, op. cit., p. 498.

335   "stomach for": Van der Kiste, *Princess Victoria Melita,* p. 136.

PAGE

335   "*My dear George*": Windsor Royal Archives, RA GV Q1550/XiX
         319, Grand Duchess Victoria Feodorovna to King George V
         of England, January 29, 1919.

337   "with feelings of": Van der Kiste, *Princess Victoria Melita*, p. 140.

337   "*Together with my*": Windsor Royal Archives, RA GV Q1550/XIX
         320, King George V of England to Grand Duchess Victoria
         Feodorovna, March 13, 1919.

339   "the insistent urging": Massie, op. cit., p. 499.

339   "*Dear George*": Windsor Royal Archives, RA GV AA43/298,
         Grand Duchess Victoria Feodorovna to King George V, July
         22, 1919.

341   "was powerless to": ibid., p. 145.

FORTY: *A Searching Wind*

342   "most hospitable": Van der Kiste, *Princess Victoria Melita,* p. 145.

342   "were naturally tired": Kirill, *My Life in Russia's Service,* p. 219.

342   "was a severe": ibid., p. 218.

343   "her once plump": Van der Kiste, *Princess Victoria Melita,* p. 145.

343   "an awful little": Pakula, *The Last Romantic,* p. 301.

344   "*Oh, life is*": ibid., p. 19.

345   "rejoicing over the": ibid., p. 301.

345   "She continues to": ibid., pp. 301–302.

346   "bowed and broken": Van der Kiste, *Princess Victoria Melita*, p. 146

346   "receiving a letter": ibid.

346   "provoking an international": Pakula, op. cit., p. 305.

347   "I hope God": ibid.

347   "at the mercy": ibid.

349   "I have had": Windsor Royal Archives, RA GV CC45/583, Queen
         Marie of Roumania to Queen Mary of England, March 10,
         1920.

349   "reminded them of . . . before": Kirill, op. cit., p. 230.

350   "a popular and": Duff, *Hessian Tapestry,* p. 349.

FORTY-ONE: *The Phantom Throne*

351   "pleasant in small . . . time": Kirill, *My Life in Russia's Service,*
         p. 230.

351   "there was hardly": ibid.

352   "she was never": ibid., p. 148.

352   "After years of": Meriel Buchanan, *Queen Victoria's Relations,* p. 205.

352   "indulged his passion": Van der Kiste, *Princess Victoria Melita,* pp.
         148–49.

PAGE

352   "Residenz-Stadt": Kirill, op. cit., p. 230.

352   "his circle of": Van der Kiste, *Princess Victoria Melita*, p. 149.

352   "formed a barrier": ibid.

354   "would provoke interest": ibid.

354   "some of her": ibid.

354   "What a curious": Pakula, *The Last Romantic,* p. 399.

354   "would sometimes watch": Van der Kiste, *Princess Victoria Melita*, p. 149.

354   "that support for": ibid., p. 150.

355   "shattered": ibid.

355   "unable to cross": Pakula, op. cit., p. 311.

355   "badly lined, overworked": ibid.

355   "as a means . . . luxury": ibid.

356   "brought only suffering": Kirill, op. cit., p. 220.

356   "save his country": ibid.

357   "There are no": Van der Kiste, *Princess Victoria Melita*, p. 150.

357   "*Our hope that*": Kirill, op. cit., pp. 247–248.

358   "was bitterly contested": Van der Kiste, *Princess Victoria Melita*, p. 151.

358   "sufficient authority to": Kirill, op. cit., p. 221.

358   "less reactionary in": Van der Kiste, *Princess Victoria Melita*, p. 153.

358   "there was no": ibid., p. 151.

359   "he should begin": Kurth, *Anastasia,* p. 128.

359   "that Coburg": Van der Kiste, *Princess Victoria Melita*, p. 152.

359   "If he and": Kurth, op. cit., p. 82.

359   "Nothing can be": Kirill, op. cit., p. 222.

FORTY-TWO: *An Empress Without a Crown*

361   "credited with all": *The New York Times,* December 9, 1924.

361   "a very strong": Van der Kiste, *Princess Victoria Melita,* p. 154.

361   "did nothing to": ibid.

362   "Remember, Kirill, you": ibid.

362   "reports on the": Kirill, *My Life in Russia's Service,* p. 230.

362   "lived in the": ibid., pp. 230–31.

362   "I often saw": ibid., p. 231.

362   "considerable space . . . confusion": Van der Kiste, *Princess Victoria Melita,* p. 154.

362   "simply in recognition": *The New York Times,* October 28, 1924.

362   "an outspoken attack": Van der Kiste, *Princess Victoria Melita,* p. 155.

363   "the peculiar position": *The New York Times,* November 2, 1924.

363   "was fostering his": Van der Kiste, *Princess Victoria Melita,* p. 155.

363   "had always opposed": ibid., pp. 155–56.

PAGE

363   "became alarmed for": *The New York Times,* November 2, 1924.

363   "under the pretext": ibid.

364   "while his wife": Van der Kiste, *Princess Victoria Melita,* p. 156.

364   "he was given": *The New York Times,* November 2, 1924.

364   "Tell them of": ibid., November 30, 1924.

364   "always self-conscious": Van der Kiste, *Princess Victoria Melita,* pp. 116–17.

365   "purely social and . . . foundation": ibid., p. 157.

365   "I am here": *The New York Times,* December 7, 1924.

365   "to invoke the": ibid.

366   "In accepting this": Kirill, op. cit., p. 231.

366   "an exceptional woman . . . contact": ibid.

366   "close-fitting": *The New York Times,* December 7, 1924.

366   "tall, rather thin": ibid.

366   "suggesting that all": Alexander, *Always a Grand Duke,* p. 133.

366   "made large personal": Van der Kiste, *Princess Victoria Melita,* p. 158.

367   "I am immensely": *The New York Times,* December 8, 1924.

367   "The singing": ibid.

367   "Every sane person": *The New York Times,* December 10, 1924.

367   "Shopping? They don't . . . serious": *The New York Times,* December 8, 1924.

368   "the homage of": Van der Kiste, *Princess Victoria Melita,* p. 159.

368   "misjudged the intricate": ibid.

368   "by coincidence or": ibid.

369   "a brave on . . . know": ibid., p. 160.

369   "bolstered up effectively": *The New York Times,* December 12, 1924.

369   "The leaders of": ibid.

369   "Soft murmurs of . . . ancestors": Van der Kiste, *Princess Victoria Melita,* pp. 160–61.

370   "looked much better": ibid., p. 161.

370   "Americans everywhere have . . . well-informed": ibid.

370   "a cause of . . . time": Kirill, op. cit., p. 231.

370   "If everybody copied": *The New York Times,* December 24, 1924.

370   "had not asked . . . received": Van der Kiste, *Princess Victoria Melita,* p. 161.

370   "everywhere I went": *The New York Times,* December 24, 1924.

370   "America needs nothing": ibid.

FORTY-THREE: *Sea of Dreams*

372   "some five hundred": Alexander, *Always a Grand Duke,* p. 135.

373   "the legitimate successor": ibid.

PAGE

375   "a number of": Kirill, *My Life in Russia's Service,* p. 232.

375   "were very pleased": ibid.

375   "the republic could": Van der Kiste, *Princess Victoria Melita,* pp. 162–63.

375   "unemployed royalty, it": *The New York Times,* December 9, 1924.

375   "to some place": Van der Kiste, *Princess Victoria Melita,* p. 163.

375   "the Bavarian ministers": ibid.

376   "a martyr to": ibid.

376   "had all developed": Kirill, op. cit., p. 232.

377   "far more lively . . . relations": ibid.

378   "dared to beat": Van der Kiste, *Princess Victoria Melita,* p. 163.

378   "drudgery of post-war": ibid., p. 164.

378   "works of an": Kirill, op. cit., p. 232.

378   "to keep the": Van der Kiste, *Princess Victoria Melita,* p. 162.

378   "as if he": ibid., p. 164.

378   "in constant dread": ibid.

378   "the experience might": Fenyvesi, *Royalty in Exile,* p. 253.

379   "Ducky is in": Windsor Royal Archives, RA GV AA/43/314, Queen Marie of Roumania to King George V of England, November 29, 1925.

379   "Mummie is as": Romanian Archives, Grand Duchess Kira to Queen Marie, June 19, 1925.

380   "this may be . . . repays it": ibid., August 12, 1927.

380   "taming the wilderness": Van der Kiste, *Princess Victoria Melita,* p. 162.

380   "this forlorn stranger . . . England": ibid., p. 165.

380   "a quiet, austere": ibid., p. 166.

380   "unobtrusive": ibid.

381   "as talkative": ibid.

381   "looking for a": ibid.

FORTY-FOUR: *Kirill's New Clothes*

382   "to be the": Kirill, *My Life in Russia's Service,* p. 233.

382   "great love and": ibid., p. 232.

382   "with all of": ibid.

383   "Taking it upon": Van der Kiste, *Princess Victoria Melita,* p. 167.

383   "should have had": Vorres, *The Last Grand Duchess,* p. 182.

383   "Tsar Kyrill, Keeper": Van der Kiste, *Princess Victoria Melita,* p. 167.

383   "For the poor": Viktoria Luise, *The Kaiser's Daughter,* p. 112.

383   "an event of": Kirill, *My Life in Russia's Service,* p. 233.

PAGE

383   "the Fundamental Laws": ibid.

384   "the success of": ibid., p. 234.

384   "just another Russian": Van der Kiste, *Princess Victoria Melita*, p. 168.

384   "the phantom capital": Alexander, *Always a Grand Duke*, p. 135.

384   "Shadow Emperor . . . pathos": Van der Kiste, *Princess Victoria Melita*, p. 169.

384   "highly overrated at": Alexander, *Always a Grand Duke*, pp. 137–38.

384   "be enforced solely": Van der Kiste, *Princess Victoria Melita*, p. 169.

385   "*Each morning, the*": Alexander, *Always a Grand Duke*, p. 138.

385   "Personal Letter from . . . Harlem": ibid., p. 139.

385   "*And there is*": ibid., pp. 140–41.

386   "Nothing is real": ibid., p. 141.

386   "a very tall . . . czar-like": ibid.

386   "expected from the": ibid., p. 148.

386   "vaguely suggestive of": ibid., p. 147.

386   "affairs of state": ibid., p. 149.

386   "a huge and": ibid., p. 148.

387   "the age-worn . . . duties": ibid., p. 142.

387   "a wisely disillusioned": ibid., p. 143.

387   "*I am working*": ibid., pp. 142–43.

387   "implicit confidence in": ibid., p. 147.

388   "managed to spend": Pakula, *The Last Romantic,* p. 392.

388   "the same extraordinary": ibid., p. 129.

388   "was not particularly": ibid., p. 311.

FORTY-FIVE: *The Betrayed*

389   "with great success": Kirill, *My Life in Russia's Service,* p. 234.

390   "It was a marriage": ibid.

390   "I dare say": Ponsonby, *Henry Ponsonby,* p. 200.

391   "fall prey to . . . existence": Van der Kiste, *Princess Victoria Melita*, p. 171.

391   "I often feel": Elsberry, *Marie of Roumania,* p. 234.

392   "Never, even in": ibid., p. 235.

392   "The Solitary Nest": Pakula, *The Last Romantic,* p. 332.

392   "Die Kaiserin aller": Van der Kiste, *Princess Victoria Melita*, p. 172.

393   "gouty septuagenarian did": ibid.

393   "expressing anger and": ibid.

393   "errand of mercy": Pakula, op. cit., p. 392.

393   "had an overwhelming": ibid.

393   "it would seem": ibid.

394   "by inches.": Elsberry, *Marie of Roumania,* p. 264.

394   "some sort of": Pakula, op. cit., p. 392.

394   "anger and sadness": Van der Kiste, *Princess Victoria Melita,* p. 173.

394   "to keep an": Pakula, op. cit., p. 392.

394   "the most unforgiving": Van der Kiste, *Princess Victoria Melita,* p. 173.

FORTY-SIX: *Among the Ruins*

395   "a meaningless pantomine": Van der Kiste, *Princess Victoria Melita,* p. 174.

396   "It is a": Windsor Royal Archives, RA GV CC45/934, Victoria Feodorovna to Queen Mary of England, October 12, 1934.

396   "thoroughly enjoyed": Kirill, *My Life in Russia's Service,* p. 235.

396   "no conversations passed": ibid., p. 236.

396   "conceived an immense": ibid.

396   "always had a": Van der Kiste, *Princess Victoria Melita,* p. 175.

397   "abundance of kin": Kirill, op. cit., p. 236.

397   "bastion of stability": Van der Kiste, *Princess Victoria Melita,* p. 176.

397   "proud to remember": ibid.

397   "If only you": ibid.

398   "*I am so glad*": ibid., pp. 177–78.

399   "had known so": ibid., p. 178.

399   "the daughters of": ibid.

399   "*We were very*": ibid., pp. 178–79.

FORTY-SEVEN: *Lilies at Amorbach*

402   "causing great anxiety": Kirill, *My Life in Russia's Service,* p. 237.

402   "quite a shock": ibid.

402   "felt very nervous": Ibid.

402   "I'm so sorry": Van der Kiste, *Princess Victoria Melita,* p. 181.

402   "to spoil the . . . will": Kirill, op. cit., p. 238.

403   "had taken a": ibid.

403   "The days that": ibid.

403   "dance his": Pakula, *The Last Romantic,* p. 404.

403   "When told by": Elsberry, *Marie of Roumania,* p. 265.

403   "It makes all": ibid.

403   "*The whole thing*": Van der Kiste, *Princess Victoria Melita,* pp. 182–83.

404   "She died at": Elsberry, op. cit., p. 265.

405   "a bitter, disappointed": Meriel Buchanan, *Queen Victoria's Relations,* p. 206.

PAGE

405   "passionate, often misunderstood": Van der Kiste, *Princess Victoria
            Melita*, p. 184.

405   "always hated being": Pakula, op. cit., p. 406.

FORTY-EIGHT: *Sunset at St. Briac*

406   "terrible to enter": Kirill, op. cit., p. 239.

406   "where her spirit": ibid.

406   "acutely lonely": Van der Kiste, *Princess Victoria Melita*, p. 185.

406   "joy knew no": Kirill, op. cit., p. 241.

407   "a virtual skeleton": Van der Kiste, *Princess Victoria Melita*, p. 185.

407   "a national sorrow": Kirill, op. cit., p. 244.

409   "the only way": Van der Kiste, *Princess Victoria Melita*, p. 189.

Bibliography

Alexander, Grand Duke of Russia. *Always a Grand Duke.* New York: Farrar and Rinehart, 1933.

———. *Once a Grand Duke.* Garden City, N.Y.: Garden City Publishing Company, 1932.

Alice, Princess of Great Britain. *For My Grandchildren.* Cleveland: World Publishing Company, 1967.

Alice, Grand Duchess of Hesse and the Rhine. *Biographical Sketch and Letters.* London: William Clowes and Sons, 1884.

Almedingen, E. M. *The Emperor Alexander II.* London: The Bodley Head, 1962.

———. *The Empress Alexandra.* London: Hutchinson, 1961.

———. *An Unbroken Unity: A Memoir of the Grand Duchess Serge of Russia.* London: The Bodley Head, 1964.

Annual Register, 1872–1907. London, *The Times.* A yearly almanac of events.

Argyll, John. *V.R.I. Queen Victoria, Her Life and Empire.* New York: Harper and Brothers, 1901.

Aronson, Theo. *Grandmama of Europe.* London: John Murray Company, 1973.

Ashdown, Dulcie. *Victoria and the Coburgs.* London: Robert Hale, 1981.

Bagger, Eugene. *Eminent Europeans.* New York: G. P. Putnam's Sons, 1922.

Balfour, Michael. *The Kaiser and His Times.* Boston: Houghton Mifflin, 1964.

Balsan, Consuelo. *The Glitter and the Gold.* New York: Simon and Schuster, 1956.

Battiscombe, Georgina. *Queen Alexandra.* Boston: Houghton Mifflin, 1964.

Beal, Erica. *Royal Cavalcade.* London: Paul and Company, 1939.

Benckendorff, Paul. *Last Days at Tsarskoe Selo.* London: Heinemann, 1927.

Bennett, Daphne. *King Without a Crown.* Philadelphia: Lippincott, 1977.

———. *Vicky, Princess Royal of England and German Empress.* New York: St. Martin's Press, 1971.

Benson, E. F. *Queen Victoria's Daughters.* New York: Appleton-Century, 1938.

Bercovici, Konrad. *That Royal Lover.* New York: Brewer and Warren, 1931.

Berkson, Seymour. *Their Majesties!* New York: Stackpole Sons, 1938.

Bernardy, Françoise de. *Albert and Victoria.* New York: Harcourt, Brace, 1953.

Bibesco, Marthe. "Ferdinand of Roumania." *The Saturday Evening Post,* Aug. 27, 1927.

———. *Royal Portraits.* New York: Appleton, 1928.

———. *Some Royalties and a Prime Minister.* New York: Appleton, 1928.

Billington, James H. *The Icon and the Axe.* New York: Knopf, 1966.

Bing, Edward, ed. *The Letters of Tsar Nicholas and Empress Marie.* London: Ivor Nicholson and Watson, 1937.

Bocca, Geoffrey. *Kings Without Thrones.* London: Weidenfeld and Nicolson, 1959.

Bolitho, Hector. *A Biographer's Notebook.* New York: Macmillan, 1950.

———. *The Letters of Queen Victoria.* New Haven: Yale University Press, 1938.

———. *The Prince Consort and His Brother.* London: Cobden-Sanderson, 1933.

———. *Roumania Under King Carol.* London: Eyre and Spottiswoode, 1939.

Botkin, Gleb. *The Real Romanovs.* New York: Revell, 1931.

Brooke-Sheperd, Gordon. *The Last Habsburg.* New York: Weybright and Talley, 1968.

———. *Uncle of Europe.* New York: Harcourt Brace Jovanovich, 1976.

Buchanan, Sir George. *My Mission to Russia and other Diplomatic Memories* (2 vols.). London: Cassel, 1923.

Buchanan, Meriel. *Ambassador's Daughter.* London: Cassell, 1958.

———. *The Dissolution of an Empire.* London: John Murray, 1932.

———. *Queen Victoria's Relations.* London: Cassell, 1954.

Buckle, George, ed. *The Letters of Queen Victoria.* London: John Murray, 1926.

Bülow, Prince Bernhard von. *Memoirs,* 1897–1903, vol. 1. New York: Putnam, 1931.

———. *Memoirs,* 1903–1909, vol. 2. New York: Putnam, 1931.

Burgoyne, Elizabeth. *Carmen Sylva.* London: Thornton Butterworth, 1940.

Burton, Sir Richard. *Narrative of a Trip to Harar.* London: Royal Geographical Society, 1855.

Buxhoeveden, Baroness Sophie. *The Life and Tragedy of Alexandra Feodorovna, Empress of Russia.* New York: Longmans, Green, 1928.

Bykov, P. M. *The Last Days of Tsardom.* London: Martin Lawrence, 1934.

Callimachi, Princess Anne-Marie. *Yesterday Was Mine.* London: Falcon Press, 1952.

Carol I, King of Roumania. *Reminiscences.* New York: Harpers, 1899.

Cartland, Barbara. *The Scandalous Life of King Carol.* London: Frederick Muller, 1957.

Chamberlin, William Henry. *The Russian Revolution* (2 vols.). New York: Macmillan, 1935.

Charques, Richard. *The Twilight of Imperial Russia.* Fair Lawn, N.J.: Essential Books, 1959.

Cherniavsky, Michael. *Tsar and People.* New Haven: Yale University Press, 1961.

Churchill, Winston. *The World Crisis: The Aftermath.* London: Thornton Butterworth, 1929.

Constantine, King of Greece. *A King's Private Letters.* London: Eveleigh, Nash and Grayson, 1925.

Cookridge, E. H. *From Battenberg to Mountbatten.* New York: John Day, 1968.

Cornwallis-West, Mrs. George. *The Reminiscences of Lady Randolph Churchill.* New York: Century, 1908.

Corti, Egon. *The Downfall of Three Dynasties.* New York: Books for Libraries Press, 1970.

Cowles, Virginia. *The Last Tsar.* New York: G. P. Putnam's Sons, 1977.

————. *The Last Tsar and Tsarina.* London: Weidenfeld and Nicolson, 1977.

————. *1913: An End and a Beginning.* New York: Harper & Row, 1967.

————. *The Romanovs.* New York: Harper & Row, 1971.

————. *The Russian Dagger.* New York: Harper & Row, 1969.

Curley, Walter J. P. *Monarchs-in-Waiting.* New York: Dodd, Mead, 1973.

Custine, Marquis de. *The Empire of the Czar.* New York: Doubleday, 1989.

Daggert, Mabel Potter. *Marie of Roumania.* New York: George H. Doran, 1926.

Daisy, Princess of Pless. *Better Left Unsaid.* New York: Dutton, 1931.

————. *From My Private Diary.* London: John Murray, 1931.

Dehn, Lili. *The Real Tsaritsa.* London: Thornton Butterworth, 1922.

Dewhurst, Jack. *Royal Confinements.* New York: St. Martin's Press, 1980.

Diesbach, Ghislain de. *Secrets of Gotha.* New York: Meredith Press, 1967.

Dobson, Christopher. *Prince Felix Yusupov.* London: Harrap, 1989.

Duff, David. *Hessian Tapestry.* London: Frederick Muller, 1967.

———. *Victoria and Albert.* New York: Tappinger, 1972.

Easterman, A. L. *King Carol, Hitler and Lupescu.* London: Gollancz, 1942.

Edward, Duke of Windsor. *A King's Story.* New York: Putnam, 1947.

Elsberry, Terrence. *Marie of Roumania: The Intimate Life of a Twentieth-Century Queen.* New York, St. Martin's Press, 1972.

Ernst Ludwig, Grossherzog von Hessen und bei Rhein. *Erinnertes.* Darmstadt, West Germany: Eduard Roether Verlag, 1983.

Eulalia, Infanta of Spain. *Court Life from Within.* London: Cassell, 1915.

———. *Courts and Countries After the War.* New York: Dodd, Mead, 1925.

Fenyvesi, Charles. *Royalty in Exile.* London: Robson, 1981.

———. *Splendor in Exile.* Washington, D.C.: New Republic Books, 1970.

Fisher-Galati, Stephen. *Twentieth-Century Rumania.* New York: Columbia University Press, 1970.

Fischer, Henry W. *The Private Lives of William II and His Consort.* London: Heinemann, 1904.

Fischer, Louis. *The Life of Lenin.* New York: Harper Colophon, 1965.

Florinsky, Michael. *The End of the Russian Empire.* New York: Collier, 1961.

Frankland, Noble. *Imperial Tragedy.* New York: Coward-McCann, 1961.

Fulford, Roger, ed. *Dearest Child.* London: Evans Brothers, 1964.

———. *Dearest Mama.* New York: Holt, Rinehart and Winston, 1969.

———. *Hanover to Windsor.* New York: Macmillan, 1960.

———. *Your Dear Letter.* London: Evans Brothers, 1971.

Fulop-Miller, René. *Rasputin: The Holy Devil.* New York: Garden City Publishing Company, 1928.

George, Grand Duchess of Russia. *A Romanov Diary.* New York: Atlantic International, 1988.

Gernsheim, Helmut, and Alison Gernsheim. *Victoria R.* New York: G. P. Putnam's Sons, 1959.

Gilliard, Pierre. *Thirteen Years at the Russian Court.* New York: George Doran, 1921.

Gollwitzer, Heinz. *Europe in the Age of Imperialism: 1880–1914.* New York: Norton, 1969.

Gore, John. *King George V.* London: John Murray, 1941.

Gorer, Geoffrey, and John Rickman. *The People of Great Russia: A Psychological Study.* New York: Norton, 1962.

Graham, Stephen. *Alexander of Jugoslavia.* London: Cassell, 1938.

Gunther, John. *Inside Europe.* New York: Harpers, 1938.

Haldane, J.B.S. *Heredity and Politics.* New York: Norton, 1938.

Harcave, Sidney. *First Blood: The Russian Revolution of 1905.* New York: Macmillan, 1964.

Hatch, Alden. *The Mountbattens.* London: Hutchinson, 1982.

Hobsbawn, E. J. *The Age of Empire.* New York: Pantheon, 1987.

Hoppe, E. O. *In Gypsy Camp and Royal Palace.* London: Methuen, 1924.

Hough, Richard. *Louis and Victoria: The First Mountbattens.* London: Hutchinson, 1974.

————. *The Mountbattens.* New York: Dutton, 1975.

————, ed. *Advice to My Granddaughter: The Letters of Queen Victoria to Princess Victoria of Battenberg.* London: Heinemann, 1975.

Hynes, Samuel. *The Edwardian Turn of Mind.* Princeton, N.J.: Princeton University Press, 1968.

Ileana, Princess of Roumania and Archduchess of Austria. *I Live Again.* New York: Holt, Rinehart, 1952.

Jonescu, Take. *Some Personal Impressions.* London: Nisbet, 1919.

Judd, Denis. *The Eclipse of Kings.* New York: Stein and Day, 1976.

Jullian, Philippe. *Edward and the Edwardians.* New York: Viking, 1967.

Kedward, H. R. *Fascism in Western Europe: 1900–1945.* New York: New York University Press, 1971.

Kennan, George. *Russia Leaves the War.* Princeton, N.J.: Princeton University Press, 1956.

Kerensky, Alexander. *The Catastrophe.* New York: Appleton, 1927.

————. *Russia and History's Turning Point.* New York: Duell, Sloan and Pearce, 1965.

————. *The Murder of the Romanovs.* London: Hutchinson, 1935.

King, Stella. *Princess Marina, Her Life and Times.* London: Cassell, 1969.

Kinross, Lord. *The Windsor Years.* New York: Viking, 1967.

Kirill, Grand Duke of Russia. *My Life in Russia's Service—Then and Now.* London: Selwyn and Blount, 1939.

Knox, Sir Alfred. *With the Russian Army.* New York: Dutton, 1921.

Kroll, Maria, and Jason Lindsey. *Europe's Royal Families.* London: Country Life Books, 1979.

Kschessinska, Mathilde. *Dancing in Petersburg.* Garden City, N.Y.: Doubleday, 1961.

Kurth, Peter. *Anastasia: The Life of Anna Anderson.* London: Jonathan Cape, 1983.

Laver, James. *Edwardian Promenade.* London: Edward Hulton, 1958.

Lee, Arthur Gould. *Crown Against Sickle.* London: Hutchinson, 1950.

————. *Empress Frederick Writes to Sophie, Her Daughter, Crown Princess and Later Queen of the Hellenes.* London: Faber and Faber, 1955.

————. *Helen, Queen Mother of Roumania.* London: Faber and Faber, 1956.

Longford, Elizabeth. *Louisa, Lady in Waiting.* London: Jonathan Cape, 1979.

————. *Queen Victoria: Born to Succeed.* New York: Harper and Row, 1964.

————. *Royal House of Windsor.* London: Weidenfeld and Nicolson, 1974.

Magnus, Philip. *King Edward the Seventh.* London: John Murray, 1964.

Mallet, Victor, ed. *Life With Queen Victoria: Marie Mallet's Letters from Court, 1887–1901*. Boston: Houghton Mifflin, 1968.

Manchester, William. *The Arms of Krupp*. Boston: Little, Brown, 1964.

Marie, Grand Duchess of Russia. *The Education of a Princess*. New York: Viking, 1931.

———. *A Princess in Exile*. New York: Viking, 1932.

———. *Things I Remember*. London: Cassell, 1931.

Marie, Queen of Roumania. *Crowned Queens*. London: Heath Cranton, 1929.

———. *Story of My Life* (2 vols.). New York: Charles Scribner's Sons, 1934–1935.

Marie-Louise, Princess. *My Memories of Six Reigns*. New York: Dutton, 1957.

Martineau, Mrs. Philip. *Roumania and Her Rulers*. London: Stanley Paul, 1927.

Marye, George. *Nearing the End in Imperial Russia: 1914–1916*. Philadelphia: Dorrance, 1929.

Massie, Robert K. *Dreadnought*. New York: Random House, 1992.

———. *The Last Courts of Europe*. New York: Vendome Press, 1981.

———. *Nicholas and Alexandra*. New York: Atheneum, 1967.

Mazour, Anatole. *Rise and Fall of the Romanovs*. Princeton, N.J.: Van Nostrand Press, 1960.

McNaughton, Arnold. *The Flight of the Romanovs*. London: privately printed, 1979.

———. *Kings, Queens and Crowns*. London: privately printed, 1977.

Moats, Alice Leone. *Lupescu*. New York: Henry Holt, 1955.

Moorehead, Alan. *The Russian Revolution*. New York: Harper & Row, 1958.

Morris, Charles, and Murat Halstead. *The Life and Reign of Queen Victoria*. New York: Macmillan, 1959.

Mossolov, A. A. *At the Court of the Last Tsar*. London: Methuen, 1935.

Narishkin-Kurakin, Elizabeth. *Under Three Tsars*. New York: Dutton, 1931.

Nicholas, Prince of Greece. *My Fifty Years*. London: Hutchinson, 1926.

Nicholas II, Emperor of Russia. *Journal Intime*. Paris: Payot, 1925.

Nicolson, Harold. *King George the Fifth*. London: Constable, 1952.

Obolensky, Serge. *One Man and His Time*. New York: McDowell Obolensky, 1958.

Paget, Walpurga. *Embassies of Other Days and Further Recollections* (2 vols.). New York: George Doran, 1923.

Pakula, Hannah. *The Last Romantic: A Biography of Queen Marie of Roumania*. New York: Simon and Schuster, 1984.

Paléologue, Maurice. *An Ambassador's Memoirs* (3 vols.). London: Hutchinson, 1923–1925.

Pares, Bernard. *The Fall of the Russian Monarchy.* New York: Vintage, 1961.

————. *A History of Russia.* New York: Knopf, 1960.

————. *The Letters of the Tsaritsa to the Tsar: 1914–1916.* London: Duckworth, 1923.

Peter II, King of Yugoslavia. *A King's Heritage.* New York: G. P. Putnam's Sons, 1954.

Ponsonby, Arthur. *Henry Ponsonby, Queen Victoria's Private Secretary.* New York: Macmillan, 1943.

————. *Letters of the Empress Frederick.* New York: Macmillan, 1930.

Pool, James, and Suzanne Pool. *Who Financed Hitler.* London: Raven, 1979.

Pope-Hennessy, James. *Queen Mary.* New York: Knopf, 1960.

Pridham, Francis. *Close of a Dynasty.* London: Wingate, 1956.

Queux, William, ed. *The Secret Life of the Ex-Tsaritza.* London: Odhams, 1918.

Radziwill, Catherine. *The Intimate Life of the Last Tsarina.* London: Cassell, 1929.

————. *Nicholas II, Last of the Tsars.* London: Cassell, 1931.

————. *The Royal Marriage Market of Europe.* New York: Funk and Wagnalls, 1915.

————. *Secrets of Dethroned Royalty.* London: The Bodley Head, 1920.

————. *Those I Remember.* London: Cassell, 1924.

Rasputin, Maria. *My Father.* London: Cassell, 1934.

Reid, Michaela. *Ask Sir James: Sir James Reid, Personal Physician to Queen Victoria and Physician-in-Ordinary to Three Monarchs.* London: Hodder and Stoughton, 1987.

Remak, Joachim. *The Origins of World War I.* Hinsdale, Ill.: The Dryden Press, 1967.

Riasanovsky, Nicholas. *A History of Russia.* New York: Oxford University Press, 1963.

Rodzianko, M. V. *The Reign of Rasputin.* London: Philpot, 1927.

Rohl, John C. G., and Nicolaus Sombart. *Kaiser Wilhelm II: New Interpretations.* Cambridge: Cambridge University Press, 1982.

Roosevelt, Blanche. *Elisabeth of Roumania.* London: Chapman and Hall, 1891.

Rose, Kenneth. *King George V.* London: Weidenfeld and Nicolson, 1983.

Rowland, Peter. *Lloyd George.* London: Barrie and Jenkins, 1975.

Russell, Phillips. *The Glittering Century.* New York: Charles Scribner's Sons, 1936.

St. Aubyn, Giles. *Edward VII.* New York: Atheneum, 1979.

Sazonov, Serge. *Fateful Years.* New York: Stokes, 1928.

Seton-Watson, Hugh. *Eastern Europe Between the Wars.* London: Cambridge University Press, 1945.

Seton-Watson, R. W. *Roumania and the Great War.* London: Constable, 1915.

——. *Sarajevo: A Study in the Origins of the Great War.* London: Hutchinson, 1922.

Smith, Hedrick. *The Russians.* New York: Times Books, 1976.

Spiridovich, Alexandre. *Les Dernières Années de la Cour de Tsarskoie-Selo* (2 vols.). Paris: Payot, 1928.

Spiro, Edward. *From Battenberg to Mountbatten.* London: Arthur Barker, 1966.

Stephan, John J. *The Russian Fascists: Tragedy and Farce in Exile.* New York: Hamish Hamilton, 1978.

Stephenson, John, ed. *A Royal Correspondence: The Letters of King Edward VII and King George V to Admiral Sir Henry F. Stephenson.* London: Macmillan, 1938.

Stone, Norman. *Europe Transformed: 1878–1919.* Cambridge, Mass.: Harvard University Press, 1984.

Sulzberger, C. L. *A Long Row of Candles: Memoirs and Diaries.* New York: Macmillan, 1969.

Summers, Anthony, and Tom Mangold. *The File on the Tsar.* London: Gollancz, 1976.

Sykes, Christopher. *Nancy: The Life of Lady Astor.* London: Collins, 1972.

Taylor, A.J.P. *The Last of Old Europe.* New York: Times Books, 1979.

——. *The Struggle for the Mastery in Europe: 1848–1918.* London: Oxford University Press, 1971.

Taylor, Edmund. *The Fall of the Dynasties.* Garden City, N.Y.: Doubleday, 1963.

Tisdall, E.E.P. *Marie Feodorovna, Empress of Russia.* New York: John Day, 1958.

——. *Royal Destiny.* London: S. Paul, 1955.

——. *Queen Victoria's Private Life.* London: Jarrolds, 1961.

Trotsky, Leon. *The History of the Russian Revolution* (3 vols.). New York: Simon and Schuster, 1932.

Tuchman, Barbara. *The Guns of August.* New York: Macmillan, 1962.

——. *The Proud Tower.* New York: Macmillan, 1966.

Tennyson, Alfred. *A Welcome to Her Royal Highness Marie Alexandrovna, Duchess of Edinburgh.* London: Henry S. King and Company, 1874.

Vacaresco, Hélène. *Kings and Queens I Have Known.* New York: Harper and Brothers, 1904.

Van der Kiste, John. *Edward VII's Children.* London: Sutton, 1989.

——. *Princess Victoria Melita.* London: Sutton, 1991.

——. *Queen Victoria's Children.* London: Sutton, 1986.

—— and Bee Jordaan. *Dearest Affie.* London: Sutton, 1984.

Viktoria Luise, Princess of Prussia. *The Kaiser's Daughter.* Englewood Cliffs, N.J.: Prentice-Hall, 1977.

Viroubova, Anna. *Memories of the Russian Court.* New York: Macmillan, 1923.

Von der Hoven, Helena. *King Carol of Romania.* London: Hutchinson, 1940.

Vopicka, Charles J. *Secrets of the Balkans.* Chicago: Rand, McNally, 1921.

Vorres, Ian. *The Last Grand Duchess.* London: Hutchinson, 1964.

Warth, Robert D. *The Allies and the Russian Revolution.* London: Cambridge University Press, 1954.

Wheeler-Bennett, John. *King George VI.* New York: St. Martin's Press, 1958.

Whittle, Tyler. *The Last Kaiser.* New York: Quadrangle–Times Books, 1977.

Wilson, Colin. *Rasputin and the Fall of the Romanovs.* New York: Farrar Straus, 1964.

Wilton, Robert. *The Last Days of the Romanovs.* London: Thornton Butterworth, 1920.

Windsor, Dean of, and Hector Bolitho. *The Latter Letters of Lady Augusta Stanley.* London: Eyre and Spottiswoode, 1942.

Witte, Sergius. *Memoirs.* New York: Doubleday, 1921.

Woodham-Smith, Cecil. *Queen Victoria, Her Life and Times* (2 vols.). New York: Hamish Hamilton, 1972.

Yousoupoff, Prince Felix. *Lost Splendor.* London: Jonathan Cape, 1953.

————. *Rasputin.* New York: Dial, 1927.

SPECIAL SOURCES

Royal Archives, Windsor Castle
Romanian Archives, Bucharest, Romania
Library of the British Museum, London
Astor Papers, Reading University, England
Hesse Archives, Darmstadt, Germany
Coburg Archives, Coburg, Germany

Index

ABOUT THE AUTHOR

MICHAEL JOHN SULLIVAN was brought up in Europe and the United States and has attended university in California, Texas, England, and Switzerland. He holds a Master of Arts degree in modern European history and has done extensive graduate study in philosophy, psychology, and communication arts. He began his writing career doing interviews and feature stories for national magazines.

Based in Southern California, Mr. Sullivan spends part of the year living in Hawaii and traveling to his favorite destinations: Europe, New England, and the American South.

ABOUT THE TYPE

This book was set in Bembo, a typeface based on an old-style Roman face that was used for Cardinal Bembo's tract *De Aetna* in 1495. Bembo was cut by Francisco Griffo in the early sixteenth century. The Lanston Monotype Company of Philadelphia brought the well-proportioned letterforms of Bembo to the United States in the 1930s.